James Picciotto

Sketches of Anglo-Jewish History

ISBN/EAN: 9783337132996

Printed in Europe, USA, Canada, Australia, Japan

Cover: Foto ©ninafisch / pixelio.de

More available books at **www.hansebooks.com**

James Picciotto

Sketches of Anglo-Jewish History

SKETCHES

OF

ANGLO-JEWISH HISTORY.

BY

JAMES PICCIOTTO.

LONDON:
TRÜBNER & CO., LUDGATE HILL.
1875.
[*All rights reserved.*]

TO

SIR MOSES MONTEFIORE, BART., F.R.S.

&c. &c. &c.

THIS BOOK IS RESPECTFULLY

𝔇𝔢𝔡𝔦𝔠𝔞𝔱𝔢𝔡

AS A HUMBLE TRIBUTE OF ADMIRATION AND VENERATION

FOR HIS UNIVERSAL AND HEROIC CHAMPIONSHIP

OF THE JEWISH CAUSE,

FOR HIS PURE AND LOFTY PHILANTHROPY, AND

FOR HIS UNIVERSAL BENEVOLENCE,

BY THE AUTHOR.

PREFACE.

It is singular that few enlightened and wealthy communities know so little of their own early history, as the Jews of Great Britain. Yet few races indeed present more vicissitudes for description, or possess records offering a more interesting and extended field for investigation. Perhaps the mart, the exchange, the counting-house, may have absorbed, in former times, and under especial circumstances, energies which, if directed to literary pursuits, would have deserved and commanded success. Certain it is that no chronicler has narrated the earlier struggles of the Jews when they returned to these isles after centuries of banishment, and no writer has attempted to depict the gradual rise and progress of the Jewish community in London. Nay, the archives of the older Synagogues, which are treasures of curious information, remained until the present time buried in obscurity, their very existence being scarcely known. Some few of the elder officials had a glimmering of their contents, but to the vast majority of even the Jews themselves these books were as hidden and impenetrable as the Vedas or the Zend Avesta. In addition to being jealously guarded, they were written in the Spanish and Portuguese languages, or in the Jewish-German dialect, which rendered them thus necessarily understood but by few. The author has had the privilege of being permitted not only to inspect these valuable registers, but to study them closely, with the kind assistance of the Synagogue officials; and months have been devoted to this labour. At the same time, he made continuous and diligent researches in all quarters where information on the subject that engrossed his attention was likely to be obtained. Libraries, public and private, were ransacked; friends good-naturedly unlocked ancient memories of past events on his behalf, and placed the correspondence of departed relatives at his disposal; eminent members of the Jewish community volunteered valuable information. Great care has been exercised to ensure accuracy; and it has been sought, so far as practicable, to obtain a confirmation of all statements and communications before any fact has been held out to the public as authentic.

The result of the labours of the author appeared in print in the *Jewish Chronicle*, in a series of papers entitled "Sketches of Anglo-Jewish History." As these papers were written *pari passu* with the progress of the researches, they necessarily bear the character of journalistic essays, rather than of a complete history. Whilst, therefore, the work in question does not aspire to rank as a regular history, the author claims to be the first Israelite who has given a full and connected account of the vicissitudes passed through by the Jews of Great Britain, from the days of the Saxon kings until the middle of the present century. He also claims to have brought to light a mass of original information, the very existence of which was all but unsuspected. These papers, therefore, must prove of greater interest to Jews than to Christians. But though they were written by a Jew for Jews, the author trusts that Christians, whose faith was founded by members of the Jewish race, will find in these chapters, in addition to that which is entirely new, much that may be of interest also to them. He hopes that as Christians learn to know better, they will also learn to like and appreciate better, Englishmen of the Jewish faith, whose inner life has unreservedly been laid open before them; and that the former may look with a less prejudiced eye on the foibles of the latter. He trusts that Christians may respect and esteem the many good qualities which their Jewish fellow-countrymen possess, sympathise with them in their struggles to elevate themselves, and heartily stretch forth to them the hand of friendship.

The writer, by permission of the late Editor of the *Jewish Chronicle*, now offers "The Sketches of Anglo-Jewish History" to the public in a separate form. These articles have been carefully revised, facts re-arranged in a closer chronological order, important additions made, errors rectified, and the general utility of the work has been considerably enhanced.

CONTENTS.

CHAP.		PAGE
	INTRODUCTION	1
I.	THE RETURN OF THE JEWS TO ENGLAND .	25
II.	THE FIRST SYNAGOGUE IN LONDON . . .	32
III.	STRUGGLES AND SUCCESSES—KING CHARLES II. AND THE JEWS	39
IV.	THE ALIEN DUTIES	46
V.	ANECDOTES — CONVERSIONS — LEARNED RABBIS — NEW SYNAGOGUES	52
VI.	HEBREW CAPITALISTS	58
VII.	SPECIAL LEGISLATION — JEWISH LOYALTY — CONTINUED PREJUDICES—ENEMIES AND FRIENDS . .	65
VIII.	COMMUNAL CHARITIES—INTERNAL LEGISLATION . .	74
IX.	THE NATURALISATION BILL OF 1753 . . .	80
X.	REPEAL OF THE NATURALISATION BILL—LITERATURE OF THE BILL	86
XI.	POSITION OF THE JEWS—BARON D'AGUILAR .	92
XII.	JEWISH MARRIAGES	100
XIII.	ORIGIN OF THE BOARD OF DEPUTIES . . .	113
XIV.	THE HISTORY OF THE DEPUTIES OF THE BRITISH JEWS .	122
XV.	THE EARLY DAYS OF THE GREAT SYNAGOGUE . .	132
XVI.	PROGRESS OF GERMAN CONGREGATIONS . .	138
XVII.	CONVERSIONS—JEWISH LITERATURE—THE GREAT SYNAGOGUE AGAIN	143
XVIII.	THE PORTUGUESE JEWS IN THE MIDDLE OF THE EIGHTEENTH CENTURY	149

CONTENTS.

CHAP.		PAGE
XIX.	AGAIN WITH THE PORTUGUESE JEWS	157
XX.	JOSEPH SALVADOR — HONORARY OFFICES AMONG THE PORTUGUESE JEWS	161
XXI.	SWEDEN AND THE JEWS—PORTUGUESE RELIGIOUS AND EDUCATIONAL INSTITUTIONS—DR KENNICOTT	167
XXII.	CONGREGATIONAL CHANGES—THE JEWS OF PORTUGAL—JEWISH OFFENDERS — THE JEWS AND THE LORD MAYOR	175
XXIII.	A NOBLE PROSELYTE	183
XXIV.	A NEW IMMIGRATION—ECCLESIASTICAL LOSSES AND OFFICIAL CHANGES—CEMETERIES AND BODY-SNATCHING	190
XXV.	CONVERSIONS	196
XXVI.	THE PURIM RIOTS—THE BERNAL FAMILY	205
XXVII.	SAMUEL MENDOZA—THE SHECHITA—SYNAGOGUE DIFFERENCES	212
XXVIII.	THE RICARDO FAMILY—THE ALIEN BILL—SYNAGOGUE FINANCE	219
XXIX.	SYNAGOGUE PROGRESS—TWO JEWISH WORTHIES	225
XXX.	FRIENDS AND VINDICATORS OF THE JEWS	234
XXXI.	CONVERSIONIST ATTEMPTS—PRIVILEGE OF PRISONERS—THE JEWS' HOSPITAL—A BAAL SHEM	241
XXXII.	THE GOLDSMID FAMILY	249
XXXIII.	A SCHEME FOR IMPROVING THE CONDITION OF THE POOR	257
XXXIV.	THE GREAT SYNAGOGUE IN THE NINETEENTH CENTURY	264
XXXV.	THE PORTUGUESE SYNAGOGUE IN THE NINETEENTH CENTURY	270
XXXVI.	JEWISH VOLUNTEERS—WRITERS ON THE JEWS	275
XXXVII.	RISE OF THE LONDON SOCIETY—THE DUKE OF SUSSEX—A WEDDING AND A MURDER—A NOBLE-HEARTED JEW	283
XXXVIII.	THE CASE OF HARPER'S CHARITY—THE LAWS OF THE GREAT SYNAGOGUE—UNION OF THE CITY ASHKENAZIM CONGREGATIONS—IRREGULAR MARRIAGES	289
XXXIX.	ISAAC D'ISRAELI AND HIS FAMILY	295
XL.	J. KING AND JEWISH WORSHIP—SIR MAURICE XIMENES—MORDECAI RODRIGUEZ LOPEZ	302

CONTENTS.

CHAP.		PAGE
XLI.	A CHIEF RABBI AND A HAHAM	307
XLII.	JEWISH WORTHIES — THE REV. SOLOMON LYON — EMMA LYON—MICHAEL JOSEPHS—ARTHUR LUMLEY DAVIDS	313
XLIII.	THE JEWS IN HAMBURG AND IN LISBON—THE SHAARE TICVA SCHOOL—AN UNLAWFUL MINYAN—GIFTS TO THE SEPHARDI SYNAGOGUE	319
XLIV.	MOVEMENTS IN THE PORTUGUESE CONGREGATION— PARTIES IN THAT COMMUNITY—PROGRESS OF THE SEPHARDIM—SIR MOSES MONTEFIORE	325
XLV.	NEW ASHKENAZI INSTITUTIONS—SYNAGOGUE LIBERALITY	332
XLVI.	TESTIMONIAL TO SIR MOSES MONTEFIORE—SYNAGOGUE IMPROVEMENTS	338
XLVII.	SIMON SOLOMON — ISAAC GOMES SERRA — ABRAHAM MONTEFIORE—NATHAN MEYER ROTHSCHILD	341
XLVIII.	BLOOD ACCUSATIONS IN THE EAST—MISSION OF SIR MOSES MONTEFIORE	347
XLIX.	SOME MORE JEWISH AUTHORS	359
L.	THE REFORM MOVEMENT	367
LI.	THE WEST LONDON CONGREGATION OF BRITISH JEWS	374
LII.	THE CIVIL AND POLITICAL RIGHTS OF THE JEWS	386
LIII.	REMOVAL OF JEWISH DISABILITIES	394
LIV.	THE JEWISH PRESS	402
LV.	CONCLUSION	410
	LIST OF AUTHORITIES AND SOURCES WHENCE THE FACTS AND INFORMATION CONTAINED IN THIS WORK HAVE BEEN GATHERED	415
	INDEX	417

SKETCHES

OF

ANGLO-JEWISH HISTORY.

INTRODUCTION.

THE early history of the Jews in this country is necessarily obscure and uncertain.

It has been surmised that the ancient Jews traded with the ancient Britons, and that the former visited and even dwelt in this island. This is pure speculation. Leaving on one side legendary times, we find the presence of Jews in England under the Saxon Kings fully attested. The first mention made of the Jews in any document connected with English history, is found in the canons of Ecbright, Archbishop of York, which contain an ordinance that no Christian shall presume to eat with a Jew or shall judaise, whatever that may have meant. These canons were issued in the year 740 or 750 C.E., for the government of the province of York. We see therefrom that not only there were Jews in England at that period, but that they were deemed of sufficient importance for the ruling powers to warn the guileless Christians against their seductions.

It is related in the history of Croyland Abbey that in 833 Whitglaff, King of the Mercians, having been defeated by Egbert, took refuge in that Abbey, and in return for the protection and assistance received, he granted a charter to the monks of Croyland, confirming to them all lands, tenements and gifts bestowed upon them by his predecessors and their nobles, by Christians and by Jews. It is asserted that the

Jews were banished from England at the beginning of the eleventh century and that they returned with William the Conqueror. This statement has not been satisfactorily proved; but certainly many Jews settled in this country under his reign. He encouraged their immigration from Rouen; and he appointed a city, the name of which has not been preserved, for their residence in England. Numerous Jews subsequently took up their abode at Oxford. They became possessed of most of the houses in the parishes of St Edward and St Aldate there, which were from this circumstance called Great and Little Jewries. They also erected a Synagogue. Some of their houses being frequented by scholars for purposes of instruction, in course of time they came to be distinguished by the name of halls, as Moyse's Hall, Jacob's Hall, and Lombard's Hall.

Under William the Conqueror, William Rufus, and Henry I., the Jews were well treated, and increased in numbers and in wealth. It is astonishing what sums of money, enormous for those days, the Jews commanded. William Rufus, who was far from being a devout Catholic, especially befriended them. He even shocked the feelings of the enlightened populations of the day, by holding public intercourse with the enemies of Christ. He ordered a theological contest to take place in London between Christian bishops and Jewish rabbis, and he swore by the face of St Luke that if the rabbis conquered, he would become a Jew. The controversy was carried on in fear and trembling by the bishops, but happily the Jews were covered with confusion. At least so say Christian historians. The reader may perhaps remember the answer of the lion, when a man showed him the figure of a brother lion subjugated by a hunter. It is you who have painted the picture, the Jews may truly say to the Christians. Indeed the Jews had the audacity of alleging that the supposed victory had been won by fraud, and that in reality they had themselves obtained the best of the argument.

Rufus was not in good odour with the Church, and he was looked upon as little better than a Jew. He promised the Israelites, of course for a "consideration," not to permit any of their body to embrace Christianity. A certain Israelite offered the King 60 marks to induce his son Stephen, who had abjured the paternal faith, to revert to Judaism. Said the King to the youth : " Get thee hence quickly and obey, or by St Luke's face I will cause thine eyes to be plucked out of thine head." The bold youth, instead of obeying the imperious monarch, reproved him for not being a good Christian, and insisted on following his new religion; upon which, it is said, the King allowed him to depart, returning to the father one-half the sum paid. Rufus gave the priests still greater offence by not filling up bishoprics as they became vacant. He retained in his own hands the incomes of the empty sees, which were sold to the highest bidders. Meanwhile the benefices were farmed out to Jews. It appears that the latter were making great progress and even gaining proselytes. The Church, alarmed at the ground won by the Jews among Christians under the reign of Henry I., sent monks to preach against the Israelites in various cities. At this period the latter had only one burying ground in all England, and thither they were constrained to carry their dead from all parts of the country. It was called Jews' Garden, and was situated in St Giles', Cripplegate, on the spot occupied by the present Jewin Street in London.

The tranquillity and protection enjoyed by the Jews under the first three Kings after the Conquest, soon came to an end. Their hopes of enjoying a permanent and safe asylum in England were frustrated. Their persecutions began, and increased in proportion to their wealth. Enormous taxes and contributions were laid upon them, and their payment was enforced by cruel outrages and unendurable bodily torture. Crimes of every kind, the most absurd and the most groundless, were laid to their charge, and were eagerly believed by an ignorant and fanatical population. Riots were excited against them on the most frivolous pretence, or without any at all. Their houses were periodically pillaged and burnt, and they themselves outraged and murdered. The history of the Jews of those days presents an almost uninterrupted record of deeds of blood and rapine, perpetrated too often in the name of religion, by the followers of a creed which theoretically preaches charity and love to all men. In the ninth year of Stephen, the Jews for the first time were accused of the crime of crucifying a child at Norwich. The reason alleged for the supposed deed was that it was intended in derision of the crucifixion of Christ. Similar atrocities were attributed to the Jews at Gloucester and at St Edmondsbury. One of the imaginary victims was canonised, and his tomb became a seat of miracles as active as the shrine of our Lady at Lourdes. Other charges at random were laid at the door of the Jews.

One day the complaint was that they had advanced money to some adventurers who proceeded to Ireland against the King's orders. Another time it was that they had received in pledge some of the holy vessels in the church of St Edmondsbury. At each accusation treasure was squeezed from the unhappy Jews. There was method in the madness of their persecutors, for the offences of the Jews were never detected unless the King's coffers were manifestly empty. At one time Henry II. extorted a large sum from them, banishing those who did not comply with his requests. On a subsequent occasion a tallage of a fourth part of their goods was levied from them. When funds were required for the King's journey to the Holy Land, an especial tax was raised for the purpose. The whole population of the kingdom was assessed at £70,000, while the share of the Jews amounted to £30,000 according to some authorities, or to £60,000 according to others. Individual Jews too were heavily fined. One Jurnett, a Jew of Norwich, was mulcted at different periods in the then very considerable sum of 7525 marks. During this reign the Jews were permitted to purchase ground for cemeteries outside all the cities in which they dwelt.

The accession of Richard I. to the throne was celebrated by wholesale massacres of the Jews. The King, of whom England is so proud, was a zealous Christian, and he entertained a proper hatred against the Jews. He issued a proclamation forbidding any Jews to enter the palace at Westminster during the coronation. The Jews augured ill from this beginning; and to endeavour to soften the King's heart, some of their principal men gathered from various parts of the country. Attired with brave apparel and loaded with rich gifts, they ventured to approach the gates to wait for the arrival of Richard. The crowd behind, swaying and surging in its excitement, pushed the Jews within the prohibited precincts. The attendants forcibly dragged forth the hapless suppliants, and showered heavy blows on their devoted heads. The mob beset them, fell upon them, wounded some and killed others. A report was now raised that the King had ordered all the Jews to be put to death for disobedience to his commands. The populace began their work of destruction. The Jews were maltreated and killed. Their houses were found to contain immense wealth behind plain exteriors, and they were plundered and burnt. The children of Israel had thriven notwithstanding all ill-usage, and their silver had proved inexhaustible, like the oil of the Shunammite. After numerous Jews had perished with their families by sword and by fire, the King despatched Ranulf de Granville, Lord High Steward, with some of the chief nobility, to quell the riot. The mob paid no attention to the King's representatives. A considerable force was sent to the city next day, when the work of destruction had been completed, and after the blood of Jews had flowed in torrents. Killing was no murder in those days as far as Jews were concerned. Some of the rioters were apprehended, but it was not considered worth while to punish them, for their victims had only been Jews. Three men were hanged, one because he had robbed a Christian dwelling, and the other two because by setting fire to the house of a Jew, they had endangered the safety of the neighbouring Christian habitations. A few Jews had sacrificed their faith to save their lives. A certain Benedict who had submitted to baptism, prayed the King to be permitted to return to his former creed since he had acted on compulsion. The King referred the question to Baldwin, Archbishop of Canterbury, who with blunt good sense exclaimed: " Why, if he is not willing to become a servant of God, he must even remain a servant of the devil." Benedict, however, soon afterwards died from the effects of the ill-treatment he had suffered.

The example of London was sooner or later imitated by several country towns. Wherever intending crusaders appeared, the Jews fell victims to popular fury. Fierce soldiers and fanatic monks who had taken up the cross, preached against the Jews. *Autos da fé* were performed at Norwich, Stamford, St Edmondsbury, Dunstable, Lynn, and York. Cries of " Death to the Jews " rang throughout the length and breadth of the land. At York especially a fearful tragedy was perpetrated. The mob began as usual to follow their pastime of plundering and burning Jewish houses. The dwelling of Benedict, who had already succumbed in London, and who was a native of York, was sacked and destroyed, and his widow, children, and numerous relatives were slaughtered like wild beasts. The popular frenzy increased, and the Jews, with their portable treasures, took refuge in York Castle. They had reason to suspect that the governor was secretly plotting for their surrender, and that a considerable part of the booty was to be the price of his treachery. During the temporary absence of the governor, the Jews closed the gates against him. The sheriff of the county happened to be at York with a number of armed men. It was represented that the Jews had perpetrated an insult on the King's authority. The sheriff was persuaded by the governor, and an order for the attack was given. The mob joined the soldiers in the onslaught. When the sheriff perceived the mad fury of the mob and the storm he had raised, he repented the order, and publicly revoked it. It was in vain. The rabble could not be refrained. The Church joined in the assault. "Destroy the enemies of Christ! Destroy the enemies of Christ!" shouted a canon of the Præmonstratensian Order, as he rushed to the front rank of the assailants. Daily the priest was at his post, until a stone rolled from the battlements over his head and silenced his zeal for ever. The Jews fought with desperate valour. They offered large sums of money for their lives, and for once Jewish precious metal was refused. When they saw their inevitable doom staring them in the face, a council was called. A rabbi, a man of great learning, asked whether it was not better for the children of Israel to render up their souls voluntarily to their Maker, than to submit to the tortures to be inflicted by their enemies. Those who were not willing might leave. With few exceptions the assembly assented. To find a parallel for such conduct, we must refer back to the days of the siege of Jerusalem. Every head of a family cut the throat of his wife and children, and then cut his own. The survivors threw the dead bodies over the heads of their enemies. They then burnt their apparel, cast their treasures into the sinks, and set fire to the castle. The rabbi was left to the place of honour. He killed Joachim or Jacinus, one of the principal Jews of York. Joachim was a friend of Benedict, with whom he had been to London, and he had narrowly escaped from death during the massacre of the Jews in the capital. The rabbi then met death at his own hands. The few remaining Jews ran to and fro on the battlements amidst the flames, beseeching for their lives, and offering to receive baptism. Their terms were accepted, but no sooner were the assailants admitted within the gates, than the poor wretches inside were all slain.

The King sent directions to his chancellor, the Bishop of Ely, to inquire into the matter, and to punish the offenders. These as usual escaped, some having fled to Scotland, others pursuing their journey to the Holy Land, while those who were captured were released on their own recognisances. The governor of the castle was deprived of his office, and the principal inhabitants of York paid a fine to the King. These were the only penalties inflicted for a barbarous outrage that cost the lives of 1500 peaceable individuals, whose only crime was that they belonged to that race whence had sprung the founder of Christianity!

Richard I. on his return from Palestine took the affairs of the Jews into his own hands. They became subjected to certain special regulations, and were to be regarded as private property of the Crown. The King appointed itinerant Justices to make inquiries into all the disturbances that had broken out in his absence. They were to take an account of the property that had been stolen from the Jews, and also of the debts owing to all members of the community on mortgage or otherwise. In the same year were passed decrees for the registration of all the estates and possessions of the Jews. No bond was to be valid unless executed in the presence of two Jewish lawyers, two Christian lawyers, and two notaries. Special Justices were also instituted for the Jewish Exchequer, *Scaccarium Judæorum*. Their office seems to have consisted not only in collecting the funds payable by Jews to the national Exchequer, but in trying actions at law wherein a Jew was concerned. Originally the office was entrusted to Jews, and in the great Roll of the tenth year of Richard I. we find that Benedictus de Talemunt and Josephus Aaron, two Jews, were termed *Justiciarum Judæorum.* Subsequently, Jews and Christians were employed conjointly, but often Christians alone. Their annual salary was fixed at forty marks, which was the sum enjoyed by the barons, though doubtless their perquisites were considerable.

The bonds or contracts between Jew and Christian were called Starrs, from the Rabbinical Hebrew term Shetar, which signifies a contract. Three copies were usually made of these securities, one of which was deposited with the creditor, one with a magistrate, and the third with a person of note. The term Star Chamber, subsequently given to a court of law, is probably derived from the name of the apartment where these *Starrs* were deposited for safe keeping.

The foreign commerce of the Jews acquired considerable importance under the reign of Henry II., and enabled them to amass wealth, notwithstanding the periodical and systematic spoliation which they underwent. The Jews were the first to introduce into this country the use of bills of exchange. It was not only in trade that the Jews surpassed the Christians. The former constituted the most enlightened portion of the population of Europe. They were the principal factors of civilisation. No educated classes existed in those days. The priesthood, with a few honorable exceptions, were steeped in fanaticism and ignorance. The higher classes consisted of amiable and indolent bullies, who, under the pretence of redressing wrongs, wandered about Europe, leading a very questionable existence under the title of knight-errants, and of robbers who, rejoicing in the names of earls and barons, enriched themselves by preying upon their weaker neighbours. The little learning that was found in the world dwelt mostly among the Jews and the Moors. The Jews in Spain held the principal chairs of mathematics in the Mahomedan Universities of Cordova and Seville. The Jews of that country were pre-eminent in all the sciences then known, and their brethren abroad drank also freely from the tree of knowledge. Jews taught geometry, logic, and philosophy in the Universities of Oxford and of Paris. They instituted schools or colleges in London, York, Lincoln, Oxford, Cambridge and Norwich; and thither flocked Jew and Gentile to hear distinguished rabbis expound the principles of arithmetic, of

Hebrew, of Arabic and of medicine. The celebrated Aben Ezra visited England, it is believed, in 4919 A.M., or 1159 C.E., and here he delivered some lectures and wrote two works in Hebrew. The skill of Jews as physicians in the dark ages has often been mentioned. King, baron and knight, were glad to summon them to their side when sick or wounded. The Jewish leech, by the numerous cures effected through his superior attainments, excited the envy and animosity of the monks who professed to restore health through the aid of relics. The Jews, it was rumoured, were acquainted with cabbalistic secrets and with ungodly sciences; their cures were carried out by incantation and witchcraft, and in time the Jews to their other virtues added that of being sorcerers.

It is probable that John Lackland before his accession to the throne of England had had many dealings with the Jews. He was accustomed to "borrow" from them, and he knew full well their financial value. He was afraid lest they should take alarm at the persecutions of his predecessors, and betake themselves to other lands, with their gold and their silver and their precious jewels. Whether John laid a crafty plan to entice Jews into this country, and then wring from them their hard-earned treasures; or whether at first he really did mean well towards them, and then his weak vacillating nature was moved to cruelty by stern necessity, we are unable to say. Certain it is that in the beginning of his reign he appeared determined to win their confidence and to attract foreign settlers to these shores. He seemed to heap favours upon them. He gave them the right of electing a presbyter or high priest, or in other words a chief rabbi. When a certain Jacobus or Rabbi Jacob was appointed to the office, the King gave him a patent with a safe conduct, in which he addressed the rabbi in affectionate terms and styled him *dilectus et familiaris noster*. The King in the second year of his reign also signed two charters, one extending to the Jews of England alone, and the other comprising those of Normandy. The Jews might dwell freely and honorably where they chose. They might hold lands and be entitled to all their privileges as in the time of Henry II. If a Jew died the King would not disturb his possessions, provided he had heirs who could answer for his debts and forfeitures. The oath of a Jewish witness was to be as valid as that of a Christian witness. Actions at law, where Jewish interests were attacked, were to be tried before a jury of Jews. All the King's subjects were bidden to defend the Jews and their chattels as the property of the King. The Israelites paid the King for these privileges a sum of 4000 marks. When in the fifth year of his reign the citizens of London heaped indignities on the heads of the Jews, John sent a sharp reprimand to the Mayor, in which he stated that he attributed the late outrages to the fools and not to the wise men of the city, and he ended by placing the Jews under the Mayor's protection.

These measures of conciliation had the desired effect. Jews came over from the continent, and relying on the King's favour, applied themselves to the pursuit of wealth. True, their position was insecure, and the people scowled at them with hatred and jealousy. But they looked upon the promises of the King as their safeguard, and they were tolerably easy. A sudden change came over John. He met opposition on every side, and here were subjects for whom no one would lift up a finger. The Jews became his victims. If formerly they were scourged with whips, now they were scourged with scorpions. A tallage of 66,000 marks was laid upon them, which was an immense sum for those days. Nearly every Jew, man, woman, or child, was dragged to jail and put to torture. Estates were confiscated, and barbarous torments were employed in dragging forth from them the secrets of their wealth. In a great many instances the victims were deprived of an eye. Abraham was the name of the unhappy Jew of Bristol, who lost one tooth a day by refusing to give up the sum demanded, until seven teeth having been torn from his aching jaw, he saved his one remaining molar by paying a ransom of 10,000 marks. Again and again John extorted money from the Jews, and when he was unable to reach them they were pillaged by the barons. The King plundered the Jews because they were his property. The barons robbed them because they were the property of their enemy the King. The warriors of the Magna Charta understood so little the commonest principles of freedom, that whilst they were in London to collect their forces they sacked the houses of the Jews, and after carrying away all their portable valuables they rased these dwellings to the ground, and took away the stones to strengthen the city walls.

A favourite practice of King John had been to grant any habitation or property belonging to a Jew, and by him tenanted, to some minion of his, as it suited his whim or his interest. For any man may give away his own, and the Jews were only chattels of the Crown. However, the rights of the King as derived from Jewish claims, pressed too heavily on the debtors, and when the Great Charter was signed, two clauses were introduced regulating these questions. If a man died indebted to a Jew, the latter was to receive no interest until the heir became of age. The wife was to attain her dower, and the children their maintenance; and the debt was to be liquidated from the residue of the estate. Altogether the power of the creditor was sensibly diminished.

Happier days for the Jews seemed to break in the early days of the reign of Henry III. The Earl of Pembroke, and afterwards his successor Hubert de Burgh, administered the kingdom for the Royal Minor with fairness and impartiality. The Jews were treated as members of a common humanity, and not as wild beasts to be hunted down and killed. Measures were adopted for their especial safety. Those who were confined in prison were released. In each town where Jews lived twenty-four burgesses were chosen to protect their persons and property. The Israelites were exempted from the jurisdiction of the ecclesiastical courts. The old Justices in the Exchequer were dismissed for corruption, and others supposed to be more immaculate were appointed. Finally, and that was a questionable measure, the Jews were ordered to wear a special badge over their attire, consisting of two broad slips of linen or parchment affixed to their breasts. This cannot be considered otherwise than as a mark of degradation. The reason alleged for the regulation was that the Jews might be recognised without difficulty, so that there should be no pretext for their ill-usage.

Once more the Jews were encouraged by good treatment to immigrate into this country. As we have said, the Jews understood the elements of trade better than their Christian neighbours. By means of their superior knowledge, and by their correspondence with their brethren in all the then known parts of the globe, the former were enabled to undersell the latter. The Christian followed the dictates of his pocket rather than those of his conscience, and preferred purchasing from the Jewish merchant any commodities he might need rather than from his fellow-believer. The Jews by the operation of this and other causes gathered fresh enemies. Hatred, jealousy, fanaticism and ignorance surrounded them on all sides. Some of their coreligionists were imprisoned on their landing in England, by the Warden of the Cinque Ports, and their effects were pillaged. They were eventually released by order of the court upon consenting to enter their names upon the Rolls of the Justices of the Jews, and not to depart the country without permission. The ecclesiastical authorities took umbrage at the countenance given by government to the Jews. Stephen Langton, Archbishop of Canterbury, and Hugh of Wells, Bishop of Lincoln, issued an order prohibiting Christians to buy from Jews, or to sell them provisions, or to hold communication with them, the latter being excommunicated for their infidelity and usury. The Jews were not cultivators of the soil; they did not grow corn or oats, and had these mandates been strictly obeyed they must needs have met with the fate of Count Ugolino. There are indeed on record several instances of Jewish families who dragged themselves about the country, vainly applying for food, until one by one the wretched children of Israel sank and perished from absolute starvation. Happily all Christians did not implicitly follow these inhuman injunctions. In the majority of instances provisions were supplied to the Jews for love or money; probably for money rather than for love. Meanwhile they applied to the crown for relief; and directions were dispatched to the sheriffs of the different counties and cities to prevent the prohibitions in question from being enforced.

Seven years afterward a change occurred in the direction of affairs. The tolerance extended to Jews was changed for exaction and oppression. Their wealth offered too great a temptation to a needy King. All their actions were distorted into crimes; even their suing a religious corporation on its bond was alleged as an offence, and led to an accusation of forgery against the Jews. In the year 1230 they were constrained to

give up to the crown one-third part of their movables. The
King generously gave them permission to build a Synagogue.
A magnificent fane was erected. As soon as completed, it
was seized and granted to the brothers of St Anthony of Vienna
to be converted into a church, which was annexed by Edward
IV. to Windsor College. At a subsequent period, another Synagogue was appropriated by the Friars Penitent, and turned
into a chapel. Scarce a year was allowed to pass without taxes
to a grievous amount being extorted. The King was continually
in want of funds to celebrate a marriage in his family, to undertake a journey, or to discharge a debt. Whenever any royal
festivities gladdened the land, it was the Jews who paid the
piper. The taxes against them were enforced by imprisonment,
by confiscation of their property, and by seizure of their wives
and children. Heavy sums were demanded as penalties for real
or imaginary offences. They were accused once more of crucifying the children of Christians, and of stealing Christian infants
to perform upon them the covenant of Abraham. When the King
was distressed for lack of means on the eve of his marriage with
Eleanor of Provence, it was discovered that the Jews of Norwich,
who were wealthy, had circumcised a Christian boy. Seven
Jews were brought before the King on this absurd and ludicrous charge, and were condemned to be drawn and quartered, and, of course, to have their property confiscated. Some
years afterwards, in 1240, a similar offence was laid at the
door of another rich Jew of Norwich, named Jacob. A boy,
nine years old, declared he had been similarly treated when
he was five years of age. The Bishop of Norwich acted as
judge, and the Archdeacon and priests as witnesses. It may
be imagined how the Jew fared at the hands of so impartial
and merciful a tribunal. Notwithstanding that medical evidence did not confirm the boy's contradictory story, the sham
trial ended as might be expected, by the execution of Jacob
and of other Jews, and by the confiscation of their estate.
The Jews were, moreover, accused of plotting against the
State and of attempting to overturn the government. It was
alleged that they had collected together large quantities of
combustible materials at Northampton for the destruction of
London by fire. Upon these baseless and astounding charges
many Jews were burnt alive, and their effects seized. Matthew

Paris, the historian, who was an eye-witness to their sufferings, concludes thus an account of the King's extortions as practised on that unhappy race: "Non tamen abrando vel excoriando sed eviscerando extorsit."

In 1234 and in 1236 heavy tallages were laid on the Jews. The King and the people seemed to consider their wealth as practically inexhaustible, and even as being gotten by supernatural means. While the heir of a baron paid for his barony only 100 marks, and the fee of a knight was 100 shillings, the daughter of Hamon, a Jew of Hereford, paid to the king as a relief the sum of 5000 marks! Aaron of York, one of the richest Jews of England, had contributed to the royal treasury within seven years 30,000 marks of silver for the King, and 200 marks of gold for the Queen. He compounded subsequently with the King to be free from taxation by payment of 100 marks annually. The ordinary currency then consisted of silver pence called easterlings, while gold was exceedingly scarce, and usually imported from abroad. The Jews were at different epochs accused of clipping the coinage, but this seems so far from having been their practice, that in the twenty-second year of this reign, they presented £100 to the King, praying that all Jews found defacing coin might be banished from the realm.

In the twenty-fifth year of the reign of Henry III. (1240 C.E.), the *Parliamentum Judaicum* was summoned. The King sent writs to the sheriffs of each county, commanding them to return before him at Worcester on Quinquagesima Sunday, six of the richest Jews from every town, or two only from such places where they were but few, to treat with him concerning his own as well as their benefit. The hopes of the Jews rose high on their being called to take part in the King's counsels. Perhaps their years of bondage were over, perhaps better days were about to dawn for downtrodden, persecuted Israel. Great was their disappointment and sore was their trouble, when they found that supplies were the burthen of his most gracious Majesty's speech. He had brought them together to think of the ways and means of furnishing him with 20,000 marks. Six among them were appointed collectors. They might assess the sum among themselves as they pleased, but the cash must be forthcoming in two instalments within a stated period, otherwise their persons would be answerable to the King. The required amount was not delivered on the stipulated day, simply because the funds could not be gathered; and the unhappy collectors paid the penalty of disobedience to impossible commands. They were thrown into prison with their wives and children until the whole sum was squeezed from the Jews.

These chapters present a melancholy sameness. Our narrative is a tune played on one string, spoliation. Almost yearly did the King make fresh calls on the unhappy Jews to provide for his personal necessities, until the barons insisted on inquiring whither had disappeared the large sums which the King had extracted from the Jews. The King was constrained to allow one of the Justices of the Jews' Exchequer to be appointed by parliament. This Act proved of no benefit to the Jews. Funds were needed to repress incursions from Wales, and 8000 marks were demanded from them, under penalty of transportation to Ireland. They were prohibited at the same time from removing their families from their ordinary places of abode. During the ensuing three years no less a sum than 60,000 marks was squeezed from the Jews.

A Jew known as Abraham of Berkhampstead had been imprisoned for treating with contumely an image of the Virgin, and for ill-treating his wife, who would not follow his example. He was released by the aid of Richard Earl of Cornwall, on payment of 700 marks. The Jews opposed Abraham's liberation from jail, he being a man of ill-repute, and bringing discredit on their race; whereupon the same man, to revenge himself, laid information as to imaginary plots on the part of his co-religionists, and what was more to the purpose, he gave detailed accounts of their wealth and where they stored their treasure. Then followed rigid investigations as to the value and nature of the property of Jews, which ended in fresh calls being made on their purse.

The oppression suffered by the Jews became utterly unbearable, and they were compelled to cry out in agony. They were expected to coin gold, when in reality the competition of the Caorsini or Pope's usurers had materially detracted from the profits of money-lending. In vain did the Jews crave for permission to depart, and seek an asylum elsewhere. Proclamations were issued forbidding any Jew to leave England without the King's license. The principal Jews were summoned before Richard Earl of Cornwall—the King's brother—whose private coffers were well filled, and they were threatened with confiscation and death unless they supplied him with the sum demanded. Elias their presbyter or high priest (probably Chief Rabbi), a venerable old man, stood up and spoke warmly in expostulation. He prayed for a safe conduct to quit the country, as his brethren had determined to leave, rather than submit to impossible demands. Their trade was ruined, they could scarcely exist, they were beggared, and if they sold their skins they could not gather the sums exacted. The poor rabbi, exhausted by his own energy, was carried away fainting. Earl Richard did not appear to press heavily on the Jews, and was not himself harsh against them. Subsequently, on a renewal of the King's demands, they presented his Majesty with a memorial addressing him thus: "Sir King, we see thou sparest neither Christians nor Jews, but studiest with crafty excuses to impoverish all men. We have no hope of respiration left us, the usurers of the Pope have supplanted us. Permit us to depart out of the kingdom with a safe conduct, and we will seek for ourselves such a mansion as we can, be it what it may." This speech was bold for a people who had lived under the direst bondage and oppression. The King received the memorial with a burst of anger. He shrieked complaints as to the debts that bound him, which amounted to 200,000 if not 300,000 marks. "He was a maimed or deceived King; he was but half a King. He was deceived on every side. He must have money from any person or by any means." These undignified complaints of a weak King, ended in his mortgaging the Jews to his brother Richard for an advance of 5000 marks. They were evidently considered as serfs, who could be transferred from one person to the other as security for a loan of money. Again at a subsequent period, Earl Richard advanced 6000 marks on their security to the King, without pressing too hard on the Jews.

The Caorsini, as we have said, were the financial rivals of

the Jews. The Caorsini were so called from the city of
Cahors in France, though in point of fact they were Italian
merchants in the service of the Pope. These benevolent individuals would advance money to the necessitous without
interest, and consequently they were not amenable to the
usury laws. Only they would make loans for exactly one-half
the period required by the borrower, extending the time as
much as desired on payment of a commission for damages of
fifty per cent. per annum or five per cent. per month. In
addition they charged to the debtor the expenses of the keep
of the merchant, his servant and his horse, for so long as the
principal remained unpaid. The Caorsini rolled in wealth,
the people cried out, and the government tried to expel the
disinterested money-lenders; but they were the servants of
the Pope, and no one dared lift up a finger against them.
Well might Jews chuckle at Christian notions on usury. It
was a truly edifying spectacle to perceive the Vicar of Christ
on earth, the representative of Him who preached lowliness,
poverty, and charity, and who said that it was easier for
a camel to pass through the eye of a needle, than for a rich
man to go to heaven, amassing treasure at the expense of
the needy. The unhappy Jews who were permitted to follow
no other avocation than dealing in money, who were shut
out from all ennobling pursuits, who were made to pay with
silver for mere existence, for questionable protection, for the
very air which they breathed, were branded as usurers. His
Holiness the Pope sanctioned plunder and extortion by the
practices of which he benefited; but he was infallible, and
all his acts were pious deeds.

The oppressions to which the Jews fell victims continued.
Westminster Abbey was rebuilt, and though heretics could
not be admitted within its precincts, their funds were as
useful as those of true believers; so the Jews were made to
contribute to the pious work. The widow of an opulent
Jew of Oxford was constrained to give considerable sums,
and all Jews of means furnished compulsory assistance in
proportion.

The exactions practised on the Jews rendered them obnoxious
to the inhabitants of the towns where they dwelt. The Jews
actually disbursed the amounts requisitioned, yet large sums

B

were withdrawn from the district, and the whole neighbourhood became impoverished. Many towns applied for charters exempting them from the presence of Israelites. Members of that unhappy race wandered about the country with their families, houseless and vainly seeking for shelter. In many places they were treated with open violence. On the sorriest pretext they became victims to every kind of cruelty and rapacity, and hundreds fell under the fury of an ignorant and fanatical mob. At Norwich, at Brentford, at Oxford, the Jews were thrown into dungeons and their houses pillaged on the most frivolous excuses. At Lincoln, a rumour was spread that they had crucified a boy eight years old. He had been fattened with white bread and milk—so it was alleged—he had been scourged, crowned with thorns, he had been made to drink gall, and at last his side had been pierced with a spear. This highly probable story found universal credence. The Jews were tried on this charge after the fashion of the day. That is to say, they were placed under torture, until unspeakable physical agony tore from them a confession of their imaginary crime. The master of the house where the dead child was discovered, was tied to the tail of a horse and torn to pieces. Eighty-eight of the richest Jews of Lincoln were dragged to London in chains as accomplices, and were drawn and quartered, and their bodies hanged on entirely new gibbets. Twenty-three more Jews were consigned to the Tower of London to wait for a similar fate. As for the young martyr it was proved that the earth would not receive his remains, and as often as they were interred they were again vomited forth. So he was duly canonized, and his tomb in Lincoln attracted crowds of devout pilgrims.

At Oxford the Jews met with another disaster. It was alleged that during a procession of the chancellors, masters and scholars, accompanied by the clergy, to the relics of S. Frideswide, an individual said to be a Jew snatched a cross from its bearer, trampled upon it, and broke it in pieces. We do not know whether in those days Jews were allowed to be present at religious processions, but at all events, no Israelite would have been insane enough to expose himself to certain death. But when accusations were brought forward against Jews, mere probabilities were not studied, and the wildest charges were made and believed, without the slightest evidence. Fortunately they escaped a massacre in this instance. They were ordered to provide funds for the erection of a cross of white marble with a gilt image of the Virgin and Child, and also to give a silver cross to be borne in future processions before the masters and scholars. As the means required were not forthcoming, all the Jews were arrested and sent to gaol ; and as they pleaded inability, all their property in the hands of third parties was seized. The statue was completed after some delay and erected before Merton College.

The Jews were mercilessly bandied about in a royal game of financial shuttlecock and battledore. From the King they were transferred to his son Prince Edward, and by him to some Caturcensian merchants, until the Crown seized them again. Each temporary owner sought to enrich himself at their expense. In the civil wars that raged in the latter years of Henry III., they as usual proved the severest sufferers. The King seized their money to fight the barons : and the barons stripped the Jews because they had assisted the king. After the battles of Lewes and Evesham, the Jews of London, Lincoln, Northampton, and Cambridge, were robbed of their portable wealth ; and the richest among them were carried away until released by heavy ransoms. The populace, on witnessing the ill-usage of the Jews, concluded that they were not entitled to the protection of the law, and, imitating their superiors, they pillaged and maltreated the Jews on their own account.

The King recollected that the Jews were Crown property, and he awoke to the folly of allowing others to injure that property. He gave permission to the Jews who had sought safety in the Tower and elsewhere to return home. By his orders Parliament restored to them their goods and chattels. They agreed to pay to the King £1000 to be free from taxes for a certain period, on condition that during that time the King should neither undertake a crusade nor set out for a foreign journey. The temporary lull in the persecution of Jews lasted but little, and the rapacity of Henry III. became greater than ever. A few individual Israelites were especially exempted from chronic extortion by favour of some member of the Royal Family. At the instance of the Church the religious and personal liberty of the Jews was restricted at the end of the reign. They were not allowed to build schools, except where they already existed. They were commanded to pray slowly in the Synagogues, so that no Christian ears might be shocked by the sound of prayers to the Lord of Israel. No Christian was to serve a Jew or abide with him in his house, and no Christian woman was to nurse or suckle the child of a Jew. No Jew or Jewess should eat meat in Lent, or enter church or chapel, or dwell in any place except where they resided before, without the permission of the King.

Another heavy blow to the Jews proved the last statute enacted by the King on their affairs. This law prohibited Jews from holding any longer any freehold in any manor, lands, tenements, &c., whatever the origin of the property might have been. They were only allowed to retain the houses where they dwelt. All their lands were taken away from them. Those on which they had advanced money on mortgage to Christians, were returned to their owners on receipt of the principal without interest.

After this the King levied new taxes, punishing with a kind of fury the defaulters; that is, those who were too poor to satisfy his greed. Even the bitterest enemies of the Jews, the Caorsini, and the monks, pitied the lot of the wretched Jews, for their fate in the last days of Henry III. was indeed bitter. The sums extracted by the King from the Jews were enormous. Payments have been recorded to the amount of 214,825 marks of silver, as well as £1000 and some small sums in gold. In addition, the community on repeated occasions were called upon to contribute a third or a fourth of their total property, and private individuals were continuously and heavily taxed. Considering the value of money in those days, our Jewish readers will form some notion as to the sacrifices borne by their ancestors in this country.

The death of Henry brought momentary relief to the Jews, but, alas! it was only momentary. Royal proclamations brought forth promises of protection to Jews and Christians, to prove as usual empty words. Edward I. determined to obtain from the Jews only the sums he required, so as to gain popularity. The registers of the Jews were examined, a new tallage was imposed upon them, and payment enforced with the greatest severity. The goods and chattels of the Jews were levied in satisfaction of the King's demands; and if they proved insufficient, banishment or imprisonment followed. These measures were so ruthlessly applied by the clerical tribunal appointed to carry them out, that even the King himself took compassion, and some Israelites were released by his orders. In answer to popular complaints against the Jews, the King, in the third year of his reign, passed the so-called *statutum de Judaismo*. It was enacted therein that no Jew should practice usury; that no distress for debt to a Jew should be so grievous as not to leave the debtor the moiety of his lands and chattels; that no Jew should have power to sell any house, rent, or tenement without the King's leave. Jews might purchase houses in cities as heretofore and take leases to farm land for ten years. They might carry on mercantile transactions in cities, provided they were not talliable with the other inhabitants of the city. They might reside only in such towns as were the King's own. All Jews above seven years were to wear two tablets of yellow taffety on their breasts; the order soon afterwards was extended to females, and all Israelites above the age of twelve were to pay at once the sum of threepence to the King.

Efforts were made to convert the Jews to Christianity. Dominican friars offered to preach before the stubborn Jews, and the latter were ordered to go to church and listen to reason. Until then, Jews adopting Christianity forfeited the whole of their property. As an inducement, neophytes at this period were allowed to retain one-half of their possessions, the remainder being allotted to the house of converts established in Chancery Lane in the previous reign. It does not appear that many Jews were tempted to embrace a new dispensation, the followers of which seemed, in those days, to pride themselves on their rapacity, their cruelty, and their inhumanity.

The Jews remained subject to heavy tallages and fines. Their money chests were examined by order of Government, and their effects were seized and appropriated. Moreover, they were accused of various crimes, especially of clipping and falsifying coins. As we have already said, when the Jews were concerned at that period, accusation meant condemnation. On the most slender grounds two hundred and ninety-four Jews, in London alone, were put to death in one year. A new source of extortion now arose against that unhappy race. They were threatened to be charged with coin-clipping, unless they purchased silence. The King then ordered that thenceforth no Jew should be answerable for any offence committed before. A Jew so accused, however, should pay a tax to the King. In the sixteenth year of his reign the principal Jews of the realm were thrown into prison one night, and were only restored to freedom on payment of £20,000. At the same time popular clamour against the Jews became more and more widely spread and violent. The clergy and gentry joined the people in demanding the expulsion of the Jews. Edward, to satisfy his French subjects, had already exiled the Israelites from his continental dominions. On his return to London he was received with signs of joy and approbation for so noble a deed. Before this feeling could subside, the King was induced to sign a decree for the final banishment of the Jews from England. The pressure must have been great to impel so sagacious a monarch to kill the hen with the golden eggs. It was commonly reported that the Jews had eaten his people to the bones, and that they had caused great hardships to the country. What the Jews had endured at the hands of King, nobles, clergy, and people, nobody thought it worth while to consider. This unhappy people had laboured for centuries to enrich the King and the state. Tolerated only because they yielded so much treasure, the children of Israel were regarded as common property and common prey. It would not be surprising if, under these circumstances, some few of them had resorted to illicit practices to gather those precious metals with which they purchased their very existence. It is probable too that the populace shouted for the expulsion of the Jews, in order to cancel the debts which they owed to the hated Israelites. In return for this act of grace, the King received from the commons one-fifteenth of their goods, and the clergy, in token of their approval of so much mercifulness, made him a gift of one-tenth of their personalities. The decree of the King commanded that all Jews with their families should quit England before the Feast of All Saints. As a matter of generosity, Edward permitted them to take with them a part of their chattels and sufficient money to defray the expenses of the journey. All their houses and the great mass of their property and treasure were appropriated by the King. True, he promised the Church liberal grants from the vast wealth he had plundered, but his words remained only empty promises. He bestowed dowries on three of his daughters who married at that period; and the Court of Queen Eleanor became renowned for the splendour and magnificence of its gold and silver plate. We do not suppose that King Edward bore any especial animosity against the Jews. He desired to court popularity, and he found means which easily fulfilled his object and enriched him in addition. The fable of hero worship is now exploded. The so-called heroes of the Middle Ages stand now in their true lights. We see them as they were—insolent, rapacious, and unprincipled tyrants, whose virtues, if they happened to possess any, were overshaded by their crimes.

The people of England did not allow the Jews to depart in peace. They persecuted them, ill-treated them, and robbed them of the few coins that had been spared to them. The King gave the principal Jews a safe conduct, which was not always respected. They fell victims to numerous outrages. A story is told of the master of a vessel who took a number of Jews on board. He stopped at Queenborough, and went on shore, followed by the Jewish passengers. As the tide was rising the master and crew returned to the ship, leaving behind the Jews, unconscious of their danger. Too late they entreated the mariner to save them. He laughed and jeered, and told them to call on Moses who had led them through the Red Sea. Consigning them to their fate, he sailed away with their small remaining effects. The master unfortunately boasted of his valiant feat, when, it is said, he was arrested, tried, and hanged for murder. According to another version, however, he was rewarded by the King. The number of Jews who quitted England in 1290 is differently estimated at 15,060 or at 16,511 persons. They went principally to Spain, Sicily, Africa, and the east. Their valuable libraries were appropriated by Convents, the richest of them being those of Stamford and of Oxford.

One or two authorities have attributed the banishment of the Jews to the fact that a Dominican friar, being enamoured of a Jewess, became a convert to Judaism, and subsequently sought safety in flight. This act, it is alleged, being regarded as a slur upon the Church, caused its high dignitaries to bestir themselves, and thus they induced the King to sign the edict for the banishment of the Jews. This version is derived from a Jewish writer. However romantic the story may be, it seems to us improbable and far-fetched; and being uncorroborated by sufficient testimony, we cannot think it deserving of credence.

For two centuries there must have been few, if any, resident Jews in this country. In the course of time, however, their commercial pursuits and their enterprising nature must have brought occasionally some Israelites to these shores. During the reign of Queen Elizabeth, Jews began to visit England freely, and we hear of their presence in these realms. History tells us that Queen Elizabeth confided the care of her health to a Jewish physician, Rodrigo Lopez; for in those days Jewish doctors were in fashion with crowned heads, just as French cooks have been in more recent times. A conspiracy was organised against Rodrigo Lopez by jealous courtiers. He was accused of an attempt to poison the Queen, and his fate being resolved upon, it became easy to justify legal murder by sham evidence. Probably individual Jews were tolerated in England at that period in the same way as they remained unmolested in Spain under Queen Isabella. Some Israelites doubtless dwelt in England prior to the advent of Oliver Cromwell, or under the Commonwealth. We know that in 1650 a Jew, named Jacobs, first introduced the use of coffee in this country by opening a coffee-house at Oxford. It was only under the Protectorate that organized efforts were made by Jews from abroad to regain a footing in this country.

CHAPTER I.

THE RETURN OF THE JEWS TO ENGLAND.

No complete and authentic account of the circumstances attending the re-establishment of the children of Israel in this country, during the seventeenth century, can be discovered. It appears that negotiations were held at the time of the Commonwealth between some foreign Jews and the British Government, with reference to the re-admission of the former into this country. Wild reports were circulated concerning the wealth of the Jews in those days, and we find historians gravely asserting that the Israelites offered to advance to Parliament £500,000, requiring in return the cession of St Paul's Cathedral, to be converted into a Synagogue, and moreover, the Bodleian Library at Oxford! Parliament, according to the story, did not seem at all scandalised at the demand for the grandest national temple and the richest national library, but insisted on increasing their stipulated price to £800,000. It is difficult to say whether there is any substratum of truth in this statement, or whether it is wholly mythical. Certain it is, that some correspondence did take place between the Jews of Amsterdam and Oliver Cromwell, who gave them permission to send over an agent to represent their interest.

Menasseh ben Israel was in this instance the champion and representative of Judaism. He was born in Spain or Portugal about 1604; and his family was connected with that of the illustrious Isaac Abarbanel. His father, a rich merchant, succeeded in effecting his escape into Holland with his household. Menasseh was educated under Rabbi Isaac Uziel, and pursued his studies with such success that, at the age of eighteen, he was appointed preacher and expounder of the Talmud, in the Synagogue of Amsterdam, in the place of his ancient master. Before Menasseh was twenty-eight years old, he published in Spanish the first part of his *Conciliador*, of which a Latin version was issued on the following year by Dionysius Vossius. This work was recommended to the notice of biblical scholars by Grotius, who did not disdain to consult Menassch ben Israel on the thorniest points of theology.

In 1656 Menasseh wrote his Apology for the Jews in English. At that time he had already printed sixty other books in English, Hebrew, and Spanish. The Inquisition had confiscated his paternal estates in the Iberian peninsula, and during his latter years, he was constrained to exchange the study of the mental treasures he loved so well, for the merchant's ledger, and, as some say, for the watchmaker's workshop. He died in Amsterdam, shortly after his return from his mission to London, either in 1657 or 1659. He was the author of numerous works of a philosophical, historical, and critical nature; he was a profound Hebraist, an adept in hermeneutics, and a graceful scholar. He was well versed in several languages, ancient and modern; and he was intimate with some of the great thinkers of the day. Grotius valued his friendship, and Gaspar Barlæus said of him:

> "Si sapemus diversa Deo vivamus amici,
> Doctaque mens pretio constet ubique suo,
> Hæc Fidei vox summa mea est : Hoc credo Menasse,
> Sic ego Christiades, sic eris Abramides."

These liberal sentiments—uttered in the days when the Holy Inquisition was periodically consigning to the flames scores of Jews and heretics, and when to belong to the race that gave a Messiah to the Christians was to be subjected to degradation and persecution—caused considerable trouble to poor Barlæus, who was fain to conceal as much as possible his indiscretion.

We will not dwell on the various interviews of Menasseh ben Israel with Cromwell before the Privy Council and the eminent magistrates, the wealthy merchants, and the erudite divines summoned to meet him. We will only repeat some of the arguments employed in favour of his cause by those who supported his proposals. The Israelites should be admitted " because their brothers we are of the same father Abraham; they naturally after the flesh, we believers after the spirit. Because many Jews are now in very great straits in many places, multitudes in Poland, Lithuania, and Prussia by the late wars, by the Swedes, Cossacks, and others being driven away from thence. Hence their yearly alms to the poor Jews of the German Synagogue at Jerusalem hath ceased, and of seven hundred widows and poor Jews there about four hundred have been famished, as a letter from Jerusalem to their friends relates. Also the Jews in Spain, France, Portugal, and in the Indies under the Spanish crown; if they are professed Jews they must wear a badge of it, and are exposed to many acts of violence and cruelties, to avoid which many dissemble themselves to be Roman Catholics; and then if in anything they appear Jewish they forfeit goods if not life also. Now some of these entreated Rabbi Manasseh to be their agent to entreat this favour for their coming to England, to live and to trade here."

Such was the unhappy condition, as described by Christians, of the descendants of Abraham. Contemned, reviled, pillaged, murdered, neither their property nor their lives were safe except in a few places, such as Leghorn and Amsterdam, when they humbly applied to be received on the shores of Albion. Their "proposals" were unpretending enough; they only prayed to be permitted to erect a Synagogue wherein to worship the God of their fathers; to traffic in merchandise, to be protected in limb and chattel, to bury their dead. They begged also that any law existing against them be repealed, and they proffered in order to save the State from unnecessary trouble, that the heads of the congregation should arrange all disputes or differences arising between its members.

During the debate at Whitehall on the re-admission of the Jews within the British realm, popular feeling seems to have been engaged on both sides of the question, and it found its vent in a number of pamphlets that were issued from the press. Among the most strenuous opponents of the return of the children of Israel was conspicuous the noted Prynne—he who forfeited his position at the bar, as well as his ears, for writing "the Histrio-mastix" or "Players' Scourge." On one occasion he was interrogated by the Rev. M. Nye, the rector of Acton, who held totally different views on the subject, as to whether he knew of any law against bringing in the Jews? Upon which Prynne replied that whatever might be the opinion of others, he was himself certain that they could only be brought in by Act of Parliament. This consummation, he added, he would struggle against and withstand to the utmost of his power, for he would fain save his country from the disgrace of harbouring clippers, forgers of money, and men that had crucified living children. Partly for this laudable purpose, and partly to thwart Cromwell, whom he suspected, and probably justly suspected, of favouring the Jews, he composed a small book entitled: " A Short Demurrer to the Jews, &c.," wherein he set forth all that could make the name of Jew odious. Prynne displayed in this diatribe that partiality and virulence of temper, accompanied with that want of judgment, which are remarkable in all his writings. He was answered by one Thomas Collier, who, dedicating his effusion to Oliver Cromwell, satisfactorily proved that the descendants of the Patriarchs—notwithstanding all arguments to the contrary—ought to receive a shelter in this country.

The Judges declared that there were no laws prohibiting the Jews from dwelling in England. Nevertheless, the repeated conferences of the Privy Council, which lasted between the 4th and 18th December 1655, ended without producing any immediate result. There must indeed at one time have been a decision in favour of the Jews, for Evelyn says, under date of the 14th December 1655: " Now were the Jews admitted." Bishop Burnet, moreover, writes that, " he (Oliver Cromwell) brought a company of them (Jews) over to England, and gave them leave to build a Synagogue." On the other hand, the *Political Mercurius*, a kind of journal published at the time, and the *Harleian Miscellany* most distinctly aver that on the 18th December 1655, the Lord Protector dismissed the assembly without having arrived at any conclusion, because the Council were of two or three distinct opinions. The *Harleian Miscellany* further adds: " Rabbi Manasses remained in London some time, but he had received no reply to that date (1st April 1656) which was, according to Holy Scripture, 14th or 15th Abib, the first month also called Nissan, when the feast of Passover was to be kept. Many Jewish merchants had come from beyond the seas to London, and hoped they might have enjoyed as much privilege here, in respect of trading, and of their worshipping the God of Abraham, Isaac, and Jacob here in Synagogue publicly, as they enjoy in Poland, Russia, and other places. But after the conference and debate at Whitehall was ended, they heard by some that the greater part of the ministers were against this, therefore they removed hence to beyond the seas, with much grief of heart that they were thus disappointed in their hopes."

Who was the writer of the above passage we are not told; but had he been a Jew he could not have spoken more feelingly and sympathisingly. This, at all events, renders clear one point, and that is, that there were other Jews in England at the time in addition to Menasseh ben Israel. In fact, we are distinctly assured by some authorities, that another party of Jews came over contemporaneously to that of the rabbi and physician, headed by "one of their most learned rabbis," who is not named. Their ostensible object was to establish a company to trade with the Levant. Their real object was said to be to inquire into the pedigree of the Lord Protector, and to prove him, if practicable, *a descendant of the Messiah.* The same individuals are asserted to have negotiated at a private interview with Cromwell, for the purchase of the valuable library of the University of Cambridge. They obtained permission to repair to that city, and they examined and took catalogue of the most valuable books. After a time they appear to have established themselves at Huntingdon, Cromwell's birthplace, to inquire as to his supposed descent from the Messiah. The research was not conducted with sufficient prudence, and the subject of it soon became known. Cromwell found himself exposed to public raillery, and he commanded them to return to London, where he summoned them before the Privy Council and ordered them to depart the country.

Leaving aside the absurd fable of the Jews seeking for a Messiah in Oliver Cromwell, or the still greater absurdity of their looking for his descent from a Messiah, who, according to Jewish belief, never existed, we gather from the legend that separate attempts, in addition to those made by Menasseh ben Israel, were effected by other Jews to obtain a footing in England. In what precise year the Jews first openly commenced residing in the British Islands, we have no means of ascertaining. Probably some few families remained in England from the time of Menasseh ben Israel, though the Jews did not take up their abode in any number in this country until the Restoration. The "Merry Monarch" proved himself a wise monarch in this one respect, for he extended his ægis over the persecuted race, and displayed a tolerance and foresight scarcely expected from a prince of his character. One of the great bugbears of the opponents of the admission of the new settlers, was the fear lest the wicked Jews should seduce and corrupt good Christians and turn them to their own faith. It must have been to guard against the possible dangers of such occurrences, that we find the most stringent enactments passed by the early lawmakers of the Israelites, under the severest penalties in their power to inflict, against the reception of proselytes into the community. This principle has been so rigidly adhered to even to the present day here, that the spiritual guides of the Jewish community have ever persistently refused to admit strangers to the rites, privileges, and duties of Judaism.

Before the end of 1660 the Jews had attracted some public attention, for whilst on the one hand, Thomas Violet, a goldsmith, petitioned the King for their expulsion and the confiscation of their property, on the other, an order of the Lords in Council was presented to the House of Commons, recommending to the House to take measures for the protection of the Jews. The narrow-minded goldsmith's petition did not have a successful issue, and the descendants of the patriarchs were not molested. It has been asserted that as early as 1656 there was a Jewish place of worship in London, but we cannot find that this statement is borne out by facts. On the contrary, considering the very limited number of Israelites that could then have been discovered in this capital and their precarious position, we are inclined to question the accuracy of this assertion.

The earliest authentic record of a Jewish Synagogue in London dates from 1662. The building, which was situated in King Street, Aldgate, consisted merely of a house temporarily fitted up for the purpose. The number of the children of Israel then existing in this country seems to have been somewhat differently estimated. Dr Chamberlain stated that there were thirty or forty families at most, whilst one Thomas Greenhalgh, who visited the Synagogue in the above year, narrated that he found therein upwards of " one hundred men apparently of affluence, and the ladies were very richly attired."

The oldest congregation in London, it is known, is that of the Sephardim or Spanish and Portuguese Jews. Its founders came over from Holland, but also, to a limited extent, from Portugal and from Italy. Indeed, when it became understood that the Jews were tolerated in Great Britain, many of their less fortunate coreligionists on the Continent crossed the Channel to establish themselves here, induced partly by their unsafe position at home, and partly from a desire to extend their commercial transactions in a country which was already acquiring a reputation for enterprise and industry. No doubt the original immigrants hither from Amsterdam were men of means, intelligence, and education, and they were very careful to preserve the high standard of their body, which accounts for the somewhat exclusive character of their legislation.

CHAPTER II.

THE FIRST SYNAGOGUE IN LONDON.

It has been difficult to ascertain who were the first Jewish immigrants into this country, after the time of the visit of Menasseh ben Israel. But Emanuel Mendes da Costa, an eminent natural philosopher of the eighteenth century, bequeathed among his papers a curious note. This document is neither more nor less than a list of the names of the original Jewish settlers in this country—a most interesting and important document. It is impossible for us to ascertain its accuracy; we can only say that its learned possessor seemed to place entire faith in its correctness. Accepting, then, the authenticity of the information, it confirms our assertions that the re-establishment of the Jews in Great Britain took place under the reign of the gay Charles, and not under the protectorate of the stern Oliver, though the exact year is not fixed. This list had been handed by Dr Chauncey to Mr Mendes da Costa. It is evidently written by a foreigner, possessing only a slight acquaintance with the English tongue. At the same time the orthography of the day is followed, in so far as any recognised form of orthography is adopted. We will transcribe the document literally:—

"The widow Fendenadoes with her tow sons and tow servants, Leadenhall Street.
   Sinor Antony Desousa, Boshapgat Street.
   Sinor M'uell Rodregoes, Crechurch Laine.
   Sinor Samuell Devega, in Beues Marks, great, jeweller.
   Sinor Antony Rodregus Robles, Duck's Plate.
   Sinor Josep   ⎫   Deohnezous
   Sinor Mihell ⎭   Duck's Plate, brothers.
   Sinor Duart Henrycus.

THE FIRST SYNAGOGUE IN LONDON. 33

    Sinor Perera } Brothers at a Plum-
    Sinor Perear } bers in Chreechurch.
    Three mor Jewes. Merchants at the sam hous.
    Sinor Dn. Diego Rodrego Aries, Fanchurch Street.
    Sinor Dormedio and Sin Soloman, his son, St. tellen's.
    Sin. Soloman Frankles, Fanchurch Street.
    Sin. Manuel de Costa Berto, Duck's Plate.
    Sin. Doctor Boyno, Phision to the Jews, Duck's Plate.
    Sin. Steauen Rodregoes, near Algat.
    Sin. Franco Gomes, St. Mary Acts.
    Sin. Moses Eatees, Chreechurch Lane, a Jewish Rubay.
    Sin. Beniman Lewme, Chreechurch Laine.
    Sin. Aron Gabey, Duck's Plate.
    Sin. Domingo Deserga, Duck's Plate.
    Sin. David Mier, Leadenhall Street.
    Sin. Moediga, Clerk of the Synagogue.
    Most have wifes and sarvants——."

Some of the above names are easily recognisable through their grotesque disguise; others are more puzzling. We find no such patronymics as Deohnegous (Dionisius?), or Boyno, or Henrycus, in the early records of the Portuguese congregation. These Jewish visitors appear nearly all to have been of Spanish or Portuguese origin, with two or three exceptions; such as Solomon Frankles (Frankel), Beniman Lewme (Levin), and David Mier. Neither can we state whether they all remained in this country. Some of the Sephardic names became well known in the community; of others no trace is left, and it is not at all impossible that a few families may not have found sufficient temptation to take up permanently their abode in the British capital.

This would help to dispose of a statement attributed by the learned author of the "Anglia Judaica," to Haham Netto, that in 1663 the whole number of Jews in London did not exceed twelve.

There must be some misapprehension in the matter, for the learned Rabbi could scarcely have made a report so inaccurate. Even in 1662 we have the testimony of Christian observers, which we have already cited in our previous chapter, to the effect that the Synagogue in King Street was well attended, and that on one occasion upwards of one hundred men were there worshipping their Creator. Twelve men surely could never have formed or supported a Synagogue;

C

their presence would not have been known or felt in this country, neither do we see any reason to disbelieve the allegations of Christian eyewitnesses, who could have no reason to exaggerate numbers or make wilfully false declarations. In conclusion, we are able to ascertain by contemporary statistics, that twelve children were born in the Jewish community in 1663. Now in London, the births average about 139,000 yearly, in a population of say three millions and a quarter. In the same proportion twelve births would represent a population of nearly 280 individuals, which is much nearer the mark, and which agrees with the statement made by Thomas Greenhalgh. In conclusion, the individuals above named, with their wives and servants, must, among themselves, have numbered a hundred.

During the same year, 1663, the Hebrews in London were pained by the public conversion to Christianity of an Italian Rabbi named Moses Scialitti. This individual was baptized upon Trinity Sunday at St Margaret's, Westminster, by the Rev. D. Warmestre, Dean of Worcester, his sponsors being George, Lord Bishop of Chester, and Samuel Collins, Doctor in Physic, and his godmother, Lucy, Countess of Huntingdon, daughter of Sir John Davies, the Irish Attorney-General. The Rev. Paul, *alias* Moses, Scialitti, subsequently addressed a letter to his former coreligionists, explaining the cause of his adopting a new faith, and exhorting them to follow his example, and to come within the true fold. His advice does not appear to have gained many followers, and only three or four conversions among the Jews occurred at this period. One of these converts was a wealthy merchant named Dupass, or more probably De Pass or De Paz, as the name was originally spelt.

In the following year, in 1664, the Jews in England were rapidly increasing in number, and a regular constitution was drawn up and adopted in the congregation. The necessary funds were secured by the imposition of a kind of income-tax, consisting of a very small percentage, levied on all goods bought or sold, and also by the addition of one farthing for every pound of meat consumed by the community. Then two wardens and a treasurer were appointed, and the first officials in the Portuguese congregation whose names have been recorded were David Abarbanel Dormido, Mosseh Baruh Lousada, and Elias de Lima. When the congregation was duly organised, it was found necessary to procure the services of a spiritual guide to expound the Jewish law, and to recite the prayers in Synagogue. There being no one suitable in London, the services of a Rabbi from Amsterdam were secured, and Haham Jacob Sasportas was the first religious head of the Sephardim in our capital. Haham Sasportas was a pious man, and, moreover, a great talmudist. This gentleman was engaged to deliver Dinim (decisions) daily, to teach Gemara, and to officiate as Hazan; whilst his son, Samuel Sasportas, undertook the office of supplying meat to the Jews according to religious custom.

The most important duty of the ruling spirits of the congregation was the preparation of a code of laws to determine the functions of honorary and of paid officials, the principles which should regulate the conduct of different members of the congregation towards each other and towards the outer world; and finally, to provide for the management of the Synagogue economically and religiously. The Roman Republic had shown its wisdom in its veneration for custom; and no nation has followed with more implicit obedience and reverence the decrees of immutable custom than the Jews. In this especial case, however, written legislation was required, and the instances of the ancient communities of Venice and of Amsterdam were imitated.

The task of the founders of the London congregation was unquestionably an arduous one. They were persons of unblemished character, but their brethren might be expected to gather thither from distant lands, tempted by the display of religious toleration, or by the hope of realising a fortune. There might be arrivals of ignorant fanatics from the wilds of Poland, or of unlettered traders from Turkey, of men who were unacquainted with Western manners and civilization. The heads of the Jews were constrained to remember that they were strangers in a foreign country, surrounded by a population, which, if not openly hostile, at all events, eyed them with distrust and jealousy, and where the slightest offence against the laws of the land might entail misery and expulsion to all of their race. Moreover, they dwelt in the midst of easily-aroused Englishmen, and not of phlegmatic Dutchmen, and in the bosom of a nation wherein reigned at the same time the extreme of licentiousness and disbelief, and the extreme of religious hypocrisy. The gay courtiers of fair Albion worshipped as their divinities only Bacchus and Venus. The gloomy saints prayed to a Lord of their own selection, that he might smite all those whose theological opinions were not in exact accordance with their own. The lower classes were divided by a strong sectarian spirit, each sect believing itself the only one chosen for salvation, while all the others were doomed to everlasting punishment. Popular pastimes were rough and cruel, and personal violence was resorted to on the slightest provocation. Bull-baiting, cock-fighting, and pugilistic encounters were the ordinary diversion of the people, occasionally varied by the finding and roasting of a witch at the stake.

It will be easily perceived how precarious was the position of the new immigrants, and how guarded their every act had to be, not to imperil their safety. It was in this spirit of cautious prudence that the founders of the Portuguese congregation approached their task. The laws they promulgated may be roughly classed into three divisions, viz.:—

1. Those regulating the internal service of the Synagogue.
2. Those providing for the maintenance of the congregation, and the raising and administration of its funds.
3. Those finally laying down a basis for the social conduct of Jew towards Jew and towards Christian.

It is these last that mainly deserve our attention, as throwing some light on the spirit in which the Israelites met the peculiar circumstances that surrounded them. A Jew was not to be allowed to take legal proceedings against a brother in faith, unless the question at issue had been argued first before the *Parnassim* (wardens). Should a settlement not be arrived at, then only each party might be at liberty to have recourse elsewhere. The Mahamad (Council) was endowed with extensive powers, and practised a mild and paternal despotism. No Jew was to be permitted to hire a horse or rent a house from a coreligionist without the consent of the ruling powers. Moreover, no Jew should venture to print books in any language, be it English,

Latin, or Hebrew, unless his work had obtained the sanction of the same authority. Too much knowledge was not considered beneficial in those days, and ignorance was deemed safer than the handling of dangerous topics.

As may be imagined, the intercourse between Jew and Gentile was hemmed in by many restrictions. It was strictly forbidden to a son of Israel to raise any religious discussion with a Christian, or to endeavour to convert him, or to admit him to the covenant of Abraham, or to speak in the name of the nation to a stranger, or to write defamatory libels concerning him, or to intermarry with him. The Jews, finally, were strenuously discouraged from infringing the laws of the country; and it was decreed that "should any Jew be arrested by justice for thieving, swindling, or any other evil-doing, expecting that the nation would aid and abet him in perpetrating these villanies, it is firmly resolved that neither time nor money shall be expended in assisting him, and that he shall be left to be chastised according to his crimes."

The punishment for infraction of any of these edicts consisted either of fines, with deprivation of all Jewish rites until their payment, or of the application of *Beracha*, as Herem (excommunication) was euphemistically designated. This punishment will probably appear in our days as too serious to be indiscriminately awarded to heavy and to light offences; but in justice to the early Jewish settlers in Great Britain, we must remind our readers that their chief men possessed no other means of enforcing their decrees, that they had neither soldiers, nor jailers, nor watchmen at their disposal, and that they had to rely on moral means in the absence of physical means of coercion. It was better to appeal to the desire implanted in the human heart for religious consolation, and to its natural longing for the society of members of the same race and creed, than to the dread of the prison-house or the hulks. Finally, we must reflect that the Jews had to maintain their high character for honour and honesty; to avoid coming into conflict with the prejudices and notions of their fellow-townsmen; and to eschew affording offence by word or deed to those who had admitted them in their midst. The main object of the first Israelites in this country was to traffic in merchandise, and to live in peaceful obscurity following the precepts of their faith.

We learn from chroniclers of the time, that the conduct of the Jews was irreproachable, which confers no small praise on the prudence of the immigrants and on the wisdom of their chiefs.

The original laws or *Ascamoth* were first promulgated in Spanish; subsequently they were written in Portuguese. They were altered from time to time as the occasion required, but they were preserved in one or other of the above languages until the year 1819, when they were rendered into an English guise.

CHAPTER III.

STRUGGLES AND SUCCESSES.—KING CHARLES II. AND THE JEWS.

So many years had elapsed since the Jews had publicly and avowedly dwelt in Great Britain, that on their re-establishment in this country, their persons and their ceremonies were eyed with no small curiosity by the inhabitants of London, to whom Jewish customs were necessarily as little known, as are to us of the nineteenth century the rites attending the worship of Buddha or Bramah. The Synagogue in King Street became a kind of show-place, whereto resorted substantial citizens, gay gallants and fashionable ladies, who visited thither just as they went to see the handsome Kynaston at the Cockpit Playhouse in Drury Lane, or to hear the dignified Betterton at the Duke's Theatre in Lincoln's Inn. Even Mr Secretary Pepys himself considered the Jews' Synagogue as worthy of his inspection, for he tells us that he proceeded thither on the 14th October 1663, after dinner, with fair Mistress Elizabeth and Mr Rawlinson. The garrulous secretary to the Earl of Sandwich does not appear to have been edified by the spectacle that there met his view. Thus he writes: "I saw the men and boys in their vayles and the women behind a lattice out of sight; and some things stand up which I believe is their law, in a press, to which all coming in do bow; and at the putting on their vayles do say something, to which others that hear the priest do cry amen, and the party do kiss his vayle." From the date and the description given, we gather that Secretary Pepys' visit must have occurred in the afternoon of the last day of Tabernacle (Simchath Torah), for he continues: "And anon their laws that they take out of the press are carried by several men, four or five burthens in all, and they do relieve one another, and whether it is that every one desires to have the carrying of it, thus they carried it round about the room while such a service is singing." The absence of decorum must have been very apparent, for it struck Mr Samuel Pepys, who in these words comments upon it: "But Lord! to see the disorder, laughing, sporting, and no attention, but confusion in all their service, ... and indeed, I never did see so much or could have imagined there had been any religion in the whole world so absurdly performed as this."

Doubtless, had the worthy secretary to the Navy lived at the present time, he would form a very different opinion on that point, and he would be satisfied with the improved order that prevails in Jewish Synagogues during service; but in those days the noise and loud talk that so shocked him were seemingly the ordinary accompaniments of divine worship. The Synagogue authorities endeavoured to remedy this evil by passing stringent enactments which, in conjunction with a sense of propriety on the part of the congregation, it is hoped may have had the desired effect. It must be said, on the other hand, that the presence of a concourse of curious sightseers was not at all likely to promote the religious feelings of the congregants. Indeed, the latter abuse became so great, that in 1665 a law was made to the effect that no member should bring with him any ladies, nor rise from his place to meet them, nor make room for them, nor introduce any gentleman without the express sanction of the Mahamad (Council), for it was the desire of that body to preserve the sacred character of the locality—a fact that at times both Jews and Christians seem to have overlooked.

The original laws or *Ascamoth* of the Portuguese community were signed by the wardens and thirteen of the elders. Among these signatures we remark such well-known names—at least to the Sephardim—as Lousada, Gomez Serra, Netto, Barzillai, Mendes, Nunes, and Azevedo. All these patronymics are still in existence, either in this country or on the Continent. It is a recognised fact that the Spanish and Portuguese Jews were the first to adopt surnames, while their Eastern brethren, and those of Germany, were only addressed by their own biblical names. In Spain the Jews who occupied important and influential positions found it advantageous to call themselves by the appellatives borne by Christian families with whom they came into contact. Thus it happens that numerous Christian Spanish houses bear to the present day those cognomens that are so familiar all over the world, wherever a Portuguese Synagogue rears its head. This, however, may be explained, in some instances at least, by the fact that there is a considerable stream of Jewish blood flowing in the veins of some of the most ancient families in the Peninsula. The Jews of Italy have mostly designated themselves by names of cities, which may be exemplified by such instances as those of Modena, Perugia, Alatri, Piperno, &c. This custom has been also accordingly adopted by the Jews of Germany, as Cleve, Worms, Neumegen, sometimes with some little modifications, as in the cases of Berliner, Wiener, Danziger, &c.

The early members of the Portuguese congregation in London were evidently not only in affluent circumstances, but also were disposed to liberality in all that regarded their faith. When the first balance-sheet of the expenditure for communal purposes was prepared in 1665, there was found to be a considerable deficit. This was at once made up by a subscription, to which twenty-three members, each one according to his means, contributed. Moreover, when it was considered necessary to double the communal impost, the additional burden was cheerfully accepted; and also a house-to-house visitation was instituted to assist in raising funds for the poor. Indeed, the requirements of the needy were carefully attended to, as is customary among Jews. In 1666—the year of the great fire of London—was founded the Hebra of Bikur Holim, or society for visiting the sick; a code of laws was framed for its guidance, and an honorary officer was appointed to direct the affairs of the brotherhood.

Nor were the intellectual wants of the community neglected. A school was established as soon as the first house of worship had been erected; the Rabbi of the congregation, notwithstanding the very modest salary he received, devoted several hours daily to the religious instruction of the children; and, to impart greater efficiency to the system of education pursued, a warden was appointed to supervise the establishment.

The community was evidently increasing in number and wealth, for the temporary building wherein the children of Israel addressed their prayers to the God of their forefathers in time became too small, and in the year 1676 a new and larger Synagogue was inaugurated. The funds required for the purpose seem to have been obtained partly by especial contributions, and partly by the payment in advance of five years' impost. No contractor was engaged for the construction of the sacred edifice, but a number of tradesmen and workmen were employed under the inspection of an architect. The exact site of this Synagogue we are unable to verify at the present moment. It is generally believed to have been raised on the same spot as the previous temporary structure, but is stated by some to have been situated in Heneage Lane. Even this last Synagogue could not have been very large, for in 1699, or twenty-three years after its opening, it was found requisite to erect another, which is the building in existence at the present moment in Bevis Marks.

Thriving as the Jewish community was under Charles II., its prosperity was not uninterrupted, nor was its political position so secure as not to give rise to frequent anxiety.

Among its internal concerns, its rock ahead was the influx of foreign poor. Then as now, various expedients were tried, and tried in vain, to check an organised immigration of paupers. Ordinances after ordinances were promulgated by the Synagogue authorities, but apparently with little effect, to judge from the frequency with which other enactments for the same object followed. In 1670 it was found necessary to decree that all foreigners coming from abroad for assistance, should depart within five days from the shores of England; that they should not be permitted to enter Synagogue in the meanwhile, and that the Zeddaka (poor fund) should allow them all it could spare. Soon afterwards it was ordered that no foreigner should be admitted as member of the congregation, or even be allowed to attend divine service, until he satisfied the wardens as to his possession of the means of subsistence. Nevertheless, poor Jews from Holland and Poland continued to flock over, and additional laws were made on the subject, probably with as little result as the previous enactments. Members of the congregation were strictly enjoined not to raise subscriptions for any foreigners, nor to canvass in their favour, nor in any way to encourage their presence. The success achieved by these new measures is not recorded, but it cannot have been great, otherwise further legislation in the same sense would not have been continued.

The Jews, as we have seen, were far from enjoying a secure position, and occasionally they were thrown into a fright by being threatened with expulsion, and with confiscation of their property. These storms happily subsided peaceably, and it must be owned that the King persistently refused to give countenance to the machinations of the enemies of the Jews. In 1664 a petition was presented by Emanuel Martinez Dormido, and two others, probably the wardens, on behalf of the Jews for protection, and leave to trade in the kingdom. The petitioners set forth "that they had long traded there, and behaved with due obedience to the laws; but Mr Ricault and others threatened seizure of their estates, and say that both life and estate are forfeited; the Earl of Berkshire says he has a verbal order from His Majesty to prosecute them, and seize their estates unless they come to an agreement with him." No doubt this was a speculative attempt on the part of that shrewd nobleman to obtain a handsome sum from the Jews on the plea of shielding them from persecution. If so, the attempt failed, for the King in Council replied that he had issued no such order, and that they might enjoy the same favour as before, so long as they demeaned themselves peaceably, and obeyed the laws.

In 1670 the Jews had acquired sufficient importance to induce the House of Commons to direct that an inquiry should be made as to their number, and on what terms they were permitted to reside here. The report, however, was not published, and thus we have lost some valuable information.

An old friendship subsisted between the Jews and Charles II. It is said that the Jews of Amsterdam had advanced him 1,000,000 gulden (about £84,000) to assist him in returning to England, and that he granted them a charter permitting them to settle in this country. It is alleged that a copy of this charter is still in possession of the Jews of Amsterdam. Moreover, the presence of two Jews among the retinue of the Queen may have had some influence in inducing him to extend his protection to their brethren.

When Catherine of Braganza was on her way to become the consort of the King of England, during her journey through New Castile, she was attacked by erysipelas. The physician of King John IV. of Portugal was sent for to heal her. His name was Antonio Mendes, and he was a Jew. He gained favour in the sight of the princess, who made him a member of her household, and appointed his brother Andrea Mendes to be her chamberlain. Catherine desired that they should accompany her to England, and settle there. The two brothers consented to this proposal. They subsequently summoned their third brother to establish himself in England, and he acceded to their wishes. Then all three threw off their assumed garb, and openly proclaimed themselves as Jews. Probably the royal lady may have been somewhat shocked at finding herself attended by heretics, but she does not appear to have dispensed with their assistance on that score. Her Majesty, though not by any means beautiful, possessed a youthful, innocent, and fresh countenance, which was very captivating to a *blasé* man of the world like Charles Stuart; and not seldom her modest and simple charms prevailed over the bold shamelessness of a Castlemaine, the saucy effrontery of a Nell Gwynne, and the meretricious smiles of a Louise de Querouaille. It is not at all improbable that the Queen may have exercised her influence in favour of the Jews. Antonio and Andrea Mendes appear to have taken active part in the affairs of the Jewish community of England, for we find their names mentioned more than once in the early records of the Spanish and Portuguese congregation. Subsequently the Mendes family repeatedly intermarried with that of Da Costa, as we shall see in its place, and their common descendants became known by the two surnames.

The King evidently preserved a certain amount of goodwill towards the Jews, and the Jews seized every opportunity of demonstrating their loyalty and gratitude towards the King. Sometimes the expression of their feelings took a singular shape.

It is recorded that in the year 1678 Rabbi Jacob Jehudah Leon, of Amsterdam, dedicated to His Majesty a small pamphlet, entitled "A relation of the most memorable things in the Tabernacle of Moses and the Temple of Solomon, according to Scripture." This effusion was forwarded to the King with a model of Solomon's Temple constructed by Rabbi Leon, and accompanied by an address wherein he says "the holy vessels, garments, and utensils thereof are delineated and set forth to the life, and which was graciously owned with devout affection thirty years ago and upwards by that serene Queen, your Majesty's mother; so be pleased, most noble prince," &c. To us this appears a strange gift to address to the protector and companion of the witty and profligate Rochester and the accomplished and equally profligate Buckingham; to the royal lover of Nell Gwynne, the sauciest of orange-girls, of the handsome and rapacious Lady Castlemaine, of the scheming Louise de Querouaille, of *La belle* Stuart, and of various other equally meritorious ladies. We do not know what reception the King gave to this singular present. His Majesty was really good natured, and no doubt the model was duly accepted, and his sense of filial duty may possibly have caused him to prize an object that had appertained to his royal mother.

CHAPTER IV.

THE ALIEN DUTIES.

The Jews of England, it must be owned, ever obtained protection from the Stuart Kings against the persecution of their too zealous subjects. In 1673 the Jews were indicted for worshipping in public in their Synagogue, probably at the instigation of persons of the same class as those who institute proceedings against Sunday trading, in the belief that they only serve their Maker when they inflict pain on their fellow-beings. The consternation of the children of Israel may well be conceived. To renounce their newly-adopted country, or to renounce the worship of the Lord of Abraham, Isaac, and Jacob, seemed the alternative forced upon them. There could be no hesitation as to their choice. They petitioned King Charles, that during their stay in England they might remain unmolested, or that time be afforded to them to withdraw from the country. The King appeared well disposed towards them, and on the 11th February 1673, His Majesty decided in Council "that the Attorney-General stop all proceedings, and that they receive no further trouble in this behalf." In 1685 a similar misadventure occurred to the Israelites, for thirty-seven of their merchants were suddenly arrested on one occasion in the Royal Exchange, under the statute 23 of Elizabeth, for not attending any church. Happily they were not at the mercy of the fanatics who once more interrupted their tranquillity. They dwelt not in a country where it was considered " an Act of Faith " to broil alive a certain number of its citizens because they happened to hold theological opinions at variance with those of the majority. The Jews addressed themselves to the new King, James II., beseeching his support and countenance for the exercise of their faith. On the 13th

November, the King in Council ordered "that the Attorney-General do stop the said proceedings;" His Majesty's intention being that they should not be troubled on this account, but they should enjoy the free exercise of their religion whilst they behaved themselves dutifully and obediently to his government. This appears to have been the last time when the Jews were avowedly molested on what is conventionally termed religious ground. We say conventionally, for there is no creed that enjoins harassing and tormenting human beings belonging to another race, and least of all, Christianity, which lays claim to especial mercy, charity, and love for all mankind.

During the reign of James II., the question of the levy of the Alien Duties was the question that, most of all others, engrossed the attention of the Jews. The King had granted them letters of denization, which relieved them from the payment of the special tax on all goods exported by foreigners. This proceeding was resented by the English merchants, who were apprehensive lest the same duties should also be remitted upon all merchandise imported. The representatives of British commerce petitioned against this measure, alleging "that the remission of duty inwards or outwards would be injurious, and a means of the diminution of the revenue, and would throw the mysteries of our artificers into the hands of foreigners, to the ruin not only of the trading and working people at home, but also of the several English factories abroad. The petition was signed by Sir Mathew Andrews, Sir Benj. Newland, Sir Thos. Griffith, Sir John Chapman, Sir Henry Tulse, Sir Robert Jeffrey, Sir Samuel Dashwood, Sir Benjamin Ayliffe, and fifty-seven others. A similar address was also presented apart by the Hamburgh Company, the Eastland Company, and the merchants of the West and of the North of England. Notwithstanding all these efforts, prompted by a rivalry of calling, the petitioners were unsuccessful in their endeavours to maintain the communal disabilities of the Jews. Nor does it appear that the direful calamities foreseen by those liberal-minded traders ever fell on British industry and enterprise, which on the contrary attained considerable development at this period.

In the commencement of the reign of William III. the Jews still received the royal countenance in the matter. Mr Thomas Pennington, one of the officers of the Custom House, acquainted the King, through one of the Lords of the Treasury, that, though the clauses of exemption from payment of alien duties granted to the Jews in their patents of denization by King Charles II. and King James II. *non obstante*, the statutes were void at the demise of the first and abdication of the last, and that His Majesty had neither confirmed those *non obstante* clauses nor granted any new patents of denization with similar clauses, yet the Jews presumed to enter their goods since His Majesty's reign in their own names, paying only English duty, by which means goods so entered became forfeited. His Majesty, in answer to this, vowed that he would not abate the Jews of threepence of what was due to himself, which was a moiety, and he ordered Mr Pennington to enter an information in the exchequer for £58,000. Nevertheless, the Jews had so much influence at Court and among the Commissioners of Customs, that for a long time they baffled all the efforts of their enemies. They succeeded in procuring an order of Council, not only against the information brought by Mr Pennington, but against all others that should be brought against their nation on the same grounds.

In vain Mr Pennington addressed a short petition to the Council, while the order was pending, praying that both parties might be heard. In vain he urged time after time that his petition might be considered. When the case came on, the matter was passed without any debate. The petition was brought forward of Antonio Gomez Serra, Phineas Gomez Serra, Andrew Lopes, Antonio da Costa, Joseph Bueno, Menasse Mendez, Antonio Correa, and several others, making twenty merchants in all. Among other allegations, it was urged in that document that the petitioners had been lately arrested in His Majesty's name by one Thomas Pennington, for vast sums of money, being the value of all goods exported and imported since 11th December 1688, that the said Thomas Pennington had brought information of *devenerunt* against them in the Court of Exchequer, which greatly impaired their credit and stopped their trading; that as to the duties inwards most of them were free denizens, and therefore discharged from paying any more customs than his Majesty's natural-born subjects, and those that were not denizens had paid duty; and that as to alien duties outwards, they had been taken off by Act of Parliament in King Charles' reign, and by proclamation in the late reign, as greatly prejudicial to the exportation of the woollen manufacturers, and it was never demanded. His Majesty in Council assembled, on the 26th February 1689, after due deliberation, was graciously pleased to order that Sir George Trewby, his Attorney-General, do cause *nolle prosequi* to be forthwith entered upon said information, or any others brought against the petitioners upon the like accounts, it being his Majesty's pleasure that they enjoy full benefit of their respective letters patent.

The triumph of the Jews was of brief duration. The battle of the duties was not over. The English merchants, with the proverbial tenacity of their race, which does not know when it is defeated, renewed their efforts to place the Jews at a disadvantage. They industriously spread rumours that the Jews had obtained a decision in their favour by openly bribing personages in high office, and that the whole proceeding was very discreditable to the Government. They addressed the King, holding forth that were the order in question to be carried out, his Majesty would lose £40,000 by not prosecuting for the forfeiture already past, and that the duty thereby cut off for the future would amount to, at least, £10,000 per annum; that these sums would have to be made up by the people of England; that the balance of trade would be broken, and the Jews let loose to overrun the trade of the English merchants both at home and abroad; that most English merchants had estates in land as well as stocks in trade, and paid taxes for them, whereas rich Jews " were past finding out," and it would grieve the English to pay any new taxes if Jews were illegally exempted from payment of any ancient duties. The Commissioners of Customs represented these matters to the Council, and exercised such pressure, that notwithstanding all the efforts of the Jews, the foregoing order was superseded, to the great joy of the Christian merchants. The

King decreed, at a Council held at Hampton Court, on the 14th October 1690, that the Lords Commissioners of the Treasury do give directions to the Commissioners of Customs and other officers for collecting all such duties as are by law payable for goods of native product or manufacture of this kingdom that shall be exported, notwithstanding the order of the 22d January 1665, or any other direction to the contrary.

This unfavourable conclusion of a prolonged struggle must have proved a heavy blow to the Jews. As we have seen, they not only forfeited thereby £40,000, but their future commercial operations would be taxed to an amount estimated at £10,000 per annum. We have no means of judging as to the extent of the injury inflicted upon them by this adverse decision. We are able, however, to form some idea of the financial position of the Jews at this period, by referring to their assessment for communal purposes. Thus, in the year 1677, no fewer than twenty members of the congregation were assessed at £20 each for their share of the half year's communal impost. The largest contributor to the fund was Solomon de Medina, the eminent merchant and army contractor, who was taxed at £28. This income-tax was calculated on the basis of 4s. for every £100 on all merchandise bought and sold, 2s. for every £100 on goods in transit, and 1s. on bullion, plate, and jewellery; and it was assessed on the half-yearly returns rendered by the merchants themselves. Reckoning this impost at an average rate of 2s. 6d. per £100, a payment of £20 for a period of six months, would represent transactions to the extent of £32,000 per annum, a by no means despicable amount for those days. In the following year, Sir Solomon Medina paid an impost of £50 for six months, the result of operations reaching to £80,000 per annum, which figure merchants of two centuries since must have regarded as altogether beyond the common range. This well-known individual, to whom we shall revert more fully hereafter, was the first Jew who received the honour of knighthood.

It is clear, therefore, that the commercial dealings of the Jews were of sufficient importance in 1678, and *a fortiori* ten years later, when their numbers had further increased, their trade must have assumed still greater proportions. The check they received by the reimposition of the alien duties, was surmounted in time, and that enterprising race, notwithstanding its having been—to use a sporting expression—so weightily handicapped, in a few years, by dint of superior energy, industry, and perseverance, showed again to the front.

CHAPTER V.

ANECDOTES.—CONVERSIONS.—LEARNED RABBIS.—NEW SYNAGOGUES.

The old penal statutes against the Jews of the time of Edward I. long remained unrepealed, though apparently allowed to fall into desuetude, and their existence was openly adverted to by the enemies of the Jews so late as the reign of the First George. One of these enactments forbade the Jews to appear in public without a yellow badge, under pain of forfeiting their lives. Amidst a series of laws, equally rational and merciful, it was decreed that no Jew should sue a Christian in his own name, but only in the King's name, and with the royal licence. The knowledge of this fact, suggested to an ingenious Christian, who happened to be indebted to an Israelite, a new way to pay old debts, with a saving-clause for his conscience. Legal proceedings were taken by the clamorous Hebrew, and the case came for hearing before Chief Justice Jeffreys—the judge of "bloody assize" notoriety. The defence was simple enough. A Jew had no right, according to the laws of England, to bring an action against a Christian. The Chief Justice inquired of the defendant whether he had any other plea to urge. "No, my lord, I insist on this plea," replied the honest debtor. "Then," shrieked the judge, "I tell you that even according to your defence, you must pay his demand, for he did not bring the action against a Christian, but against a Jew, and one greater than himself."

For once, perhaps, one of the greatest bullies that ever sat on the judicial bench was right. But the sentence, just in itself, was supported by arguments more offensive to the plaintiff, than the allegations of the defendant.

Notwithstanding the eventual decision of William of

Orange in the matter of the alien duties, there is no reason to doubt his favourable disposition towards the Children of Israel. Indeed, it is asserted, that without the assistance of the Jews of Amsterdam, the King could never have reached the throne of England, for his intended expedition was at a standstill for want of funds, until they advanced some very large sums. If such was the case, the loans in question must have been effected to the government of the republic, and not to the Stadtholder personally; for we are informed by Lord Macaulay, that soon after the Chief Magistrate of Holland had ascended the throne of England, the English Parliament voted a grant of £600,000 to repay the Dutch Republic for the costs of the expedition. At all events, William must have well known the great benefits that the presence of the Jews had conferred upon Holland. He must have seen with his own eyes the enterprise and the industry, the financial genius and the honesty—ay, the honesty, of that much maligned people, to whom his native country was so greatly indebted. He must have perceived how materially they had helped in rendering that small strip of marshy land that struggled for bare existence against the all-devouring sea-waves, one of the wealthiest states in Europe, the flag of which rode proudly over every ocean. Doubtless, King William had to yield to pressure in the question of the alien duties. But when the inhabitants of Jamaica petitioned his Majesty to order the Jewish settlers to quit their homes, and leave their property at the disposal of the patriotic natives, he most positively declined to entertain their application.

Another instance also is recorded of the King's prudent forbearance towards the Jews. In 1689 two millions were voted by Parliament for the conquest of Ireland. The difficulty was how to procure the money. A new assessment was made on real property; a poll-tax was levied, and extra duties were laid on tea, coffee, and chocolate. All these sources of revenue proving insufficient, it was proposed to tax the Jews to the extent of £100,000. The Jews at once petitioned the King, and declared that they could not afford it, and they would rather leave the country at once than be ruined. Wise statesmanship showed that such a tax would be little better than confiscation, and it was eventually abandoned.

We may here observe that singularly enough, while few English Jews selected the army as a profession, the sister service found much favour in their sight. Our co-religionists have furnished several distinguished naval officers to their country. Among these we may name Commodore Chamberlain, who flourished at the time of William and Mary: and in our own days we have known several Israelites holding commissions in the British navy.

It has been remarked by some writers that in the reign of King William III. and Queen Anne, there were many conversions of Jews to Christianity. Now we have grounds for believing that the number of these conversions was much exaggerated. Few names of note have been handed down to us as appertaining to persons who forsook their ancient religion at that period. We shall hereafter fully analyse the subject of conversions from the old faith to the new dispensation. We shall merely observe at present that obvious reasons for the adoption by some stray members of a barely-tolerated race of the external religion of the country which tolerated them, will suggest themselves to all readers.

Some of the conversions were evidently of a hollow nature, and cases are known of "converted" individuals, who, before their death, desired to return to the old persuasion. Among these we may adduce the example of Mr Dupass, to whom we adverted in a previous chapter. This gentleman, who was a Dutch merchant of means, had come to England at the time of the Restoration, and had then embraced Christianity. As a reward for this act, he had been appointed a clerk in the office of the Secretary of State, Sir Lionel Jenkins. Dupass became a court favourite, and married a wealthy English lady. According to a writer, who is a bitter enemy of the Jews, these latter persecuted him until he went to India, and there he was driven to seek re-admission into Judaism. Mr Dupass died in that country, and we are told that the wicked Jews who held his property declined to give it up to his widow until constrained by proceedings at law.

The influx of Jews from Lithuania and Germany became greater and greater towards the end of the seventeenth century. The aristocratic Sephardim, whose ancestors had banqueted with sovereigns, and held the purse-strings of kings, looked with some disdain on their poorer and humbler brethren—the plebeian Ashkenazim, who had dealt in worn garments or huckstered in petty commodities on the banks of the Vistula, or in German Ghettos. The Portuguese did not allow the Germans to have any share in the management of congregational affairs. It was especially enacted that the latter, who probably were neither very refined nor very cultivated, should not be allowed to hold office in the Synagogue, nor vote at meetings, nor be called to the Law, nor receive *Mitzvoth* (religious honours), nor make offerings, nor pay imposts. The Germans, in point of fact, were treated as belonging to a lower caste, and the only functions that a member of that nationality was permitted to fulfil were the useful, albeit lowly, duties of beadle, which were actually entrusted to a German—a certain Benjamin Levy. In time the Germans resolved to establish a Synagogue of their own, as our readers will see in due course.

The Spanish and Portuguese Jews were fortunate in obtaining the services of men of great learning and piety as Rabbis of their congregation. Among these we may name Rabbi Jacob Abendana, who was elected Haham, or Ecclesiastical Chief, in 1680. He was distinguished by his profound knowledge of Hebrew, and he rendered the " Cuzari " into a Spanish dress. His brother Rabbi Isaac Abendana settled soon afterwards at Oxford, where he became professor of Hebrew. He is said to have been an indefatigable writer, and he translated the " Mishna " and the " Commentaries of Maimonides " into Spanish. He also produced a work entitled, " Discourses on the Ecclesiastical Polity of the Jews," which caused some sensation among Christian scholars.

The most eminent Haham or Chief Rabbi that the Sephardim ever possessed in this country was unquestionably Rabbi David Nieto. He was a philosopher, physician, poet, mathematician, astronomer, and theologian. Like many other great men among the Jews, he showed that faith and science may go hand-in-hand together, and, whilst being the spiritual guide of his flock, he did not disdain to heal their bodily infirmities. The Rabbi was practising medicine at Leghorn, and had written in his own language an erudite work entitled, " Pascologia," demonstrating the errors that had crept into the calendar from the Council of Nice to 1692, when he was summoned to preside over the Spanish and Portuguese Congregation, London. In the English capital he composed a book called the "Matteh Dan," which is a kind of supplement to the well-known "Cuzari" of Rabbi Yehuda Halevy, and has for its object a vindication of the Oral Law. He, moreover, gave forth another work in Hebrew, the "Aish Dath"— "Fire of the Law," which was aimed at a Rabbi of heterodox opinions, named Nehemiah Cheyon. The heresies of this individual served as a theme for the lucubrations of another Rabbi, Haham Joseph Ergas. This work is said to be well written, but conceived in an intemperate spirit. The printing of these early Hebrew books was attended with great difficulty, and reflected great credit on the energy and perseverance of their authors; for there were no Jewish compositors in those days, and Christian workmen, being ignorant of the Hebrew letters, committed numberless typographical errors, requiring the revision of many proof-sheets.

Hebrew genius and learning were honoured in England even during the early part of the 18th century. Among the talented Jews who acquired a reputation with English *savants* we may distinguish Daniel Israel Laguna, who published in 1720 a metrical version of the Psalms, under the title of "A Faithful Mirror of Life;" a work that was highly commended. Then another Portuguese Rabbi, Jacob de Castro Sarmiento, attracted general attention for his profound erudition, and his extensive acquirements in natural science and philosophy. He was elected a member of the Royal Society, and an honorary diploma was conferred upon him by the University of Aberdeen; facts that speak well, not only for the appreciative discrimination of Englishmen of letters and science, but also for the spread of liberality and religious tolerance.

During the first year of Rabbi Nieto's residence in England, an important event occurred in his congregation. A new Synagogue was inaugurated. The increase in the community had of late years been so rapid, that, in 1698, it was resolved to raise a new place of worship. In that year the wardens and elders summoned a meeting of the members, and applied to them for the payment of the sums they had subscribed towards a building-fund. On the 12th February,

1699, a contract was signed by six representatives of the Synagogue, viz., Antonio Gomes Serra, Menasseh Mendes, Alfonso Rodriguez, Manuel Nunes Miranda, Andrea Lopez, and Pantaleao Rodriguez on the one part; and Joseph Avis, carpenter, on the other; for the construction of the new Synagogue. It is related that the builder, who was a Quaker, returned to the Portuguese authorities, on the day of the opening of the Synagogue, the profit he realised on the contract. He would not retain to his own use any of the gold intended for the erection of a fane to God. The cost was to be £2750, and the payment to be effected in seven instalments. On the 13th November of the same year, a lease was signed by the same gentlemen for the land on which the Synagogue was to be raised—for sixty-one years certain, and the remainder, viz., thirty-eight years at the election of the Jewish representatives, was granted by Lady Ann Pointz, *alias* Littleton, and Sir Thomas Pointz, *alias* Littleton, for the site of Plough Yard, in Bevis Marks, at £120 per annum. The leasehold, we may add, was afterwards converted into a freehold property.

During the progress of the new building, the old Synagogue was becoming too small for the congregation. It was so crowded that the wardens were ungallant enough to exclude the ladies from divine service, and they ordered that the men should temporarily sit in the ladies' gallery, the old entrance thereto being bricked up, and another ingress being opened from the men's side. The new Synagogue was in time completed, and was consecrated in the year 1702. Curious to say, Queen Anne presented a beam to the new Synagogue, which is still to be found in the ceiling there. Many of the original benches were brought thither from the old Synagogue, and some of the brass candlesticks had been conveyed over from Holland. With the exception of some unimportant alterations in the shape of the windows and other minor matters, the old edifice remains there unaltered to the present day; and it is there that the ancient Portuguese community still assemble to pray to the God of Israel.

CHAPTER VI.

HEBREW CAPITALISTS.

The success achieved by Jews in commercial and financial operations has been regarded at all times and in all countries as an especial grievance, by some at least of their Christian neighbours. We will not discuss whether such feelings as envy and jealousy may not have some share in the half ludicrous, half bitter lamentations on the supposed great wealth of the Jews, lamentations which are occasionally wailed forth from some Gentile journal, more remarkable for fiery zeal than tolerance or discretion. The greed, the love of gold, of the Jews has formed the theme of many an invective thundered against that unhappy race. Comparatively few writers have rendered them the common justice of admitting that the greed or love of gold of Gentiles has been quite as great; and if a few Hebrews have occasionally realised exceptional fortunes, it has been because they possessed exceptional foresight, perseverance, industry, and courage.

The eighteenth century has furnished several examples of financial genius among the Jews. Among the men who made their mark in their day and who gained a place in history, we will mention first the " Jew Medina," who lived in the reign of Queen Anne, and to whom we have already adverted. It is recorded in British annals that in the year 1711 the Duke of Marlborough was attacked in Parliament for receiving from a Jew a yearly payment of the sum of £6000. The keen general, who hungered as sharply after the precious metal as any Israelite, replied that the money had been applied towards obtaining trustworthy information. During the enquiry that followed, the curious fact was brought to light that, since 1672, the Jews of Amsterdam had handed over annually an amount of between £5000 to

£6000 to the commander of the Dutch forces, an office vested in 1711 on the conqueror of Blenheim. These and other discoveries made as to the Duke's rapacity, were so handled by his political opponents that the haughty John Churchill fell for the time into disgrace. The Jew who accompanied the Duke of Marlborough in all his campaigns, and who administered to the avarice of the great captain, was Sir Solomon Medina, he who for years had been the largest contributor to the funds of the Sephardic Congregation. This enterprising gentleman is the " Jew " who at one period held contracts to supply the army with bread. Sir Solomon Medina amply repaid himself for the advances made to Marlborough by forwarding expresses bearing intelligence of some of the most glorious battles ever won by English bravery; and Ramilies, Oudenarde, and Blenheim contributed as much to the wealth of the Hebrew as to the glory of England. Sir Solomon Medina bequeathed a considerable fortune at his death; and we believe his descendants eventually left the pale of Judaism.

Menasseh Lopez was another member of the Portuguese community who acquired riches by superior sagacity and courage. He was a successful dealer in stock, when one day rumours of the death of Queen Anne were circulated. The tidings produced a sudden panic in the capital. The train-bands desisted from their exercises: eager crowds flocked in alarm at the street corners, and the funds fell with suddenness. Gentile speculators became intimidated, and did not muster sufficient resolution to operate. Stock was openly offered at rapidly diminishing prices, and no one had the boldness to purchase, until Lopez and other Jews stepped forward to buy all the government securities they could obtain. The news in time was discovered to be false; public agitation quietly subsided, and a rebound upward occurred in every kind of stock. Lopez by his nerve and discernment cleared very large profits on this occasion; and he became the possessor of a fine property. Of that other Menasseh Lopez, sprung from the same stock, who came many years afterwards, we shall speak in its proper place.

Pre-eminent among the Hebrew capitalists of last century

ranked Sampson Gideon, for that was the name by which the great " Jew broker " was known in the Gentile world. He was the "greatest Roman of them all." He was the Rothschild of the day, the friend of Walpole, the pillar of state credit. His operations were executed on a scale that was then considered gigantic. During the crisis that followed the South Sea Bubble, Gideon was anxiously looked up to, but he was as firm as a rock, as impenetrable as a sphinx. It is said that he rendered Sir Robert Walpole considerable services at this time, not only in a private capacity, but also in materially assisting the minister in allaying public alarm, and in restoring general confidence. It is noteworthy that the Jews, with their commercial insight into the real nature of undertakings, held aloof from the South Sea Scheme and its sequel which promised sudden riches to all. When the whole nation was infected in an astonishing degree with the spirit of stock-jobbing; when Exchange Alley was crowded with statesmen and clergymen, whigs and tories, churchmen and dissenters, sober merchants and fashionable ladies; when other employments and professions were utterly neglected; when new companies started up every day under the highest auspices; when the Prince of Wales was constituted Governor of the Welch Copper Company, the Duke of Chandos headed the York Buildings Company, and the Duke of Bridgewater formed another for building houses, the Jews appeared to preserve their calmness and perspicacity in a remarkable degree. They did not allow themselves to be carried away by the universal passion for gold, nor to be led into the vortex that dragged thousands upon thousands into destruction. When the crash came, and disappointment, rage and despair preyed upon numberless victims, the Jews reaped the fruits of their caution. Insolvencies were exceedingly numerous, but not a single Hebrew name is perceived in the list of bankrupts.

It is related of Gideon that in the panic that accompanied the advance of the Pretender to London in 1745-46, he purchased stock when everybody else was eager to sell. The consternation was general. The King was trembling, the prime minister was wavering, and the funds were offered at any price. Sampson Gideon went to Jonathan's and bought all the government securities he could obtain; he advanced every guinea he possessed, he staked his credit, and he held as much stock as all the remaining speculators put together. The Pretender soon after retired, and Gideon nearly doubled his fortune! Some months before the revolution, this enterprising financier had borrowed, to carry out some operation, a sum of £20,000 from Mr Snow the banker. When the Pretender was marching on the capital, Mr Snow wrote to Sampson Gideon in tones alternately piteous and offensive, requesting an immediate return of his advances. Mr Snow not only really required the money in his own bank in this emergency, but he was afraid of losing it altogether. Gideon quietly proceeded to the Bank of England, and obtained therefrom twenty £1000 notes, which he rolled around a bottle of smelling-salts, and forwarded to the dismayed banker. The latter, reanimated probably more by the sight of those crisp pieces of paper than by the pungent scent of the stimulating agent, addressed immediately a gushing letter to Gideon, vowing everlasting gratitude. Sampson Gideon, it is well known, was the ancestor of the Eardley family, on the female side, and he purchased the Belvedere Estate at Erith, which remained until late years in the possession of his descendant, Sir Culling Eardley, Bart. Sampson Gideon espoused a Christian lady, and his son, Sampson, was baptized and raised to the peerage under the title of Baron Eardley. One of the daughters of Lord Eardley was united in matrimony to a gentleman bearing the not uncommon name of Smith, and who was created a baronet in 1802. Mr Smith became Sir Culling Smith, Bart.; he eventually styled himself Sir Culling Eardley, and is the progenitor of the present representative of the title.

One day in Heshvan, 5514 (1754), while the elders were holding a meeting, a notary entered and delivered a communication to the President. It was from Sampson de Rehuel Abudiente, resigning his membership of the congregation. The letter caused little surprise and was not taken into consideration for three weeks, when the tendered resignation was accepted. The withdrawal of Sampson Abudiente was received without comment, for he had long ceased to take part in Jewish affairs. Sampson Abudiente had become a great man. No longer was he seen in the Jewish quarters with his basket in his hand; no longer did he wend his way to Synagogue on Friday evenings; and his seat in the house of prayer was tenantless. Sampson Abudiente had grown into a power on 'Change. Sampson Abudiente, whose sordid and mean attire had passed into a proverb, was the friend and confidential adviser of the Prime Minister of England. Sampson Abudiente was now called Sampson Gideon. The strange foreign designation had become distasteful to him, and he had adopted a patronymic more suitable to English ears. But he had never ceased to be a Jew, and it was not that he loved Judaism the less, but that he loved wealth and worldly honours the more. In former days he had desired to purchase a landed estate and found himself surrounded by difficulties. It was a disputed point whether a Jew could legally own landed property. By using his great influence with Sir Robert Walpole, he had obtained a special Act of Parliament authorising the vendor to transfer to him, Sampson Gideon, the rich acres he coveted. But this process was uncertain and unsatisfactory. It was his ambition to be the founder of a great family. He was anxious to secure his millions to his children. To cut away all difficulties he brought them up to the Christian faith. As it happened, his plan did not attain the end he coveted. Poetical justice usually occurs only in the third volume of a novel, or at the close of a melodrama, for in reality it is seldom visibly carried out in actual life. It is worthy of remark, that Sampson Gideon's eldest son, Lord Eardley, left no male issue; and, consequently, the title became extinct, and the vast wealth accumulated by the "Jew broker" went to enrich strangers. A baronetage by the female side and a burdened estate are all that are left now of the financier's ambitious dreams.

As we have already said, Sampson Gideon had never forsaken Judaism, and until the time of his withdrawal from the synagogue, in 1754, he continued to pay regularly his tax (finta) to the Portuguese congregation. He also was employed as broker to buy or sell the communal funds when needed. Even after his retirement he remained a Jew at heart, and until his last day he retained a singular hankering after his race. When Sampson Gideon, in 1763, was summoned to join the greater number, his will brought to light in an unexpected manner the state of his feelings. His executors forwarded a copy of his will to the authorities of the Spanish and Portuguese Congregation, with a request that orders might be given for the interment of the deceased. The following paragraph was found in that document: "To my executors—£1000 to be paid by them and applied to and for the use of the Portuguese Synagogue in Bevis Marks, London, in case I shall be buried in the Jews' burying-place at Mile End, in the *carreira* (regular row of graves), with the right of a *guebir* (member), and an *Escaba* (or prayer for the dead) said every Kippur." The reply of the Portuguese elders was brief and dignified, and to the effect that orders had been given to the keeper of the burying-ground at Mile End to let the grave be open according to the desire of the deceased, and that his remains would be treated as those of any other member. Then Phineas Gomes Serra, a gentleman belonging to one of the first families of the community, came forward and stated that a certain sum offered annually by him in the name of "Peloni Almoni"—as anonymous donors were designated—in reality was contributed by the late Sampson Gideon, who had thus regularly kept up his payments as member. Here we have, indeed, a strange phenomenon. A man who would be a Jew, and would not appear a Jew; who believed in Judaism, and brought up his children to Christianity; who moved for years solely among Christians; and yet who craved to be laid in his last sleep beside Jews. Perhaps Sampson Gideon when he entertained his lordly and honourable guests at Belvedere House, Erith, was a less happy man than when he trudged on foot to Synagogue. Who can tell the struggles that tore his bosom between religious faith and worldly ambition, between conscience and self-aggrandisement! No better lesson on the emptiness of human ambition, on the vanity of human pride and greatness, can be furnished, than is afforded by the career of Sampson Gideon.

According to Jewish custom, only a plain stone points out to visitors to the Portuguese cemetery at Mile End, the site of the grave of the great financier. And every year during the evening of the solemn Fast of Expiation, a short prayer is recited at the Portuguese Synagogue for the soul of Sampson de Rehuel Abudiente.

CHAPTER VII.

SPECIAL LEGISLATION—JEWISH LOYALTY—CONTINUED PREJUDICES—ENEMIES AND FRIENDS.

During the first half of the eighteenth century the legislature of the country commenced to take notice of the existence of the Jews, and passed several enactments applying solely to the ancient people of God. In the year 1715, it was represented to both Houses of Parliament, that the severity of Jewish parents was a great hindrance to the children being converted to the Christian faith. It was firmly believed by some well-meaning enthusiasts, that were Jewish youths and maidens assured of not forfeiting their share of their father's fortune, they would forsake in crowds the old faith to adopt the new dispensation. An Act of Parliament therefore was passed, to the effect that if the child of any Jewish parent became a Christian, or was desirous of embracing Christianity, he might compel such parent, upon applying to the Lord Chancellor, to make due provision for him.

It does not appear that this law caused any especial number of conversions. On the contrary, about three years after this there was a groundless rumour that the Jews had converted several Christians. We know that such an occurrence could not be; but a credulous individual, more fanatical than prudent, published a small anonymous pamphlet, frantically inveighing against Jews and Judaism, and dedicated this lucubration to "the reverend clergy, and particularly the members of the Convocation." The author observed with "wonder and strangeness that amidst a multitude of outcries for reformation, they had still left the greatest work of all undone, namely, the suppression of the Jews, and until that were accomplished, all other attempts would be to little purpose." The poor man, in a state of great alarm, thus

E

concluded, not without indulging in a sly hit against his own clergy—"The suffering of the Jews to erect a new Synagogue in the heart of the City of London is such encouragement to Judaism, that enemies of the Church of England say that if rabbis and priests of Jews had but as ancient pretensions to church livings and ecclesiastical dignities as popish priests, our most spiritual Lords the Bishops would be as energetic in expulsion of Judaism as they were in King William's time for the excision of Popery."

We hardly know which is the more entertaining: the intense dread of the Jews experienced by the author, or the simplicity with which he attributes to his own priesthood an overwhelming desire for a monopoly of the loaves and fishes.

Some of the laws in question were framed to grant to the Jews some slight instalment of the commonest rights.

In Great Britain, as in some other European kingdoms, the Government has been usually in advance of the population in their treatment of the Jews. In England, in France, in Italy, the rulers fully acknowledged the title of the Jews to the citizenship of their country, while the inhabitants eyed them suspiciously as aliens. Indeed in most states the law recognised the equality of the Hebrews to the remainder of their countrymen, when society failed to admit it.

In the year 1723 the British Government carried through Parliament an Act which, albeit apparently of small importance, was yet of great significance, for therein it was proclaimed for the first time that the Jews were British subjects. This Act determined that "whenever any of his Majesty's subjects professing the Jewish religion shall present themselves to take the oath of abjuration, the words 'on the true faith of a Christian' shall be omitted out of the said oath, and the taking of it by such persons professing the Jewish religion, without the words aforesaid, in the manner as Jews are admitted to be sworn to give evidence in courts of justice, shall be deemed a sufficient taking." Here we have a beginning of religious tolerance. The rights of individual conscience are conceded, and the scruples of even a Jew are respected. Moreover, we notice that the obnoxious words had been previously left out on taking oaths in Courts of

Law, so that the Hebrews already possessed some privileges, which on this occasion were extended and further sanctioned by the legislature.

The next concession in this direction was in 1740, when another Act of Parliament granted the rights of natural-born subjects of Great Britain to those Jews who had already resided in the American Colonies, or who had served as marines during the war in British ships for two years.

No state, we may here remark, ever had cause to regret its due recognition of Jewish claims. Loyalty is a quality essential in the Hebrew race. The Jews have invariably paid implicit obedience to the powers that be, as they have always supported public order. In a republic, the Jew is a moderate republican; in a monarchy, he is a consistent constitutionalist. A Hebrew *sans culotte* would have been as curious a phenomenon as a religious reformer in the chair of St Peter. In this country, as elsewhere, the Jews, whenever treated with common humanity, have been ready to shed their blood and to expend their treasure on behalf of the legal authorities. The attachment of the Children of Israel to the House of Brunswick is notorious. Not that they had any ground of complaint against the last two Stuart Kings, who, as we have already seen, displayed towards them a wise tolerance. But Dutch William, and the House of Hanover which succeeded him, represented the cause of progress, liberty of conscience, and religious equality, while the last James allied himself to bigotry and fanaticism and narrow-minded despotism. The Jew, though quiet and orderly, is no humble submissive slave; and the natural inborn love of independence of his race will lead him ever to prefer that form of government which is most in accord with his desires and requirements. A Jew will not join any revolutionary movement against constituted authorities, but he will be more zealous in his allegiance towards those who are willing to concede that amount of political and religious freedom to which every sane adult is entitled. Thus it happened that the Jews were constantly willing and ready in every emergency to take up arms in defence of the British throne in general, and of the Guelph dynasty in particular. The Jews in 1745-46 honourably distinguished themselves in taking part in the common danger against an enemy who represented a retrograde movement in civilisation. The lower classes in the community enlisted themselves in the city militia. Those of higher rank entered into associations of all kinds, whilst those whose condition made them more useful in following their own callings, every way promoted whatever was thought serviceable to the Government. Public credit was sinking, the run on the Bank of England was unceasing, and the drain of specie was becoming so serious, that a stoppage of the bank was generally apprehended. The Jews imported specie, and brought it to that establishment, which proceeding materially contributed to the restoration of national credit. Many people, indeed, solicited the Jews to let them have the gold and silver, so that they might have the merit of taking it to the bank themselves. The situation was so critical, that it was not sufficient to bring in supplies, unless a stop were put to the continual demand. It is useless to pump water from a disabled bark unless the leak be stopped. Some persons, whether actuated by malice or panic it does not appear, exposed some bank-notes publicly for sale at a discount. Twelve merchants, two of whom were Hebrews, formed at once a union, each member of which signed an undertaking to accept bank-notes in payment at par. This resolution saved the sinking credit of the country, and the union was joined by numerous patriotic traders, among whom figured all the principal Jewish commercial and financial men. Moreover coin was scarce in the Treasury, and immediate calls for it were pressing. Coercive measures would have been simply destructive, for they would have increased the alarm of the people, and occasioned a renewed run on the bank. A subscription was opened in the city by Government to borrow money on the land-tax. The conditions of this loan were by no means favourable to the lenders; nevertheless, the Hebrews came forward freely and subscribed fully one-quarter of the required amount. The conduct of the once persecuted race seems to have been duly appreciated, for when it was resolved to present an address to the King, a Jew was elected as member of the committee that was to head the merchants on that memorable occasion, an honour that would not have been paid to the despised race unless its zeal and loyalty had gained general approbation. In conclusion, two wealthy Israelites had armed two vessels in the river for the purpose of privateering, and also for loading goods for foreign markets. When it became known that ships were required to prevent the enemy from landing, the owners tendered the vessels, so fitted out at their cost, to the Government, sacrificing their private advantage to the necessities of the country. Nevertheless, the patriotism of the Jews was soon forgotten, for when, in 1753, the Naturalisation Act passed, the greater—or the most noisy—part of the population was up in arms against the obnoxious law, and peace was not restored until the slight boon conferred on the Hebrews was revoked by Parliament.

In the beginning of this century, when all England was thrown in a fever of alarm by the anticipation of a never-intended invasion by the "Corsican Ogre," the Jews eagerly enlisted themselves among the volunteers. In 1848, when some silly and mischievous demagogues desired to convince the country forcibly that prosperity, independence, and ample labour would be magically bestowed upon all by the adoption of the several points of the Charter, numerous Jews were observed patrolling the streets with the special constable's badge round their arms and the emblematic staff in their hands. Finally, when, a dozen years ago, England awoke to its unprotected condition, Jewish young men stepped forward by hundreds, and leaving the fascinating pursuits of pleasure and the engrossing cares of business, stood arrayed side by side with the flower of British youth, prepared to incur any sacrifice on behalf of their native land.

We must not believe that the position of the Jews in England during the first half of the eighteenth century was especially enviable or brilliant. No doubt many Israelites were gathering hither from the Continent; which, however, is rather a proof of the inferiority of their condition in the rest of Europe, than of the abstract goodness of their condition in England. Though Government protected the Jews from actual ill-usage, social prejudices against them broke out occasionally, hampering their every movement, and surrounding them with difficulties. In the year 1715 a Jew applied to be admitted as broker in the City of London, when a petition was presented against that application by the brokers. It commenced thus:—" Reasons offered humbly to the Lord Mayor and Court of Aldermen against a Jew (who is a known enemy to the Christian religion) his being admitted a broker." The reasons alleged were six in number, and were in substance as follow:—1. That the brokers were limited to 100, and that the Act of Parliament made no mention of Jews or other foreigners. 2. That of the Jews that were brokers, not above one-half were " of any advantage to the merchants in any branch of trade whatsoever." 3. That for drawing and remitting money to and from foreign countries the Jews might be serviceable; but that there were twice as many " Jew brokers " as were required, which was the cause that one-half of them became addicted to stock jobbing, and had recourse to irregular practices. 4. " That no branch of trade will not receive detriment by admitting Jew brokers." 5. That the Jews were neither free of the City nor of any livery company, and paid very little towards public support; whereas the petitioners were house-keepers, freemen, liverymen, who paid scott and lott, and had a right to the immunities and privileges of Englishmen that Jews had not. 6. That Jews had no right to immunities and privileges, as would appear from the many statute laws in force against them, which were printed in 1703, and dedicated to Convocation.

This curious document brings forward several interesting facts concerning the Jews. In the first place, we perceive that the pursuit of a broker was much in favour among the Hebrews, and greatly resorted to by them. Then we observe the numerous restrictions that hemmed them in in the battle of life, and the prejudices that were rife against them; and, in conclusion, we learn that many penal enactments still existed at that period in the Statute-Book rendering the property of that race insecure, and their lives barely safe. This petition was not successful; for the Corporation of London, with that liberality which has generally characterised its conduct towards the Jews, took no notice of it, and granted the application to the Hebrew broker.

Occasionally some voice from the crowd was raised against

the Jews at this period; and an anonymous pamphlet was published a few years later, in which it was stated that " the Jews, by their corrupted charms and secret intrigues, though they have no manner of right to live here, do boldly presume not only to engross the principal part of our trade, but are now admitted, as some say, to shares in the East Indian, African, Hudson's Bay, and Hamburgh Society." From this and other analogous sources we gather that, notwithstanding so many adverse circumstances, the Jews, by their natural sagacity and indomitable energy, had already acquired an important position in British commerce; that they had engrossed the Portugal and Barbary trade to themselves; that they were running a close race for that of Spain; that they had got into their hands Barbadoes and Jamaica; and that by their foreign relations they regulated the course of the Exchanges. We are also apprised that the Jews were shareholders in many of the principal companies; but that as all Jews had been declared traitors by an Act of Edward I., they could own no property. Therefore they were liable, at the King's pleasure, to have all their funds seized. All the joint concerns in which the Jews possessed any interest were, moreover, subject to the same risk. We do not learn that the Jews were ever practically despoiled in this manner at this period; and their enemies take care to inform us that the former played their cards so well, by professing friendship with all religions, that they were growing into favour with both laity and clergy.

The Jews, at the same time, were not without friends and supporters. In 1736 a singular pamphlet was published. It attracted much attention at that period. It is addressed to " the Rev. High Priest of the Church by law established," and it is signed by "Solomon Abrabanel, in Synagogue Lane, Bury Street, the 12th day of the 12th month of Adar." Internal evidence would lead us to the belief that this little treatise was not written by a Jew, and it appears the production of a practised writer. It is composed in a forcible, half-jocose, half-satirical style, that reminds us of the diatribes of the great Dean of St Patrick. We question whether a Jew —even had he possessed the necessary abilities—would have ventured at that time to make use of some of the bold expressions therein contained. There was, however, a family of the name of Abrabanel in existence among the Israelites; but whether any member of this family lent his name to the pamphlet, we are unable to say. The essay is a representation of the grievances of the Children of Israel under the penal laws, and prays for the repeal of the Test Act. This slight work ran through seven editions. We shall give some brief extracts, as specimens of its language and line of reasoning. " You avow that the Christian religion *was never intended to leave the rights of mankind in a worse condition than it found them, and since 'tis proposed* that no religious opinion shall be any longer a civil disqualification, we hope, sir, that you will be our patron on the principle of universal charity, and that as Paul gloried in being the apostle of the Gentile, you will think it no dishonour to be the Bishop of the Jews, and that we may say of you, Behold an *Israelite* in whom there is no *guile*. . . . . You have laid hold of the promise made to *father Abraham*, and have taken the Kingdom of Heaven as your inheritance; you have converted our *moiety* of the *Bible* to your own use; you have seized upon *Moses* and *Aaron*, and the *ten commandments*, which were our natural property, and placed them over the *communion tables;* yet make this pretence of Christian communion a reason for excluding us from the advantages of the commonwealth, so that our law and our prophets can afford us no protection though you have exalted them. You have robbed us of our priesthood, Urim and Thummim, and of our tithes also, yet give us nothing in exchange but *damnation*, as if Satan could be such a fool as to take us when we lost all." After justifying the act of the Jews in condemning Jesus to death in incisive terms that cannot be adverted to here, and dwelling on the equality of Jew and Christian, the writer continues—" It is true we are charged with too violent a passion for the *mammon of unrighteousness*, but that we find the most sanctified Christians, in respect of worldly lucres, as little scrupulous of taking the profit to themselves as they are of throwing the scandal upon us. We get what we can, and keep what we get, not by any principle of religion, but of convenience, which principle reigns in as full perfection amongst the saints at

Hackney, as among the Children of Israel in Bury Street or Duke's Place."

The author then suggests that Jews should be appointed tithe-collectors, for they would afford no more offence than the generality of church officers; he deplores the scant courtesy shown by dissenters towards Jews; he gives a brief sketch of the history of the Jews in England, and thus he concludes his essay in a humorous strain—" When a petition for the Repeal of the Test Act shall be about to be presented, we intend on that day to march in a solemn procession from our Synagogue in Bury Street, with our priests and our law and Aaron's bells at the head of us. If this *moving* appearance shall not have its effect, we must give up all hope of being restored to our national rights. We hope you will imitate the Apostle Paul, who unto the Jews became as a Jew, that he might gain the Jews; and if you protect the Children of Israel in this emergent affair, we will promise you, whenever you come amongst us, the first cut of the Paschal Lamb, and the chief seat in the Synagogue."

CHAPTER VIII.

COMMUNAL CHARITIES—INTERNAL LEGISLATION.

During the earlier half of the eighteenth century, while the Jews were surely, if slowly, strengthening their outward position in this country, their inward or communal existence was acquiring a vigorous development in proportion to their increased numbers and importance. Comparative prosperity did not cause the Children of Israel to forget the Lord of their forefathers. They obeyed His precepts, and manifested their reverence for Him by dedicating to Him various houses of worship; while they displayed their love for their suffering fellow-beings by founding a number of institutions for the relief of the unfortunate, the sick, and the aged.

In the beginning of that century, in addition to the German Synagogue in Broad Court, Duke Street, and the Portuguese Synagogue in Bevis Marks, we find recorded the existence of a smaller house of prayer in Coleman Street. A contemporary Christian writer adverts to it as a proof of the spread of Judaism; but at the present day we are unable to fix on its precise site, or state whether it belonged to the one or the other of the two Jewish communities. We are apprised by another authority that the German Synagogue was by no means so imposing in appearance as the Synagogue of the Portuguese, and that the new edifice wherein the latter gathered to pray was about twice the size of the Ashkenazi Schule.

The German Israelites were rapidly increasing, owing to a considerable immigration; and in 1722 they reconstructed their Synagogue on an enlarged scale, and they consecrated it with great solemnity. Even this new arrangement proving insufficient for their wants, in 1726 another Synagogue was erected near Leadenhall Street, and became known as the Hambro Schule.

The Portuguese remained content with their one grand old building, which appeared enough for their congregation. The Sephardim, if they did not raise new temples, probably performed as good work in the sight of God, for they took tender care of His forlorn creatures. Various noble institutions arose for the education of the young, and for the relief of the poor, the sick, and the aged. In 1703 they founded the Orphan Society, or " The Gates of Light and the Father of the Fatherless." The object of the charity, as its name purports, is to maintain, educate, and apprentice a number of orphan boys, who are admitted by the votes of the subscribers.

Then in 1724 another society was brought into existence, which grants annually a dowry of £60 to one or more fatherless girls of the Portuguese congregation, and distributes the small gifts of £1 to every poor woman lying in at the hospital, and 5s. to every individual above ten years old undergoing confined mourning. Subsequently, in the year 1730, a wealthy and generous personage, Isaac Da Costa Villareal, made a liberal endowment for the education and clothing of twenty poor female children of the same congregation. The Villareal school—the pupils of which are distinguished by their neat though old-fashioned garb—is under the management of a committee of ladies, who devote much thought and time to the welfare of the future mothers of Hebrew workmen. The family of Villareal, we may remark, was one of the most ancient and honourable among the Portuguese. The Villareals had occupied some of the highest posts at the Court of Portugal, and when driven from the banks of the Tagus by the implements of torture and blazing stakes of the Inquisition, they brought away with them a great name and a considerable fortune. In England their blood became allied to Albion's proudest aristocracy, and we believe that it flows through the veins of at least two members of the British peerage.

The condition of poor damsels seems to have received considerable sympathy, for six years after the establishment of the Villareal school, another association was created for the purpose of furnishing marriage portions to the extent of £80 to destitute orphan girls of the Sephardic congregation.

It was in 1747 that first originated the Portuguese "House of the Sick," the *Beth Olim*, one of the most useful and noblest foundations in that congregation. Therein the sick are tended with care and skill, and their suffering is alleviated by the visits of relatives and the knowledge that, should God please to summon them to His Presence, their last hours would be soothed by the countenance and prayers of their brethren of the House of Israel. Under that roof needy married women are assisted in bearing the curse of Eve ; in that building, broken-down, decayed persons of both sexes find an asylum for their old age ; and finally, in the surgery of the hospital gratuitous advice and medicine are supplied to the patients who cannot be admitted within its walls.

In 1749 the "Society of Good Deeds," *Mahasim Tobim* was established. The good deeds here assume a variety of shapes. Poor boys of the Spanish and Portuguese congregation are apprenticed to suitable trades. Small sums are advanced to the industrious poor ; rewards are granted for satisfactory behaviour to servants and apprentices, and outfits are provided for boys leaving the country. After this a long pause occurs, and we hear of no new charitable associations until 1778, when a union was founded, "That giveth Bread to the Hungry," for distributing a certain number of loaves weekly to the Portuguese poor.

We have so far seen how the Jews augmented in numbers, and how they were provided for in sickness and in poverty ; let us now inquire how they were disposed of after death. When the first Hebrews had come over from Holland, they had purchased for 999 years a piece of land at Mile End to serve as a "Beth Haim," a House of Life. This is the cemetery of the Sephardic congregation. It has in recent times been extended by the acquisition of an adjoining tract of land. The hospital to this day stands in a corner of the original estate. Until 1738 all the Jews in London interred their dead in the same locality. At about that period the Germans, who possessed their Synagogues and institutions apart, began availing themselves of a separate place of burial. We will here observe, that among the muniments of the Spanish and Portuguese community is found a conveyance of a certain space of ground in the city of Dublin, bought in 1748, for the purpose of conversion into a cemetery; and we believe that the same land is now employed for that identical object by the Dublin congregation.

We are unable to ascertain positively whether any Jews dwelt in Dublin in the above year, but indubitably some Israelites frequently visited that city. It is related that a learned rabbi came over from the Irish capital to confer with the London rabbis, a fact that would encourage the belief that there were on the banks of the Liffey resident Jews. During the middle of the eighteenth century the Jews unquestionably spread throughout the country, and they established themselves in fewer or greater numbers at Canterbury, Chatham, Cambridge, Bristol, Exeter, Edinburgh, Glasgow, Ipswich, Liverpool, Manchester, and Plymouth.

Among the Portuguese community the elders continued to exercise a paternal sway over the other members, which, however childish and irksome it may appear to us, in reality must have proved beneficial, for it certainly helped to maintain the high character of the congregation. It is evident—and the fact is confirmed by Gentile writers—that the Spanish and Portuguese Jews were held in greater repute, socially and commercially, than their less fortunate German brethren, which result may, perhaps, be partly attributed to the less stringent rule of the German authorities.

The Sephardic governing body, at the period of which we are writing, directed a number of enactments against a variety of offences. It was prohibited to advance funds on post obits, or otherwise to young men of expectation, who in their turn were enjoined not to borrow cash from moneylenders. Clandestine marriages were held up to reprobation. Interference in parliamentary or municipal elections was strongly condemned, and betting was strictly forbidden. The betting to which the Israelites were addicted at this time —let us hasten to state—does not appear to us in these days of plunging as of a very formidable nature. The young Jews of the day did not lay or take odds on turf events, neither did they back the favourite pugilist for the next encounter in the ring, nor the most strutting cock for the following fight in the pit. They simply wagered as to the day of arrival of the Dutch mail, an incident which seems to have happened with sufficient irregularity to warrant its causing some excitement.

The infringement of these ordinances was naturally attended by proportionate penalties. *Herem,* or excommunication, was no longer applied so freely as it was two or three generations before. Money-fines, and mere exclusion from Synagogue, seem to have had sufficient deterrent effect to maintain a wholesome discipline. We perceive in one instance that a certain individual had been debarred from attending the Portuguese Synagogue at Bever's Marks—as some writers spelt the name—owing to an accusation under which he laboured of being *particeps criminis* in an abduction case. The young lady was recovered, and returned safely home to her parents, upon which the person in question humbly petitioned the "Very Magnificent Gentlemen of the Mahamad" to open to him once more the gates of the House of Prayer. The request of the petitioner was not granted, probably because his innocence was not so clear to the eyes of the Parnassim or Wardens as to his own.

We have already observed that the fear that Jews should pervert Christians to their own tenets was one of the principal bugbears raised by the opponents of the admission of the Jews into England in Cromwell's time— wherewith to alarm the credulous and the ignorant. The Sephardic authorities had always been strenuous in their endeavours to avoid affording any umbrage to their Christian friends. In 1751 the question arose again, as it had nearly a century previously, and the Sephardic chiefs thought it their duty to adopt new measures on the subject. They addressed, at the same time, to the heads of the Ashkenazi community, the following curious letter in English, which we reproduce verbatim:—

LONDON, 27*th December* 1751.

GENTLEMEN,—Being persuaded that you will join with us in all things that tend to preserve the present happy toleration, we take this opportunity to acquaint you as worthy representatives of your congregation, of a growing evil among us, viz.: that of permitting proselytes, for which end we have heard that two or three Christians have come hither from Norway with that intention, and lest these practices should extend to English proselytes, which is contrary to the express condition annexed to our first establishment here, we have thought proper to forbid in our Synagogue any from aiding and assisting them therein in any manner whatsoever, under the penalties as we send you enclosed. We do not doubt that you will also concur with us to endeavour to prevent the same from taking effect amongst you in the manner that may be judged most expedient. We pray God to preserve you for many years, and believe us to be, Gentlemen, your friends and humble servants,

A. DE CASTRO, for the Congregation.

We formerly remarked that we could find no trace of the *express condition* above adverted to, and we can only confirm our opinion on the subject. Whether this condition be traditionally understood or otherwise, certain it is that our spiritual guides of all communities in London have steadfastly refused to admit converts from Christianity into the covenant of Abraham.

The communication herein given was accompanied by a copy of the resolutions voted on the subject by the Mahamad. The two documents were duly acknowledged by the chiefs of German congregations, who, perfectly agreeing in the view of the case adopted by their Portuguese brethren, framed some ordinances in an analogous sense.

CHAPTER IX.

THE NATURALISATION BILL OF 1753.

Not many measures caused greater commotion in London, or gave rise to warmer discussion, than an Act of Parliament which merely proposed to grant a few, only a few, of the privileges of Englishmen to a very limited number of foreigners. Neither the Repeal of the Corn Laws, nor the introduction of Free Trade, nor the passing of the Reform Bill caused more excitement in their day than the question as to whether or not some scores of Dutch or German Jews were to be allowed to go through costly proceedings to acquire the right of holding property in England.

In the year 1753 the House of Lords passed a bill, permitting those Jews who had resided for three years in England, and not absented themselves therefrom for more than three months at one time, to be naturalised by Parliament. The bill having received the sanction of the Upper House, was despatched to the lower and more popular assembly, usually supposed to be the more liberal of the two. On the 16th of April the bill was read for the first time, and a number of violent debates ensued, in which was exhibited more passion than patriotism, more sound than sense. The ministry was under the guidance of Mr Pelham, who, with his brother, the Duke of Newcastle, held the complete control of public affairs. Reports of Parliamentary proceedings were not then permitted to be avowedly published. No public journal ventured to print the speeches of British peers or commons, but the sayings and doings of the Parliament of Lilliput, during the earlier half of the eighteenth century, were made known to the public through various periodicals and magazines. Among the names of the orators of that famous legislature, readers of the present day would scarcely recognise personages who had made their mark in the history of these realms. Who would discover in *Hurgo Castrolet* the witty and polished Earl of Chesterfield, or in *Hurgo Santhepo* the accomplished Earl of Stanhope: though, through the thin disguise of *Sir Retrob Walelop*, it is not difficult to detect the future Earl of Orford.

We cannot consequently read in their entirety the debates that occurred on this question. But we know that an exaggerated and factitious importance soon became attached to this bill, as if the very fate of the whole country depended on its issue; and that an amount of fallacies was uttered on the subject, and a degree of ignorance displayed, that would fairly astonish an ordinarily educated individual of the present generation.

A petition, signed by above one hundred merchants and traders of the City of London, was presented to Parliament in favour of the bill during its discussion. This petition was followed by another in the same sense, to which subscribed upwards of two hundred persons, consisting of merchants, traders, manufacturers, shipwrights, and commanders of vessels, many of whom were said to be "people of the greatest fortune, judgment, and abilities." It was urged in that document, among other reasons, that the passing of this measure would "increase the shipping and encourage the exportation of the woollen and other manufactures of this kingdom, of which persons who profess the Jewish religion have for many years last past exported great quantities."

The City member, Sir John Barnard, spoke vehemently against the bill, prophesying a thousand calamities should it be allowed to become law; and the Corporation of London, contrary to its customary liberality and toleration, strongly opposed, with all its powerful influence, the intended enactment. Sir Crisp Gascoigne, the Lord Mayor, presided over meetings of Aldermen and Liverymen, and exhorted the citizens to resist the poor little concession about to be made to the Jews. Petitions—presaging the direst consequences from such dangerous generosity—were drawn up and eagerly pressed upon the House of Commons. Counsel was heard and evidence was examined. Notwithstanding all opposition, Government courageously persevered in its action. The bill was committed: it passed through all its various stages with some modifications, and within five weeks it received the royal sanction.

The Act in question was entitled "An Act to permit persons professing the Jewish religion to be naturalised by Parliament, and for other purposes therein mentioned." The bill was at best of limited advantage to the Jews, for it was of a permissive kind, and only the wealthy could have set in motion the machinery necessary to obtain the desired naturalisation. Then the privileges of Jews were curtailed, for they were placed under special civil and political disabilities, and they were debarred from purchasing or inheriting " any advowson or right of patronage or presentation or other right or interest whatsoever in any benefice, prebend, or other ecclesiastical living or promotion in school or hospital."

It is difficult in our time to understand how a boon so grudgingly bestowed upon an inoffensive race, and of so slight a nature, could have attained so high a degree of unpopularity. Reports exaggerating its effects were industriously spread throughout the length and breadth of the land. The enemies of the Jews joined hands with the enemies of the ministers, and actively circulated a number of fables so wildly absurd, so palpably improbable, that nothing but violent party spirit, gross ignorance, and blind prejudice could have induced any reasonable being to place belief in them.

It was alleged by the opponents of the measure that the naturalisation of the Jews was not consistent with the Christian religion, and was repugnant to the constitution of Great Britain. That it would diminish the consumption of ham, bacon, and brawn, and thus materially injure the trade in those commodities. That it was an act against the will of God; it was flying in the face of prophecy, which declares that the Jews should be a scattered people, without country or fixed habitation, until they should be converted from their infidelity, and gathered into the land of their forefathers; that the Jews would become so numerous as to exclude all Protestants from the home or any other trade. That so many rich Jews would come over to

England that they would purchase all the lands in the kingdom, and influence elections, so that no one would be chosen unless in their interest; that they would become members of Parliament themselves, and reach the highest posts under government. That a number of poor Jews would flood the land and devour it like locusts; that they would deprive of bread the natives who earn their livelihood by work, or else bring such a mass of pauperism into the country as to greatly impair its resources, spread misery, and seriously augment taxation. That Jew brokers, usurers, and beggars, would flock hither, robbing the real subjects of their birthrights, disgracing the character of the nation, endangering the constitution of Church and State, and proving an indelible reproach to the established religion of the British realms. That the Jews would multiply in number, increase in wealth, and gain power to such an extent as to acquire great personal importance, introduce universally their customs, and render Judaism the fashionable religion of the English. That they would engross all the foreign commerce of the realm, and that the Spaniards and Portuguese would be greatly offended at the refuge afforded in England to a people whom they had driven away from their kingdoms, where they would not be tolerated. That the Jews were more ready than any other people on earth to betray intelligence; and that should a Jew be found in the councils of the country, or in any branch of government wherein he could arrive at a true state of affairs, it would be in his power to betray the counsels and secrets of the nation to every court in Europe. That to harbour a Jew was, in the words of Innocent III., when he expelled that race from Rome, to receive "mus in pera, serpens in gremio, ignis in sinu." Finally, that by bringing the Jews into England, with them would be brought the curses that have pursued them through all countries and for so many ages, and the same part would be acted as that of Julian the Apostate, when he invited them to gather in his empire and erect a temple.

It was impossible to stem the torrent of popular fanaticism. In vain it was represented by reflecting and outspoken men, in reply to these ludicrous, contradictory, or malicious misrepresentations, that the Act would produce a very inconsiderable effect, that the number of Jews that could avail themselves of its provisions must necessarily be very restricted, and would exert no perceptible influence in the destinies of Great Britain; that rich Jews desired to be naturalised, not to be enabled to sit in Parliament, enjoy posts of honour and profit, or obtain possession of all the estates in England, but to labour no longer under a stigma, to be treated by Protestants with the same respect as they displayed towards each other, and to be suffered to live in peace, in case some few of them purchased lands; that in the actual state of public feeling, scarcely any wealthy Jews would venture to settle in England, and that in point of fact, new emigrants of that class from distant countries ceased to arrive, preferring to proceed to Holland, where they were welcomed, and to France, where the laws, promulgated under Kings Henry III., Louis XIV., and Louis XV., secured them some immunities and rights.

In vain it was repeated that commerce and manufactures would be greatly benefited by the establishment here of a number of industrious traders, who not being manufacturers themselves, but exporters and importers, would necessarily increase and encourage English production. That should a Jew ever become member of Parliament, he would give his vote on that side of the question which should appear to him most advantageous to the society of which he would then be member; that should the subject under discussion be one connected with trade or finance, he would be especially qualified to illustrate and point out the merits or defects of the proposal under debate, and that it would be no easy matter to puzzle his understanding with sophistical arguments. That the Jews were the most peaceful sect in England; Sampson Gideon was the father of the poor, and his charity was as boundless as his fortune; the generous and noble members of the Mendes family with Franks, Salvador, and others, were famed far and wide for their beneficence and largeness of mind, and when the nation had been in need, they had proved its friends indeed, and had furnished the State with ample funds. In conclusion, it was asserted that Jews, being induced to take up their abode in England, might the more easily receive the Gospel; and one of their defenders thus ended an emphatic appeal in their favour—" No doubt they (the Jews) labour under most unhappy prejudices, but for these they must answer to their Maker. Suppose our Saviour himself now was to appear where the Orthodox court is established, and was to preach against the temporal kingdom which has been erected upon the simple principles of His gospels, don't you think it probable He would be taken into the hand of the Corregidor, and be made a spectacle as an *auto-da-fé?*"

In time the scanty concession to the Jews became more and more generally disliked. As the controversy grew hot between their supporters and enemies, the popular clamour arose with greater intensity and fury. The opponents of the measure grew in number and in violence. An outcry against it was heard throughout the country, and the hostile majority soon silenced the friendly minority. Reproaches were heaped on the heads of the Ministry who had introduced so hateful an enactment, and the two brothers who held the helm of the affairs of the State were alarmed at the effect this clamour might have on the next election, which was approaching.

CHAPTER X.

REPEAL OF THE NATURALISATION BILL—LITERATURE OF THE BILL.

THE Ministers, frightened at the storm they had raised, became as eager to annul the unpopular measure as they once had been eager to make it law. At the very opening of the parliamentary session in 1754, the Duke of Newcastle, immediately after the customary address to the Crown had been voted, abruptly presented a bill for the repeal of the obnoxious Act, which, he said, had been used by the disaffected as a handle to produce general discontent. The work of the previous session was undone with far more speed than it had been done. All were ready with more or less ardour to throw stones at the very enactment which the majority of them had supported but a brief year before. At first the clause in the bill disabling all naturalised Jews from purchasing, inheriting, or holding any advowson, or presentation or right to any ecclesiastical benefice or promotion was allowed to stand separately. Subsequently it was argued that such a clause remaining unrescinded might imply that Jews being especially debarred from the possession of any ecclesiastical right of presentation, might be considered as having the power of purchasing and inheriting lay property in the kingdom. This illusory advantage was more than ought to be accorded to miserable Jews, and the whole Act of Naturalisation was revoked without exception. A few only among the Peers had the courage to oppose such unworthy and pitiful submission to external pressure. Among these was honourably distinguished Earl Temple, a nobleman of high abilities, who in an eloquent discourse, powerfully though vainly espoused the cause of the unfortunate Jews.

In the Lower House members of all parties vied with each other, and with members of the Upper House, in displaying their detestation of this ill-fated Act. The British

Parliament hastened to obey the voice of the people as if it had been the voice of God, and not the voice of interested agitators and ignorant fanatics. On the very first day of the session, Sir James Dashwood, an influential member of the Opposition, gave notice that immediately after the Address to the Throne had been voted he would propose a measure of very great importance. After that proof of loyalty to his Majesty had been given, Sir James Dashwood rose again, and having dwelt on the just and general indignation caused by the Act of the preceding session in favour of the Jews, he asked that a certain early date should be fixed for taking that Act into consideration. It was inconsistent with the rules of the House to fix a date for the purpose, but the general motion was seconded by Lord Parker, who was his political opponent, and it was unanimously accepted.

Meanwhile the Lords had hastened to frame a bill, which they transmitted to the Commons, who saw no objection to it with the exception of the preamble, which excited a strenuous opposition. It was thus worded—" Whereas an Act of Parliament was made and passed in the twenty-fifth year of His Majesty's reign intituled an Act to permit persons professing the Jewish religion to be naturalised by Parliament and for other purposes therein mentioned; and whereas occasion has been taken from the said Act to raise discontents and disquiets in the minds of his Majesty's subjects, be it enacted," &c. This introduction, which happened to represent the truth, was stigmatised as a reflection upon the former opponents of the bill in particular, and the body of the people in general. Sir Roger Newdigate moved the substitution to the previous form of the following words—" Whereas great discontents and disquietudes had from the said Act arisen." A violent debate ensued. Mr Pelham and Mr Pitt resisted the amendment, which was rejected. The bill, as originally drawn up, was in due course read a third time, and obtained the royal approbation.

This humiliating concession did not satisfy the nation, which seemed to look upon the Jews as so many ogres ready to devour with an insatiable appetite the inhabitants of England, and to seize upon their goods and chattels. An attempt was made to repeal the Act of 1740, which allowed those who had resided for seven years in any of his Majesty's colonies to become free denizens of Great Britain without taking the Sacrament. A sudden alarm was conceived at the dangerous tendency of this law. In the House of Commons motions were made for the production of papers concerning the working of the Act. It was ascertained that though theoretically many Jews were entitled to claim this privilege, practically very few availed themselves of their right, which could only be attained with much trouble, and at a considerable cost. Nevertheless Lord Harley moved for leave to bring in a bill to repeal that part, and Sir James Dashwood and the Earl of Egmont spoke in the same sense. The eloquence of Mr Pelham and of Mr Pitt prevailed, and the majority saved Parliament from the disgrace of persecuting the weak to curry favour with the strong.

The Naturalisation Bill, like all questions which greatly excite the popular mind, produced a special literature of its own. It was attacked and defended, censured and praised, abused and commended. Not only the then existing organs of the press took the one or the other side of the controversy, —it was mostly the other side,—but a number of persons in private or public life rushed into print, sometimes to enlighten, more frequently to bewilder or further prejudice the public mind. The *Gentleman's Magazine*, the *Westminster Journal*, the *London Evening Post*, distinguished themselves for the bitterness of their invectives against the Jews. The *General Evening Post* and the *Public Advertiser* had the courage to open their columns to those who dared speak the truth to an ignorant multitude.

There was little variety in the arguments employed by the opponents of the Act of 1753, but their language had the merit of diversity of expression. Some writers exercised considerable ingenuity in culling the most forcible terms of abuse to be found in the vernacular, and applying them to the Children of Israel. The expressions of forgers, clippers, blasphemers, murderers, were amenities commonly showered on their devoted heads. One gentleman, more penetrating than the rest, discovered that not only the Jews were unclean in person, that they squinted, and were awkwardly built, but that there was a demoniacal leer in their eyes which marked them from the rest of mankind.

Others spoke far more moderately and reasonably, and supported their view of the case without heaping a volley of insulting epithets on an unoffending race. A generous individual went even so far as to assert that good qualities might be possibly found in Jews, and that he had actually heard of the existence of one truly good Jew. This Israelite was Benjamin Mendes da Costa, a man endowed with a large heart, and whose unbounded charity in its most extended form had endeared him to Jew and Gentile. Mr Da Costa, we will add, took an active part in communal matters, and we shall have hereafter frequent occasion to refer to his name.

Among the supporters of the bill, we often perceive an apologetic deprecating tone, as if they were ashamed of the cause they were defending. In some instances the attempted advocacy was carried on in such an hesitating or questionable manner, as to render it difficult to ascertain whether the writers were blundering friends or malignant enemies. We have heard the story of an Irishman, who on recommending a friend to a position of trust in a warehouse, asserted that his companion was incapable of stealing, for he was always in a state of such complete drunkenness as to render him absolutely unable to commit a theft.

A parity of reasoning was followed by a certain person who alleged in favour of the measure that it might very safely be passed, for the Jews, who were a very subtle and deceitful people, were hated and detested by all who professed themselves Christians, whether Protestants or Papists; and they knew so well the feelings they inspired, that they would take good care to stay away from England, notwithstanding all concessions made to them. Another writer, before breaking a lance on behalf of the Jews, observed that, after all, the devil was not so black as he was painted, and that Israelites probably would not prove to be so totally devoid of conscience, principle, and honour as they were represented. Some men, however, with a liberality and freedom of thought not often met with in those days, espoused the cause of the Jews on its own merits, in language elevated and refined, and with arguments drawn from Christianity itself. One of the warmest supporters of the Jews deserves honourable mention, for he suffered in person for the nobleness of his sentiments. A clergyman of the Established Church, the Rev. Josiah Tucker, M.A., Rector of St Stephen, Bristol, and chaplain to the Bishop of that diocese, ably and temperately vindicated the Jews from the numerous foul and baseless calumnies hurled against their devoted heads. Whereupon the generous mob seized the minister who had preached Christian charity and toleration towards the race that had produced the founder of Christianity, and maltreated him until he with difficulty escaped with bare life.

Some wit and coarse humour were brought to bear in the controversy, mostly on the side of the opponents of the Naturalisation Bill. It was so easy to make butts of the victims to the persecution of ages. The following lines, which are a fair specimen of the satire then in vogue, were circulated in some of the periodicals of the day :—

> " Thus step by step a nation is undone,
> And prodigals lose what their fathers won.
> A Jew, a Turk, or devil may come here
> And naturalise ; it will not cost him dear."

The dreadful menace herein implied has been realised, and we are happy to say that, albeit Jews and Mussulmans have acquired the rights of Englishmen, we do not perceive any signs of immediate ruin in the prospects of the British Empire.

Those who were alarmed at the possibility of the Judaisation of the English nation anticipated the most serious and melancholy consequences from the passing of the bill. A number of squibs were composed, representing the condition of England a hundred years thence; and as most of our readers have the opportunity of judging how far the facetious prophecies therein contained have hit the mark, we will cull some samples of those witticisms of last century. " From the *Hebrew Journal*, published by authority.—' This is to inform the public that the good ship *Rodrigue, alias Salvador*, Emanuel de Fonseca, commander, 1100 tons burthen, 50 guns, Jewish built, a prime sailor, having excellent accommodation for passengers, is now lying at Mr Caneo's dock, at Limehouse, ready to take in those Christian families that may be inclined to transport themselves into any part of Turkey, as choosing to live under a Mahommedan rather than a Jewish government. It is proposed that this ship shall return, loaded with a proper number of foreign Jews, against the next sessions of Parliament. All Christians, therefore, who are disposed to leave the once Christian kingdom of Great Britain, are desired to apply every first Sunday in the month to Mr Lopez d'Almeida, who is never absent from his counting-house, in the Old Jewry, on that day; at Solomons' Coffee-House, near the Custom House; the Francos' Head Tavern, in Fenchurch Street, or Sampson's Coffee-House, in Exchange Alley, where attendance is given every day in the week, the Jewish Sabbath excepted.'"

"On Wednesday last, died at the seat of His Grace the Duke of Hebron, in Barkshire, Sir Nadab Issachar, Attorney-General. He was esteemed a sound lawyer, an able politician, and a friend to the Sanhedrin. He is succeeded in his office by Moses da Costa, Esq., of Lincoln's Inn."

"On Monday last a dispensation passed the Great Seal, to enable Abraham Levi to hold a living in the Synagogue of Pauls, together with the rectory of the Rabbi in the diocese of Litchfield."

"Last night the bill for naturalising Christians was thrown out of the Sanhedrin by a great majority."

"At two o'clock this morning, died at his house in Grosvenor Square, the Right Hon. the Earl of Balaam, Baron of Zimri, and Knight of the most Noble Order of Melchisedek. He married Miss Bathsheba. . . . His lordship's remains are to be interred in Westminster Abbey, and we hear that he has left an estate of £100,000 per annum."

The humour herein displayed is not of a high class, but it tends to show the kind of fears that were entertained in all good faith by numbers of persons of average intelligence 120 years ago. If the writer were now to arise from his grave, he might experience some temporary consternation in beholding a Jew, an observing Jew too, dispensing even-handed justice in the High Court of Chancery. But on glancing round him, with the single exception of that one point, in which, curiously enough, he came near the mark, he would no longer be dismayed at the possible encroachments of the Jews, and would return in peace to his long sleep.

CHAPTER XI.

POSITION OF THE JEWS—BARON D'AGUILAR.

THE ill effects of the repeal of the Naturalisation Act soon became apparent. The Jews in general, notwithstanding the wealth possessed, and the consideration enjoyed by a small number of their body, were looked upon more than ever as aliens, as interlopers, as suspected foreigners. It was regarded as a doubtful question whether even English-born Jews were entitled to any of the rights of Englishmen. In the face of the several enactments of the Legislature, which had apparently settled the question in the affirmative, new doubts were raised and many politicians obstinately denied that an Israelite could possibly be considered as a Briton. A spirit of persecution against the Jews became manifest, and a tendency to reduce their scanty privileges was visible. Thus when a rich Jew, named Elias de Pass, bequeathed the sum of £1200 for the erection of a Hebrew College, the Government refused to allow a proper application of the legacy. The authorities discovered that to raise a Hebrew College was to encourage superstition, which was contrary to law. In accordance with an old Act of Parliament, the bequest of £1200 was seized, and without the slightest reference to the testator's desires, the sum was devoted to the Foundling Hospital. This unjust and arbitrary act of Government, created a considerable impression at the time, and proved a check—happily only temporary—to the destination of sums for religious or charitable objects.

Let us now endeavour to ascertain what was the state of the Jews of England when George II. reigned, and the great Mr Pelham governed. Their number then, in this country, was estimated at between six and eight thousand souls. The population of the British islands at that period was reckoned at about 8,000,000 of inhabitants. The increase of the Jews during the last 120 years in English soil is by no means extraordinary, for while the general population has quadrupled, the Jews have perhaps quintupled in number. Considering the important and incessant immigration from the Continent that flowed in during the second half of the eighteenth century and the first quarter of the nineteenth, the result, probably, scarcely equals that attained by the inhabitants of the British Isles, with whom the tide has largely streamed outward.

In 1753, according to an authority avowedly hostile, there were only twenty opulent families among the Jews; then followed about forty brokers, some of whom were not deemed among the most honourable in their profession. Finally came a train of hawkers, pedlars, traffickers in every imaginable commodity in every imaginable way. It was represented that not more than ten Jewish houses of business of any great note were in existence. Some able and learned men were recognised among the Hebrews, some being physicians and some merchants. The Jews were said not to practise agriculture or manufacture; nor to serve in the army or navy. It was commonly reported that Jewish property, to the extent of £2,000,000, was invested in English stock, a considerable portion of which sums, however, belonged to foreign Israelites. One Jew was reputed to possess £200,000 in the funds.

According to more friendly—and probably more accurate—writers, many affluent families, some of which were very rich, flourished among the Jews. They were not allowed to possess landed property, and the first of the nation, Sampson Gideon, was constrained to obtain an express Act of Parliament in his favour, permitting the seller to convey to him a certain estate.

Herein we are enabled to furnish a list of the principal Jewish merchants of the day, some of whom rivalled in the extent of their transactions the foremost English houses in the City of London. Abraham and Jacob Franco, Francis Salvador, Joseph and Jacob Salvador, Benj. Mendes da Costa, Aaron Franks, Levy and Reuben Salamons, Isaac Lamego, Gonzales and Da Costa, Pereira and Lima, Jacob

Fernandez Nunes, Moses Lamego, Abraham Osorio, Daniel Mendes Seixas, Moses Franks, Isaac Levy, Joseph Treves, Abraham Fonseca, Jacob Levy Sonsino, Judah Supino.

It has been averred that wealth, when not invested in real property, seldom remains for above a century in the hands of one family. The fact certainly receives full confirmation in the present instance. Not only not one of the above Jewish firms is now to be discovered, but even their very names—with two or three exceptions—have disappeared from the face of the earth. The descendants of the Francos have long forsaken the God of their forefathers, and changed their appellation. The name of Salvador, once the representative of generosity, kindliness, and courtliness, is only known now in connection with a building on an old site in the city. The patronymics of the other Portuguese merchants are recollected in the congregation merely from their being painted on the walls of the vestry-room; and few now living have ever heard of the hospitable and charitable house of Franks.

Some of these great merchants, we are aware from other sources, left large fortunes; and though we may not accept literally the fact that there were a hundred other Hebrew firms with means as considerable, we may safely affirm that this picture of the Jews is not distant from the truth. It was calculated that full one hundred families would each expend annually between £1000 and £2000, and that estimating the number of Jewish families at 1000, excluding the poor, their average outlay might be fixed at the moderate rate of £300 for every Jewish household, which would produce a total of £300,000 distributed annually by the Jews throughout the land. The Jews paid all duties and taxes and assessments. In addition, they supported their own poor. They clothed and fed them in health, relieved them in sickness, buried them in death. The foreign commerce of the Jews was reckoned at £1,500,000 yearly. The trade with Jamaica was principally in Hebrew hands, and in that island about two hundred Jewish families resided and had been naturalised.

Many of the above-named Hebrew merchants possessed a high reputation for integrity, benevolence, and largeness of heart. Foremost in their ranks shone conspicuously Benjamin Mendes da Costa, to whom we adverted in a previous chapter as the "one truly good Jew," who in his own resplendent virtues would have sufficed to save the whole nation from obloquy. The family of Mendes da Costa was one of the most ancient and honourable among the Portuguese Jews. The noble figures of grand old Alvaro da Costa, of the gifted Antonio Mendes, physician to Queen Catherine of Braganza, and of the courtly Andrea Mendes, her chamberlain, rise before our eyes; and we cease to wonder that the family of Mendes da Costa should have enriched the Jewish community with so many eminent men. Emanuel Mendes da Costa was another distinguished member of that family. He was the grandson of Alvaro da Costa, who had wedded the sister of Antonio Mendes, and who quitted Portugal in 1692. After spending ten years at Rouen in Normandy, the Portuguese merchant immigrated with his family into England— then a land of promise to the hunted, persecuted Jews. Here the old stock took root, and spread forth a number of branches in various directions. Alvaro's son Abraham or John Mendes da Costa, married his cousin, a daughter of Dr Mendes, and became in 1717 the father of Emanuel, who shone as a botanist, a naturalist, a philosopher, and as collector of anecdotes of literati, and of valuable notes and MSS. Emanuel Mendes da Costa contributed many valuable papers to the *Philosophical Transactions* and to other scientific publications. It was in the library of this gentleman that the list of the original Jewish settlers in this country was found. The collection of printed books and MSS., and engravings and drawings of natural history, which had cost Emanuel Mendes da Costa many years to gather, was of great value. At his death it was brought to the hammer, and dispersed among numerous purchasers.

Several other members of the community also enjoyed great personal consideration. Much prejudice, however, was still rife against the Jews, and with the exception of a favoured few, who were admitted into the higher ranks of society, the great bulk of the ancient people were eyed by the British vulgus as outcasts and Pariahs with whom it was discreditable to consort. We have read a letter written by a gentleman at Isleworth to a friend in town, in which he says that he would have found the country very pleasant had he not had the mortification of seeing the finest seats in possession of the Jews. Since the last Act—the Naturalisation Bill—they had grown very familiar. The Jews had come between the wind and his nobility, and he did not like it. Let us give the concluding paragraph in the missive in his own words—" M—s H—t (Moses Hart) and A—n F—s (Aaron Franks) at the last vestry held here, mingled with the rest without opposition, though two clergymen and Justice B— were present. No less than a coach-load of them (Jews) last Thursday assembled at a clergyman's house very near us to play cards." Had the writer lived at the present day, he would be far more startled and shocked at the spectacle of a Jewish Member of Parliament making eloquent speeches to an attentive House, a Jewish Lord Mayor admitting within the City precincts a foreign potentate, and a Jewish judge presiding over one of the highest courts in the realm.

Among the not numerous Israelites who moved on nearly equal terms with the aristocracy, we may mention Mrs Judith Levy, daughter of Moses Hart, founder of the first German Synagogue in London. She was the widow of Elias Levy, a wealthy financier, and sister-in-law to Isaac and Aaron Franks. This lady, who lived to a great age, enjoyed an income of £6000 a year, and dwelt in great splendour. She frequented many of the nobility's routs, and played half-guinea quadrille with the Countess of Yarmouth, Lady Holdernesse, Lord Stormont, and other persons of quality. She was exceedingly charitable and warm-hearted, and she distributed to her indigent relatives upwards of £1000 per annum. Her greatest delight was in rendering happy those that surrounded her. She died when ninety-seven years old, in January 1803, at her house in Albemarle Street, and she was interred with Jewish rites at Mile End. She left no will, and her fortune was inherited by John Franks, who was remarkable for benevolence, and who followed her noble example, dispensing substantial relief to hundreds of Jews and Christians without distinction of creed.

Notwithstanding all drawbacks, wealthy Jews came occasionly to settle in England. In the year 1756 Baron d'Aguilar arrived in London with his numerous offspring, consisting of twelve sons and daughters, and he was said to have brought with him an immense fortune. Moses Lopez Pereira was descended from an ancient Portuguese family. He first visited London in 1722, and then proceeded to Vienna, where he farmed the tobacco and snuff duties. Being successful in his undertakings, he gradually became a great favourite of the Empress, and was appointed her treasurer. The Emperor Charles VI. conferred upon him the title of Baron d'Aguilar, which, according to a writer, had formerly existed in his family. Baron d'Aguilar died in 1759, and his eldest son, Ephraim d'Aguilar, succeeded to his title and to a large share of his riches. Young Ephraim was then only twenty years old, and two years before, in 1757, he had become naturalised, and had wedded the daughter of Mr Moses Mendes da Costa, a lady who brought him the princely dowry of £150,000. The Baroness died in 1763, leaving several young children, who inherited the whole of their mother's wealth. The eldest of his daughters became the wife of Admiral Keith Steward, who was possessed of great property in Scotland; and the second bestowed her charms and her fortune upon Dr Ewart, Physician-General to the establishment at Bengal. For some time D'Aguilar took part in the communal life of his co-religionists, and we find his name in the list of the treasurers of the Synagogue. Several of the minutes of the proceedings of the Mahamad bear the signature of Ephraim d'Aguilar—a neat and clerkly handwriting, not at all like the production of an ill-regulated, badly-disciplined mind. D'Aguilar was elected Warden in 1765, when he declined to serve, and refused on technical grounds to pay the fine. Eight days were given him to accept or submit to the penalty. He evidently complied with the law, and later on he was again made Warden.

In 1767 Ephraim d'Aguilar married the relict of Mr Benjamin Mendes da Costa. She was a very good and accomplished lady, and was possessed of £10,000 and £1000 per annum, which sums were happily settled upon her for her sole use. For some years the young Baron lived in great style in a mansion in Broad Street Buildings, which had been built by his father-in-law, Mr Moses M. da Costa. He kept several carriages, and maintained a retinue of twenty-four servants. The loss of a large estate in America, and other causes, induced him suddenly to change his mode of living. On the expiration of the lease of his house, he renounced the character of a gentleman, and became rude, slovenly, and careless of his person and conduct, totally withdrawing himself from his family connections and the gay world.

Baron d'Aguilar budded out into one of those eccentric characters that appear inexplicable to the philosopher and the psychologist. He affected an appearance of poverty, albeit he was in affluent circumstances. He parted from his wife, and for twenty years forgot her existence. He suddenly recollected her, and visited her one day. Subsequently, he frequently dined with her, and finally he took up his abode altogether with the lady, apparently to render her life a burden. His pleasure appeared to be to give her pain. He tormented her and distressed her in every way in his power. He locked her up for three days, and the Baroness was constrained to flee through the window. She had long discovered the difference between her second and her first husband, the "one truly good Jew," and she had recourse to legal proceedings in her own defence. The lady had the whole court in her favour, and thenceforward she was freed from any further persecutions from her tyrannical spouse.

The Baron purchased several houses in various parts of London, while he resided in Shaftesbury Place, Aldersgate Street. He converted some ground into a farmyard, near Colebrook Row, Islington; he filled it with domestic animals, which he declined to feed and refused to sell, until they were converted into living skeletons. Withal, incredible as it may seem, he was really benevolent and charitable. His donations to the poor were numerous, and his good deeds were performed unostentatiously. He opened an asylum in his own establishment for the destitute poor, especially females, and many unhappy beings were saved by him from distress or destruction. Charity covers a multitude of sins, and let us hope it redeemed his transgressions. He died on the 16th March 1802, in Shaftesbury Place, after an illness of seventeen days. He would light no fire in his house, notwithstanding the severity of the weather, and it was thought he perished for want of proper care and treatment. His remains were interred in the Sephardic Cemetery at Mile End, whither they were followed by a few mourners in half-a-dozen coaches. Much valuable property was discovered in his dwelling after his death. Among other objects were discovered a quantity of cochineal and indigo worth £10,000, and jewels estimated at £30,000. The present General d'Aguilar is descended from one of the elder sons of Ephraim d'Aguilar. Among the Sephardic Congregation there are still living the representatives of a younger son, who remained stanch adherents to the old faith.

Baron d'Aguilar was a most singular character—a combination of vice and virtue, of misanthropy and benevolence, of cruelty and kindness, of avarice and liberality. He was a Harpagon, with a good deal of the Cheeryble and a tinge of the Squeers in his composition. In his earlier days he associated with his co-religionists. Subsequently he completely disregarded Jewish observances, and ceased to follow Hebrew rites. He neglected to give his daughters any religious education, and he married them without the pale of their race. The history of Ephraim Baron d'Aguilar, if it does not adorn a tale, will, to the thoughtful mind, assuredly serve to point a moral.

CHAPTER XII.

JEWISH MARRIAGES.

FROM the settlement of the Jews in England down to our own time, that is, to the passing of the Registration Acts in the reign of William IV., the question as to the validity of Jewish marriages has been one of vital importance to the community. Abstract questions as to whether foreign Jews were legally admissible into the kingdom, and entitled to dwell therein without an Act of Parliament, had always afforded matter for ingenious speculation to the lawyers of the time. Practically it mattered little whether it was held with Prynne in his celebrated " Demurrer," that as the Jews were banished by an Act passed in the reign of Edward I., they could only be readmitted by its repeal; or whether it was maintained with Lord Coke in his " Institutes," that the statute " De Judaismo " imposed such onerous disabilities upon them that they migrated from England of their own accord. We do not believe in the correctness of Lord Coke's version, and we have already laid before the reader a brief account of that event, as gathered from the best authorities. It was, however, all important to the Jews that the State should recognise the validity of marriages performed amongst themselves according to the rites of their religion, as upon such recognition depended the legitimacy of their children, the right of inheritance, the devolution of property, and even their individual status in a court of justice.

By the ancient common law of England, which had been revived after the Restoration, there were three modes of entering into matrimony—(1) By public solemnisation *in facie ecclesiæ*; (2) By clandestine celebration; and (3) By consent of parties, called consentual marriages. The civil marriages before justices of the peace, which prevailed during the Commonwealth, had been abolished, and the Registration Acts placing Jewish marriages on an equality with those performed in church did not yet exist. It would have been an act of profanity for Jews to wed in church, and an act of indelicacy as well as profanity to have had the marriage service read clandestinely by a parson. It was essential to the Jews that marriages performed according to the rites of their religion should be recognised as valid by the courts of law. Yet, by the law as administered in the temporal courts, no marriage was held valid unless celebrated by a clergyman in holy orders, episcopally ordained. No ceremony in church was then necessary, but any person once ordained by virtue of his orders—which no degradation could extinguish—was enabled to unite a couple behind a hedge, in a field, or in a tavern, in a prison, or in a drawing-room. The evils arising from the solemnisation of secret marriages had become so glaring as to attract the attention of the Legislature. The sons and daughters of noble or wealthy houses were daily seduced in their affections, and inveigled into matches laden with shame and infamy. A band of profligate miscreants, the refuse of the clergy, men abandoned to all sense of decency and decorum, frequently prisoners for debt and crime, hovered about the verge of Fleet Prison to intercept customers, and united couples for life, without license or question, to the scandal of religion and the disgrace of their cloth. Young and inexperienced persons of both sexes were tempted by the facilities offered to them by wretches without honour or principle, to indulge in a passing fancy or a questionable inclination, and so wreck for ever their chances of happiness in this world. The conjugal infidelities, the misery, the sin, the crimes, caused by these practices, were seriously undermining the morality of the country. Never, not even in the profligate times of Charles II. and his minions, had the nuptial knot been so little respected. Marriage itself was falling into disrepute. A work was published in defence of the holy tie that joins together two human beings for better and for worse, and therein it was actually alleged that it would be a pity to abandon altogether the old practice of marriage, for it did occasionally serve to good purposes. A remarkable case of a scandalous nature was presented before the House of Lords as an appeal from an inferior court, and Lord Chancellor Hardwicke determined to terminate these abuses. To that effect he framed a bill, which eventually became law, after passing the ordeal of warm debates and undergoing many modifications. Of the nature of the provisions of Lord Hardwicke's Marriage Act we will speak hereafter.

Before this period the Ecclesiastical Courts were the only tribunals in matrimonial questions, and remained so until their jurisdiction was abolished, when the present court of marriage was established. The legality of Jewish marriages could only be tried in these courts, while their validity would merely incidentally arise in the Courts of Common Law. By the Ecclesiastical Courts consensual marriages were regarded as complete in substance, but not in ceremony. As a matter of discipline, it was enjoined in such courts that the ceremony should be performed by some one in orders, in proof of a consensual marriage. As regards property, legitimacy of children, and disabilities of coverture, the temporal courts held that a consensual marriage gave no rights. No cases relating to the marriages of Jews can be found earlier than the reign of George II. But the question as to the validity of a Jewish marriage must have been considered as early as the reign of William III. In 1695, when England was engaged in a death struggle with Louis the Great of France, and when funds were sadly needed to pay soldiers and feed sailors, an Act obtained the sanction of Parliament granting duties to the Crown on all marriages, and levying a tax upon bachelors.

Though the Common Law Courts did not hold any one to be married unless the ceremony had been performed by an individual in holy orders, yet as Jews, Papists, and Quakers did marry according to their own rites, Parliament resolved that Jews and others should pay the marriage-tax. With a consistency equalled only by its liberality, the Legislature declined to recognise such persons as legally married. The money of the Jew would certainly be received, but then the rights of a civilised being, not to say an Englishman, would be withheld from him. So it was enacted that if Jews lived together as man and wife, they should be subjected to the tax. At the same time there was inserted in the Act one of those ingenious saving clauses which gladden the heart of the lawyer and perplex the mind of the judge. It was provided in this Act "that nothing contained in it should be construed to make good or effectual in law any such marriages of Jews or pretended marriages, but they shall be of the same force and virtue as they would have been if this Act had never been passed." What force or virtue was attached by law to such a marriage? That question the Legislature left undecided. In this position of affairs it happened that the first recorded case referring to a Jewish marriage came before an English tribunal. That was the once famous suit of Da Costa v. Villareal, which, it is stated, caused considerable excitement in the courts, and doubtless acquired great notoriety in its day in the Jewish community. Both parties were members of the highest families in the Portuguese Congregation.

Mrs Catherine da Costa Villareal was the daughter of Moses or Anthony da Costa, an opulent merchant, who had attained the dignity—unusual for a Jew—of director of the Bank of England. This Moses or Anthony da Costa had contracted a union with his cousin, Catherine Mendes, who was born in the royal palace of Somerset House, and who was named Catherine because the royal Catherine herself, the dark-skinned but not unpleasing consort of the fickle Charles, had stood her sponsor. Catherine da Costa Villareal, a lovely bride at eighteen, a wealthy and beautiful widow at twenty-one, had no lack of admirers. The lady, on being free, promised Jacob Mendes da Costa to espouse him at the termination of her widowhood of twelve months, provided her father consented. The gentleman was her first cousin, and the brother of the Emanuel Mendes da Costa of whom we have already spoken. At the expiration of the stipulated period, Mrs Villareal, availing herself of the privileges of her sex, flatly refused to maintain her promise. Mr Da Costa, actuated by love either for the person or purse of the lady—her purse, we may remark, was uncommonly weighty—proceeded against her in the Ecclesiastical Court to constrain her to fulfil her engagement. The cause was tried in the Court of Arches, that is, the Court of the Archbishop of Canterbury, in the year 1733. It was objected by the lady's counsel, that as the persons were not Christians, and that the alleged promised marriage was to be performed according to the rites of the Jews, and not in *foro ecclesiæ*, the Court of Arches had no jurisdiction. The Court, however, decided that if it had full proof that the parties had bound themselves to each other in marriage, and that at the end of the time agreed upon Mr Da Costa had demanded, and Mrs Villareal had refused, a fulfilment of her promises, the Court possessed authority to enforce it, though the parties were not to be married in church.

When the case came on for hearing, the Court ruled that as the lady's promise was conditional, and not absolute, it was not binding upon her, and dismissed the application. In vain the baffled suitor addressed himself to the Court of King's Bench to obtain compensation for his wounded feelings. The action he brought against the lady for breach of promise was unsuccessful. Lord Hardwicke, the future Lord Chancellor, and then Chief-Justice of King's Bench, gave judgment that the sentence of the Court of Arches was conclusive evidence that Mrs Villareal was not bound by such promise, and nonsuited the plaintiff, who was left without further remedy. When Lord Hardwicke had decided that a woman's promise was not binding upon her conscience unless accompanied by indisputable legal forms, Mrs Catherine da Costa Villareal married Mr William Mellish, a gentleman belonging to a family of great commercial standing, and who had himself filled some high functions under Government. Subsequently this lady not only embraced Christianity herself, but brought to the baptismal font the two children who had been left to her care by her first husband, a girl and boy of tender years, who were named Elizabeth and William. Elizabeth grew up as comely as her mother, and a coronet rested on her brow as the wife of Lord Galway, to whom she bore several children.

Four years after this decision, Mrs Andreas, a Jewess, sued her husband in the Consistory Court of the Bishop of London for restitution of conjugal rights. Before the Court could decree the restitution prayed for, it was necessary to prove that Mrs Andreas possessed marital rights. The learned doctor of law who appeared for Mr Andreas objected that as the parties had been united according to the forms of the Jews, and not of the Church of England, the Court could take no notice of such marriage, and Mrs Andreas could not establish a case against her husband in the Ecclesiastical Court. But the court held that the parties were duly bound according to Jewish forms, and the lady obtained the desired redress. Let us hope that circumstances may not have caused her afterwards to repent of her success.

Such was the state of the marriage laws in the country in general, and among the Jews in particular, when Lord Hardwicke in the year 1753 introduced his celebrated Act. This important measure completely revolutionised the common law of England as affecting marriages, which hitherto had rested on the old canon law of the church. Before this Act was passed a marriage was valid by the mere consent of the parties, or by the presence of a priest in orders at any time or place. The inconveniences and hardships, both to married persons and their children arising from the existing law were glaring; and of the frightful abuses and immorality caused by it we have already spoken. Lord Hardwicke's Act struck at the evil from its very root. Consentual marriages and suits to compel celebration of the same in *facie ecclesiæ* were abolished in England, and all marriages were declared null and void unless performed by a priest in orders, under banns or license, according to the liturgy of the Church of England. No alteration of the law was made in Scotland, where Gretna-Green marriages flourished until within memory of the present generation. The disorders resulting from the state of the law north of the Tweed have long proved favourite themes for the imagination of novelists, and recently they were powerfully depicted in Mr Wilkie Collins' tale and drama of "Man and Wife."

In the greater part of the British Islands, the trade of Fleet or hedge parson became extinct. Considerable hardship was however inflicted on Dissenters and Roman Catholics, for the law constrained them to marry according to the prescribed service, or renounce wedlock altogether. If the Jews had not been exempted from the operation of this Act, no valid marriages could have been contracted by them.

The influence of the Jews was brought to bear on the Government, and their exertions were successful, while Dissenters obtained no immunity, albeit some of their body sat in the House of Commons. The same Lord Chancellor who had brought in the Naturalisation Bill, again befriended the Jews with characteristic enlightenment. In a specially introduced clause, the eighteenth, it was declared that nothing in the Act should extend to any marriage among persons professing the Jewish religion, when both parties were of that faith. Though by this enactment marriages between Jews were not expressly declared valid, they were excepted from the operations of the Act which abolished consentual marriages. Hitherto the marriages of Jews, not being performed by a clergyman in orders, had been deemed consentual marriages, and as such had been acknowledged by the Ecclesiastical Courts. The exemption of the Jews from Lord Hardwicke's law was hereafter held by such courts to be by implication a statutable recognition of the validity of Jewish marriages.

For nearly forty years after the passing of this Act, no cases relating to Jewish marriages seem to have arisen, but between 1790 and the commencement of the present century several very important cases appeared before the English courts. In 1794 the suit of Vigevena and Silverra v. Alvarez was instituted in the Prerogative Court, to decide who should be entitled to the property of a deceased Israelite. The claimant represented himself to be the legitimate son of the person whose property was disputed. The question turned on the legitimacy of one whose parents had been wedded according to Jewish law. It was objected that persons coming before the Ecclesiastical Courts to claim any right by marriage, must show the marriage to have been in conformity with the rites of the Christian Church.

To this it was replied, "that the peculiar and fundamental tenets of the Jews were averse to the use of such rites, and it was unreasonable to maintain that their marriages according to their own rites should not be valid; that the Jews had always existed as a separate community, and were entitled to have their marriages tried by their own law." The judgment of the Court, delivered by Sir William Wynne, solemnly declared the legal effect of Lord Hardwicke's Act upon Jewish marriages. "There is no case," enunciated the Judge, " in which a Jew has been called upon to prove his marriage. If there had, I conceive the mode of proof must have been conformable to the Jewish rules. The Marriage Act lays down rules for all marriages excepting those of Jews and Quakers. There is no comparison between Jews and Dissenters. Jews are anti-Christians, Dissenters are Christians. Here the parties are alleged to be married according to the rites and ceremonies of the Jewish Church, which I hold to be sufficient."

Lord Stowell acted in the well-known cases of Lindo v. Belisario and Goldsmid v. Bromer on the doctrines here established, that Jews were entitled to try and prove their marriage according to their own code. These cases are most interesting, not only because the judges of the Consistory Court of the Bishop of London referred a question of law to a Jewish Beth-Din (Ecclesiastical Court), but also because, when the evidence of custom was conflicting, the judgment of a Beth-Din was deemed conclusive by a Christian Ecclesiastical Court.

In the year 1793, Miss Esther Lindo, a minor, was prevailed upon to consent to a clandestine marriage with Mr Mendes Belisario. The young lady met by appointment her lover at the house of his brother ; then Mr Mendes Belisario, before two credible Jewish witnesses, asked Miss Lindo whether she understood the purport of the proceedings, and on receiving an affirmative reply, he placed a ring on her finger, repeating at the same time in Hebrew the formula used in the celebration of Jewish marriages. There was no Ketuba (contract), Khupa (canopy), nor the seven nuptial blessings. It was a Mekadish or irregular Jewish marriage, recognised by Jewish law if contracted in accordance with its ordinances. Immediately after the ceremony the newly united couple separated, never again to enjoy each other's society. Miss Lindo was an orphan and much younger than her alleged husband. When her guardian learned what had taken place, he resolved that the marriage should never be completed. On the question being referred to the Portuguese Beth-Din, they pronounced the ceremony to be a doubtful betrothment, without declaring whether it constituted the relationship of husband and wife. To further secure the lady against the enterprises of her husband, the ægis of the High Court of Chancery was thrown round her. That Court, which disposes of the substance of so many orphans, accepted her as a ward. Lord Loughborough, then Lord Chancellor, prohibited Mr Belisario from having access to her, and ordered that Mr Abraham de Mattos Mocatta, her guardian, should institute a suit in the Consistory Court to test the validity of the marriage. A suit of jactitation of marriage was thereupon commenced in the Court of Consistory, and the case was tried by Lord Stowell, one of the greatest jurists that ever adorned the bench. Consentual marriages amongst Jews being recognised, and the Ecclesiastical Courts having held that Jewish marriages were to be tried by Jewish law, Lord Stowell had to decide whether there had been between Miss Lindo and Mr Mendes Belisario a valid marriage. With that diffidence which characterises great minds, Lord Stowell entered into the investigation with doubt, being, as he said, fearful that in applying the principles of Jewish law he might run the risk of mistaking those principles, and that his decision might affect a very numerous and respectable body of people, as he designated the Jewish community. The question was reduced to this issue : whether a Mekadish without being followed by consummation constituted a valid Jewish marriage. Various Jewish authorities, ancient and modern were consulted, the opinions were taken of Mr Julian, Mr Almosnino, and Mr Delgado, the members of the Portuguese Beth-Din ; of Mr Is. Jimenez, ex-Chief Rabbi of the Portuguese Congregation at Hamburg, of the Rev. S. Lyon of Cambridge, and of other learned rabbis. The certificate of the Beth-Din of 1776 was handed in as evidence proving that a Mekadish between a certain Benjamin Henriques and a lady had constituted a valid marriage. Authorities as usual disagreed. The rabbis took opposite views on the question. Maimonides was at variance with the Talmud, and the Hebrew text of the great philosopher and the Latin text of his translator again differed.

Lord Stowell was perplexed. The difficulties of the case will remind the reader of a celebrated instance in modern days, where a similar question was solved in three distinct ways by three British courts of law. Much interest was at one time felt in these islands as to whether Miss Theresa Longworth possessed legally the right of designating herself the Hon. Mrs Yelverton. It will be recollected that an irregular Scotch marriage had taken place between the lady and Mr Yelverton. On her applying to the tribunals of her country to obtain public recognition of her position, it was ruled by a Scotch court that she was not married in Scotland, by an Irish court that she was married in Ireland ; and by the highest English court, the House of Lords, that she was not married either in England, Scotland, or Ireland.

No wonder that Lord Stowell and the Jewish Beth-Din were puzzled. Lord Stowell, who evidently only sought for further light, proposed to the Beth-Din a number of questions relating to Jewish marriages for their decision. After carefully considering the replies of the Beth-Din, the court delivered judgment. In the opinion emitted by that body, it was stated that the law of Moses did not prescribe any formal ceremony of marriage, but there were legal institutions to which the Jews adhered in practice, and which must be considered as having the force of law, and there were the laws derived from the institutions of the rabbis ; that as consummation had not taken place, Mr Belisario had no right to demand of the lady to perform the duties of a wife ; that there had been only a betrothment, that the contract was determinable at will, and the wife might decline to continue to be his partner.

Lord Stowell, on delivering judgment, adverted to the necessity for a court of law, when dealing with Jewish rites and ceremonies, to consider not alone the law of Moses, but the laws of the recognised rabbinical authorities. His Lordship thought that the finding of the Beth-Din must be considered as a judicial opinion, and not that of an individual ; as an authoritative opinion, not only conveying knowledge, but also sanctioned by the qualifications of probity, learning, and judgment, which must have recommended the individuals to the stations entrusted to them. Lord Stowell then confirmed the decision of the Beth-Din, and declared Miss Lindo not to be the wife of Mr Belisario. The wifeless husband appealed from this decree to the Court of Arches, where in 1796 Lord Stowell's judgment was confirmed by Sir William Wynne, the judge of that court. The unhappy man, who was sincerely attached to the lady, continued for some years to struggle against these adverse decisions, but his efforts were necessarily hopeless.

The first petition for divorce among Jews was filed in 1794 before Lord Stowell. The plaintiff in that suit was Baroness d'Aguilar, who instituted proceedings against her husband, Baron Ephraim d'Aguilar, charging him with cruelty and adultery. In our preceding chapter we gave a brief sketch of the strange career of this worthy. When his wife escaped from his power, she was seventy years old and infirm in health. The sympathies of the court were enlisted in her favour, and the levity displayed by the respondent was sternly reproved by the judge. The marriage had been contracted in 1767, according to Jewish rites, and Lord Stowell now decreed its dissolution. Objections were taken on the ground that the marriage had not been performed in church, but Lord Stowell in giving judgment declared forcibly the civil rights of the Jews. "The marriages of the Jews," said he, "are expressly protected by the Marriage Act, and persons of that persuasion are as much entitled to the justice of the country as those of any other. Jews have the same rights of succession to property and of administration as other subjects, and they come to the Ecclesiastical Courts to have such rights secured. Many of them are possessed of considerable property, and they have the same rights to transmit it as others. It would be hard, therefore, if they had not the same mode of securing the legitimacy of their children, and consequently if the same rights of divorce did not belong to them."

Hardly had the excitement in the community attending this case and that of Lindo v. Belisario subsided, when public attention became engrossed in the story of Miss Goldsmid and Mr Bromer. In 1798, Miss Maria Goldsmid, a daughter of one of the most influential families among the Jews, with all the susceptibility and inexperience of sweet sixteen, was captivated by the charms of Mr David Bromer, one of her father's clerks. This enterprising gentleman, who visited the family of the young lady, succeeded in inducing her to agree to marry him clandestinely. For this purpose Mr Bromer accompanied Miss Goldsmid in a coach to the "Shakespeare Tavern," Covent Garden, where two Jewish witnesses, named Levy and Hess, were in attendance. Before these persons the bridegroom placed the mysterious golden circlet on the bride's finger, pronouncing at the same time the Hebrew words constituting the ceremony of Kedushim. Meanwhile arrived Mr George Goldsmid, the lady's father, who broke up the young couple's happiness by taking away the bride. Moreover, Mr Goldsmid brought a suit of jactitation of marriage in the Consistory Court of London, to declare the marriage invalid. It was proved that the ceremony at the tavern was defective, owing to the disqualification of the witnesses. Such disqualification might proceed from certain degrees of consanguinity to either of the parties who marry, or from nonconformity with the ceremonies of the Jewish religion. Evidence was given to the effect that the mother of Levy, one of the witnesses, and the mother of Bromer, the bridegroom, were sisters; and that Hess, the other witness, did not conform with the practices of the Jewish religion, for he profaned the Sabbath and ate forbidden meats.

Lord Stowell decided that, according to precedent, the validity of the marriage must be tested by Jewish law. The Beth-Din of the German Congregation declared the marriage to be void on the above grounds, and the Portuguese Beth-Din concurred with that judgment. It was urged on behalf of Mr Bromer that the law enunciated by the Beth-Din was most unreasonable. Lord Stowell declined to discuss the reasonableness of Jewish law, which must be taken as it is found. He considered that the Beth-Din was a tribunal of great authority on matters of Jewish law; at the same time he did not think the law so unreasonable, for its object was to render clandestine marriages almost impossible, and such marriages are admitted to be evils in all civilised countries. Consequently Lord Stowell pronounced against the validity of the marriage.

In the reign of George IV., Lord Hardwicke's Act was modified and amended, and the exemption in favour of the

Jews was re-enacted. That law remained in vigour until the passing of the Marriage and Registration Acts in the reign of William IV., which now regulate all marriages under these Acts; the marriages of Jews properly solemnised are placed on an equality with those celebrated in church. At the same time an Act was passed declaring good all Jewish marriages previously performed, so as to remove doubts with reference to the validity of consentual marriages in the temporal courts. The history of Jewish marriages illustrates the history of the Jews struggling in the courts of law for a recognition of their civil rights, as the history of the Oaths Bill embodies the history of their struggles in Parliament to obtain their political rights.

CHAPTER XIII.

ORIGIN OF THE BOARD OF DEPUTIES.

IF union be strength, organisation is certainly power. During the first half of the eighteenth century, whenever the Jews had occasion to address themselves to the Government of the country, each man was his own representative. The Jews as a body possessed no recognised medium of communication with the outer world. When questions arose affecting Jewish interests, desultory steps were taken—when taken at all—by isolated individuals, and often failed for want of concerted action. Sometimes an influential capitalist was applied to in order to intercede with Government on behalf of his less fortunate brethren. Sampson Gideon among others rendered his race many a service by availing himself of the favour his wealth gained for him in high places, to obtain a hearing for the Children of Israel. We may add that Jewish financiers have ever been ready and willing to uphold the cause of their faith; and in latter times, we all know how the illustrious houses of Goldsmid, Montefiore, and Rothschild have warmly espoused the defence of their oppressed and down-trodden race in the days of its sore trouble and anguish.

In the year 1745–46 some political events occurred which taught the Jews the necessity of concentrating their forces, so as to attain the best results from them. It has been alleged that the Irish are the only nation who have never ill-treated the Jews. To this statement it has been replied that the Irish have seldom possessed the opportunity. For our part, we have no desire to endorse any such ungenerous remark, and we are glad to acknowledge any acts of friendship and kindliness towards the Jews, without too minutely investigating all the causes that might have converted present good into potential evil. It may be that a certain affinity exists between the Irish and the Hebrew character. At all events, the Irish in 1745, unlike the English in 1753, did not consider that the naturalisation of the Jews would either Judaise their country or straightway bring it to spiritual and material perdition. On the 18th November 1745, Mr Morgan introduced into the Irish House of Commons a bill for the Naturalisation of persons professing the Jewish religion. At the same time was presented a bill to accept the solemn affirmation of Quakers instead of an oath. The bills were speedily carried through their several stages, and passed on the 25th November, but they were thrown out by the Peers. Mr Morgan, nothing discouraged, again brought forward the Jewish Naturalisation Bill on the 18th March 1746; and the Irish Commons, to show their determination, carried it through in three days without a dissentient voice. It was in vain. It was thrown out again by the same power, but only by a small majority. There were very few resident Jews in Ireland at that time, and so this result was not of great practical moment. Nevertheless, the congregation at Bevis Marks, considering the principle at stake, was much annoyed at this disappointment. It was believed that, had proper measures been adopted, the votes required to secure success in the Upper House might have been obtained. As other movements in the same direction were anticipated, "a Committee of Diligence" was appointed by that community to represent the interests of the nation, and to seize every opportunity to establish its freedom. The duties of this committee were to watch over the affairs of the Jews, to grasp at every chance for improving their condition, and to protect them against any danger. To enable the committee to carry out this somewhat extensive programme, considerable faculties were given to that body. They were free to act as best seemed in their judgment; they were empowered to engage the assistance of men of law and of letters, and they were promised sufficient funds to satisfy lawyers and writers. They were recommended to keep a minute-book, but they were politely told that they need not show it to their constituents. The gentlemen who were elected by the elders to fulfil these responsible functions were five in number. They were Benjamin Mendes da

Costa, Daniel J. Rodriguez, Jacob Fernandez Nunes, Jacob de Moses Franco, Jacob Mendes Pacheco. The noble and universally-respected Benjamin Mendes da Costa, to whose virtues we have more than once paid a befitting tribute, was elected president. Doubtless the committee did bestir themselves, though unfortunately success did not crown their efforts. Another attempt was made by the persevering Mr Morgan in favour of the Jews in the Irish House of Commons. In December 1747 the Jewish Naturalisation Bill was once more agreed to by that branch of the Legislature, to be rejected, as before, by a stubborn Upper House, notwithstanding the exertions of the Committee of Diligence. But we need not wonder at it when we consider that a whole century of progressive enlightenment has not softened down the prejudices of caste, and that in England the same attempts had to be repeated again and again, to meet the same repulses, until the torrent of public opinion came and swept off all further resistance.

The proceedings of the committee were not regularly chronicled. That they were not idle is evident from the fact that the elders of the congregation were called upon to liquidate the expenditure incurred by their delegates, and which amounted to some hundreds of pounds. The functions of this body appear to have expired in due course.

In 1760 another body was created, destined to attain a far different and more vigorous existence, and from that period the political representation of the Jews may be said to date. An institution that has since grown and become powerful, thus acquired a name if not a local habitation—an institution that has flourished and increased in importance until it has become a Jewish parliament, reflecting the views of most of the principal congregations in the kingdom.

George III. had ascended the throne of England, when the elders of the Portuguese community appointed seven delegates to offer their respects to his Majesty. These gentlemen were authorised to act on behalf of their co-religionists in other matters too; but they were instructed not to seek new privileges or advantages without consulting with the elders. The persons named as " Deputies of the

Portuguese nation" were Jacob de Moses Franco, Benjamin Mendes da Costa, Jacob Nunes Gonzales, Moses de Joseph da Costa, Joseph Jesurun Rodrigues, better known as Joseph Salvador, Isaac Jesurun Alvarez, and Isaac Fernandez Nunes. Mr Jacob Franco was elected president; but on account of his advanced age, his attendance at meetings was excused. Mr A. de Castro, secretary to the congregation, fulfilled the same duties to the committee.

The first meeting of the *Deputados* was held on the 19th November 1760, and the urgent affair on hand, that of the presentation of an address of congratulation to his Majesty, was satisfactorily settled. To Mr Salvador were intrusted the preliminary steps for procuring an audience for the Jewish deputation, and he was perfectly successful in his mission. The Duke of Devonshire, Lord Chamberlain of his Majesty's household, received Joseph Salvador most affably, and assured him of his great respect for the Jews. Two days afterwards, a deputation, consisting of Benjamin Mendes da Costa, Joseph Salvador, and two other members of the committee, waited upon his Grace of Devonshire with the address for the King. This kind of composition seldom contains any novel conception or originality of thought. The document in question stated that "the Portuguese Jews most humbly begged leave to condole with his Majesty on the demise of the late king, whose sacred memory would ever be revered, and to congratulate his Majesty on his accession to the throne of these kingdoms; humbly craving the continuance of his Majesty's favour and protection, which they hope to merit by an unalterable zeal for his Majesty's most sacred person and service, and by promoting to the utmost of their abilities the benefit of his Majesty's realms."

The Duke of Devonshire, with the sanction of the Duke of Newcastle, presented the address to his Majesty. When the deputation returned to pay their respects to the Lord Chamberlain on the 23d November, his Grace assured them that his Majesty had been pleased to accept, with great pleasure, the respectful expressions of the Hebrew community; his Majesty felt a regard for the Jews; he was aware of their good qualities, and he would always bear them in his favour and his estimation.

Meanwhile, the German Jews, who had borne no part in these festive proceedings, complained that they had had no opportunity of testifying *their* loyalty to the Royal Family. In truth, hitherto the somewhat haughty Sephardic Jews had looked upon their pushing, thriving, and rising German brethren with a rather doubtful eye : very much in the same way, perhaps, as a marquis of ancient descent regards from his paternal acres the ambitious and self-asserting manufacturer, who buys all the land around him, and erects a mansion as fine as that of the nobleman. Nevertheless, the application of Aaron Franks, who, as we already know, was one of the most influential members of the Ashkenazi community, was treated with due consideration. A meeting of the *Deputados* was summoned, and Mr A. Franks and Mr Levy Salomons were invited to attend. These two gentlemen were told that the address had been presented in the name of the Portuguese nation ; that the Dutch (German) nation might do likewise, or they might join the Portuguese in offering their condolences and congratulations to the Dowager Princess of Wales. Mr Franks and Mr L. Salomons asked that both nationalities among the Jews should henceforth act in concert in all public matters, to which proposal it was replied that the *Dutch* possessed no public body with whom to communicate. It was then stated by Franks that his community would also elect a secret committee.

Joseph Salvador then proceeded with A. Franks to wait upon Sir Wm. Irby, the Chamberlain to her Royal Highness, to inquire when they might present their services to the Princess. On Thursday, December 11, 1760, Joseph Salvador, with A. Franks and H. Isaacs, had the honour of kissing the hands of her Royal Highness, and of the Duke of York and the Princess Augusta, by all of whom they were received with the greatest affability and condescension. The courtiers also treated the Jewish deputation with considerable kindness and regard. No doubt the Jews were strangers at Court, and were eyed with some curiosity, such as might be excited now in fashionable *salons* by the presence of a couple of Chinese mandarins or a few secretaries of the Japanese mission. But the Jewish delegates were lionised and petted, and took their departure with all the gratification that usually falls to the lot of flattered deputations.

The names of the members of the secret committee of the Germans were duly communicated to the Portuguese. The representatives of the Duke's Place Synagogue were Aaron Franks, Naphtali Hart, Moses Franks, and Michael Adolphus; while the congregation in Magpie Alley (Hambro Synagogue) chose as its agents Henry Isaacs, Levy Salomons, and Abraham Elias.

The Portuguese Deputies became now a fixed institution. Ample faculty for action was accorded to them. Leave was granted them to expend from time to time such sums as might be needed. They were desired to keep records of their proceedings, which, as in the case of the Committee of Diligence, they were not bound to show. Joseph Salvador, who acted as honorary secretary, entered into correspondence with the Germans, and a definite understanding was arrived at between the two sections of British Jews. The Portuguese Deputies formally passed the following resolution, which was duly notified to their German brethren: "December 14, 1760. Resolved that whenever any public affair should occur that may interest the two nations, we will on our parts communicate to the Committee of the Dutch Jews' Synagogue what we think proper should be done, and we desire the same gentlemen may do the same, and make a minute thereof." To this document were appended the signatures of the Portuguese Committee, and of Aaron Franks and Henry Isaacs on behalf of the Germans.

Such, then, is a brief sketch of the origin of the body now known as the London Committee of Deputies of the British Jews, a body which has been graced by the presence of most of the greatest and best men that have risen in Israel for upwards of a century, and which has been for many years, and was until lately, presided over by one of the most eminent and noblest philanthropists ever bestowed by a merciful Providence on a suffering race.

It would be impossible to attempt to give here even the most succinct account of the proceedings of the Committee of Deputies. An intelligible record of its transactions would be in itself sufficient to fill the pages of a volume. Within the space allotted to us we can only furnish a general idea of the kind of work performed by the British Deputies, barely touching upon the principal events brought before that body, from the day of its creation until the middle of the present century.

The immediate cause of the assembling of the Portuguese Deputies was to present a loyal address to the Crown. To testify to the fidelity and attachment of the Jews to the throne of Great Britain, whenever a suitable occasion arose, became one of the practices of the Deputies. In England, as in France, the monarch never dies. The records of the Deputies present a series of addresses of congratulation and condolence to the reigning sovereigns of Great Britain on their accession to the throne, and on every auspicious and inauspicious event that happened in their lives. "The first gentleman of Europe," the "Sailor King," and the exalted lady upon whose brow now rests the diadem of the vast empire where the sun never sets, all duly received the humble homage of the Jews.

There is a simple faith in the divine right of kings apparent in the language with which our ancestors addressed royalty that is quite refreshing in the present day of cynicism and rationalism.

Assuredly we should not now advert to the reign of George IV. in the following strain : " The mild and paternal rule of our late sovereign has indelibly impressed on the minds of his people feelings of veneration and duteous affection, and placed his cherished memory among the fond recollections of departed happiness, and to none of his loving subjects is his name more endeared than to the members of the Jewish community, who dwell with delight and gratitude on the protection and favour they have enjoyed during his glorious reign." This Johnsonian period was penned as late as 1830, on the demise of the august individual of whom it has been written :—

> "A noble, nasty course he ran
> Superbly filthy and fastidious ;
> He was the world's first gentleman,
> And made the appellation hideous."

Though the Committee of Portuguese Deputies had been

established to protect English-Jewish interests, that body soon became the recipient of requests of assistance from their less fortunate brethren abroad. From 1760 to 1874, from the Jews of Jamaica to the Jews of Roumania, the representatives of the Portuguese, and subsequently of the British Jews, under whatever designation they may have been known, have always been looked up to by distressed Israelites in the four quarters of the globe for support and help in every emergency. Oppressed Jews from the tropical clime of the Antilles; tortured Jews from the Biblical city of Damascus; starved and ill-treated Jews from the gorgeous land of Ahasuerus; vilified and pillaged Jews from the wild plains of the Danube, — have all in turn piteously lifted up their voices to London for aid. It must be said that the Deputies have never hesitated to succour their afflicted co-religionists so far as lay within their very limited powers. They have usually laudably exerted themselves on behalf of the harassed Children of Israel, albeit we cannot conscientiously say that they have invariably attained a conspicuous success in their undertakings of this nature. We may assume that all commendable zeal on their parts has been displayed, and that the failures have been caused by the limited sphere of action of the Deputies. In truth, with reference to foreign affairs, they have confined themselves to seeking the intervention of the Foreign Office, which has been granted or declined, according to circumstances. Whether the Deputies might have found other available means of action at hand is a question we need not here discuss. The creation of that institution was for a specific purpose, and the expediency of extending its general scope was a matter for the consideration of its members.

The Deputies had not been appointed many months when they were called upon for their good offices by the Jews of Jamaica, who had been ill-treated on some occasions. The first intercession of the Portuguese Deputies on behalf of their brethren was successful, and renewed security was promised to Jewish life and property in that colony. The Jewish inhabitants of Port Mahon, in the island of Minorca, who complained in 1766, among other hardships, that they were not permitted to erect a synagogue, were not so fortunate.

The Deputies, after waiting on the Duke of Richmond, Colonial Secretary, found themselves constrained to tell their co-religionists, that sufferance was the badge of their tribe, and all they could do for the Jews of Minorca was to give them some excellent advice. It may interest some readers to learn that the then Duke of Richmond was the brother of the beautiful Lady Caroline Lennox, who in 1740 escaped from the window to wed Henry Fox, the father of Charles James Fox; and of the lovely Lady Sarah Lennox, who might, had she so chosen, have worn the royal diadem of England on her brow, as queen to the fascinated George III.

The meetings of the Deputies were held at very uncertain intervals, and for many years they were, "like angels' visits," few and far between. From this period the Deputies do not appear to have been called together again until the 11th November 1778. When they met at that time the congregation in Magpie Alley nominated as Deputies of their nation Isaac Isaacs, Aaron Norden, and Joseph Gomperts. These German representatives did not form part of the body, and only attended when they were especially invited. The minutes, too, had hitherto been kept in Portuguese, and it was now for the first time that they began to be reported in English.

It is curious to observe that at this period Joseph Salvador applied to know how he was to act towards Baron d'Aguilar, who, having been elected Deputy, took no notice of the communications made to him. The Baron, however, did attend one or two meetings later on, in 1783, but he soon withdrew from the Deputies, as he did from Israel.

CHAPTER XIV.

THE HISTORY OF THE DEPUTIES OF THE BRITISH JEWS.

WHEN the political representatives of the Portuguese community reassembled in the year 1789—a year memorable for the new principles fraught with evil and fraught with good that were proclaimed before a wonder-stricken world—not one single member of the original *Deputados* was left alive. The last to disappear was Joseph Salvador, who had suffered great reverses of fortune. Another generation of men had sprung up, who " knew not Joseph," and for the first time we perceive the names of E. Baruch Lousada, of David Samuda, of Daniel de Castro. The meetings of the Deputies continued to be held at the residence of the president, and Moses I. Levy was elected to that office. The representatives of the German synagogues were Eleazer Isaac Keizer and Lyon de Symons for the Duke's Place Synagogue, and Joseph Gompertz and Eleazer Philip Salomons for the Fenchurch Street or Magpie Alley Synagogue, as it was variously called.

It may be noted that the delegates of the Ashkenazi Congregation really formed no part as yet of the Sephardic deliberative body. They attended meetings when it was thought needful to summon them, which was probably left to the discretion of the president. On great occasions, too, Nathan Solomons, the *rosh* or principal of the New Synagogue in Leadenhall Street, was called in for consultation. These gentlemen, nevertheless, by their energy and zeal, soon acquired great influence in Jewish affairs, and thereafter played an important part in them. When the next address of congratulation was voted to George III., on his recovery from one of his fitful attacks, Mr Levy, the president of the Deputies, and Messrs Gompertz and De Symons, were deputed to express the joy of the Jews at his Majesty's restoration to health. The Hebrew representatives met a most courteous reception at the hands of the authorities, as they had done on former occasions.

There is little worth reporting in the transactions of the Deputies at this period. In the last decade of the eighteenth century they seemingly came together on only one occasion —in November 1795. A bill had been introduced in the House of Commons, entitled the Sedition Bill, and the Jewish community were doubtful as to the interpretation of a certain clause. The Deputies bestirred themselves; they made respectful representations to Government, and eventually the questionable clause was abandoned.

In 1801, Moses I. Levy retired on account of ill-health, and Naphtali Basevi was named president.

In 1802 a question arose which threatened to create a bad feeling between the two sections into which the Hebrew community in London was divided. Happily moderation and good sense prevailed, and the branches of the family of Israel, agreeing to differ in certain unimportant details, continued their harmonious intercourse, which even became closer and closer. It was proposed by the Germans to merge together by Act of Parliament all the Jewish charities in London. This scheme was abandoned in deference to the opposition manifested thereto by the Portuguese community, through their representatives, the Deputies. These proceedings— which throw considerable insight into the respective positions of Sephardim and Ashkenazim—will be duly set forth by us in their proper place, our object in this chapter being limited to recording the acts of the Deputies.

In 1805 we find a prosecution was ordered against the printer of the *St James' Chronicle* for the publication of some offensive letters against the Jews, signed "Catharticus." An apology, though somewhat tardy, was obtained, and thus the matter terminated.

It was at this time that the Committee of Deputies began to acquire greater development and importance. The Portuguese themselves saw the necessity of placing the institution on a broader basis, just as the Conservatives were foremost of late years in granting extended suffrage; and the following letter was forwarded to the principal German congregations in Great Britain:—

"We, the undersigned, appointed by the elders of our Portuguese Jew nation by the appellation of *Deputados*, for the purpose of watching all Acts of Parliament, Acts of Government, laws, libels, addresses, or whatever else may affect the body of Jews, are desirous of acting with complete unison in all public concerns, therefore deem it necessary to assume the liberty of soliciting that your congregation in concert with the others will be pleased to appoint such gentlemen as you may think proper under the same denomination, that we may request their attendance as occasion requires, and have the pleasure of joining in all transactions that may concern us as one body. Should you think proper to comply with our recommendation, we beg you will transmit us the names of the gentlemen so appointed.—Signed R. Brandon, N. Basevi, Moses Lindo, jun., Jacob Osorio, Moses Mocatta, and Jacob Mocatta."

Thus, at last, the barriers of exclusiveness were thrown down, and all Jews of the British Empire acquired political equality, as they had ever been civilly and religiously equal. We do not know whether the response to this invitation was as hearty as it deserved to be, for no meetings were held until 1812. Then for the first time the "German" Jews took their seats in the national representative body side by side with their Portuguese brethren, and voted on equal terms. The first German members of the Board were Moses Samuel, Samuel Samuel, M. Levy Newton, Joseph Cohen, N. Hart, Levy Salomons, M. Salomons, Gabriel Cohen, G. Levien; and they represented the three German synagogues in the city.

One of the earliest acts of the renewed and reinvigorated assembly was the election of a deputation to wait on some respectable Quaker to ascertain the sentiments of the Society of Friends on a pending bill in Parliament referring to the rights of marriage, baptism, and burial. The result of this mission was not recorded.

In 1820 the name of Rothschild was first brought into connection with the Deputies. When an address was about to be presented to the throne, on the accession of George

IV., on the death of his father, Mr Joseph Cohen enlisted the influence of his kinsman, Mr N. M. Rothschild, who introduced to the Right Honourable Nicholas Vansittart, Chancellor of the Exchequer (afterwards Lord Bexley), two members of the United Deputies, viz., Mr Moses Lindo, jun., president, and Mr Joseph Cohen, vice-president and hon. secretary. The address was eventually presented through Viscount Sidmouth, Secretary of State for the Home Department, by Messrs M. Lindo, jun., J. M. da Costa, sen., Samuel Samuel, Naphtali Hart, M. L. Newton, and Joseph Cohen, and it was received with every mark of approbation.

In April 1828 we perceive for the first time the appearance among the Deputies of the great philanthropist Sir Moses Montefiore. Three gentlemen were elected members of the Board, and they were Messrs Moses Montefiore, C. C. Michols, and Myer Salomons. On the 28th April a meeting was held to consider a bill then under discussion in Parliament, for repealing so much of several Acts as imposed the necessity of receiving what is called the sacrament of the Lord's Supper as a qualification for certain offices. Now there was an opportunity for endeavouring to obtain a removal of the disqualifications pressing upon the Jews. A petition was ordered to be prepared by the solicitor to the Board, Mr Pearce, and a sub-committee, consisting of Messrs M. Lindo, jun., Joshua Van Oven, and Moses Montefiore, were elected to present it to the House of Lords, to protect the interests of the Jews.

The next meeting took place on February 5, 1829. Mr Isaac Lyon Goldsmid attended, and reported the steps he had adopted since the introduction of the bill on the previous April for the relief of Dissenters. He stated that the words "upon the faith of a Christian," in that bill, placed the Jews in a much worse position than before. He also informed the meeting that he had had occasional interviews with several members of both Houses, and he read various letters addressed to him by Lords Holland, Lansdowne, and Suffield, Messrs Gurney, Baring, Martin, and others, containing assurances of their aid and support in any measure that might be submitted to Parliament for the relief of the

Jews. Mr Goldsmid then intimated that he had reason to calculate on further powerful influence through Mr Moses Montefiore. It was considered by the meeting that the time appeared propitious for the advancement of the civil interests of the Jews of the United Kingdom, and it was determined to take steps in that direction. The epoch for triumph, however, had not yet arrived, and years elapsed before the Jews obtained a recognition of their civil rights.

From this period the history of the United Deputies of the British Jews becomes intimately connected with the history of the prolonged struggle for the removal of Jewish disabilities. Not to tread over the same ground twice, we will reserve our account of the part borne by the Deputies in those momentous questions until we relate the details of the long and arduous fight. The Deputies were not idle. They appointed sub-committees, drew up petitions, presented them to various authorities—from the Archbishop of Canterbury to the Chancellor of the Exchequer; held many consultations with Mr I. L. Goldsmid (Baron de Goldsmid), and his son Mr F. H. Goldsmid (Sir Francis Goldsmid), with Mr D. Salomons (Sir David Salomons), and many others. The Deputies exerted themselves with creditable energy, and had the appearance of doing a great deal. But as we are the chroniclers and not the panegyrists of that body, as we desire to treat the subject with all impartiality, we are bound to state that we fail to perceive that the efforts of the Deputies contributed, to any great extent, to the removal of Jewish disabilities. Probably their endeavours deserved success; assuredly they did not command it. With all the respect inspired by the illustrious names that have graced that assembly, we must confess that it was not the Deputies of the British Jews, in their corporate capacity, that endowed their brethren with civil and political life. No; that series of glorious achievements was accomplished by a few solitary individuals who bore the brunt of the battle—and conquered. It is to the unceasing exertions of a Goldsmid, a Montefiore, a Rothschild, a Salomons, a Van Oven, that the Jews owe their emancipation. It is to these and other equally high-minded men, who made heavy sacrifices in time and in fortune, that Israel is deeply indebted, and not to a number of gentlemen, who in their corporate capacity displayed much timidity, and acted as if they were fettered by a dread of responsibility and by a lack of funds.

In April 1835, on the resignation of Moses Mocatta, the president, the Deputies honoured themselves, and conferred a great benefit on Israel, by electing to the vacant post one who was destined to play so beneficent and commanding a part in Jewish affairs, viz., Moses Montefiore. At the same time, it was considered that the institution needed a thorough remodelling. A sub-committee was delegated to investigate the question, and its scheme for an amended system of Jewish representation was accepted at a full meeting of the Deputies. The name of Committee of Deputies of the British Jews was then adopted. The Portuguese Congregation was empowered, according to the new rules, to elect seven deputies; the Great Synagogue was to appoint an equal number, and the Hambro and New Synagogues in proportion to their standing were to be satisfied each with four deputies. The expenses were to be defrayed, one-third by the Portuguese Synagogue, and a similar share by the Great Synagogue; while the remainder was to be borne by the other two German congregations. Provisions were made for the admission into the new body of such other Jewish congregations as might desire the privilege; and the Deputies were authorised to take such measures as they might deem proper, in all cases tending to promote the welfare of the Jews.

Mr Moses Montefiore was elected president, and Mr D. Brandon was requested to act as honorary secretary. One of the first acts of the Deputies was to forward circulars to all the synagogues in the kingdom, inviting them to send deputies to the Board. The Western Synagogue approved the constitution, and elected as their representatives Messrs John Levy and S. Ellis. The response from the country congregations was by no means as favourable as might have been anticipated; want of funds and want of public feeling combined in causing them to hold back. Another attempt was made in 1838 to induce those communities to join the London synagogues, and strengthen the Jewish representative body, but with little success. The answers were far from encouraging. Edinburgh declined to appoint deputies; Birmingham came to no decision; Sunderland chose a deputy, but soon after withdrew him on the score of poverty. Liverpool took time to consider the subject; Gloucester merely acknowledged the circular; Yarmouth was not in circumstances to comply with the request; and Chatham refused altogether.

On the 31st August 1835, an Act was passed prohibiting marriages of consanguinity, an Act which laid the foundation for much misery, and which perpetrated as flagrant an injustice as ever was committed by a legislature. For Jews especially to be forbidden from performing certain acts, sanctioned by Jewish law, is an unquestionable interference with the rights of conscience. It is to be regretted that the Deputies did not display more vigour and energy at the proper time, when, not impossibly, Jews might have been exempted from the action of this obnoxious law. As it was, the Deputies proceeded on the principle of shutting the stable door after the flight of the steed. A year after the passing of Lord Lyndhurst's Act, the eyes of the Deputies were open to its consequences, and a sub-committee was nominated to move in the matter, but, as might be expected, without success. At this time, too, the Act for the Registration of Marriages became law; this Act regulates the marriages of Jews, and it is known as the 6 and 7 William IV. We spoke of it at length in our chapter on Jewish Marriages.

It may interest some members of the present generation to learn that the deputation elected to prepare an address of congratulation to Queen Victoria on her accession to the throne in 1837, consisted of Messrs Moses Montefiore, Abraham Mocatta, Solomon Waley, Louis Lucas, Hananel de Castro, Solomon Cohen, John H. Helbert, and Daniel Mocatta.

In the year 1838 the transactions of the Board had increased so much that it was considered desirable to appoint a salaried secretary. The gentleman selected for that office was the late Sampson Samuel, who after a very brief period declined to receive the small salary allotted to him, but continued to afford the Deputies for a long time afterwards his able and zealous services gratuitously. It must be mentioned, however, that subsequently Mr Samuel was presented by the Deputies with a testimonial in the shape of a silver tea service. In the same year Baron L. de Rothschild was elected deputy for the Great Synagogue, and Mr David Salomons for the New Synagogue. Mr Salomons, in the temporary absence of Mr Moses Montefiore, was named president, but after fulfilling those functions for one or two meetings, he resigned, whereupon the honour was conferred upon Mr J. G. Henriques.

Contemporarily with these events some changes were effected in the constitution and by-laws of the Board. One of the new regulations was to the effect that the Committee of Deputies of British Jews constituted itself the sole medium of communication between the Jews and Government. This unfortunate clause gave great offence to Mr I. L. Goldsmid, who addressed a letter to Mr Ansell, the secretary of the Great Synagogue, containing a formidable bill of indictment against the Board. The sins laid to the charge of the Board were rather of omission than of commission.

Mr I. L. Goldsmid had devoted money and time from night to night to carry through the House of Commons three different bills for the relief of Jewish disabilities, while he had found among the most influential members of the Board of Deputies a certain unwillingness to devote personal exertions, and a total refusal of pecuniary assistance. Mr Goldsmid, after enumerating all the privileges enjoyed by the Jews, and which the Deputies had not obtained, declared that he could not consent to intrust his political interests to the Deputies. He would feel the deepest concern in separating himself from a body with which his father and family had been connected for so many years, and hoped the obnoxious regulation would be rescinded, and a declaration made that no persons by becoming or continuing members of a synagogue were precluded from taking, either separately or in concert, measures with respect to the civil rights of the Jews.

The communication containing these remarks caused great impression when read before the Deputies. Whether from alarm or pure good-nature, we are unable to say, the Deputies hastened to invite Mr I. L. Goldsmid and his son, Mr F. H. Goldsmid, to a conference. It was then alleged by the Deputies that the clause in question did not bear the construction placed upon it by Mr Goldsmid; but "to make assurance doubly sure," the obnoxious expressions were altered to meet Mr Goldsmid's views. Mr I. L. Goldsmid was at this period elected a deputy for the Great Synagogue in conjunction with Mr S. I. Waley, but he declined to accept the office. In 1839, Mr David Salomons, who had carried on for some years, unassisted, his struggles on behalf of Jewish civil rights, found it expedient to request the support of the Committee of Deputies. The Court of Queen's Bench, he stated, had decided in favour of his construction of the Act with reference to the aldermanic gown. The Court of Exchequer Chamber had reversed that decision, four judges having given judgment for, and seven against, him. The last resource was an appeal to the House of Lords. Several Peers, and among them Lord Brougham and Lord Cottenham, had promised him their countenance. He, Mr Salomons, had incurred great expense to try that important question, and he was not willing to go further. He considered that the Board should now take up the question, and appeal to the highest jurisdiction in Great Britain. The Board of Deputies, however, was far from adopting the same view of the question as Mr Salomons. His proposal was discussed and declined, on the ground that it would be more expedient to seek relief by legislative amendment.

A memorable epoch now occurred in the annals of the Committee of Deputies of the British Jews. We use the expression "memorable," because the Board took a leading part in a moment of the highest importance, and towards this assembly the eyes of all Israel were turned with an eager, beseeching look. A piercing, deep cry of anguish from the far East had caused a thrill of pity and horror through the hearts of Western Jews. Some of their innocent brethren in a semi-civilised country had been barbarously tortured to force from them a confession of a crime which they had never perpetrated.

On the 28th April 1840 a meeting was held at the residence of Sir Moses Montefiore, to which were invited several gentlemen of eminence, in addition to the members of the Board. There were gathered Sir Isaac L. Goldsmid, Messrs Isaac Cohen, David Salomons, A. A. Goldsmid, Dr B. Van Oven, Dr Loewe, several members of the Portuguese Congregation, and last, and assuredly not least, Monsieur Cremieux, the celebrated French jurisconsult, and vice-president of the "Consistoire Central des Israelites Français." M. Cremieux was afterwards Minister of Justice in Paris under the Government of 1848, and in our days was the colleague of M. Gambetta. The heart-rending account of the persecution of the Jews of Damascus for the supposed murder of Father Thomas was communicated to the meeting in the plain, unvarnished language in which those unhappy Israelites besought and implored the help of their more fortunate coreligionists in Europe.

Certain resolutions suited to the urgency of the case in hand were unanimously and heartily adopted at the meeting. As, however, the history of the affair of *Il Padre Tommaso* appertains to the history of Judaism, and not to that of any especial institution, we will defer giving a succinct relation of that tragic occurrence till its proper time and place.

Here we must part company with the fortunes of the London Committee of Deputies of the British Jews, heartily desiring to it prolonged existence and renewed vitality. In questions of general importance the acts of the Deputies will be embodied in the records of the acts of the Jewish public; while in internal questions the more modern proceedings of that body will be sufficiently remembered by our Jewish readers, or might form part of polemics which we have no wish to revive.

CHAPTER XV.

THE EARLY DAYS OF THE GREAT SYNAGOGUE.

THE spectacle presented by the struggles of the first German Jewish settlers in this country differs as widely from that offered by their Portuguese brethren as a Flemish interior by Cuyp—plain, homely, rough, and yet clearly displaying in the figures delineated some of the qualities that make up a nation's greatness—differs from the representation by Rubens of an imposing municipal gathering at the Hague, adorned with a crowd of richly-attired personages. Yet both paintings only bring forth the various virtues of one race, and describe various phases of the same national life.

The original immigrants into England from Germany and Poland were undoubtedly placed at a great disadvantage as regards the Spanish and Portuguese settlers. These latter were usually men of wealth, of polished manners, of old lineage, whose ancestors anciently had figured at courts, and who in modern times had constituted an aristocracy of commerce in Holland. The former were persons whose forefathers for ages had been subjected to every kind of degrading persecution, and had been debarred from pursuing any ennobling avocations; persons who themselves had neither been endowed by their fathers with worldly goods nor with liberal knowledge. Nevertheless, to their credit be it said, these German Israelites, uncouth, illiterate, narrow-minded and poor, as the greater part of them must have been; friendless, without resources, and ignorant of the English language, as they unquestionably were; by dint of strict frugality, of unceasing activity, of indomitable energy, of considerable innate if uncultivated abilities, succeeded in acquiring more or less considerable fortunes, and in raising themselves to positions of trust and honour.

For a long time prejudice against them lingered in the breast of the proud Sephardi, even until after the traits that had inspired this ungenerous feeling had ceased to exist. The question became then merely a question of caste. Many old-fashioned Portuguese Jews at one period held themselves socially aloof from their Ashkenazi brethren, and would no more have given to one of the latter their daughter in marriage than a Brahmin would have affianced a dusky child of his to a Sudrah. As the German community advanced in enlightenment and grew in wealth and numbers, the barriers separating them from the older established branch of their race in England were gradually thrown down. When the former section of the English Jews had outstripped the latter in material advantages and external influence, it would have been too palpably absurd for the minority to affect a superiority, which no longer existed, over the majority. All distinctions gradually disappeared. From the beginning of the present century concord and amity have reigned among the Jews of Great Britain, who have united in working together for the moral and intellectual advancement of their race. The one blot in the harmony existing in Israel that formed the solitary, though important exception, to the good feeling reigning among the Jews, will be duly recorded in its place.

The German and Polish Jews, at the time of William III., as we related in a former chapter, that is to say, as soon as they were in sufficient number in this country, became desirous of establishing for themselves a place of worship, entirely independent of their Spanish and Portuguese brethren. So early as the year 1692 they were wont to assemble for prayers—which they intoned in their own manner—in a house in Broad Court, Mitre Square, where for a period of about thirty years they held divine service. These immigrants from the banks of the Oder and the Vistula were tolerably numerous, albeit almost destitute of means.

Probably not half-a-dozen men in affluent circumstances flourished in their midst. The richest among them was named Moses of Breslau in the Synagogue, while to the outer world he became known as Moses Hart.

He was a remarkably shrewd and able man, and the English Government of the day learned to appreciate his talents.

Hart was connected by marriage with Benjamin Levy, who at that period was a great financier, and also a promoter of the East India Company.

Mr Levy is said to have procured the charter for that great corporation, and to have his name inscribed second in their books. Mr Hart increased in wealth, and when Lord Godolphin was High Treasurer in the reign of Queen Anne, a place under Government was conferred upon him, whereby he obtained great honour and affluence. In 1720 he built for himself a handsome house at Isleworth. In the year 1722, the community having altogether outgrown their temporary house of prayer, Moses Hart, actuated by a feeling of religious zeal, generously contributed a liberal sum which materially helped to raise a special and permanent edifice dedicated to divine worship. This was inaugurated on the eve of New Year in 1722. The lineaments of Moses Hart have been handed down to us in a picture presented by Mr Joshua Van Oven to the Great Synagogue. From the left wall of the vestry-room, near the door, Moses Hart eyes the visitor with quiet curiosity. A shrewd countenance surmounted by a flowing periwig, according to the fashion of the day; yet a countenance by no means vulgar or commonplace. Moses Hart moved among people of quality, and no doubt he had acquired an air of distinction. He appears to have lived to a great age, for in 1756 he desired to be excused from further attending Synagogue affairs, on the score of his failing health; as well he might indeed, for he must then have been very aged.

The first wardens elected for the Synagogue were Lazarus Simon, Isaac Franks, and Abraham Franks; Myer Polak was appointed treasurer. The rate of expenditure was by no means regulated on an extravagant scale, and the salary of the first reader was fixed at the very moderate sum of £30 per annum; while the services of the second reader were valued at exactly one-half that amount. The Germans, following the example of the Portuguese congregations, as soon as they had acquired sufficient importance as a separate body, proceeded to draw up a code of laws for their internal guidance. These regulations throw not a little light on the usages and customs of the Ashkenazim of 1722.

A curious practice obtained in those days of throwing sweetmeats upon a bridegroom when he was called up to the law, though we are unable to say whether to inure the happy man to the sweets of married life, or, on the contrary, to offer him some compensation for that bitterness of spirit which is not unfrequently induced by the connubial condition. The practice was found indecorous, and was strictly prohibited. We believe, however, that even in comparatively modern times it was occasionally followed in German congregations when the bridegroom went to the law on *Simchat Torah*—on the rejoicing of the law. The sense of refinement or propriety on the part of the worshippers does not appear to have been very great, for they were strictly enjoined not to chew tobacco in synagogue, nor to attend divine service wearing slippers or caps. Gentlemen having frequent occasion to undertake journeys to the Continent were not to be elected treasurers. Travelling was insecure in those days, and it was impossible to say what mishap might occur to an official who exposed himself to such risks. Marriage was considered to add to the qualifications for teaching, as no bachelor was allowed to remain an instructor of youth for more than three years. The authority of the Rabbi was considerably restricted. He was not permitted to place any one in Herem or excommunication without the sanction of the Parnassim or wardens, nor to perform marriage or pronounce divorce, nor to interfere in any quarrel. The civil authorities were evidently desirous of curtailing the power of the ecclesiastical authorities, and the latter were made entirely dependent on the former. Though we are by no means advocates of absolute ecclesiastical power, we question whether a spiritual guide, who is the humble servant of the delegates of his flock, can fulfil conscientiously his mission, and whether he can preserve his own dignity and maintain a high tone of religious feeling in his congregation. We believe that the restrictions placed on the actions of the Chief Rabbis were the cause of much mischief during the last century, and eventually induced the resignation of one of them—the learned Rabbi Hirsch. The pastor who was at the head—at least nominally—of the German community when the Moses Hart Synagogue was opened, was called Rabbi

Uri Phaibul, and it would appear that his post was by no means a bed of roses. No fewer than ninety-seven ordinances and regulations were promulgated at the beginning by the rulers of the Great Synagogue, and from time to time these were modified or new laws introduced.

In the year 1735 the sale of the offices of bridegroom of the Law and of the Sabbath of Genesis (Hatanim) was discontinued, and those distinctions were conferred by election or rotation. It is curious to remark that the then doctor of the congregation—a gentleman who received £30 per annum—was accustomed to take his seat among the wardens and to vote in all matters brought before the Council, as if he were one of the leaders of the community, and not one of its most inadequately-salaried officials.

As the German congregation increased in numbers, not only the house of worship became crowded, but also the House of Life, as the Jews poetically term the cemetery for our dead. In 1748, Moses Hart, Aaron Franks, and H. Franks were appointed a sub-committee to buy some land for a cemetery. This object they carried out in due course, and we find that in the following year the sum of £174 was paid for the purchase of ground for the purpose. This land was situated in the Alderney Road, Mile End Road, and it has long since ceased to receive the dead.

In 1745 the earliest German charitable institution was called into being. It was entitled *Akenosath Berith*, and it furnished a small gratuity to necessitous German women in childbed, providing at the same time a Mohel to perform the covenant of Abraham.

In the year 1758 the Chief Rabbi of the German Congregation, Rabbi Hirsch, the father of Dr Solomon Hirschel, was in receipt of £250 per annum, £150 of which was contributed by the Synagogue in Broad Court, also called the Synagogue of Moses Hart, and £100 by the Hambro, or, as it was termed, Wolf Prager's Synagogue. Considering the value of money in those days, and the limited means at the disposal of the community, the stipend of the "German" Chief Rabbi was not to be despised. Indeed many a worthy and hard-working minister of the Church of England would gladly even now attain a benefice productive of that amount.

The ground on which the Great Synagogue is erected belongs to the Corporation of the City of London. In 1760 a perpetual lease was granted by the Court of Common Council to the authorities of the Synagogue at a very moderate annual rental, the lease being renewable every fourteen years on payment of a fine of £30. It is only at the present moment that the leasehold is being converted into a freehold, by the payment of a final sum to the Corporation, which we understand to be very reasonable. Thus henceforth the chief German Synagogue, like the chief Portuguese Synagogue, will stand on property belonging to its own community.

CHAPTER XVI.

PROGRESS OF GERMAN CONGREGATIONS.

The Jews have not, as a rule, displayed against each other that fraternal hatred which so frequently breaks out between members of the same sect or race. But there is a certain episode in the chronicles of the Great Synagogue which displays a feeling much resembling hate on the part of the authorities of that congregation, against some of their brethren. In the year 1761 the German community in London was acquiring a considerable development in number and resources. The two synagogues then open were becoming insufficient for the rapidly-increasing worshippers, and possibly some of these were not altogether satisfied with their ruling powers. At all events certain members of the existing synagogues united with some freshly-arrived immigrants to establish a new house of prayer. The indignation manifested by the heads of the Duke's Place Synagogue appears to have been warmer than the circumstances warranted. A meeting was held on the 19th August 1761, in which the wardens and elders of the German community arrived at the following resolution: "Whereas certain persons unworthy of our countenance and protection have formed themselves into a society calling themselves a congregation at Buckler's Hall; we do hereby strictly charge our priest, now and hereafter, that he does not directly or indirectly, or other in his name or with his knowledge or permission, officiate either publicly or privately in the service of marriages, burials, circumcisions, or other acts of priesthood, for any person whatever belonging to the said society. And to prevent any persons from unwarily joining with that society, we order that this resolution be read publicly two Sabbaths successively in our synagogues, that none may plead ignorance thereof. And we further order that a copy of this resolution be forthwith delivered to the Mahamad (Council of Wardens) of the Portuguese Synagogue, desiring their concurrence in supporting and maintaining with us the good order of our respective communities."

The new congregants were by no means alarmed at the opposition of the older establishments, and pursued their plans without heeding the harmless thunderbolt that was hurled at their heads. In June 1762 the first stone of the New Synagogue was laid with great ceremony at Buckler's Hall (since Sussex Hall), facing Cree Church in Leadenhall Street, and a considerable sum of money was collected on that occasion. The holy edifice was duly completed and was consecrated with much pomp. The relations between the New Synagogue and the parent congregation were then, and continued for many years to be, on an unsatisfactory footing. Jealousy, which equally affects the infant in arms and the experienced man of the world, caused Duke's Place to look askance on Buckler's Hall, while the latter regarded the former with unconcealed resentment for its attempts at extinguishing its existence. During last century, and even subsequently, the New Synagogue possessed its own independent Rabbi. But all rivalries have an end; with the rise of a new generation all past animosity was mutually forgiven and forgotten, and when the Great Synagogue in 1792 found itself for a lengthy period without a spiritual chief, it did not disdain to engage the services as Dayan of the Rabbi of the New Synagogue. We will, moreover, do the Duke's Place Synagogue the justice of recording that even when the ill-feeling between the ancient and modern congregations was at its height, no formal Cherem or excommunication was pronounced.

The foundation of the New Synagogue withal did not inflict any material injury on the old places of worship. On the contrary, it stirred up a spirit of emulation among the members of the principal German congregation, who in 1763 resolved to enlarge their house of prayer. An adjoining piece of ground was at once purchased. At a meeting held in August of that year many gentlemen came forward with liberal donations, and fifteen generous persons subscribed among themselves a total of £2000 towards the requisite fund; a most liberal sum, considering the relative value of money and other surrounding circumstances.

It was not uncommon at this period for Christian visitors to attend Jewish synagogues, and descriptions of Jewish festivals occasionally found a corner in the periodical literature of the day. Thus we learn "that on Saturday the 6th October 1764 the Jews kept their annual day of fasting and humiliation in order to atone for their sins of last year, as instituted by Moses in the 16th chapter of Leviticus. It was observed so strictly that there was not an Israelite to be seen in the streets from six o'clock in the previous evening until seven on that night. Many of them were in synagogue all that time, and none of them during that interval did eat, drink, or take a pinch of snuff."

We are not informed in which particular synagogue the writer witnessed this impressive sight, which evidently struck him, but we have no doubt that all other Hebrew places of worship would have presented on that sacred day an equally solemn spectacle. We are apprised by the same source that the Feast of Tabernacles was also celebrated with similar devotion, and that the Jews strictly fulfilled the enjoined ordinances by taking their meals during the whole period of that holiday not in their houses, but in "tents or tabernacles" erected for that purpose in their yards. The Succoths or tabernacles were then, as at present, decorated with fruits and flowers, and all friends entering were hospitably pressed to take some refreshment.

A profound veneration for the ceremonies commanded by the precepts of their law is a remarkable feature in the Jewish character, a feature that has been neither obliterated by persecution nor by emancipation, by the depth of ignorance nor by the height of civilisation. It has been said of the Jews, by one evidently not too well disposed towards them, that, "however deficient they may be in other respects, they at least strictly keep up the outward prescribed forms of their religion, which we wish could be said of numbers that profess one preferable." However questionable this praise may be, it pays at least a just tribute to one undoubted

Jewish virtue, which is thus acknowledged by those who display no special love towards Judaism.

Rabbi Ziwy Hirsch, as we have already stated, was so hampered and trammelled in his acts by the control exercised over them by the wardens and elders of his community, and he found his position so little to his taste, that in 1764 he resigned his post. Rabbi Ziwy Hirsch proceeded then to Berlin, and he subsequently became Chief Rabbi of that city. When this learned man quitted the English shores he had already an infant son, named Solomon, who was destined thenceafter to occupy the honourable position of Chief Rabbi of the German Jews in London, under the title of the Rev. Dr Hirschel. The latter gentleman therefore could boast of being an Englishman by birth, of which title we believe he was very proud.

After the retirement of Rabbi Hirsch, Rabbi David Tabil Schiff Cohen was called upon to direct the religious affairs of the Great Synagogue. He was appointed to his functions in February 1765. His portrait may be seen to the present day in the vestry of that congregation. A dark and somewhat heavy countenance with a black beard, and a square, massive jaw, indicating a certain strength of will. Above this picture we behold another canvas, whence the mild eyes of a predecessor, Rabbi Uri Phaibul or Phaibush, look down with benignant repose on the visitor.

One of the early duties devolving upon Rabbi Tabil Schiff was the dedication of the rebuilt and enlarged synagogue in Duke's Place. This ceremony was celebrated with much splendour in August 1767, before a crowded congregation. Christian friends of the Jews have always expressed admiration for the mode in which Jewish divine service is conducted, and the chanting of Hebrew prayers usually impresses them favourably. Mirabeau says in his Letters from England that the psalmody of the English synagogue surprises one by the sweetness and agreeable simplicity of its modulation. On the occasion of which we are speaking, several Christian visitors attended, and described themselves as having been much edified at the proceedings. The solemnity was adverted to in a flattering manner in the periodical press of the day, and it was stated in a contemporary publication that "the prayer for their Majesties and Royal Family, which was always read in their liturgy in Hebrew, was at this time pronounced by the Chief Rabbi in English, and was followed by Handel's coronation anthem, performed by a numerous band of eminent musicians. The procession and other ceremonies in the synagogue were accompanied with several anthems and choruses by the same performers."

CHAPTER XVII.

CONVERSIONS—JEWISH LITERATURE—THE GREAT SYNAGOGUE AGAIN.

To convert a Jew to Christianity has been for ages the supreme ambition of certain enthusiastic and no doubt sincere, albeit mistaken, Christians. To save a soul from everlasting perdition must clearly be good work for those who follow the very uncomfortable and uncharitable tenet that all who differ from them in their theological views, or even in their definition of such views, are to be condemned to suffer the perpetual tortures of the fiery city in the sixth circle of Dante's "Inferno." Among the individuals who have held these opinions we will mention a certain Edward Goldney, an affluent merchant, who flourished nearly 120 years ago. This gentleman bestirred himself zealously to save the Jews from the fate awaiting them in the nether world. He wrote a friendly epistle addressed to them, and dedicated to the Archbishop of Canterbury. Therein he recommended the Primate to show great courtesy and hospitality to the Jews, and to entertain their principal men to sumptuous banquets, prepared according to Jewish law, in the expectation perhaps that good cheer and choice vintages might soften the obdurate Hebrew heart. It does not appear that his Grace acted upon the suggestion at the time, nor have we heard that the plan has been tried at any more modern period. Mr Goldney, who was not a Lessing, had more than one interview with Rabbi Aaron Hart, believed to be related to Moses Hart, the founder of the Great Synagogue. The aged Rabbi, who is described as a man of venerable aspect, declined to discuss the question with Mr Goldney. He merely observed that his father, grandfather, and great-grandfather were Jews, and that he continued in the religion to which he had been born, as he would, had his creed been any other. The reply did not satisfy Mr Goldney, who considered it "a poor, low, mean answer from a gentleman of his years." The Gentile, however well-intentioned, evidently did not possess a very brilliant intellect; and he did not understand that the Jew desired to avoid a controversy that would lead to dangerous ground. An Irish prelate, the Bishop of Clogher, also made some efforts to lead away the Jews from the old faith to the new dispensation. But it does not seem that these endeavours were attended with success, even according to the construction of their authors. That some Jews have swerved from the religion of their ancestors is an undoubted fact, and, as we have already said, we shall treat at length the subject of Jewish conversions in a future chapter.

While the Jews in England were increasing in numbers and wealth, rumours reached them from the far East, denoting in one remote spot an exactly reverse condition of affairs. That there have been Jews for many years in the interior of India is a well-ascertained fact; and we have ourselves beheld native Jews scarcely to be distinguished in form and feature from pure-blooded Hindoos. A traveller from East India, on his arrival in London in the year 1764, communicated some curious information to the periodical press. A republic of Jews then existed at Patna, capital of the kingdom of Behar. These Israelites, who formed a state within a state, had once numbered 60,000 families, and had constituted a powerful and semi-independent community; but at the time of which we are speaking they had dwindled to 4000 families. They still possessed, near the Nabob's palace, a synagogue, in which their records were preserved, engraved in copper-plates in Hebrew characters. These Jews professed to be able to trace their history from the time of Nebuchadnezzar. They stated that they appertained to the tribe of Menasseh, a part of which, by order of that haughty conqueror, had travelled to the most eastern province of his empire, and thence had proceeded southward, ultimately reaching the banks of the Ganges. The journey from Babylon had been performed by 20,000 souls—men, women, and children—and it had taken three years to accomplish. Their records, which had been kept in Hebrew, had been translated into the ordinary language of the country. We see no reason to question the accuracy of this "traveller's tale;" and we entertain no doubt that descendants from that community still exist in India, though we are unable to say whether there be at present a Jewish congregation at Patna.

At about this epoch the British Jews were becoming better known, and more respected among their Gentile fellow-countrymen, and they even made some endeavours to introduce in England an appreciation for the noble and grand literature of ancient Israel. It was partly in furtherance of such views, and partly as a recognition of the tolerance of the British people, that in the year 1760 an individual, named Solomon da Costa, presented a valuable collection of about 200 Hebrew MS. volumes to the trustees of the British Museum. Many of these books bore on their covers the royal arms of England, and the Jewish community of Amsterdam had intended to offer them to Charles II. as a token of their gratitude for his benevolence toward their race. In consequence of the king's death, the plan was naturally abandoned. It was destined for Mr Da Costa, who had become the possessor of the books, to increase their number, and to tender this acknowledgment to the English nation, at the same time that he furnished additional scope for the student of the sacred language and literature. The letter of the donor accompanying the gift is still preserved at the British Museum, and is couched in the hyperbolical and somewhat inflated style, so much affected in the East. To afford our readers some idea of the style of this singular communication, we will quote the opening paragraph:—" Go, I pray thee, see the presence of those in whom there is wisdom, understanding, and knowledge; behold they are the honourable personages appointed and made overseers of the great and noted treasury called by the name of the British Museum. The Lord preserve them! Amen. Saith the man Solomon, son to my Lord and Father, the ancient honourable, devout, meek, and excellent Mr Isaac Da Costa, surnamed Athias, of the city of Amsterdam, of the people scattered and dispersed among all nations; of the captivity of Jerusalem, which is in Spain." The collection was much prized for its literary worth, and also as a proof of the good feeling of the Jews towards the people of England.

At the same time original composition was not neglected among the Jews of England during the second half of the 18th century, and various Hebrew works issued from the several presses at the disposal of both Ashkenazi and Sephardic congregations. Native writers do not seem to have compared favourably with foreigners in this respect. The two principal works of those days were the production of foreigners, published in England. In 1766 was brought out a volume of poems by Ephraim Luzzatto, an Italian, which are stated to breathe the spirit of pure poetry, and to be penned in a correct and classical diction. Then a few years later on, in 1771, a learned German, named Levysohn, who was then studying surgery under the celebrated John Hunter, wrote a philosophical treatise, entitled Maahmar Hatorah Vehachochma: an essay on the Law and on Science. Levysohn's book, albeit displaying considerable ability and erudition, was not well received by some of his brethren, who regarded him in the light of a dangerous innovator. Levysohn returned to his native city, Hamburg, where he became an eminent physician, and it is said that he discovered the use of chocolate, and acquired considerable affluence. In his later days he expended much money in collecting books, and was known as the possessor of a valuable library of Hebrew works, which he bequeathed to the Beth Hamedrash in Hamburg. Levysohn, we will remark in conclusion, lived and died a zealous Jew.

Among the productions of English Jews of that period the most valuable seem to have been the Kehilath Yahacob, a vocabulary of the Hebrew language, by Jacob Rodrigues Moreira. The author was an accomplished Hebraist, and the work has been pronounced one of the best of the kind ever published in England.

The great Synagogue was far from being a wealthy body a hundred years since, and it had to carry on a continual struggle to support itself and its institutions. Legacies must have been very acceptable, and the amount of £3500 left in 1769 to the Duke's Place Synagogue by Lazarus Simon, one of its oldest members, no doubt proved a great boon. Of that sum, the interest of £1000 was directed to be applied to clothe and afford a small gratuity to six destitute men and as many destitute women; while the interest of another £1000 was to be handed half-yearly to the overseers of the poor, fourteen days before the holydays. A question arose many years afterwards, in 1808, as to whether needy candidates for habiliments to the extent of £5 yearly, might be strangers. It was then decided by a committee appointed for the purpose, that only decayed members and their widows were entitled to enjoy Lazarus Simon's bounty. Notwithstanding this and other resources, the financial position of the congregation remained in an unsatisfactory condition. In 1772, a committee of four gentlemen— viz., Aaron Franks, Naphtali Franks, Moses Franks, and Aaron Goldsmid—were empowered to grant a mortgage on the Synagogue and buildings to Edward Holms, a builder, for a balance of £1300 due to him, probably for work executed, and further to borrow from him a sum of £400 on the same security at £4 per cent. Again, in 1789, it was found necessary to raise £2000 to construct a new ark, a new reading desk, and new seats in the Synagogue. And this, too, happened only two years after the generous donation of Mrs Judith Levy, who had presented to the Synagogue the munificent sum of £4000. This lady, as our readers will recollect, was the charitable and wealthy daughter of Moses Hart, and her object was to bestow the amount required for the enlargement and repair of the Synagogue. It is said, that when the lady heard that a loan had been raised, she expressed considerable annoyance that application for further funds had not been made to her to enable her to complete the good work. Through these and through other loans, all honourably discharged, the earliest German Jewish congregation in London strove to reach, and eventually attained, through the energy and zeal of its members, to the eminent position it has so long deservedly occupied.

In the year 1770, the Great Synagogue possessed a singer so sweet voiced, that strangers went to hear him as a musical feast. His name was Myer Lyon, and he was engaged in 1667 as chorister at the modest salary of £40 per annum.

Myer Lyon's services were valued so little that in 1772, the congregation being in debt, his salary, like that of all other Synagogue officials, was reduced, and his pittance fell to £32 per annum. In 1770, the Rev. Charles Wesley, the hymn writer, and brother to John Wesley, paid a visit to the Duke's Place Synagogue, which is thus recorded in his journal—" I was desirous to hear Mr Leoni sing at the Jewish Synagogue. . . . I never before saw a Jewish congregation behave so decently. Indeed, the place itself is so solemn, that it might strike an awe upon those who have any thought of God."

Myer Lyon, the humble chorister, rose to be Leoni the opera singer. He possessed a tuneful head, and he composed light songs and sacred melodies. He adapted some Synagogue airs to church hymns; but he preserved strictly his religion, declining to appear on the stage on Friday nights and Festivals. Leoni did not remain very long behind the footlights, and in his latter days he returned to the Synagogue choir. The German congregation of Kingston, Jamaica, having applied to the Great Synagogue for a reader, Leoni offered himself in that capacity. He occupied for some time the vacant post at Kingston, and we hear no more of him in England.

CHAPTER XVIII.

THE PORTUGUESE JEWS IN THE MIDDLE OF THE EIGHTEENTH CENTURY.

It is a necessity imposed upon us by the nature of our undertaking to imitate occasionally the romancist, who, after having guided one set of characters through a series of perilous adventures, halts and takes up the thread of the story at some preceding period, to follow the fortunes of another set of characters. We have traced the foundation of the Great Synagogue from its humble beginning as a Minyan Room, to its development into an important and numerous congregation, in many respects inferior to no other Jewish community in Great Britain. Let us now turn back and inquire how the ancient body of Spanish and Portuguese Jews progressed during the 18th century. It has been said that happy is the nation that has no history. This proposition is scarcely accurate in every instance; and in the case of the Jews, if understood literally, would argue a stagnation and want of vitality by no means to be desired. Yet with respect to the Sephardim during the first half of last century, the axiom is not far from the truth, for their records glide along with a flow of smooth and uninterrupted prosperity. No perils, no persecutions for conscience's sake, no struggles against insufficient means or poverty. The budget of the Synagogue usually displayed a surplus. The impost or tax on the commercial operations of its members frequently brought in as much as £2000 a year, and some members contributed singly £100 or even £200 a year, as a small per centage on their transactions. They were rich men, and with some limited exceptions, the principal Jewish merchants belonged to this congregation. Yea, there were persons of enterprise and financial genius among the Portuguese Jews, men whose names commanded almost unlimited credit on 'Change, and whose descendants have acquired fame in the world of finance, in the forum, in the senate. But if the annals of the Portuguese congregation register few very striking events, they nevertheless hold forth a mass of matter equally interesting to both Jew and Gentile. We glean therefrom many facts throwing a light on congregational history, and we gather much curious information illustrating the manners of the time or the character of the ancestors of families, occupying in the present day important positions among the aristocracy of wealth, or title, or intellect in the United Kingdom.

The most exciting occurrence that had happened for some years among the Portuguese, was a fire in the Synagogue. On one Friday evening in the year 1738, the buildings surrounding the house of prayer were discovered to be ablaze. The alarm was soon given, and notwithstanding the imperfection of the appliances of the period for extinguishing fires, the lambent flames were soon subdued into smouldering cinders by the united exertions of firemen, soldiers, and watchmen. The roof of the Synagogue itself was injured, and a portion of the buildings attached to it, and many of the surrounding houses were reduced to utter ruin. Upwards of forty poor families were left totally destitute. A subscription was at once set on foot to furnish food and clothing to the unhappy creatures whom the calamity had deprived of their little all, and also to reward the firemen, soldiers, and others who had saved the main body of the Synagogue itself from being devoured by the flames. The damages caused by the fire were not repaired immediately, and it was not until the year 1749 that the Synagogue buildings were entirely reconstructed, at a cost of £1700. Hitherto the Bevis Marks Synagogue had been tenanted by the Sephardi congregation on a lease entered into with Sir Thomas and Lady Pointz in 1698, and which had not yet expired. It was left to one who was ever foremost in initiating good work, to secure the property to his community. Whenever any undertaking of a noble, generous, or philanthropic nature was to be established, his name would assuredly be found at its head. Benjamin Mendes da Costa in the year 5507 (1747), announced to the Elders that he had purchased the remainder of the lease of the Synagogue and its appurtenances, which he desired to transfer to the Wardens for the benefit of the holy congregation of the Gates of Heaven. The elders gratefully accepted the offer, but resolved that a subscription should be opened, so that any zealous Israelite who so wished might have an opportunity of participating in the pious work. The lease was obtained at $28\frac{1}{2}$ years' purchase calculated on the rental of £135, and it was vested in a committee consisting of Gabriel Lopez de Britto, David Aboab Ozorio, Moses Gomes Serra, David Franco, Joseph Jessurun Rodriguez, and Moses Mendes da Costa. It was not until many years afterwards that the leasehold was converted into a freehold tenure.

We have before remarked that the only fault that might be laid to the charge of the government of the Portuguese congregation, wise and temperate as it usually appeared, was the too paternal discipline with which it ruled its members, and the too stringent regulations with which it sought to bind their action. The prohibition from performing many things which to us appear very harmless, though no doubt caused by reasons which had their weight at the time, often savours of despotism and intolerance. Once a certain Moses Netto humbly begged permission to publish a translation of the prayer-book in English, which permission was at once refused. Nevertheless, some version of the Hebrew prayers found its way into an English guise, though we are unable to say whether it was through Netto or some one else. Thereupon it was thundered forth from the *Tebah* (pulpit) that all Yehidim (members) were strictly enjoined not to have so dangerous a book in their possession, and that any one perusing, buying, or selling it, would be condemned to a penalty of £5. Catholics, it is well known, are discouraged from reading the Bible in a modern language, the reason for which is obvious to the thinker. But why Jews, who have nothing to fear and nothing to conceal from the knowledge of Jew or Christian, should have placed under a ban that which should have been their pride to proclaim before the world, it is not easy to explain in our more enlightened days. The punishments for disobedience would seem to have been occasionally harsher than the nature of the offence demanded, and sometimes they verged on the absurd. On one occasion, a refractory individual was condemned not to shave for six weeks,—whatever infliction that may have been. He had not obeyed some order of the Mahamad (Council of Wardens), and he had six weeks allowed him to submit: failing to do which he would not be allowed to occupy his seat in the Synagogue, or take any part in the service, or pay his poll tax, and in case of death he would be buried "behind the board," which means in unconsecrated ground. We are not to be understood to censure the efforts made to maintain proper discipline by the rulers of the Portuguese congregation. Such a voluntary body, like a public school, could only have been kept in order by a wholesome discipline. But care should have been taken not to pull the cords too tightly lest they snapped. What we desire to state is, that paternal governments, however well-intentioned, often commit grievous mistakes, and that the petty restrictions and vexations and arbitrary regulations formerly enforced by the authorities of the various London Jewish congregations, have contributed to the withdrawal from the community of many whose secession has proved a serious loss to Judaism.

The questions of labour, of the poor, and of emigration, appear to have vexed the minds of the chiefs of the Sephardi community during last century, just as they bewilder at present other important bodies. Notwithstanding the presence of many persons in affluent circumstances among the Jews, the poor unfortunately have always been in greater numbers than the totality of the Hebrew population warranted. A hundred years ago the Jews possessed no middle class. There were perhaps 150 to 200 families that might be considered rich, about two-thirds of which belonged to the Spanish and Portuguese congregation. Then we should find at most as many families engaged in small retail trade, and finally we should see a floating mass, at least five times as numerous as the other two classes together, consisting of hucksters, hawkers, journeymen, and others, either verging on pauperism or steeped hopelessly in its abyss. To endeavour to diminish the strain of pauperism by emigration, the Sephardi congregation in 1734 appointed a committee to apply for grants of land in Georgia, which the British Government was freely distributing to intending emigrants under certain conditions. This committee remained standing for some years, but we do not gather that it led to any practical results. Three years afterwards the committee reported that some lands in Carolina had been offered to them, and that they were negotiating on the subject. In 1745 this committee was still in existence, and obtained an extension of powers and an allowance to cover expenditure. After this time we hear no more of it, and it is fair to assume that had it achieved anything worth recording, it would have been recorded. Then again, the plan was mooted of emigration to Nova Scotia, and in 1749, poor families were exhorted to proceed thither. But even a bribe of three years' zedaka (relief to the poor) failed to induce any of them to exile themselves to those distant climes. Finally, in the same year a proposal was made to raise a fund of not less than £150, to assist deserving young men of the congregation in earning their livelihood. This scheme also went the way of other good intentions, and pauperism showed no sign of abatement.

The Jews during their numerous emigrations since their dispersion from the Holy Land have usually carried with them two languages, the Hebrew and the language of their last adopted country. Thus it happens that Spanish continued for several generations to be the mother tongue of the Jews scattered in the Ports of Italy and the Levant, while German has long been the vernacular of the Israelites dwelling in Poland, in Russia, and in Hungary. In England, too, the Jews in the last century, when they were still living apart from their fellow-citizens, conversed for generations in the idiom of their ancestors. The Portuguese Jews not only kept all their Synagogue books and records in the language of Camoens, but also their private correspondence was carried on in a similar manner. Some knowledge of English they must naturally have possessed, but probably it was not very perfect. It was not until the year 5495 or 1735 that it was judged expedient to teach English to the children at the public schools. For this purpose was opened what was termed "a Writing-School," wherein the language of Shakspeare was to be taught to the sons of the poor. A grant of £20 per annum was given from the Synagogue funds, and the amount was subsequently increased to £30, and it was continued until Moses Lamego made the generous gift that bears his name. This beneficent individual, to commemorate the death of his only son, presented to the Synagogue in the year 5517 (1757) the sum of £5000 in Bank reduced annuities, the interest of which was to be distributed as follows. The interest of £4000 was to be paid yearly to the treasurer of the Orphan Society, called *Shaare Ora Veaby Yetomim*, and that of £1000 was to be applied to the salary of an English master of the Hes-Haim Schools. The name of Hes-Haim, we will explain, was formerly the generic term applied to the schools of primary instruction. When these ceased to exist in their ancient form, and the society of *Shaare Tickvá* (Gates of Hope), for the support of a Spanish and Portuguese Jews' Charity School, was established in its place, the interest of that £1000 was handed over yearly to the governors of the new institution.

Before the foundation of the "Writing School," the primary instruction imparted to the children of the poor of this congregation was of a purely religious, or of an attempted religious, character. Hebrew was the Alpha and Omega of their studies. The institution of Hes-Haim was divided into three divisions, the lowest of which was intended for the youngest children, and was styled the Aleph Beth School. In the other two sections the boys were gradually taught Hebrew prayers, the rudiments of grammar, translations from the Bible, and finally Rashi, to enable them to enter the Medrash (College). The progress of the pupils even in these limited studies does not appear to have been very profound, for we frequently perceive proposals for reform in the management of these schools. In the year 1770 new and more stringent regulations were framed for the schools. The daily working hours were increased, and one evening a week was to be devoted to additional instruction. To provide for the higher branches of Hebrew studies, Benjamin Mendes da Costa, with his usual noble generosity, had since the year 5494 (1734) founded a Yesiba, or college, entitled *Mahané Rephael*, which he liberally endowed. He handed over to trustees a sum of £3900 in South Sea Stock, which was afterwards changed into long annuities. The produce of this investment was to furnish £5 a month to be distributed among the students of the Yesiba, this allowance commencing at two shillings and sixpence each a month, and increasing according to their merit and other circumstances. A certain amount was to be expended in rolls to be given to the younger children of the public schools. Finally, the remainder of the income, to the extent of £6 per annum, was to be laid out in purchasing books for the Yesiba and the public schools. The Haham, or Rabbi, of the congregation was to preside, and receive one guinea a month for his attendances. The Yesiba of Mahané Rephael is now incorporated with the Medrash, and the students of this institution enjoy the fruit of the noble gift of the pious founder. The beneficence of Benjamin Mendes da Costa seems to have been never ending, and in the year 1762 he endowed another Yesiba, in conjunction with a pious individual named Isaac de David Levy. A sum of £30 a year in long annuities was given by the liberal donors to be distributed among the students of the Yesiba or College of Assifat Haberim, who were to attend two evenings a week, to read Arambam (Maimonides) and his Commentators. In the days of which we are writing, neither wealth nor munificence were wanting; and when any member of the Spanish and Portuguese congregation accumulated riches, one of his first thoughts was to show his gratitude to Providence by apportioning some of his gains to the service of religion or education, and to the relief of the sufferings of his less fortunate brethren.

Benjamin Mendes da Costa was one of those rare philanthropists whose every thought was directed to the welfare of others. So long as he lived, he distributed £3000 a year in charity to the poor of all creeds.

In 1764 he was summoned to receive his reward in another state of existence.

By a codicil of his will he desired his benefactions to be

continued, during the lives of the indigent families who received his bounty. Moreover, he directed that all private bills and bonds in the hands of his executors at his decease should be destroyed, and the debtors released from any obligation towards his estate. His generous principle was, that all who borrowed must be in need. Mere words must necessarily fail in rendering justice to the goodness of such a man.

CHAPTER XIX.

AGAIN WITH THE PORTUGUESE JEWS.

JACOB ISRAEL BERNAL was a well-to-do West India merchant, coming from a good and honourable stock, though not ranking in the first line of Hebrew capitalists. In 1744 he was elected to the Synagogue office of Gabay (Treasurer), but to the surprise of his colleagues, he resigned his functions in the following year. When the reason of this act became apparent, the astonishment of the Elders considerably increased. Jacob Israel Bernal had applied for leave to marry a German Jewess. For a member of the Portuguese congregation, and especially a gentleman occupying the honourable post of treasurer, to desire to wed a "Tudesco" woman (German female), was an unexampled occurrence, upon which the Mahamad or Council of Wardens could not venture to pronounce an opinion! The important question was referred to the consideration of the elders. This body, after mature deliberation, granted to the petitioner permission to wed Jochebeth Baruh, as the lady who captivated him was styled. But the Elders, to mark the sense of their disapprobation of so unequal a union, and to discourage for the future such ill-advised connections, imposed upon Mr Bernal some rather humiliating conditions. Neither the members of the Beth Din, nor the Hazanim (ministers) were to be present at the solemnisation of the marriage: the bridegroom was not to be called up to the Law in that capacity, no offerings or "mesheberach" were to be made for his health, and no celebration of any kind was to take place in Synagogue. *Nous avons changé tout cela.* Happily, at present, prejudices of this nature have long ceased to exist, and the chief distinction between the German and Portuguese Jews is that they pronounce Hebrew differently. Mr Bernal from that time forth mixed little in congregational affairs, and he must naturally have experienced some feelings of displeasure. Years afterwards his eldest son was admitted as a yahid or member, and the Bernal family long continued to be strictly observing Jews. We shall have occasion to refer again to them. Meanwhile we will observe that by the espousal of Miss Grace Osborne, daughter of Mr Bernal Osborne, to the Duke of St Albans, the ancient blood of Judah has become allied with the blue blood of the Stuarts—through the descendants of Mistress Eleanor Gwynne, the sauciest of orange girls—whatever honour that may reflect on the old lineage of the former West India merchants!

The Portuguese congregation, in its desire to serve the interests of members of limited means, consented for many years to grant life annuities on payment of adequate sums. When we employ the term adequate, we use it only as a figure of speech, for in point of fact the principals paid to the Synagogue were quite inadequate to cover the risks incurred. The laws of life insurance were imperfectly understood in the middle of last century, and, moreover, the Synagogue only undertook these operations to benefit the parties with whom it dealt. But in the long run the granting of life annuities proved a too obviously losing concern, and they were gradually discontinued. The applicants for this kind of indirect assistance were usually the widows of deceased officials, or members in somewhat straightened circumstances, or their surviving relatives, mostly females, to whom it was wished to secure a modest income.

The subject of butchers' meat is neither very lofty nor very inspiring, but as we must daily consume this commodity in more or less quantity, the subject acquires considerable importance. The history of both German and Portuguese congregations records a continual series of laments against the representatives of the Jewish slaughter-house. Here we have accusations of unlawful practices on the part of the killers; there we have complaints of irregularities in the sale of meat. At other times fault is found with the quality of the article vended, or with the price charged. Some of the evils seem to be of an incurable nature, for the Jews hear of them now as their ancestors heard of them a century since. The Portuguese authorities incurred a vast deal of pains to have the Mosaic laws enforced on the one hand, and to avoid harsh or unjust measures against killers and inspectors on the other. Committees were appointed and inquiries set on foot at different periods, entailing considerable expense on the congregation, without attaining results of a lasting nature. In 1756 a committee was elected to investigate the abuses alleged to have been introduced into the slaughter-house. It was formally stated that the flesh of improperly killed animals (Terefa) was commonly disposed of to Jews. Haham Netto, Joseph Salvador, and other members of the congregation, actively bestirred themselves on the subject, and assisted materially in bringing the truth to light. A number of persons connected with the trade, Jewish officials appertaining to the various London congregations, and even Christians, were duly examined. Some of the allegations were unfortunately found to be true, and the ecclesiastical authorities pronounced their opinion. Eventually the shochet or killer was dismissed, and several reforms were introduced in the establishment; but, from the subsequent renewal of similar complaints, it does not appear that the evil was uprooted.

The Portuguese congregation was wont to receive frequent applications for assistance from its less fortunate brethren in all parts of the world. Like the rich man, who is often surprised by the discovery of hitherto unsuspected relationship with affable and shabbily-attired strangers, the Bevis Marks Synagogue found itself the object of considerable solicitude from various quarters. The holy cities of Palestine, Newport in Rhode Island, Bohemia and Moravia, Persia, Venice, and various other places, advanced claims to the benevolent support of Bevis Marks. Funds were regularly remitted to Jerusalem, Saphet, and Tebariah, and, moreover, a duly accredited Shaliah (emissary) from the Holy Land was never dismissed empty-handed. Upwards of £800 was collected to relieve the distress of the Jews of Bohemia and Moravia, and arrangements were made with the two German congregations for the proper application of the fund. A smaller amount was sent to the Israelites of Persia. The Jews of Newport were courteously informed that a multiplicity of other calls for help prevented their request being acceded to. The Jews of Venice were very fortunate. We do not know exactly what was the nature of their needs, but they seemed to find favour in the eyes of the Elders, who, while declining to disburse any of the Synagogue funds, opened a private subscription on their behalf. Considerable sums of money, amounting to some thousands, were remitted to that city in the year 1737, and they were to be repaid in ten instalments, spread over a number of years. At first the interest on the loan was forwarded regularly, but the punctuality was short-lived. Letters from Venice were received, pleading total inability to pay. That congregation was in embarrassed circumstances, and in fact was going from bad to worse. A correspondence between the two congregations was long kept up; and the Jewish community of Venice not only did not cover the advances already made, but even applied for further advances, which we need not say were courteously but firmly refused. An arrangement was eventually entered into between debtor and creditor, and for many years certain instalments were paid more or less regularly by Venice. Gradually the matter was forgotten; the original lenders died and the borrowers too. The glories had departed from the Queen of the Adriatic, and the Jewish community had suffered with the rest of the inhabitants. So the claim has never been completely settled, and exists to the present day, though it would be impossible to ascertain what amounts are owing, or to whose representatives.

CHAPTER XX.

JOSEPH SALVADOR—HONORARY OFFICES AMONG THE PORTUGUESE JEWS.

A VISIT to the vestry-room of the Spanish and Portuguese Synagogue, Bevis Marks, must cause to the reflecting mind a sensation of awe and solemnity not unlike that experienced in wandering over a cemetery. The walls of the Council Chamber and of the neighbouring lobby are covered with inscriptions of the names of the pious individuals who in past generations bestowed their benefactions on the congregation. The men whose names figure in golden letters in those panels, once graced the room with their presence, and therein discussed the affairs of the nation. Many of them were personages famed for their wealth, their philanthropy, their public spirit. And where are they all now? Not only have they passed away, which is merely saying that they followed the ordinary laws of nature, but their very names and their very existence are only dimly recollected in our day. Few of the leaders of the Sephardi community of a century and a half, or even a century ago have left descendants in the congregation. Some of the most ancient families have wandered from the pale of Judaism, and now rank among the untitled nobility of Great Britain. Others have become victims to the inexorable decrees of fate, which seem to have pressed on the Portuguese Jews with more than usual severity, and have disappeared from the face of the earth.

Among the most distinguished families of that congregation during the eighteenth century we must mention the family bearing the name of Jessurun Rodrigues. They had originally come over from Holland, bringing with them considerable sums of money, which they invested principally in commerce, and they ranked as merchant princes among the Jews. The most noted scion of that lineage was Joseph Jessurun Rodrigues, to whom we have already adverted by the appellation of Joseph Salvador, under which guise the world knew him. He took a leading part in the affairs of his Synagogue, and he was ever to the fore when the sufferings of poor humanity were to be relieved. He was president of the congregation, and one of the most efficient members of the original Committee of Portuguese Deputies. Notwithstanding the extensive financial and mercantile transactions in which he was engaged, he devoted a portion of his time to the improvement of the condition of the needy. He not only gave largely to all existing institutions; he was ever seeking new plans for conquering the hydra-headed evil of pauperism. Now he would help to establish a new society, like that intended to assist Jewish young men in earning their livelihood by hard work, and which, unfortunately, was unsuccessful. At another time he would be found asking permission of the Wardens to enter into a speculation on behalf of some deserving families in humble circumstances. He was always a liberal donor to the necessitous. Joseph Jessurun Rodrigues was a partner in the well-known house of Francis and Joseph Salvador, which, after the death of Sampson Gideon, repeatedly negotiated loans for the British Government. We cannot tell at precisely what period the name of Salvador was first adopted, but certainly it must be in the early part of last century, though it does not occur in the synagogue registers until about 1760.

Personally, Joseph Salvador, to style him by the most familiar designation, was popular, and enjoyed considerable repute among Jew and Gentile; albeit, when he appeared in a theatre on one occasion, after the passing of the Naturalisation Bill in 1753, he and his party were hooted, and were constrained to withdraw, to the utter disgrace of the civilised and Christian audience. The principal part of his career was accompanied by unbounded prosperity. He had vastly increased the wealth he had inherited, and he was the first Jew who had been appointed Director of the East India Company. He constructed a handsome house in White Hart

Court, Bishopsgate-street, which bore until recent times, if it does not still bear, his name; and in the N.E. corner of one of the cellars may yet be seen the foundation-stone, with an inscription laid upon it by his daughter, Judith Salvador. He also was the owner of a country residence, with an extensive park, at Tooting. Joseph Salvador was less fortunate in his latter days. Misfortunes began to befall him. He lost heavily in consequence of the earthquake at Lisbon, he holding much property in various shapes in that city, though this did not appear to affect him much. It was the failure of the Dutch East India Company that brought ruin on him, and that proved almost a calamity to many of the rich Portuguese Jews of England and of Holland. This disaster was a great blow to those communities, from which they found it difficult to recover. As for Joseph Salvador, he never raised his head again. All his available property in Europe little by little disappeared; and his last days were spent in obscurity. The family were still possessed of some tracts of land in America, which were in charge of a steward. A nephew of Joseph Salvador, Francis, determined to undertake a voyage to the new continent. It is said that Mrs Joshua Mendes da Costa, a daughter of Joseph Salvador, gave up a part of her marriage-settlement to furnish funds for the expedition. Francis started to retrieve the family fortunes. In due course letters came, advising his safe arrival to the new continent, and announcing his intention of seeking his property. He never wrote again. A long silence ensued, and then it was reported that the unhappy Salvador had been murdered and scalped by Indians!

It is related that in 1802 an American arrived in Amsterdam and waited upon Mrs Texeira de Mattos, Salvador's eldest daughter, and offered her 10,000 dollars to sign a deed giving up all claim on the American property. The lady declined the transaction. In 1812 the stranger once more returned and repeated his offer. He alleged that he was the grandson of Salvador's former steward; that the land in Mr Salvador's time had been a tract of barren forests and utterly valueless; that now it was covered with villages and towns, and that he had himself a good holding title thereto. Finally he added that, during the War of Independence,

British subjects had forfeited all their rights to property in the United States, and that she could advance no claim whatever to the land. Under these circumstances Mrs Texeira de Mattos, who was eighty years of age at that time, and who had not the slightest idea as to the State or part of the Union in which the demesne was situated, accepted the sum tendered, and signed the required assignment, which thus conferred a valid selling title on the descendant of the steward. The last male representative of the family of Salvador or Jessurun Rodrigues was a member of Lloyd's, and is believed to have died about 1830. In this manner terminated that ancient and honourable lineage.

The correspondence that passed between the London Congregation of Spanish and Portuguese Jews and their foreign brethren scattered over the Old and the New World, enables us to form a fair idea of the general position of that denomination of Jews during the eighteenth century. The principal congregations of that Minhag were those of London, Amsterdam and Leghorn. These were the most independent, the wealthiest, and probably the most numerous. All the others, or the greater part of them, were more or less struggling against a number of adverse circumstances. The London congregation, though the youngest of the three above-named, enjoyed a considerable reputation for liberality, affluence and devotion to Jewish interests; so that Jews in distress addressed themselves to this body on the appearance of every difficulty. We are not speaking now of solicitations for financial help, which point we have already touched in our last chapter. We are referring at present to the applications for moral help, which were constantly arriving in London. We know the kind of letters that fame for charity brings to a private individual. The Bevis Marks Synagogue was regarded as the protector of the Jewish weak, and the redresser of Jewish wrongs in the four quarters of the globe. The Jews of Jamaica were constantly writing to request the intervention of the Jews of Bevis Marks on their behalf. For instance, in 1736 the former were groaning under severe and special taxation, when the latter prepared a petition in favour of their brethren, filled it with a number of signatures of Jewish and Christian merchants, presented it to the King, and succeeded in obtaining a removal of the grievances complained of. Then in 1753 the Jews of Barbadoes submitted their internecine quarrels to the authorities of the London Portuguese Synagogue, who paid very little attention to that storm in a teapot. The Jews of Barbadoes were very plainly told that in those days when the passing of the Naturalisation Bill had created an hostile feeling against the Jews, it was very unbecoming and ill-advised for them to dispute among themselves about trifles, and they were recommended to settle their differences quietly at home. Afterwards the Jews of New York appertaining to the congregation of *Sheerit Israel* sought in London a *Reader* or *Hazan*, and eventually received a minister at the hands of their English brethren. It would take us too long to repeat even a quarter of the demands of this nature made upon the chiefs of the Bevis Marks Synagogue, who appeared always ready in every emergency to lend countenance and support to their brethren abroad.

As will easily be understood, the Jews of last century dedicated all their attention to Jewish affairs. There was no other scope for their ambition. The Jew could not figure in the Municipal Council, in the forum, in the Senate. The only office to which he could aspire was office in the synagogue, and consequently this honour was greatly coveted. Among the Portuguese Jews the Wardens, or Parnassim, inspired considerable awe. When these officials were inducted into their charge they would take a solemn oath before the Ark to administer justly and without favour the laws of the congregation, and to respect all its customs. Gentlemen elected to these posts had to deposit £100 to contribute towards Synagogue expenditure, as the communal taxes and offerings were discharged by members twice a-year—at Passover and at New Year—and sometimes the payments were in arrear. The treasurer, or Gabay, was required to advance £600 for the same reason; but all these amounts were duly returned at the expiration of the period of office. As at one time there was some little difficulty in finding suitable Hatanim (bridegrooms of the law), a society of pious individuals was formed to offer themselves for the office whenever required. The fine for non-acceptance of the post of Wardens, or Hatanim, was £40, which sum in the latter case was divided between the ministers and the teachers. One of the duties of the Mahamad, or Council of Wardens, was to adjudge in matters at issue between the congregants of the synagogue. Multifarious were the questions submitted to the decision of that body, and they ranged from the price of a warming pan to cases of breach of promise. Usually the Wardens satisfactorily adjusted such small claims as now would be brought before a County Court; but when it was found impossible to settle any question, or the defendant declined to put in an appearance, written leave was granted to the plaintiff to sue in the civil courts of the country.

There was and there is still in the Portuguese Synagogue a special office called that of *Parnass* of the *Cautivos* (Warden of the Captives). At present this is merely an honorary title, and means only the first step in synagogal dignities. Formerly there was real earnest labour attached to the post. The synagogue was constantly receiving applications for the redemption from captivity of Jewish prisoners. Now it was to rescue some Jews that had been taken prisoners by Moorish Corsairs, and confined in chains at Tetuan. Now it was to save other Jews imprisoned at Malta; at one time to ransom Israelites undergoing duress at Tripoli; on another occasion it was to liberate Hebrews who had been taken prisoners by the Turks in their wars against the Persians. There was an especial fund set apart for this purpose, and it was regularly drawn upon. Usually the sums required were remitted to Leghorn, whence there was a considerable trade in the hands of Jewish houses with Levantine and North African ports. Jewish prisoners, we must add, were not considered worth a king's ransom, for we percieve that £80 were forwarded in 1768 to Leghorn to buy off fourteen prisoners at Malta. Probably the Jews of Leghorn contributed something towards this benevolent object; but it appears clearly that a Jew's head was not so valuable in those days as a Jew's eye was popularly represented to be.

CHAPTER XXI.

SWEDEN AND THE JEWS—PORTUGUESE RELIGIOUS AND EDUCATIONAL INSTITUTIONS—DR KENNICOTT.

It is probably not generally known that Sweden, a country that not long since indulged in special legislation against the Jews, a century and a quarter ago invited Jews to settle in and to enrich the State with their capital, their labour, and their industry. After the signature of the treaty of Nystad with Russia in 1721, Sweden, by the cession of several important provinces to the former power, lost much of its political influence, and sank into a second-rate nation. During the reign of Frederick of Hesse Cassel, the Court of Stockholm was the scene of continuous intrigues between the French and the Russian party. Great attention was bestowed upon the arts of peace; agriculture and commerce were encouraged; and the great Linnæus gave a new impulse to science. Various schemes for the promotion of trade were proposed. The legislature sanctioned, among other projects, one for the establishment of a fishing company on an extensive scale, and at the same time gave permission to wealthy Portuguese Jews to take up their abode in Sweden and all its dependencies. This last concession had been granted unasked and unsought; and the event was duly communicated to the authorities of the Portuguese community in London. This congregation, through its president, Joseph Jessurun Rodrigues (Salvador), wrote a most becoming reply to their correspondents in Stockholm, who were a mercantile firm of eminence. This document states, under date of the 2nd May 1746 " that the gentlemen of the States and the very venerable gentlemen of the Senate were sincerely thanked for their condescension in favour of the Jews, but that the continued kindness of the king and parliament (of England) did not allow them (the Jews) to leave the United Kingdom. They thought that unless some unforeseen accident occurred, few Israelites from England and Holland would proceed to Sweden, but more might go from Italy and France; and they suggested that the Swedish Government should take measures to inform the Jews of those countries of his Majesty's good will towards them. No great result, however, could be expected until his Majesty ceased to make a distinction between the rich and the poor, between financiers and hawkers." English Jews of Portuguese extraction were not tempted to leave the comparatively hospitable shore of Great Britain to visit the cold climes of the Scandinavian Peninsula, for a very moderate degree of benevolence is enough to attach the Jews to the soil in which they dwell. Moreover, it does not appear that they formed any permanent settlement in Sweden during last century. Subsequently to this period, less liberal monarchs and less enlightened legislatures placed renewed restrictions on the presence of Israelites. After the fall of Napoleon, and when the reaction came against the wide principles advocated by the French, the Jews were regarded with unqualified aversion. It was only in recent times that they first obtained toleration, and eventually gained their civil rights.

We have already adverted to the existence of Jews in Ireland in the middle of last century, and to the purchase by the Portuguese congregation of a piece of ground at Dublin to serve for the purposes of a cemetery. This purchase was effected in the year 1748, through a Mr Jacob Phillips.

After much correspondence, the Wardens of the Portuguese Synagogue authorised Mr Phillips to draw upon them for the required funds, which he accordingly did when all the conditions had been arranged, and transmitted to them the title deeds. There does not appear any reason why the Portuguese should have desired to acquire the ground beyond a general wish to benefit their race, for the Hebrew residents in Dublin were of German extraction, and the German communities in London would have been, strictly speaking, bound to assist members of their nationality in the

Irish capital. On this occasion the Portuguese Jews of London looked to no such distinction. They possessed the means, and they performed a pious action. The only acknowledgment they required was a mention that the burial ground had been bought with the money of the Sephardic Congregation of London. We gather also that about this epoch there were Jews dwelling in other parts of Ireland; for it was stated that in several cities of that island there were men who professed to be licensed to kill Jewish meat, but that the only *Shochet* or *slaughterer* legally qualified was to be found at Cork. Whence it seems that there were more Jews in Ireland in those days than we imagine.

Let us now take a glance at the religious condition of the Bevis Marks Community. After the death of the illustrious Haham David Netto, which occurred about 1728, the guidance of the spiritual affairs of the congregation was entrusted to his son, Haham Isaac Netto. This learned rabbi came to London in the year 1747, probably from a residence at Leghorn, his father's birthplace; and he was much esteemed for his urbanity and scholarship. For some years he seemed to give satisfaction to his flock; and under him there were two Dayanim or minor rabbis named Isaac del Valle and Jacob Coronel. Haham Isaac Netto appears to have been a man of amiable disposition, rather than of commanding intellect. He preferred the retirement of private life to the turmoil of public affairs, and in 1755 he found it advisable to resign his sacred functions. The reason he assigned for this act was that his own personal affairs necessitated his whole time and attention. But his conduct has been attributed to the fact that an opinion he once had emitted, having been considered as not sufficiently orthodox by some of the authorities of the congregation, these persons were induced to consult the heads of the older congregation at Amsterdam. The answer was in the main in conformity with the decision of Haham Netto. But doubts on the one side caused dissatisfaction on the other, and the Haham thought it best to regain his independence. At all events the parting took place in a most friendly manner. The Rabbi continued to dwell in London till his death; he felt much interest in educational affairs, and was frequently consulted on congregational and religious matters. The two members of the then acting Beth Din were his pupils, who followed in his footsteps and appealed to him in any difficulty. For some years no other Haham was elected. It was not until 1765 that his successor was appointed in the person of Rabbi Moses Cohen de Azevedo, one of the disciples of Rabbi Netto, and who was Rabbi of the Beth Din and Hebrew teacher in one of the schools. The ruling powers of those days accustomed to the dictates of Spanish and Portuguese etiquette, were vastly particular in laying down the law in small matters as in great matters. The more easy-going gentlemen of the present generation will hardly be able to repress a smile on learning, that on Haham Azevedo's election to his post, the elders of the Synagogue solemnly debated as to whether the rev. gentleman should wear his beard! For the sake of the ladies who may like to know how the question was settled, we will add that the meeting decided the point in the negative by a majority of several votes. When Rabbi Netto was called to his fathers in 1773, his funeral was attended by great solemnities, and he seems to have been sincerely lamented.

Though instruction in English was evidently deficient among the Portuguese boys, instruction in Hebrew superabounded. Hebrew masters were remarkably plentiful. When a vacancy for a teacher occurred on a certain occasion, no fewer than sixteen candidates presented themselves, a state of things which singularly contrasts with that which now obtains. On the other hand, if the Hebrew instruction were to be measured by quality rather than by quantity, the result arrived at would leave small cause for boasting. In Haham Netto's visits he found much more ground for censure than for commendation. The boys, to use his own forcible expression, were "steeped in crass ignorance." The pupils stopped away, and the masters did not attend; and no attempt was made at preserving a semblance of order and discipline. The same condition of affairs remained until long after the death of the worthy Haham. In 1779 a committee was nominated to inquire into the subject. In the report delivered to the elders the committee dolefully complained that of the total number of sixty-four pupils scarcely one-eighth could even read Hebrew, after an instruction of seven or eight years, and nearly all were unacquainted with the daily prayers. After lamenting the utter inutility of an establishment maintained at an annual cost of £600, the committee proposed various reforms. The principal of these were the division of the school into four different classes, each to receive instruction from a distinct teacher in a distinct classroom, and the yearly appointment of masters who, considering their posts as sinecures for life, had hitherto greatly neglected their duties. It is curious to remark that food for mind and food for body proved both sources of incessant trouble and vexation to the authorities of the synagogue. The school, like the slaughter-house, was constantly being reconstituted, to remain as faulty as before. The highest institution for learning Hebrew was the college, or Medrash, and it was reorganised in 1758. In the absence of a Haham, three students, all of whom were rabbis, were deputed to preside therein alternately; and the eighteen learners were divided into three classes. Formerly scholastic disputations were carried on at random, without plan or aim. Now, when a thesis was given forth, and after all the reasons had been alleged *pro* and *con* any particular opinion, the President and his two coadjutors were to decide the question, which, when once thus settled, was not to be renewed unless new authorities were adduced. Rabbi Cohen de Azevedo, before his election to the functions of Haham, had acted as one of the presidents. This institution undoubtedly furnished the means of acquiring a knowledge of the sayings and opinions of the Talmudists, and enabled the students to form a correct judgment on any given point, according to the principles of the Jewish oral law.

In 1768 a useful innovation was introduced in this congregation. It was found inconvenient not to know the exact ages of men and women of the congregation, and a register was established wherein were to be entered the births of all legitimate children. The date was to be inscribed both in Hebrew and in English. Each father was to pay on that auspicious occasion the moderate fee of one shilling. It was not until many years later that a similar system was adopted by the German Jews. In the year 1816 a certificate of the marriage of Moses Franks and of the birth of his children was applied for to the authorities of the Great Synagogue. It was then stated that previous to 1791 no register of births, marriages, or deaths had been kept, and that even since that date they had not been regularly preserved, only those who thought proper so to do having registered the births of their children. It was resolved on that occasion that for the future such registration should become regular and compulsory, and a committee was appointed, consisting of Messrs Hyman Cohen, Nathaniel Nathan, and Solomon Cohen, to give effect to this resolution.

Seekers after truth have existed in all ages, though not always has truth been properly understood when discovered. Among those who were desirous of ascertaining the actual facts with reference to the text of the Scriptures we may name the Rev. B. Kennicott. This gentleman, who was a clergyman of the Church of England, applied in the year 1763 to the authorities of the Portuguese Synagogue for permission to have their oldest Hebrew MS. Bible inspected by his nominee, M. Bruns. The Rev. B. Kennicott stated that he had sent M. Paul J. Bruns, of Lubeck, to Frankfort, Worms, Strasburg, Venice, Prague, Amsterdam, and other cities to visit Jewish Synagogues. His mission was to examine the most ancient MSS. of the Bible or of part of the Bible, and to see how far the passages of importance agreed with the Hebrew text as ordinarily printed. The inquiry had been carried on for three years, under patronage of the King of Great Britain and of several eminent Jews. The reverend gentleman thought that there must be some primitive MSS. in public synagogues, as well as in private hands, and he desired to have letters of recommendation from eminent Jews to their brethren abroad to assist in their researches, his object being to establish truth and do honour to the genuine words of Moses and the prophets. As may be imagined, the Portuguese elders hastened to comply with so praiseworthy a wish; and they placed at Mr Kennicott's disposal the two ministers of the congregation, the Rev. Mr de Crasto and the Rev. Mr Salom. The results of the labours of Dr Kennicott are curious. He discovered in the British Islands no fewer than 129 MSS. of the Bible or portions of the Bible, in Hebrew, and 336 on the Continent.

He collated, with the assistance of a qualified staff, nearly all these MSS. with the best printed editions of the Hebrew Bible. He examined, among other valuable MSS. the Samaritan Pentateuch, given by Archbishop Usher to Sir R. Cotton, and which was very old. Dr Kennicott's undertaking inspired general interest. Cardinal Passionei, librarian at the Vatican, placed the whole of the Hebrew MSS. in that great library at his disposal. Dr Kennicott's work was completed at the end of 1769, and had lasted ten years, as he had calculated.

The inquiry cost over £9000, and the funds were raised by a subscription, which was headed by the King. In 1776 Dr Kennicott published the first volume of his great Hebrew Bible, with its various readings; and this was followed in 1780 by the second and final volume. Dr Kennicott, who was regarded as a profound Hebrew scholar, discovered numerous inaccuracies in the Hebrew text. The Hebrew MSS. differed greatly from each other, and from the printed text. The oldest printed copies varied considerably from the latest, and agreed more with the oldest and best MSS. The conclusion Dr Kennicott drew from this was that the original text had with time become vitiated.

In the month of August during the same year, a Jewish dignitary of consequence arrived from abroad. For the first time, we believe, a foreign power despatched an avowedly Jewish representative to London, on a diplomatic mission. On the 19th of August, Jacob, son of Abraham Benider, was introduced to King George III., and delivered his credentials as minister of the Emperor of Morocco. His Maroqueen Majesty spoke most graciously of his envoy, and referred to him thus, in the missive he had forwarded to the King of England: "The bearer of this imperial letter is Jacob, the son of Abraham Benider, a person equally beloved of his sovereign and country, and who has your Majesty's interest to heart. I have entrusted him with full powers to treat, and from his knowledge of public affairs and his attention to our mutual affairs, I doubt not that he will conduct to a successful issue the negotiations I have empowered him to carry on with your Majesty's Government." We trust the Jewish envoy may have realised the expectations raised by his abilities and integrity. Certain it is that the Emperors of Morocco felt themselves justified in again confiding the representation of their empire, at the Court of St James's, to Hebrew ministers, which they did on two subsequent occasions. In 1794 the Jew Sumbal came to London, charged with a special mission to the King; and subsequently in 1827 Meir Cohen Macnin visited the same capital as the envoy of the Emperor Muley Abdelrrahman.

CHAPTER XXII.

CONGREGATIONAL CHANGES — THE JEWS OF PORTUGAL — JEWISH OFFENDERS — THE JEWS AND THE LORD MAYOR.

A SIMILAR fate is shared by families, by communities, by empires. When the highest pinnacle of prosperity is attained, and after a longer or shorter interval, a period of decay begins more or less visibly, and continues steadily if slowly. There are few instances on record of families retaining great wealth for a whole century, unless such wealth be invested in land. That is why all those who wish to found a family eagerly purchase landed estates, and probably that is why so little of the riches held by Jews during last century has been preserved by their successors of the present day. The Jews, as is well known, being debarred from owning broad acres, invested their capital in mercantile or financial operations. The exciting speculations of Change Alley offered a great temptation to the quick-witted Israelites who flocked thither from all parts of Europe. Jonathan's was thronged with Jewish jobbers, and the neighbouring alleys were crowded with Jewish beggars who sped thither to solicit alms from their richer brethren. Many Jews realised large fortunes; few retained them beyond one or two generations. When any commercial disaster happened, the Jews became considerable sufferers, as in the case of the failure of the Dutch East India Company. That the Spanish and Portuguese Jews of London sustained heavy loss on the occasion is apparent from various reasons. Not the least important of these is that at this period—between 1770 and 1780—the finances of the Synagogue were not in so flourishing a condition as was their wont. For the first time for many years we hear of a deficit in the annual estimates, and retrenchment became the cry of the day. The allowances made to various charities were diminished; the distribution of medicine and other relief to the poor, which had led to many abuses, was subjected to stringent regulations; other expenses were cut down; and the legacy fund being completed to £16,000, all further legacies were merged in the *Zedaka* or poor fund. Numerous members were in arrears to the Synagogue, which clearly points out a general cause affecting many congregants. The evil, however, was far from being irreparable, and a few years subsequently the congregation was once more in a position to make generous grants to their necessitous brethren abroad. But the palmiest days of the Portuguese commmunity were certainly over; and their co-religionists of German extraction were fast approaching them in the race in which they subsequently so completely outstripped them. It is a remarkable and curious fact that in the year 1873, the Bevis Marks Synagogue could boast of no more members than it counted in 1773; and that the quantity of Passover cakes distributed to the poor at both periods was precisely identical. Statistics it is said may be made to prove anything; but we question whether in this instance they can be made to prove that the Sephardi congregation is more numerous or wealthier at present than it was a hundred years ago. It would require much time and space to endeavour to trace why one of the two communities of Jews existing in London a century since, should have remained stationary or nearly so, whilst the other should have increased tenfold. We must of course allow for the natural difference in growth between the Spanish and Portuguese Jews, the fresh supply of whom from abroad was, if not exhausted, at all events very restricted, owing to the original source being nearly dry; and the German congregations which could draw a practically inexhaustible supply of fresh blood, from the millions of their co-religionists vegetating in poverty and ignorance in the crowded Ghettos of German cities, or in the wild plains of Poland. But one source of the stagnation is so obvious and palpable, that we cannot refrain from recording it. It is the numerous desertions that have occurred from the ranks of the Sephardi community, that are at the root of the diminished importance of their ancient congregation. It is to those who lapsed from the old path of Israel, and who forsook the old faith for the new dispensation; to those who sold their spiritual privileges for a mess of pottage; to those who deserted the Bevis Marks Synagogue and set up a new code of laws, substituting the ordinances of their wise men to the ordinances of the wise men of Israel; to those who were neither Jews nor Christians, and whose religion was their convenience, and whose God was mammon; it is to all these that the Portuguese Jews of London owe their decline from their former greatness. Neither on the other hand can we acquit from blame those who, embued with a narrow mind and an unyielding intolerant spirit, refused to make the slightest concession, and who determined, by harsh and ill-judged measures, the departure of some of their brethren from the House of Israel.

The Portuguese Jews once enjoyed decided advantages over their co-religionists of German extraction in other places in addition to London. Nevertheless the latter, over-weighted as they were in the race, by their superior industry, energy, and enterprise, everywhere reached to the front. It may not be generally known that during last century Israelites of Spanish and Portuguese origin enjoyed in Paris the especial privilege of being admitted to that city without a passport, a privilege denied to German Jews, who, on the contrary, were subject to very strict police supervision. Henry II. had granted letters patent in the year 1550 in favour of the Portuguese Jews; and these letters had been renewed from king to king. For some years this immunity had not been claimed by the Sephardi Jews, possibly through their ignorance of it. But in December 1777, M. Jacob Rodriguez Pereire of Paris wrote to the authorities of Bevis Marks to remind them of the charter granted by his most Christian Majesty to their nationality, and to hand them a copy of the regulations referring thereto. Jacob Rodriguez Pereire, we may add, was the well-known teacher of the deaf and dumb, and the grandfather of M. Emile and M. Isaac Pereire. At the same time M. Pereire informed them that a certificate signed by seven of the Elders of the congregation would entitle the bearer to enter the capital of France and to dwell therein without any other papers, and without any fear of molestation by the police. What a blessing such a boon would have proved even within the recollection of the present generation!

Even so late as this period the banks of the Tagus were not free from the presence of the " Judeo," who still dwelt in disguise on the soil of Lusitania. It is an ascertained fact that a number of families—how many it is impossible to tell—under the guise of devout Catholics, secretly worshipped in Portugal the God of Israel. From time to time one of these families succeeded in making their safe escape to a land, where the fact of their being members of a race which produced the founder of Christianity, was not deemed sufficient cause to ensure their being broken on the rack or their being roasted at the stake. A curious case is related, in which the timely intervention of the Wardens of the Bevis Marks Synagogue prevented the discovery of a family of hidden Jews in Portugal, and the almost inevitable fate that would have been their doom. A certain Israelite who had himself escaped from Portugal, and who adopted the name of James de Lemos, had a claim against a co-religionist described as Antonio Suarez de Mendoza, of Lisbon. Antonio Suarez, it appears, demurred in satisfying the demands of James de Lemos, if he did not altogether decline to acquit them. Whereupon the latter wrote to the former threatening that were he driven to despair by the continued non-payment of the sum owing to him, he would denounce the true faith of the latter to the Inquisition. The Wardens by some means heard of the menace held forth against a co-religionist, and ordered De Lemos to hand over to the *Mahamad* all the papers in his possession incriminating Antonio Suarez de Mendoza—that is, adverting in any manner to his religion. At first De Lemos refused to obey; then fourteen days were allowed to him wherein to comply. At the last moment he reluctantly gave up to one of the religious officials of the congregation the dangerous writings that might have consigned to ruin a Jewish family. These documents were retained by the Synagogue authorities for some months, and then they were returned to the owner under promise that he would never commit the rash act that once had been in his thoughts.

Poor De Lemos, who probably had never seriously contemplated betraying a co-religionist, does not seem to have recovered the sum he claimed, and eventually he fell into want, and had to be assisted by the Synagogue. Among wonderful escapes from the Iberian Peninsula, we must not fail to mention that of a boy only seven years old who fled from Gibraltar in the year 1777 because his liberty of conscience was endangered! The boy, or child rather, hid himself on board a ship about to sail for the Thames, and succeeded in finding his way to Bevis Marks. The story of Moses de Paz—for so the young fugitive was called—was very extraordinary. His family, to save their lives, had embraced Christianity, but he, child as he was, rather than forsake the creed of his fathers, had found strength and courage enough in his little heart to flee from those he loved and to face unknown perils. Of course the youthful hero was taken by the hand by the Wardens of the Synagogue, and for several years he was maintained and educated at the public expense. Whether he showed subsequently any gratitude for the benefits he received from the congregation we are unable to say; but it was not at all uncommon for individuals who had received help from the poor fund, to restore in after years to the community the sums that had been allotted to them from that source. At one time a certain person remitted more than £80 to cover charity distributed to his late father; another returned £50 which he reckoned had been expended on his mother; and a third personage forwarded back upward of £150 which he calculated his parents had cost the congregation. This gentleman rose to be a Warden of the Synagogue, and his name was, until recently, borne by his descendants in the community. These restitutions, which were necessarily effected by men who had risen from a lowly condition, were always offered in a thankful manner, and always accepted in a kindly spirit.

During the second half of the eighteenth century, the general position of the Jews in the country showed no signs of improvement. They were still debarred from political and civil rights; still the objects of social prejudices; still fettered by commercial restrictions. The privilege of being one of the twelve Jewish brokers, which was the only number allowed, was eagerly sought for, and it was always purchased by a liberal gratuity to the Lord Mayor. The sums paid on these occasions usually varied according to the elasticity of conscience, or to the wants of the " King of the City," and £2000 was frequently given by an aspiring Hebrew to be enrolled among the fortunate twelve. It is related that in the year 1774, when John Wilkes was Lord Mayor, one of the Jewish brokers happened to be lingering for some time on the point of death. That greediest and most extravagant of patriots began to speculate on the advantages to be derived from the occurrence. A rumour that Wilkes had expressed a wish for the speedy death of the Jew soon spread, and quickly reached 'Change Alley. The indignant son of the broker rushed to the presence of his Lordship to upbraid him for his unfeeling conduct. " My dear fellow," replied Wilkes, " you are mistaken ; I would rather witness the death of all the other Jew brokers than that of your father." It must be admitted that if there was little indulgence displayed toward the Jews, they were nearly always treated with strict justice. A curious instance of this will be perceived in the fact that in 1776, a woman who kept a public-house was charged at the Westminster police office with assaulting a Jew and greasing his chin with pork, for which offence the defendant was condemned to pay a fine of £10 for damages.

The Jews, though occasionally accused of petty offences, seldom rendered themselves amenable to the laws of their country for serious crimes. Jews have rarely been guilty of deeds of violence. One of the very few instances in which they are known to have spilled human blood occurred in 1771, when four Polish or German Jews were convicted of robbing the house of Mrs Hutchins at Chelsea and killing a man-servant, and were sentenced to death. A journal of the day relates that "The Recorder prefaced the sentence with a just and judicious compliment to the principal Jews, for their very laudable conduct in the course of this prosecution, and trusted no person would ignorantly stigmatise a whole nation for the villanies of a few, to bring whom to justice they had done everything they consistently could." It is to be hoped that the audience profited by the liberality of the words of the judge, who displayed at the same time charity and knowledge of human nature. The Jews were ordinarily very well behaved and orderly, but it was not surprising that among the arrivals from foreign Ghettos, some black sheep—such as exist in every community—should be found. On the Sabbath prior to the execution, an anathema (Herem) was pronounced at the Synagogue in Duke's Place against the criminals. The sentence was carried out at Tyburn on the 9th December 1771.

The Synagogue authorities of the Portuguese Congregation usually carefully avoided any conflict with the constituted authorities of the country. But of course there were exceptions. Hence, in the year 1772, a warrant was issued by the Lord Mayor to constrain the Portuguese community to maintain an individual named Uzily. This fellow, who was an incorrigible vagabond, had been refused relief by his own people, and he rendered at the Mansion House an exaggerated account of the privations he was enduring through the hardheartedness of the Jews. The *Mahamad* declined to obey the mandate of the Lord Mayor, and at once submitted a case to leading counsel. The important points on which legal opinion was solicited were the following:—1st. Whether the Jews were compelled to maintain their poor? 2d. Whether the Lord Mayor had any jurisdiction in the matter? 3d. Whether the parish could constrain the Jews to pay for the support of their paupers? All these points were answered in a manner absolutely favourable to the Synagogue authorities, and so high an authority as Mr Attorney-General Thurlow, who afterwards became the celebrated Lord Chancellor Thurlow, expressed himself thus on the question. " I am of opinion that the poor of whatever nation or religion must be maintained by the officers of the parish, where they are found, and that no other person is compellable to relieve them, except under especial circumstances, which make no part of this case." This view was also supported by another eminent authority, Mr Dunning the late Solicitor General, who stated "That the people of the Jewish nation have time out of mind had a Synagogue in the Parish of St Botolph, and paid a poor rate of £30 per annum, and that the Wardens or Elders of the Synagogue were by no means whatsoever compelled to maintain their poor." These opinions, however important they may have proved to the Jews at large, did not satisfy Uzily, for that enterprising individual once more summoned the Wardens before the Lord Mayor. That magistrate at once dismissed the case, but he recommended to the attorney representing the defendants to assist the plaintiff, if his clients could conscientiously do so. Eventually Uzily became penitent and submissive, and having publicly entreated to be pardoned by the *Mahamad*, he was placed on the roll of the Zedaka or poor fund.

Then again in 1777, the vestry clerk of Cree Church summoned the Wardens of the Synagogue for the payment of church rates. The claim was resisted. The Wardens appeared before the Vestry, accompanied by Mr Constable, their "man of letters" or attorney, and pleaded exemption. The Wardens exhibited strong opinions in their favour from several leading counsel, and at the request of the Vestry the former undertook to forward to the Vestry copies thereof for their consideration. The case of the Synagogue appeared to be good as against the Church, for no more seems to have been heard of the matter. The Jews had occasion not unfrequently to attend the Lord Mayor's Court; and as an acknowledgment of the patient hearing bestowed on their cases, and perhaps as a sense of gratitude for favours to come, the Portuguese Congregation were wont to present to the first magistrate of the city an annual gift of fifty guineas. This practice was continued till 1780, when, owing to the unfavourable condition of the finances of the Synagogue, the last deputation that waited upon his Lordship for that purpose, politely intimated to him the inability of their constituents to keep up the time-honoured custom after that year.

CHAPTER XXIII.

A NOBLE PROSELYTE.

On the 6th and 7th of June 1780, London was at the mercy of a mob roused by religious fanaticism and maddened by fiery liquors. Calamitous scenes of conflagration, plunder and slaughter were being enacted, accompanied by frantic cries of "No Popery," "Repeal the Bill," "Lord George Gordon." The prisons of Newgate and Clerkenwell were broken open, and all the prisoners therein confined let loose upon society. To pillage, to burn, to drink, to ravage, appeared to be the aims of the drunken representatives of the Protestant interest. Many houses were destroyed, among which were the residences of Sir John Fielding, the magistrate, and Lord Mansfield, with all their valuable furniture, paintings and papers. Catholic chapels were razed to the ground, and persons of that faith were in fears for their lives. Mr Langdale, a Papist and distiller, saw his premises set on fire whilst his stock was running in the gutters, and many of the rioters literally drowned themselves in gin. Members of both houses of parliament were personally ill-used, their carriages were stopped, they were constrained to alight amid the jeers and gibes of the mob, and they had to seek safety in flight. The loss of property was enormous, and at one period there were no fewer than thirty-seven conflagrations casting lambent flames towards the lurid sky. At last the government resolved to take energetic measures to restore peace and order in the capital. Troops had been summoned from the country, and magistrates were found to perform their duty. The night of Wednesday, the 7th June, presented a terrific sight. Crowds of ruffians, armed with sledge hammers and bludgeons and infuriated by gin, threw themselves on the gates of the Bank of England, to be shot down by the muskets of the soldiery. The gleam of distant fires, the cries of the countless rabble, the groans of the wounded and dying, the roar of the volleys of musketry, rendered the scene dreadful and never to be forgotten. The mob was everywhere defeated, with considerable slaughter. On the following morning London presented the appearance of a city stormed and sacked. Several partial riots again occurred on that day, but the rioters were easily dispersed by the military. On the same day the cause of all this evil, the ill-advised author of all this mischief, Lord George Gordon, was arrested in his house in Welbeck Street; and after being conducted to the Horse Guards, he was taken in the evening to the Tower, under the strongest escort then ever known to attend political prisoners.

A detailed account of the origin of the "No Popery Riots" would here be out of place, and doubtless our readers need no repetition of their history. Suffice it to say that Lord George Gordon had been elected President of the Protestant Association, a society established in Edinburgh with ramifications in all parts of England, and having for its object the protection of Protestant interests which were supposed to be in jeopardy; that Lord George Gordon determined to present a petition to the legislature for the repeal of an act passed in 1778 for relieving the Roman Catholics from some of the heavier penalties inflicted upon them formerly; that he headed a threatening procession of 60,000 petitioners to impose the will of the mob on parliament; that his inflammatory discourses aroused the passions of the multitude; that gradually many of the real Protestants who had the interests of the Church at heart, drew back, whilst the elements of disorder came forward: and finally, that notwithstanding the disavowal of the riots, printed, published, and circulated by Lord George Gordon, the thirst for plunder and bloodshed having been fairly excited in King Mob, the negligence or mistaken leniency of the government had led to the disastrous spectacles we have already adverted to. Lord George Gordon was brought up for trial by writ of Habeas Corpus on the 24th January 1781. He was charged before Lord Mansfield with levying war against the King in his realms.

The trial lasted several days and did not conclude until the 6th of February. The prisoner's counsel pleaded insanity, which plea was not exactly admitted by the jury, who nevertheless acquitted him on the score that his offence did not amount to high treason.

Much has been written on the question of Lord George Gordon's mental condition. As a member of the House of Commons, his extraordinary interruptions and unaccountable manner had afforded scope for comment; albeit his singularities in dress and appearance had furnished subjects rather for pleasantry than for serious apprehension.

Hume gravely asserts in his History of England, that this nobleman gave afterwards undoubted proofs of insanity by turning Jew. Now for a Christian to become a Jew constitutes *per se* no greater proof of madness than for a Jew to become a Christian. The border land between sanity and insanity is easily crossed over, and few can say where the exact limit lies that separates the two conditions of mind. Lord George Gordon was a religious enthusiast whose brain had been attuned to a dangerously high key. To take refuge from the doubts of one religion, divided within itself and full of uncertainties, to the bosom of another religion which is simple and homogeneous, might be considered by reflective minds rather a proof of wisdom than of folly. Conversions from the faith of the land to another faith, whose principal merit consists, or rather consisted, in its uniformity, have been justified on similar grounds, and as we think with less reason.

Lord George Gordon rigorously underwent all the rites imposed upon proselytes before he was admitted within the pale of Judaism. He was received into the Covenant of Abraham in the city of Birmingham, under the agency of Rabbi Jacob of Birmingham. Subsequently he returned to London; and having meanwhile acquired some knowledge of the Hebrew language and of Jewish ceremonies, he attended the Hambro Synagogue. He was there called to the Law and honoured with a *Meshabarach* (benediction) when he offered £100 to the Synagogue. Lord George with the restlessness that characterised him, proceeded after this to Paris, where he recklessly cast serious accusations against personages in high positions. Subsequently new proceedings were taken against him, first at the instance of Mons. Barthelemy, the French Chargé d' Affaires, for a libellous publication against the Queen of France in connection with Count Cagliostro; and secondly, at the suit of the Attorney-General, for a libel entitled the "Prisoner's Petition," reflecting on the administration of justice in this country. He was tried in the Court of Queen's Bench before Justice Buller, and found guilty on both counts. Judgment was reserved, and the prisoner being allowed to remain at large, he proceeded to Holland. Thence he went to Birmingham, where he lived as a Jew until he was apprehended in December 1787, at the house of an Israelite. When Justice Ashurst pronounced judgment, he passed severe strictures on the prisoner whom the judge "wished had made a better use of his reading the Bible, and had not used the Scripture style for the wicked purpose of promoting mutiny and sedition, and of undermining the laws of his country." The sentence of the court was very heavy. The prisoner was condemned to three years' imprisonment in Newgate for the "Prisoner's Petition," and to two years imprisonment and a fine of £500 for the libel on the Queen of France; and further at the expiration of his time, he was ordered to enter into a bond for £10,000 to keep the peace, and to find two sureties for £2500 each.

Notwithstanding the weight of the condemnation, Lord George Gordon did not appear to modify his religious views. He remained as irrepressible as ever; from his prison he sent forth handbills full of Scriptural quotations to be distributed; and he applied texts from Scripture to the state of the King. This greatly exasperated the prison authorities, and the Governor threatened him with removal to a worse cell if he did not alter his conduct; so the circulation of the handbills had to be stopped.

This singular proselyte was very regular in his Jewish observances in prison. Every morning he was seen with phylacteries between his eyes and opposite to his heart; every Saturday he held public service in his room with the aid of ten Polish Jews. His Saturday's bread was baked *more Judaico;* he ate Jewish meat; he drank Jewish wine. On his prison wall were inscribed the ten commandments;

by their side hung a bag containing his *Talith* and his phylacteries. How the gloomy years of imprisonment passed, Heaven knows! It must have been a long and dreary time for the prisoner, and only the belief that he was suffering a political and religious martyrdom could have given him the strength of living through it.

At last, on the 18th January 1793, the prisoner's sentence had expired; but before he could obtain his freedom he had to satisfy the court as to his future good behaviour. He entered the court, accompanied by his keeper and by several foreign Jews, two of whom were to be bail for him. Lord George Gordon wore a huge patriarchal beard, and carried a large slouched hat on his head. He was ordered to uncover his head, which he declined to do. The crier took off the large slouched hat, whereupon the prisoner desired the court to observe that his hat had been removed by violence. He then deliberately drew from his pocket a white cap, which he placed upon his head, tying a handkerchief around it. After this he produced a document which he laid before the court, which he said was his petition. At the same time he apologised for appearing with his head covered agreeably to the custom of the Jews. He meant no disrespect to the court, but his conduct arose from tenderness of conscience, since he had entered into the "holy covenant of circumcision." The petition was read by the officers of the court, and a great portion of it consisted of arguments drawn from Jewish sources in favour of appearing covered before all men. Lord George Gordon then entered into some details with respect to his fortune, from which it results that he possessed an annuity of £500 a year, and that his brother, the Duke of Gordon, had advanced him £500 to pay his fine. In conclusion he furnished the names of two Polish Jews who had agreed to become bail for him. Unfortunately for the petitioner these men were penniless, and could not be held responsible for any one. The Attorney-General objected to them, and an affidavit was read of their incompetence. So Lord George Gordon had to return to his prison cell. He did not long survive this disappointment. No doubt his position preyed upon his mind; he was attacked by fever, and died in November 1793, at the age of forty-three. He had studied literature in his early days, and in his varied political writings his arguments were usually sound; his language was animated, his diction correct and classical, and occasionally he showed flashes of genuine humour. Personally he is said to have been exceedingly amiable, notwithstanding the libellous publications he issued; and his conduct to his fellow-prisoners was very humane and even beneficent. A contemporary periodical says that "his last moments were embittered by the knowledge that he could not be buried among the Jews, to whose religion he was warmly attached." Lord George Gordon, we must add, does not lie in a Jewish "House of Life," as a Jewish cemetery is called; he was interred in St James' burial-ground in the Hampstead Road.

The Christian writer, whose words we quote above, probably thought with many others, how little the Jews had done for one who had become a zealous convert to their faith. But it was not callousness that caused the Jews with all their wealth to allow Lord George Gordon to perish in prison for want of two miserable bail. We have already observed the unwillingness of Jews to receive proselytes. This to a great extent arose from some real or fancied engagement contracted by the early Jewish immigrants at the time of Cromwell or of Charles II., when they settled in this country. The Jews invariably discouraged proselytes, in proof of which we will cite one instance of many we could record. We will premise that the Portuguese Jews then formed the leading congregation in this country, and that the Germans usually followed the example of the senior Synagogue. A certain Luis da Costa, a native of Portugal, appeared in 1789 before the Wardens of the Bevis Marks Synagogue, stating that he was desirous of being admitted to the Covenant of Abraham; that he had sailed in a ship from Bordeaux to Amsterdam for that purpose; that the vessel had been wrecked off Dover, and he begged to be dispatched to Amsterdam to fulfil the longings of his heart. The Wardens of the Portuguese Congregation did not deem fit to comply with this request, on the ground that they were not sure his ancestors had belonged to Israel. How much stronger would the same reasons have militated against the reception into Judaism of Lord George Gordon! We also must take into consideration motives of worldly prudence, for the conversion to Judaism of an English nobleman, the brother of an English duke, if openly abetted and avowed by the Jews, might have aroused popular vengeance against that race, and cries of "No Judaism" might have proved as disastrous to those against whom they were directed as cries of "No Popery" had been to the Catholics.

CHAPTER XXIV.

A NEW IMMIGRATION—ECCLESIASTICAL LOSSES AND OFFICIAL CHANGES—CEMETERIES AND BODY-SNATCHING.

Though the position of the Jews in England was not in itself especially brilliant or enviable, Great Britain was to the Jewish race a very Garden of Eden as compared with many other countries. What if they possessed neither civil nor political rights; if they were usually regarded by the mass of the population with a mixture of contempt, suspicion and aversion; if they had to endure slights and rebuffs with smiling lip and cringing step! At least they enjoyed under the British flag a certain amount of material prosperity. Their lives and limbs and property were safe; and above all they were permitted openly to follow the practices of their religion and to worship the Lord of their forefathers.

Painful evidence of the perils incurred by the Jews abroad was given in June 1781. One day the Portuguese Congregation received news from the Jews of Portsmouth of the arrival of a number of destitute families. The siege of Gibraltar was raging at that period, and though one of the Royal Princes of France was exchanging polite notes with Gen. Elliott, the English commander, and the besieger had chivalrously forwarded to the chief of the besieged, presents of game and fruits, the ill-starred Jews had suffered severely. Happily many families succeeded in effecting their escape, and reaching some neutral ships. Of the hair-breadth escapes and romantic adventures encountered by the fugitive Jews much has been said, and it is difficult in these traditional tales to separate actual facts from legendary amplifications. It is traditionally recorded that a ship containing some Hebrew families was captured by an armed privateer, that the Jews found themselves cast on the shores of Ireland utterly wanting the common necessaries of life; that the

Irish gave the Jews a warm and hospitable reception, and provided them with all they needed; that some Roman Catholic priests most strenuously helped the hapless Israelites by word and deed, contributing by their influence and example to the generous treatment of the scarcely welcome strangers; and that the Jews, after being liberally supplied with food and raiment, were assisted on to London by different routes. The Jews of Portsmouth were under some obligation to the Bevis Marks Synagogue, which had granted them shortly before £50 to aid them in building a new house of prayer. The Jews of Portsmouth, perhaps inspired by gratitude, treated the immigrants from Gibraltar with great kindness, and furnished them with sufficient funds to enable them to reach London. The Scrolls of the Law had been saved from the two Synagogues of the beleaguered fortress, to the great personal risk of the devout Jews, who had to cross some open spaces exposed to the fiery globes hurled against the impregnable rock, in the midst of a severe bombardment.

Among the names of the refugees we find those of Ben Oliel, Ben Susan, Almosnino, and others, since well and honourably known in the Portuguese Community. Haham Almosnino was the Chief Rabbi of Gibraltar. In London he was regarded with great consideration for his learning and piety; and his descendants became zealous, efficient, and respected officers of the congregation.

As time elapses, the laws and regulations of every community need remodelling, or at least modifying, according to the requirements of the period. In 1783 a committee was appointed to consider what alterations might be advisable in the *Askamoth* or *Laws* of the Portuguese Congregation, and a report, suggesting a number of amendments, was presented to the Elders in the spring of 1784. The proposed amendments were discussed seriatim, and many slight modifications were introduced in the regulations governing the Congregation. But the fundamental laws remained untouched. The unity of the Synagogue was strongly insisted upon, and only a majority of two-thirds of the Yehidim, or members, were allowed to order the erection of another Portuguese house of prayer. Stringent provisions again were made for raising the necessary funds, the former system of *finta*, or tax, and an impost or per centage on business carried out on commission, being retained. The powers of the Elders were somewhat enlarged, and when each member of the congregation attained to the dignity of elder, he was required to take a solemn oath before the doors of the Ark, where are deposited the Scrolls of the Pentateuch, to administer the laws of the congregation fairly and impartially, without fear and without favour, and to respect the usages of the community. We have more than once adverted to the objects of these laws, which were promulgated at a time when the fortunes of Israel were in a precarious state, and when stringent enactments became necessarily conservative measures. We are bound to state that these ordinances were not always kept in consonance with the spirit of the times, and that altered circumstances and the march of events were taken too little into account in the re-constitution of such laws.

It will be seen that the constitution of the Portuguese Jews, like that of the German Jews, was a pure oligarchy, the real power resting in the Elders, while the Wardens were little more than an administrative body. Of late years, however, with the spread of popular ideas, the Elders have of their own accord resigned some of their functions to the members of the congregation. The principle of popular election has been recognised in most institutions in this country, and it has been admitted in the Synagogue. The Spanish and Portuguese Jews, one of the most conservative bodies in England, have vested the appointment of their Wardens and treasurer in the hands of the members, and as these officials become *ipso facto* Elders of the Synagogue, it necessarily follows that the ratepayers practically become the constituents of the Elders. Among the German Jews, also, the members choose their own honorary officials; and at present the majority of contributors to a Synagogue may exercise a fair share of influence directly or indirectly in its government.

At one period the Portuguese Synagogue was deprived by death of several of its religious officials, who died within a few months of each other. The first to depart was Haham Moses Cohen de Azevedo, much respected for his piety and esteemed for his humility and modesty; qualities not always to be perceived in ecclesiastical authorities. His death occurred in September 1784. Haham de Azevedo had desired to be interred at the cost of his family, who were prepared to incur the outlay, albeit the very moderate stipend which the deceased had received had prevented him from making any provision for his wife and children. But the Elders decided that the funeral of their late spiritual chief should be performed at the public expense, and that all customary honours should be paid to his memory. The last earthly remains of the Haham were carried into the Synagogue, followed by the Wardens, Elders, and members of the Beth Din, attired in deep mourning. The Synagogue was lighted up by numerous wax tapers, and solemn hymns were chaunted. The bier was carried from the Synagogue to the hearse by the Wardens, whilst the loud tones of the *Shophar* or ram's horn resounded far and wide. In the cemetery, again, mournful dirges were intoned, with a prayer recited on the Day of Atonement (*Vayabor*), and the coffin was carried from the mortuary hall to its last resting place by the Wardens, accompanied by ringing strains from the ram's horn or cornet. Then a sermon was delivered in affecting accents, and during the Escaba or prayer for the dead, the late Rabbi received the glowing and hyperbolical titles customary on such occasions. The ceremony was most impressive and solemn, and the multitude must have been greatly affected. On the 27th of the following October died Haham I. Almosnino, of whom we have already spoken. Though this gentleman held no recognised place in the congregation, he appears to have been much esteemed; his opinion was frequently sought on religious questions, and he was treated with as much respect as if he had been Haham, or ecclesiastical head, of the community. He was followed on the 3rd of January 1785, by Israel David de Crasto, who was a Minister and Dayan—member of the ecclesiastical tribunal—and on the 26th January, by Rabbi Benjamin Dias Lorenço, another Dayan and a teacher in the schools. Public honours were paid to all these Hahamim, who had been of unblemished lives, and suitable pensions were granted to their widows.

In the year 1786 Eliau Lopes Pereira, who had for some years creditably filled the position of Secretary or " Chancellor" to the Congregation, resigned his functions. Eliau Lopes Pereira was descended from an ancient family, a member of which had received the title of Baron d'Aguilar. Mr Lopes Pereira, on his inheriting a considerable property from a relative, wrote a graceful letter to the Wardens saying that he no longer considered himself justified in accepting from the Congregation emoluments that might be of more service to another member. The "ex-Chancellor" became then an honorary officer in his Synagogue, in due course serving the offices of treasurer and Warden. It may be noted that Mr Lopes Pereira was in 1788 a colleague in the Mahamad of Mr Abraham Israel Ricardo, the father of David Ricardo, the financier and political economist, and grandfather of Mr Ricardo, the Member for Stoke-upon-Trent. At his death, Mr Lopes Pereira bequeathed a legacy of £200 to the Synagogue, the interest of which was to be distributed on certain occasions. This gentleman was succeeded as "Chancellor" by Daniel de Castro, who faithfully discharged his trust in the Congregation for many years.

Towards the end of last century, the Jews of London were exposed to one source of anxiety, which happily their descendants at this period do not experience. Body-snatching was then practised to an alarming extent; the grave was nightly made to give up its dead, and no sect and no place were secure from the operations of miscreants who dragged from their long rest the last remains of humanity, to convert them into so many gold pieces. The Jews, who feel a great veneration for the dead, took various measures against this desecration. The Portuguese Jews, when they opened their new burial ground, proposed a variety of schemes to ensure safety to all that was left on earth of those they had loved. First, it was designed to heighten the walls of the cemetery and to protect the tombs by a kind of *chevaux de frise*. These plans were dismissed as expensive and impracticable; and heavy stones weighing a ton each were placed over the graves. At one time it was resolved to fill up the spaces between the graves by blocks of stone equally heavy, and lying close together, so that there should be no room to introduce any power of leverage. Eventually the sacred contents of the "House of Life" were entrusted to watchmen.

Several persons, both Jews and Christians, were engaged for this duty. A wooden house moving on wheels and resembling a watch-tower was constructed, and thence a Jew and a Christian were conjointly to perform night duties. The watchmen were to be provided with a fireplace to warm themselves in the long, dreary, winter nights, with a blunderbuss to frighten away graveyard robbers, and bells to summon assistance. Subsequently, in 1804, the watchman was ordered to call out the time every half-hour. In the new cemetery, inaugurated in 1786, no trees were to be planted near the walls, no strangers were to be permitted to enter within the precincts under any pretence whatsoever, and every morning each tomb was to be examined separately to ascertain whether any attempts had been made to tamper with it. It is said that before these measures had been adopted, some coffins appeared to have been disturbed in their places, and some bodies displayed marks of violence. When the practice of hasty burial is taken into account, and the fact is considered that in 1779 the Portuguese authorities ordered that " to conform with the customs of the country, no interment should take place *until* twenty-four hours after death, unless on special grounds," a horrid cause for these appearances will at once suggest itself to the mind of the reflecting reader. To speak more plainly, the fearful consequences of premature burials, far more to be dreaded than the acts of body-snatchers, seem to have been wilfully ignored by the Jews of the 18th century. Who can tell now how many victims were sacrificed at the shrine of an antiquated, superstitious usage! And how many wretched beings may have perished in the agonies of suffocation, in the injuries suffered in their desperate though vain attempts to release themselves from their narrow and dreadful prison!

Among the German congregations a strict watch was established for the same purpose. A law was passed in Duke's Place Congregation to the effect that all members between eighteen and seventy years of age should in rotation perform the pious duty of protecting the dead, three members acting together. They might, however, provide substitutes; and it is not unreasonable to suppose that, judging from the ordinary standard of human nature, substitutes must have been in great demand.

CHAPTER XXV.

CONVERSIONS.

That in former times a certain number of Jews of intelligence and note left the Synagogue for the Church, is a fact which, however painful it may be to Jewish ears, must be held to be historically true. No amount of ostrich-like holding of heads in the sand, and closing of eyes to what is palpable to the rest of the world, can alter stern reality. Instead of evading a difficulty or endeavouring to pass it over in silence, it is preferable to grasp it manfully, and to discuss it calmly and impartially, employing reason instead of prejudice, and logic instead of abuse.

The apparent process through which one form of religious belief is gradually changed for another form of religious belief, has perhaps never been more vividly described than by an eminent Christian ecclesiastic in his "Apologia," which forms a substantial defence for his leaving the Established Church in favour of the Church of Rome. We will venture to say that when once the element of mystery is admitted as forming part of a creed, and indeed its very essence, reason ceases to exercise its functions, and the human mind becomes ready to accept any dogma that would not bear the process of ratiocination. Into the sincerity of the converts from the Law of Moses to the dispensation of Jesus of Nazareth, we will not undertake to inquire. A man is only bound to answer to his Maker for his religious creed, and no other man, be he rabbi or bishop, has a right to call him to account on matters of faith. While we decline, therefore, to examine this question from a theological point of view, we will lay before our readers a variety of motives and circumstances of a purely temporal nature that may account for these conversions from Judaism, and which motives must in any case have exercised a powerful influence in causing such results.

By far the greatest number of these changes of creed, or at all events of outward form of worship, were effected during the last quarter of the eighteenth century, and the first quarter of the present century. This is explicable from the general position of the Jews in Great Britain during the periods of transition. With the principal features of that position we have already made our readers familiar. What the authorities of the oldest Synagogue in London thought on the subject we can ascertain from the document we shall now bring forward. The Jews of Rome had addressed a communication to their brethren of Bevis Marks as to the status of the latter in this country; and the following is a translation of the reply forwarded to Messieurs Tranquillo del Monte and Salomone Ambron of Rome, under date of the 14th August 1787. " The privileges of the Jews in this country must not serve as a rule for their privileges in other countries, as the government is very different. Where sovereigns are absolute, the Jews may enjoy advantages to a greater or lesser extent; but in this kingdom, even if his Majesty wished to favour them, he could not do so without the consent of Parliament, consisting of more than 500 or 600 Nobles and Commons. This makes it very difficult to obtain the privileges we need, and which would be very useful to us. The only privileges enjoyed by our nation are equal to all those enjoyed abroad, and these consist of the free exercise of our religion, and the security of our property, which any one may possess without fear of king or government."

The Jews of this period knew their position, and, we believe, were not altogether discontented with it. Probably the bulk of them thought little on the matter, or considered it was the lot of Israel to suffer, and bore their fate with resignation; or they contrasted their situation with that of many of their brethren abroad, and were thankful. But in all communities there are men of keen feelings, of restless energy, of ambitious minds, and withal, of weak convictions. To these individuals, the condition of a Jew entailed continual humiliations, disappointments, and miseries. To remain on a dead level with those around them, hopeless of ever soaring higher in the social sphere, must have proved gall and wormwood to many Israelites in olden days. The mart, the exchange, the Synagogue, the domestic circle, did not suffice for their aspirations. Gold, always the pursuit of gold! And what availed their wealth when their sordid occupations were crowned with success? Their race, their religion, were insurmountable barriers frowning down against all hope of worldly advancement. The wealthy Jew was unable to serve his country, for the Senate was to him a dreamland altogether beyond his reach; the magistracy would not be contaminated by his presence; all political, civil, and municipal offices were strictly closed against him, and even society looked at him askance, and with some occasional exceptions, kept him at arm's length. Then what could he do with his sons? A university education was as unattainable as if they had been Hottentots; the army would disdain to admit Israelites within its ranks; the bar carefully excluded them; and a father could not even with safety settle upon his children landed estates. The only liberal profession they were permitted to follow was that of medicine. When a proficiency in that art had been acquired at great disadvantage, the usual difficulty stared the Jewish physician in the face. The hospitals would not open their wards to him; Christian patients would not consult him; public offices were out of the question; and Jewish young men were driven to tender their services gratuitously, or at a paltry pittance, to the authorities of their own community, merely to practise their profession.

All these difficulties and restrictions arose from one cause, one solitary cause, and one so easily removable! A tempting voice whispered a word into the ear of the Jew, a word that contained a sovereign remedy against all his vexations, all his heart-burnings. Baptism was the cure of all his moral ailments. Baptism promised to the rich the realisation of his ambitious dreams; place, honour, power, social consideration; to the poor it promised loaves and fishes for the present, and sufficient provision for the future. To both rich and poor it offered—precious boon—eternal salvation! Prosperity in this world; heaven in the next world. Assuredly a tempting bait. True, the gentlemen who embraced this opportunity of satisfying their desires, or their needs, most probably placed greater reliance on the material than on the spiritual advantages to be gained by their conversions; still it was desirable to be able to throw a sop to their conscience if it happened to cry out occasionally. After all, what had they to renounce to win these brilliant benefits? It was easy to cast off the forms of a religion that hung loosely enough around them; and a long time had elapsed since they had prayed with heartfelt fervour to the Lord of Israel. To break off early associations and memories, and feelings imbued with their mothers' milk, may have caused some pangs in the minds of the Neophytes; and the word apostate has an ugly sound. Sophistry may have offered a variety of excuses for their conduct, and gratified desires go far towards allaying scruples of conscience; *but we do not envy their death-beds.* Many a convert during his lifetime has rested his aching head on an uneasy couch of luxury. Some men are cast in a delicate mould; and when the strong passions that led them away had calmed down, and the earthly prospects that dazzled them had ceased to appear in so brilliant a light, these men must have been painfully aroused by the still small voice which rose reproachfully within their hearts. Many a deserter from Judaism in his last moments would have given all he possessed to have recalled that one step; alas! it was too late.

Conversions from the Synagogue to the Church, as our readers have perceived, occurred more frequently among the higher class of the Sephardi Jews than among a similar class of the Ashkenazim. The reason can be easily explained by a reference to the characteristics marking these two sections of English Jews, and to which we have already adverted. It were needless and invidious to say more on the subject. We will only say that the Germans, retaining some of the traits distinguishing the natives of their ancient fatherland, were more plodding, more steady, more earnest of purpose, and less ambitious than their Portuguese co-religionists of those days. The warehouse, the domestic fireside, the Synagogue, were enough to fill their minds:

accustomed to trade and to pray, their lives were absorbed by these two pursuits. And as long as they were able to advance their material interests and to worship the Lord of their forefathers, they cared for little else. Gradually the German Jews rose to higher aspirations, and they equalled in time, if they did not surpass, the mental achievements of the Portuguese. Meanwhile the former escaped the temptations to which some of the latter had succumbed. When the Jews of Teutonic descent had awakened to a new life, and had attained to the amount of culture necessary for them to shine in the Senate, the forum, or the magistracy, the barriers of intolerance that had so long excluded their race from occupying in the world the position due to their brain power, had crumbled to pieces before the light of advancing civilisation, and the Jews were enabled to follow a multitude of new paths without forsaking their religion.

Worldly considerations were not the only temptations to which Jews were exposed, speaking from a religious point of view. Another influence, sometimes even more powerful, would occasionally exercise an almost irresistible effect! The Jews of England lived apart from their fellow-subjects: nevertheless they had eyes and ears, and they were not insensible to the blandishments of beauty. The Jews have ever enjoyed the reputation of being admirers of the fair sex. Many a Samson became an easy prey to many a Delilah. The golden tresses, the sapphire eyes, the soft voices of the fair daughters of Albion did more to draw followers from the Synagogue to the Church than is usually imagined. Nor did lovely English girls disdain the considerable fortunes and dark complexions of the Jews, more especially of those of Sephardic origin. Christian children by Christian mothers were too common in the Portuguese community; the offspring adopted their mothers' faith and surname, and thus many an ancient family and great accumulated wealth have been lost to Judaism. Occasionally these descendants of Jews know perfectly well their origin, and live in friendly intercourse with professing Jews; and at other times the former disappear in the masses of population in this country, and it becomes impossible to trace their future course.

Another source of losses to the Jewish community, though to a minor degree, may be traced to the practice of sending Jewish children to Christian schools, especially to public schools. The effect of surrounding influences on children is well known. The continual allusions to Christianity, the religious observances of that faith, and sometimes the active conversionist zeal of some teacher or fellow-pupil, implant seeds that bring their fruition some day, if they do not win at once a stray sheep into the fold. We might point to several cases of secession from Judaism from this cause; and among others we might mention the instance of the family of an eminent member of the leading German Synagogue, who were lost to their ancient race from his boys being sent to Charterhouse School. Much unhappiness had been entailed on parents by such occurrences. The attention of Jewish fathers has often been called to the necessity of providing for their children Jewish training in Jewish schools. Happily this is now easily attainable, and perfectly compatible with complete secular and even scientific instruction.

So far we have only spoken of the external influences that drew members of the Synagogue into the pale of the Church. Strong as were these influences, there were others within the community itself that acted as their allies. Attractive force towards the one side, repulsive force from the other, formed a dangerous combination. The latter arose from the very nature of Jewish institutions. There is a double and constant peril in voluntary associations. If their members are not bound together by a fixed and rigid code of rules, a lack of cohesion will arise that may end in dissolution. If the rules are too fixed and too rigid, many members will not accept the trammels they impose, and disruption is threatened. Among the Jews in general, and the Sephardic Congregation in particular, to avoid the Scylla of laxity, wreck was made against the Charybdis of over-strictness. The Elders of that congregation were usually benevolent men leaning to the side of mercy. But they strictly exacted full and uncompromising obedience. Every offence of a member would be condoned, provided he made humble submission. Rebellion was an unpardonable sin. The strict letter of a conventional law was injudiciously enforced on occasions when very moderate relaxation would have prevented the loss of valuable members. Certain laws or rules not of a religious character, but of congregational polity, probably necessary and wise when they had been enacted, might advantageously have been modified when from change of circumstances they had ceased to be prudent or beneficial. Yet blind resistance was the practice to all demands for slight emendations or personal concessions. *Non possumus* was the only reply to such applications. And thus it happened that members of that congregation, whose descendants now might be gracing the councils of their race, have either seceded entirely from Judaism, or cast their tents independently elsewhere.

We have it also from undoubted contemporary authorities, from men well affected towards their brethren, that the services in the principal Synagogues were ordinarily conducted in a manner not at all likely to inspire feelings of devotion. Some of the congregants were addicted to chattering and laughing, to the annoyance of those more earnestly disposed; the readers said the prayers in a listless and indifferent manner; no choirs existed, and charity boys screamed—we cannot say sang—the sacred melodies in discordant strains, entailing acute sufferings on those who unfortunately possessed musical ears. Moreover, a long time was spent in the tedious repetition of the *Meshaberach* and mutual compliments, which practice tended to render the service tedious and wearisome. It may be observed that these are trivial matters. We do not think so. Whatever impairs the solemnity of a religious service does considerable harm, for it discourages the attendance of members whose religious ties become weakened, their interest in communal affairs is slackened, and their withdrawal from the congregation is more easily effected. We must not omit to take into account the private prejudices and crotchets of members of various congregations, which could not easily be satisfied. In all communities there are obstinate, impracticable, and narrow-minded men, who conceive mortal offence if their every desire is not instantly gratified. In voluntary associations, in such cases, refusal on the one side is followed by secession on the other; albeit such men are no loss to any religious community. These individuals are ready to change their belief as they would their coats; they usually are destitute of real faith, and they are guided in their outward form of worship by pure expediency and convenience. We have present before our eyes instances of this nature to which we will recur more fully in another paper; we will merely observe that about a century ago a member of one of the first families in the Portuguese Synagogue resigned his seat in the Synagogue only because he could not obtain a particular *mitzvah* or honour on the day of the Fast of Expiation.

We have above endeavoured to place before our readers the principal causes that have conduced to the loss from the Jewish community of a certain number of persons of that race. Though it is impossible to trace the particular motives that prevailed in each instance, we have striven to show that in the great majority of cases, these conversions were not the result of researches after religious truths, nor were they likely to shake the belief of those who have followed faithfully the dispensation of Moses.

In our days, when happily some of the causes we have enumerated are no longer at work, conversions of another and coarser type have become more frequent in this country. Powerfully organised associations, with extensive pecuniary resources at their command, send out paid officials to chase Jewish souls, and to bring them within the pale of imaginary salvation. Their instruments, chiefly apostates themselves, interpose between parents and children, and by ingenious devices, destroy the peace of families, in order to produce triumphantly at head-quarters some poor simpleton or child said to have been converted. These organisations, which all right-minded Christians condemn, have their field of operations principally among the uneducated children of the indigent and among destitute foreigners. Their salaried agents do not disdain the use of bribery and misrepresentations, and with keen mockery call their victims " Inquirers after truth." After truth indeed! Empty stomachs and half-clad bodies know better the objects of their inquiries. Ignorance and poverty brought face to face with plenty, and with a picture of comparatively brilliant prospects held before their eyes appear so easily persuaded, so thoroughly convinced, as to render it almost a pity to destroy their delusion. Yet frequently some of these dupes have conscience enough, or feeling enough left, to reconsider their position, and then often they slip away from the grasp of their would-be saviours. Thus the gains of societies' conversion are reduced to only a small figure, and their operations are supported by grossly exaggerated reports and misrepresentations. Sometimes the results are somewhat amusing. It is related that once a poor Polish Jew, who had been induced to " inquire after truth," and whose conviction had been facilitated by advances during " the inquiry " amounting to a hundred crowns, was eventually baptized. Subsequently an old acquaintance whom he met asked him whether he had discovered the truth. He had discovered an important truth, said the neophyte; he had ascertained that the old religion was just worth one hundred crowns more than the new religion, since on his making the exchange, he had received that balance. With that sum the convert soon after disappeared. We need not say that such black sheep are no loss to any flock.

In conclusion, with all deference to that very large majority of her Majesty's subjects who profess the creed of Jesus of Nazareth, we make bold to assert that had the position of affairs been reversed — had Christians dwelt in a Jewish country, subject to similar external temptations and internal influences—the Church would have yielded to the Synagogue a goodly number indeed of proselytes. That the Jews, notwithstanding all the defections suffered by the community, are still increasing in numbers, is a proof of the vitality of their race, and of the staunch adherence of the bulk of this people to their ancient form of worship.

CHAPTER XXVI.

THE PURIM RIOTS—THE BERNAL FAMILY.

In our preceding chapter we dealt generally with the subject of conversions, pointing out the principal causes that formerly powerfully influenced the Jews in forsaking the law of Moses for the dispensation of Jesus. We shall now, and again hereafter in the course of our narrative, place before our readers such particular cases of conversion as are remarkable either for their accompanying circumstances or because they form landmarks in the annals of families of note, ranking with the aristocracy of wealth or intellect of the United Kingdom.

It was once the custom among the Jews, during the feast of Purim, for unruly boys and silly men to show their reprobation of Haman's conduct by loudly knocking against the Synagogue benches during the celebration of the service. This absurd and irreverent usage had ever been opposed by the congregational authorities; and in March 1783, immediately before Purim, they issued strict orders forbidding such puerile manifestations. Nevertheless certain members of the congregation, either from mere spirit of mischief or from love of opposition, insisted on Purim eve on following a custom more honoured in the breach than in the observance. Whereupon on the morrow the ruling powers secured the attendance of a couple of constables, who, on the attempted repetition of such discreditable behaviour, very quickly removed the offenders. The *Mahamad* summoned before them the delinquents, who all, with a solitary exception, either appeared or sent complete apologies. A few of the parties were condemned to pay slight fines for their disobedience, others were altogether forgiven, and thus the matter ended so far as the public was concerned, albeit the Purim riots formed for some time a favourite topic of conversation with communal gossips. Isaac Mendes Furtado was the only individual who had rebelled against the Synagogue authorities. Furtado was a man who had acquired some wealth, which, according to his views, conferred upon him the right of treating disrespectfully the Elders of the congregation. On more than one occasion he had behaved with marked rudenesss towards them. In the present instance, though he occupied an honorary office in the Synagogue, he was one of the most prominent among the disturbers of the peace, apparently from sheer wantonness. Isaac Mendes Furtado not only declined to appear before the *Mahamad*, but wrote an offensive and scurrilous letter, evidently the production of an arrogant, unruly spirit. He had been disturbed in his devotions by the entrance of constables in Synagogue. It was not the rioters who had outraged his feelings; it was the constables. He would separate himself from so irreligious a society. He would renounce Judaism and the promised land. After a tirade of malicious accusations against the Synagogue authorities, Furtado concluded this precious document, which was signed by himself and his wife, by the expression of his firm determination not to hold any further intercourse with members of the community.

Furtado subsequently caused the open baptism of his children; and he erected certain houses at Mile End to commemorate the glorious event, designating them Purim Place. Mrs Sarah Furtado, his wife, was however interred in the Portuguese cemetery. Furtado himself was buried in Newington Churchyard, albeit it signifies little where are laid the bones of one who, never a strict adherent to his creed, eagerly seized the first absurd and worthless excuse to quit it. An indifferent Jew is hardly likely to make a good Christian. Here we behold the spirit animating at least some of the converts from Judaism. The moving springs are too apparent: laxity of principle, exaggerated notions of self-importance, unbounded pride, and expectations of worldly advancement! But a sense of religious feeling, a sincere and profound belief in the truths of Christian dogmas, a preference of the new dispensation to the old faith from pure conviction,—in vain shall we seek for them in these neophytes!

The case of Elias Curry had a very different issue, and it

came to a pitiful end. The person who had adopted this pseudonym was a native of Portugal. He had arrived into this country in extreme youth, and had received much substantial kindness from the congregation. In his after-life ugly rumours reached the authorities of the Sephardi Jews, concerning the conduct of this individual. He was a tolerably regular attendant at Synagogue; nevertheless it was asserted that he had entered the Church. A member of the congregation took considerable pains to ascertain the truth of the reports; he searched the baptismal register of various churches; and eventually he had an interview with the Rev. Mr Green, the rector or curate of West Ham parish church. Elias Curry who, contrary to Jewish habits, had been known to indulge in fiery liquors, had been heard to boast in his cups of his new faith. Mr Green admitted readily having baptized Curry; but before the latter could be recognised as a Christian, he considered it was necessary to perform again the ceremony which had not been attended with due solemnity. The clergyman moreover regretted having given any annoyance to the Jews, and did not appear especially eager to admit this black sheep into his flock. The truth was that Elias Curry had been converted to Christianity over a bowl of punch, and the rum which it contained no doubt exercised a lively influence in changing his theological opinions. The Wardens of the Portuguese Congregation did not desire to encourage a new sect of baptized Jews, who professed to be both Jews and Christians, and who were neither; so they resolved to dismiss Elias Curry from the community. This occurred early in 1785; and in the April of that year Elias Curry wrote an insolent letter to the *Mahamad*, in which with affected contempt for that body, whom he designated, by the novel designation of " little court, or tribunal of great injustice wherein Prince Satan presides as First Lord," he took leave of those to whom he was beholden for many benefits.

For once ingratitude and want of principle met with condign punishment. Elias Curry did not prosper in his new creed. He became poor; he became unhappy; he became conscience-stricken. In 1791 the burden of remorse became more than he could bear, and his heart longed to return to his old faith and early associations. He wrote a most penitent letter to the authorities of his community entreating their forgiveness, and craving to be received back into the Synagogue. He was not satisfied with the refusal he received; he prayed again to be admitted as a proselyte, which he thought would be facilitated by his being a foreigner, and he offered in vain to make any atonement, to undergo any penance. A year after this, the Elders, who would not open their arms to Elias Curry in life, granted him six feet of ground in death. At first, indeed, they refused; but the entreaties of a relative, the tears of his mother, had their effect. Three witnesses declared that the sinner had made a solemn recantation on his death-bed, and that he departed this life a sincere Jew. The Wardens consulted the Beth Din, or ecclesiastical authorities; and eventually the wretched man was interred in a corner of the cemetery. Let us hope that this example may have served as a salutary lesson, at least for a time, among men of his class, whose eyes must have been opened to the fact that apostasy does not necessarily lead to prosperity, wealth and success.

The most important loss that occurred among the Jews at this period was the secession of some members of the Bernal family, which appears to have been induced by a variety of causes. Isaac and Jacob Israel Bernal were the sons of that Jacob Bernal who had many years before asked permission to marry a German lady, which, as may be remembered, had been somewhat reluctantly granted. These gentlemen were persons of means and character, and had realised moderate fortunes in the West India trade; albeit they did not rank among the foremost men in their congregation. Mr Isaac I. Bernal became dissatisfied at his non-election to some honorary office in the institutions of his community, and on the 5th June 1786, he wrote in strong terms to the Synagogue authorities. He had been proposed twice, he said, as a Governor of the Hebra (Burial Society), and of Heshaim (Charity School), and twice he had been rejected. He had contributed annually £40 to £50 to the Synagogue funds, and yet he had been treated with great disrespect. He felt himself called upon to resent the affront. He retired from a society where he had been so ill-treated. But, he concluded, he was born a Jew, and would continue a Jew until his death. Mr Bernal's resignation not being at once accepted, he wrote subsequently another and more peremptory letter, and finally a third letter a year afterwards. In November 1787, his resignation was admitted, though the reasons were considered insufficient. At about the same period Mr Jacob I. Bernal, too, thought it fit to address the rulers of the Synagogue in a most unseemly and overbearing manner. He compared the latter to the Portuguese Inquisition for their proficiency "in the art of torturing the sensibility of religious men." He accused them "of feeling causeless hatreds like their ancestors." He said that a similar groundless vindictive spirit existed among some of them with malignant ardour. He ended by observing that "it was a serious consolation to be liberated from wanton and unmerited insults which were aggravations of their common, miserable, abject state, and he renounced any further connection with the Jewish body." The elders naturally considered certain expressions in this document as unworthy and offensive, and erased his name from the list of the members of the Synagogue.

Thus terminated the relations between the leading members of the Bernal family and the Synagogue. The cause of their withdrawal was apparently pique; but there were other and more important reasons in the background which we abstain from laying before our readers from prudential considerations. The term employed by Mr Jacob Bernal of "our miserable, abject state," affords a key to his state of mind, and we can easily understand his desire to retire from the society of those who were placed in that unfortunate condition.

We shall now give a few details of the history of the Bernal family from the time when Isaac and Jacob Bernal left the Synagogue. Isaac Bernal, albeit his anger against the Synagogue authorities was not appeased, continued to observe strictly all Mosaic precepts. He had wedded a Christian lady who seems to have accepted the Jewish religion, and his son and his several daughters followed the creed of their forefathers. Isaac Bernal having retired from general business was induced to advance a large amount (£40,000) to an Irish nobleman, at a fair rate of interest. This nobleman soon failed to pay the interest due on his debt, which in time seriously inconvenienced Bernal, and constrained the latter to fall into arrears with tradesmen and others with whom he had dealings. He dwelt at this period in a handsome residence in Great Prescott Street, Goodman's Fields, then a desirable situation and much affected by opulent Jews. The Tenterground was a well laid out public garden, with trees, flowers, and shrubberies, and was a great place of resort for the dark-eyed daughters of Judah. Isaac Bernal's creditors became first importunate and then would wait no longer. One day the bailiffs penetrated into the precincts supposed to be an Englishman's castle, and seized all their contents, from his wife's jewels to his favourite peacocks. Bernal this time narrowly escaped personal arrest; but two or three years afterwards he was less fortunate. His friends had purchased part of his property and returned it to him. For a long period he defied the bailiffs, in his barricaded stronghold, until a traitor in the camp brought him to the Fleet. The once opulent merchant still possessed friends. He was enabled to give substantial bail, and, instead of occupying a cell in the prison, he was permitted to live within the rules of the Fleet, and took up his quarters above a shop at the corner of the Old Bailey. Years elapsed; his son went abroad endeavouring to retrieve the fortunes of the family, whilst a lawsuit against his lordly debtor, and then against his executors, for the recovery of his debt, was dragging its weary length. His brother Jacob, whose animosity against his race seems to have acquired a special bitterness, endeavoured to induce him to abandon Judaism, but in vain. Isaac Bernal and his family remained attached to their faith. Probably Jacob Bernal, who had increased his fortune, assisted his brother, and his son Ralph occasionally visited his uncle. At last Isaac Bernal obtained a verdict for a very large amount for capital, interest, and costs. But he did not live long to enjoy his restored fortunes. His son came home in an almost dying state, in time to confess to his father that he had married a Christian woman; and then father and son descended to the grave within a few days of each other. In October 1820, application was made to the Synagogue authorities, by the representatives of Isaac Bernal, for the interment of the body of the deceased in the Portuguese burial-ground. For thirty-four years he had lived apart from the

Synagogue; nevertheless the request was granted: and on payment of an unimportant sum by his relatives, Isaac Bernal was permitted to sleep by the side of his forefathers. Two of his daughters became contributing members of the Portuguese Congregation until they and most of their sisters followed the destiny of their sex, and some espoused Jews and others espoused Christians.

The future of Jacob Bernal's descendants was more brilliant, and their lives were cast into pleasant places. Jacob Bernal educated his children to Christianity, though we believe his son Ralph married a Miss Da Silva, a lady appertaining to a Portuguese Jewish family. Mr Ralph Bernal became a magistrate, a land owner, and a member of Parliament. His son, Captain Bernal, married in 1844 the heiress of Sir Thomas Osborne of Newtown Anner, Tipperary, when he assumed the surname of Osborne in addition to his own, and he is now known as Mr Bernal-Osborne.

CHAPTER XXVII.

SAMUEL MENDOZA.—THE SHECHITA.—SYNAGOGUE DIFFERENCES.

The prize-ring is not a very noble arena of contest, and pugilistic encounters do not present a refined and elevated aspect of human nature. We do not propose, however, to depict in these pictures only the highest side of Judaism. It is, on the contrary, our desire to endeavour to delineate faithfully and impartially the various phases of Anglo-Jewish life, as well as to record the most interesting or curious events in which Jews participated. We will then for a short time leave the Synagogue, the council chamber, and family annals, and descend into the prize-ring. Boxing matches were formerly exhibitions much affected by people of quality, and as much patronised by the "upper ten" as now is pigeon shooting. The average Briton of the eighteenth century was not a being endowed with exquisite sensibility, and he loved to imitate his superiors. When he saw some of the oldest names among the aristocracy, with the princely George himself, the "finest gentleman in Europe," at their head, associate on terms of intimacy with professional prize-fighters, and crowd to witness the feats of their prowess, it is not surprising that plain John Bull should look upon the champions of the noble art of self-defence as heroes to be regarded with awe and admiration.

The Jews have usually excelled more in mental than in physical pursuits, and have habitually displayed more power of brain than of sinews. But Samuel Mendoza, the pugilist, proved an exception to the rule, and he became a man of mark in his day. He had already acquired some reputation, when a match was arranged for considerable stakes between him and another hero named Humphreys. On the 18th February 1788, many thousands of people flocked to Odiham, to see the encounter, notwithstanding the inclemency of the weather; and hundreds of eager spectators paid their half guineas to gain admission within the paddock. Humphreys was seconded by Johnson, and Mendoza by Jacobs. The fight commenced at one o'clock, when betting was two to one in favour of Humphreys, who was the more experienced champion. Mendoza began with great spirit, and gradually the odds changed to his side. The superior skill of Humphreys prevailed in the end, and he planted on his adversary's jaw a heavy blow that nearly disabled him. Mendoza struggled on manfully, but blinded and exhausted, he became helpless, and yielded after half an hour's struggle. £20,000 was lost in this contest, the greater portion of which was the money of Jews. Mendoza, however, would not own himself defeated. Like Bruce when he was watching the spider, he determined to try again. With the perseverance and energy of his race he worked until he obtained greater proficiency in his art, when he challenged his old opponent. The second encounter took place at Stilton, on the 6th March 1789. A spacious amphitheatre had been erected in Mr Thornton's park, capable of accommodating 3000 spectators, and all the seats were occupied. Again Humphreys' second was Johnson, while Mendoza was supported by Captain Brown, and Sir Thomas Appryce was his umpire. After a severe struggle of an hour and a quarter the Jewish champion was declared conqueror. Times truly have changed, and manners with them! Can we imagine a country gentleman now placing his park at the disposal of a mob to revel in the spectacle of a prize fight, and an officer in the army and a baronet escorting and abetting one of the pugilists! Mendoza, we will add, flourished for a long time as a successful champion, and nearly twenty years after this period we find him, during an undecided contest, again making a fierce onslaught against his antagonist, and triumphing.

Let us now return to matters more strictly concerning the Jews. The Israelites of England must confess, that they have usually found the judges of the land perfectly ready to uphold the spiritual jurisdiction of the Jewish rabbins, and to maintain the authority of the latter among their own flock. A curious action at law was tried in 1788, which indeed differed but little from another action brought on similar grounds of late years against the Chief Rabbi of the German Congregations. In the former case, a butcher, named Rodriguez, had been repeatedly discovered selling to Jews *terefa*, or unlawfully killed meat, thus perpetrating a fraud on the conscience of his customers; a much greater offence than perpetrating a fraud on their purses. A zealous Jew named Levy summoned Rodriguez before the Sephardi Beth Din (ecclesiastical tribunal), when the offence was clearly proved, and the butcher deprived of his licence. His name was denounced in the Synagogue from the pulpit, according to the custom of the day, and Jews were forbidden from purchasing any more meat from him. Rodriguez at once took legal proceedings against Levy, asking for heavy damages; and after much litigation, Levy obtained a verdict in the Court of Common Pleas. Lord Chief Justice Loughborough, afterwards Lord Chancellor, justified completely the action of the "High Priest" (Beth Din, or ecclesiastical tribunal); which view was also confirmed by all the judges of the Common Pleas, when a motion for a new trial was moved before them. It must therefore be understood that the rabbinical heads have full control in religious questions, and that the law of England will support their authority in all matters within their competence.

We have repeatedly observed that the irregularities of the Jewish butchers entailed much trouble and vexation on the heads of the various Synagogues, and each congregation was left to struggle individually with the slaughterers and butchers. An organised institution to deal with the subject was first proposed on the 19th April 1792, when two representatives from each of the three German Synagogues met to discuss this important question. We advisedly say important question, however prosaic it may seem, for matter feeds mind; and the loveliest maiden, the noblest hero, and the greatest poet would soon be reduced to inanity if deprived of the fibrous juicy flesh, that quickly becomes part of their own fibre and muscle. At that meeting Mr L. de Symons proposed to draw up a plan for the foundation of a joint board, in which all London congregations should be represented, and for the construction of a Central Hall for the sale of meat. This scheme was prepared and was submitted to the Sephardi community by Mr Bing, Secretary to the Great Synagogue. It was alleged in this document that the Portuguese Synagogue would not only save £100 which they annually expended in providing *kosher* meat for their congregation, but would even realise an assured yearly profit. The Hall to be erected was to contain twenty shops to be let to the butchers, and Christian butchers were to pay a small amount for each head of cattle they killed. Plans and estimates for the proposed market were also forwarded to the Portuguese authorities for their consideration. The scheme was found impracticable by the latter. It was alleged in reply that the building contemplated would be utterly useless if constructed; that butchers would not remove thither; that it would be highly inconvenient for families who dwelt at a distance; that on Sundays it would prove a scandal to surrounding Christians; and that Christian butchers would refuse to pay the tax to be levied upon them. The Portuguese would willingly join in the formation of a general body for the management of the Shechita (arrangements for slaughtering and preparing cattle for food *more Judaico*), but declined altogether to accept the scheme for the market. The subject did not drop at once, and Duke's Place and Bevis Marks again exchanged letters. The Germans stated that they could not separate what they regarded as two portions of one integral plan, that the three City Synagogues had resolved to construct a Hall, and that the Portuguese could join them whenever they deemed it proper. The latter replied that the necessary orders had been given to the Beth Din to consolidate the Shechita; but that there was no reason to alter the decision arrived at on the subject of the Hall. Thus the correspondence ended, not without numerous expressions of good will on both sides; and Mr de Castro, the Portuguese Secretary, stated in conclusion that " we shall be happy to cultivate that harmony and good understanding that subsist between our congregations, and which are so essential to our welfare." A subscription was set on foot among the German Congregations to obtain funds for the construction of the Hall, but with little success. About a twelvemonth afterwards another spasmodic effort was made to carry out this object. Nobody, however, believed in a Hall, and the Jewish Butchers' Hall never existed except on paper. The plan for a general Shechita Board remained in abeyance for more than a decade, and it was not until 1805 that Askenazim and Sephardim finally united to establish the body known by that name at the present day.

It will be perceived that the three City German Synagogues were acting in unison on that occasion; unfortunately such was not always the case. All Jews are not necessarily endowed with lofty patriotism, neither are their actions invariably guided by pure philanthropy. Human nature is alike everywhere; Cæsar strongly resembles Pompey, and Synagogue committees do not at all times soar above the level of parish boards. The influx of foreign poor, especially of Germans and Poles, at the end of last century, was increasing to an alarming extent. The Askenazi Jews, though augmenting in numbers and wealth, found it no easy task to cope with an evil that was yearly assuming more gigantic proportions. Each Synagogue was expected to contribute towards the relief of those wretched immigrants in life, and to their interment in death. Those nearest and dearest often quarrel with each other over some paltry pecuniary question. The principal source of wrangling among the sister congregations, was as to which should spare six feet of ground for the bones of some miserable foreigner. On some occasions these unseemly disputes led to unpleasant consequences. One evening in September 1790, a coffin was lying in the middle of Duke's Place. The parochial spirit was strong at that moment, and not one of the Synagogues would give decent sepulture to the remains of the pauper. Duke's Place considered it was the turn of Leadenhall Street, and Leadenhall Street was certain the duty devolved on Duke's Place. Meanwhile a Portuguese Jew, to save the body from being buried in a neighbouring church, gave the coffin temporary shelter in his own house. He then went to the Portuguese authorities to inform them of the occurrence. The wardens were summoned to meet at once, albeit it was nine o'clock at night. A message was despatched to the Leadenhall Street Synagogue, which was stated to be the delinquent on this occasion. Eventually one of the wardens from that Congregation and the secretary came to Bevis Marks and promised to bury the dead man, on account of the intercession of the Portuguese Mahamad, though in reality it was no concern of their Synagogue.

In June 1794, a similar case occurred, when a German child remained unburied owing to the dissensions between the Duke's Place and the Hambro Synagogues. Mr Alexander Phillips, presiding warden of the former Synagogue, came to explain matters to the Portuguese Mahamad (vestry), and said that owing to a resolution of the members of his Congregation he did not dare to inter the child; but desiring that it should be buried as a Jew, he begged the Portuguese to interpose and effect a reconciliation between the two Synagogues. A meeting was held at ten o'clock on the following morning, at the Portuguese vestry. It was attended by Mr Alexander Phillips, of Duke's Place Synagogue; Mr E. P. Solomons, presiding warden of the Hambro Synagogue; Mr Asher Goldsmid and Mr Solomon Solomons, on the part of the Germans; while the Portuguese were represented by their wardens — Messrs Emanuel Lousada, Gabriel I. Brandon, Raphael Rodriguez Brandon, A. Lopes Pereira, and Isaac Gomes Serra. It was proposed that the Hambro Synagogue should pay £50 for six months, from Nisan to Tisri, to the Duke's Place Synagogue, in consideration of which payment the latter undertook to provide for the poor. It was left to the Portuguese wardens to decide in future whether that sum should be increased. The two Synagogues were to complete an arrangement on this basis; but it was agreed that should they fail in doing so, another meeting should be held on the following Monday. The two Synagogues did not immediately arrive at an understanding, and the intended meeting was not convened, owing to the absence of Mr Joseph Gompertz, whose opinion it was desired to consult. Then the Hambro Synagogue declined to accept arbitration, like those capricious ladies who, after soliciting intervention in their domestic quarrels, are ready to repudiate such intervention if likely to end in a decision against them. This conduct so displeased Mr E. P. Solomons, that he addressed an apologetic letter to the Portuguese authorities, explaining that in consequence of such decision he had resigned his office in the Synagogue. However, an agreement on the above terms was eventually entered into by the Great and the Hambro Synagogues; and information to this effect was conveyed in a letter written in very handsome terms by the wardens of Duke's Place to those of Bevis Marks. We extract the following paragraph from that document:—" Our vestry are fully convinced that your laudable interference at the commencement, and indefatigable perseverance in offering your assistance, are some of the principal causes to which they must attribute the happy conclusion."

This letter, which contained a profusion of thanks and expressions of gratitude, was signed by Messrs Levy Barent Cohen, and Moses Samuel, the wardens.

Unfortunately such agreements as the one above adverted to were made periodically, only to be periodically disregarded.

CHAPTER XXVIII.

THE RICARDO FAMILY.—THE ALIEN BILL.—SYNAGOGUE FINANCE.

The Hebrew mind has usually displayed an extraordinary aptitude for Stock Exchange operations. The keen wit, the far-seeing vision, and the unceasing activity of the Jew, rendered him especially fit to grasp with stock-jobbing; while the boldness of his conceptions, his power of combination, and the means at his disposal of obtaining accurate information, enabled him to amass great wealth. Many Jewish capitalists came over from Holland with William III. From Menasseh Lopez to Abraham Goldsmid and Nathan Meyer Rothschild, a series of Hebrew speculators held commanding positions in Change Alley or the Stock Exchange. They followed their avocation with eager zest; and their expresses from every court in Europe outstripped Government messengers with the latest news. Stock-jobbing flourished greatly, and increased in extent in the middle of last century, notwithstanding various attempts made by the legislature to check this form of gambling. Sir John Barnard's Act—providing that no loss suffered through time bargains should be recoverable at law, and which remained in force until late years—at first proved a serious hindrance to speculation. Time bargains had originated from the period of six weeks in each quarter in which the bank books were closed, and for obvious reasons they greatly encouraged gambling. Sir John Barnard, we will observe, was for many years Member for the City of London, and he was an honest, conscientious man; albeit he bitterly opposed the Jewish Naturalisation Bill in 1753. Speculators soon accepted this Act; brokers were made responsible for the contract they entered into, and the rush to Change Alley in pursuit of Mammon became greater than ever.

Abraham Israel Ricardo was a prominent member of the Stock Exchange during the latter part of the eighteenth century. He was a devout Jew, and for many years acted as broker for the Bevis Marks Synagogue, of which he was member. His family had come over from Holland long before, and they had always strictly adhered to the tenets of Judaism. The Portuguese Congregation in those days, instead of investing all their funds in permanent securities, as at present, were wont to leave a large sum in the hands of their agent to be advanced in properly covered loans in the Stock Exchange. Abraham Israel Ricardo carried out many transactions of this nature to the great satisfaction of his brethren, and nearly every year a vote of thanks was awarded to him by the electors, for the care and zeal which enabled him to hand over to them by no means contemptible profits. Mr Ricardo's business on behalf of the Synagogue seems to have been extensive, and carried on with Jew and Christian. On one occasion we find that he lent £22,000 in consols, at a small backwardation, and £9500 bank stock at a continuation, to Mr E. P. Solomons, to whom we adverted in our previous chapter as resigning the Presidentship of the Hamburg Synagogue, when its wardens declined to accept the arbitration of the Portuguese Mahamad. Mr Ricardo had a numerous family of sons; and great was his sorrow when his child David, a bright, intelligent boy, whom he had initiated at the age of fourteen into the mysteries of the Stock Exchange, began to waver from the ancient faith of his forefathers. David Ricardo was induced in extreme youth to secede from Judaism, when his father abandoned him altogether. David's own means were narrow, but, as will easily be imagined under the circumstances, a number of influential members of the Stock Exchange readily came forward to assist him. They discovered his extraordinary powers, and they foresaw that he would prove an important acquisition to Christianity. At twenty-five years of age David Ricardo began the study of mathematics, and explored the secrets of nature through chemistry and mineralogy. Then he grew acquainted with Adam Smith's "Wealth of Nations," and the bent of his genius becoming apparent, he devoted himself to political economy, in which field he won distinction. He realised a fortune in the Stock Exchange, while his opinions on the last-named science acquired great weight. The Bank Charter was to a great extent founded on his principles, and to him the country was indebted for the original plan by which the resumption of cash payments by the Bank was effected without danger. His writings on political economy almost formed as marked an era as the work of Adam Smith. His principal production was published in 1817, and attracted considerable attention. David Ricardo in time reached the Senate, where his reputation had already preceded him, and he died in 1823, at about fifty-two years of age. At the time of his death he represented in Parliament the borough of Portarlington. His fortune was estimated at £700,000, and comprised several considerable landed estates, which were equitably distributed between his three sons; his four daughters being also adequately apportioned. David Ricardo's withdrawal was an undoubted loss to Judaism. He was an acute, patient, and comprehensive thinker on scientific subjects, though we are not aware that he had specially studied theological questions, neither do we offer any opinion to explain his change of religious views. His example was followed by most of his own brothers; and Abraham Ricardo, who lived to beyond the threescore and ten years allotted to man, had the grief of seeing son after son deserting the creed in which they had all been nurtured, and to which he himself remained faithful to the last.

During the last decade of the eighteenth century, the political position of the Jews in England appears to have been at times very far from agreeable. The French Revolution had raised its sanguinary flag. New and subversive doctrines were preached on the other side of that narrow strip of sea which divides Great Britain from the Continent; general uneasiness reigned in England; a fear of Jacobinism pervaded nearly all classes; strangers were eyed with suspicion, foreigners were often regarded as spies in disguise, and Jews, from their correspondence and relations with other states, inspired more or less open distrust. To obviate unpleasant consequences from the condition of public feeling, on Sabbath Hanucah, or during the Feast of Dedication in 1792, the Wardens of the Portuguese Synagogue instructed their Dayan,

Rabbi Hasday Almosnino, to preach a sermon, inculcating upon his audience the duty of Jews to show a firm attachment to their king and constitution. Doubtless this was intended rather to satisfy Gentile feeling than to teach Jews sentiments of loyalty, which they had always prided themselves upon possessing. At the same time the Portuguese Secretary, Daniel de Castro, communicated this resolution to Messrs George Goldsmid, Alexander Phillips, and Joseph Lazarus, the Wardens of the Great Synagogue, in conformity with a previous understanding. What steps were taken on the question we are unable to say: for Rabbi Tabil Schiff had died in 1791, no successor had been appointed, and the necessity for pulpit instruction had not yet been recognised by the authorities of the Great Synagogue. Then also, on the 19th December 1792, Lord Grenville brought forward the Alien Bill in the Lords, which gave Government control over the movements of foreigners in this country, and notwithstanding the eloquent opposition of Fox and his party in the Commons the Alien Bill became law. This measure was rigorously enforced. Occasionally King George himself did not disdain to sign an order for the expulsion of some poor Dutch or Polish Jew, whose misfortune it was not to be following some profitable calling. Such occurrences were by no means rare, and pressed heavily on the Jewish community, which had to find funds for the departure from England of these aliens, mostly men of little or no available means. Nevertheless the Jews again displayed their attachment to the throne by celebrating a special service on the 13th April 1793, the day ordered by his Majesty to be kept as a fast. King George III. and his advisers did not believe, like Napoleon, that Providence was on the side of big battalions, and they desired to propitiate Providence by prayers and humiliations.

Towards the end of the last century the German Congregations were rising in wealth, in numbers, and importance, and were rivalling in some respects the older Portuguese Congregation. The Sephardim, whatever may have been their private views, had the wisdom of accepting the inevitable, and entered into closer ties public and private with the Ashkenazim. Since 1785 the Portuguese had elected Dr Joseph Hart Myers, as doctor of their poor, a position which Dr Myers filled with much credit for many years, until constrained to resign by ill health. In 1790 that community resolved to permit the admission into their hospital of the poor of any other Jewish Congregation, on proper arrangements to cover the extra expense being effected. Then in December 1794 the wardens of the four city Synagogues decided conjointly to reduce the cost of the flour to be used for Passover Cakes on the ensuing festival, by having all their wheat ground at the same mill. It was war time, it must be recollected; flour was worth 65s. to 70s. the sack, and economy was well worth practising. The poor were not allowed to suffer on that account; the best quality of flour was employed, only, owing to its scarcity, the poor received two-thirds of their customary allowance in Matzoth or Passover Cakes, and one-third in potatoes. The tendency was clearly towards a closer connection between English Jews of German and of Portuguese stock; a temporary check to this good feeling occurring in 1802, through a circumstance which we shall in due course fully narrate, but which fortunately made no lasting impression.

When Rabbi Tabil Schiff, the German Chief Rabbi, died in 1791, his funeral was conducted with great decorum, and all the honours sanctioned by Jewish usage were paid to his remains. All the London Synagogues deputed their wardens to do homage to the virtues of the deceased Rabbi, and the Bevis Marks Synagogue was represented by their five wardens, and by the four members of their Beth Din. We have already in a former paper spoken of this pious doctor of Jewish Law, so we need not further dilate on the subject. The office of Chief Rabbi in his community remained unfilled for many years; the Rabbi of the New Synagogue being provisionally appointed Dayan of the Duke's Place Synagogue at a nominal salary. The election of a new Rabbi was mooted, but no active steps were taken until 1794, when the requirements of the Congregation were made known. Four or five applications for the office came from abroad, one of them being from Dr Hirschel, who was eventually elected. But no resolution was arrived at, at that time, lack of funds being pleaded as a reason for procrastination; and the first year of the present century still saw the Duke's Place Synagogue without a spiritual chief. In truth the finances of that Synagogue were not in an over flourishing condition. Mrs Levy's generous gift in 1787, and the subsequent loan of £2000 raised in 1789, had not sufficed to place the Synagogue in the state desired by zealous worshippers. And in November 1791, it was found necessary to borrow a further sum of £3500 to liquidate the debts incurred for repairs of the holy building. On this occasion the ingenious expedient was hit upon, in order to facilitate the operation, of taking members' notes of hand at twelvemonths' date for the amount of their subscription; such notes being renewable on payment of interest for the term of three years, when the loan itself was to be repaid. Thus some members contributed to the good work by merely lending their signatures. However, in most cases the amount subscribed was advanced in cash, and nearly £3000 were collected. The brothers Goldsmid, of whom we shall speak fully hereafter, were then rising men; and among the subscribers to that fund we find the names of Abraham Goldsmid, Asher Goldsmid, and George Goldsmid, each of whom gave £200.

At this period, too, the exchequer of the Bevis Marks Synagogue, formerly full to overflowing, did not present by any means a brilliant aspect. The offerings had fallen off, the deficits of several years had accumulated, and it was deemed desirable also to open a subscription for the amount of £2500. Neither public spirit nor wealth had become extinct in the Congregation, and the sum required was readily forthcoming.

In the year 1794, a singular compact was made by the members of the Great Synagogue to maintain the unity of their sacred institution. Whether a falling off of members was feared, or whether it had actually occurred we cannot say; but certain it is that a number of gentlemen signed an undertaking not to withdraw from the Synagogue under penalty of forfeiting £100 each. An excellent plan this to prevent desertions. An appeal to a man's purse is occasionally more effective than an appeal to his religious principles; and pique and convenience may perhaps be found not to weigh down the scale when balanced on the other side against the sum of one hundred pounds.

CHAPTER XXIX.

SYNAGOGUE PROGRESS.—TWO JEWISH WORTHIES.

ONE of the first thoughts of Jews when they congregate in sufficient numbers, is to erect a place of worship; and the beauty and size of their Synagogues may serve to give a fair idea of their numbers, means, and zeal. As we have already explained, their increase during the eighteenth century was mainly confined to the Jews of German and Polish descent; and that section of Jews from being a minority, gradually rose into being a large majority. Synagogue after Synagogue was by them raised in London and in provincial towns. One of the few places where their establishment does not appear to have been always successful was Dublin. From some unexplained cause, the Jews, who are beholden to the Irish for more than one act of true kindness, did not uniformly prosper on the banks of the Liffey. At one time, indeed—in the year 1791—the congregation had so dwindled in extent, that the Synagogue had been closed and the Scrolls of the Law had been returned to the London Portuguese Jews to whom they belonged. This temporary check must have been owing to some purely fortuitous circumstances, for Dublin has since beheld a flourishing Jewish Congregation. The Jews of Dublin, let us say, always felt a sense of friendship and gratitude towards the Jews of Bevis Marks; and even so late as 1842, the former expressed a desire to affiliate their Synagogue to the Portuguese Synagogue of London. But everywhere else, at the period of which we are speaking, the Jews with characteristic energy and activity were extending their religious, educational, and charitable institutions. Usually, as soon as the Synagogue reared its head, the school-room quietly rose at its side. The three German Synagogues in Duke's Place, Fenchurch

Street, and Leadenhall Street, had become insufficient for the crowds of worshippers who assembled thither on the days of solemn gathering to invoke the Lord of Israel. Permission was granted by the authorities of the Great Synagogue to small Congregations of foreigners to meet for prayers in suitable localities; and among others a small Polish Synagogue was built near Cutler Street, Houndsditch. The Great Synagogue itself had been enlarged and rebuilt; and its members had so multiplied that a new resting-place where they could sleep their last sleep undisturbed had to be purchased. Towards this pious object Mr Abraham Goldsmid and his brother Mr Asher Goldsmid did not fail to contribute with their customary liberality. The ground for the new "House of Life" was purchased in 1795; and a portion of the land was sublet to a Christian, with the curious proviso that a certain space should be devoted to the cultivation of willow-trees, for the use of the Congregation in their ritual observances during the Feast of Tabernacles. Then the Portuguese Congregation had ordered the reconstruction of some of the buildings adjoining their House of Prayer, at a cost of about £4000. The New Synagogue in Leadenhall Street was not behind its sister Congregations, and in 1798 the edifice was repaired and decorated in a very elegant and chaste style. The ceremony of the consecration was attended with great solemnity, and is thus described by a Christian eye-witness. "The High Priest with the subordinate rabbis, the chorus and attendants with a great number of fathers of families in the proper vestments, were at the ceremony which was affecting, grand, and awful. The music and the voices performed in the eastern manner of strophe, antistrophe, and chorus. The anthems were performed in a very superior style of modulation and harmony. A crowd of people attended, and they all conducted themselves decorously. A subscription was opened, and in about twenty minutes upwards of £200 was subscribed."

We have thus seen that the City Synagogues were flourishing, and their Congregations growing larger and richer; now we must record the foundation of a new Synagogue in another quarter of the town. It was found advisable for many Jews in trade to dwell beyond the boundaries of the city; principally in those districts where the rich, the idle, and the fashionable, meet and lounge and flirt together. These Jews lived at a distance from the City Synagogues; and not being able to walk thither, and not wishing to be excluded from the religious services to which they had been accustomed, they naturally resolved to establish a place of worship in their own locality. In the year 1797, a small Synagogue was fitted up in Denmark Court, Strand. This was the beginning of the Congregation of the Westminster Jews, now in St Alban's Place. In the above-mentioned year, the founders of the Westminster Synagogue consulted the authorities of the Hambro Synagogue on the subject, and all the three existing German Congregations resolved to act together in this question. The old communities raised no objection to the formation of another Congregation; no feelings of narrow-minded jealousy were awakened: and no laws of the Medes and the Persians enacted that Jews should assemble to pray in certain fixed spots and nowhere else. In 1798, the City Congregations entered into a temporary arrangement with the new Westminster Synagogue on a very reasonable basis. It was not until the beginning of the present century that a regular agreement was effected between the Great Synagogue—on behalf of the City Congregations—and the Westminster Synagogue.

During the same period, too, Jewish intellect was far from being idle in London. Several Hebrew works principally by German writers were published, which reflected great credit on authors, editors, and printers. Among these we must enumerate two important works by Eliakim ben Abraham, which saw the light in the year 1794. One of these was called *Milchamoth Adonai*, " The battles of the Lord," and consisted of essays on several philosophical subjects; and the other, *Maamar Beenah Laetim*, was a commentary on the most difficult passages of Daniel. The diction of these treatises has been pronounced to be chaste and elegant, and their contents to display much knowledge in science, natural philosophy, and theology. The same writer also edited other works in the holy tongue, consisting mainly of philosophy and metaphysics. But Hebrew was not the only language in which Jews wrote; and one man at least wielded the vernacular with vigour if not with elegance. We must not forget the services that David Levi rendered to Judaism; and let us pay a just tribute to the memory of a man who taught Jews to appreciate the beautiful prayers they too often addressed parrot-like to the Deity, without understanding them; and who broke many a lance on behalf of his co-religionists. Let us say a few words concerning David Levi. Born in 1742, his youth was passed like the old masters in the Talmud in the pursuit of a handicraft. Whilst struggling to earn a living as a shoemaker and a hat dresser, and surrounded with domestic cares, he found time to devote to those studies he loved so well. He first produced a volume on the rites and ceremonies of the Jews. He next published his "Lingua Sacra" in three volumes, consisting of a Hebrew grammar with points, and a complete Hebrew and English dictionary. These works are far from being the most perfect of the kind, but they form a remarkable instance of industry and perseverance in a person constrained to follow a mechanical pursuit to supply the necessities of life. He then defended his faith against the attacks of ardent sectarian, albeit modified, Christianity on the one side, and against the attacks of pure atheism on the other. Dr Priestley, the well-known natural philosopher and dissenting minister; the extraordinary man who dived into the mysteries of nature; who followed by turns the doctrines of Arius and Socinius; and who discovered new gases, desired to convert the Jews to a religion the divine nature of which he entirely repudiated. Dr Priestley, F.R.S., invited the Jews to a friendly discussion on the evidences of Christianity. Thus replied David Levi in the first of two series of letters: "I am not ashamed to tell you that I am a Jew by choice and not because I was born a Jew. Far from it, for I am clearly of opinion that every person endowed with ratiocination ought to have a clear idea of the truths of revelation, and a just ground for his faith so far as human evidence can go." In 1789, David Levi administered another rebuke to Dr Priestley, and then he broke a lance in defence of the Old Testament against Thomas Paine's "Age of Reason." David Levi was a hard worker; he gave the Portuguese Jews a translation of their prayers, and subsequently he rendered the same service to his own community. He addressed several controversial letters to Christian writers; and he published a Pentateuch in Hebrew and English with notes. He was poet in ordinary to the Synagogues, and he furnished odes as occasions required on public celebrations. The work which appears to have lain nearest to his heart was his "Dissertation on Prophecies," of which a part only had come before the world when he was stricken with paralysis. In 1801, David Levi was summoned before his Maker, whom he had humbly and zealously glorified for nearly sixty years. David Levi, though not a polished or cultured writer, was an earnest thinker, and he strove hard to benefit his community. He was the first Jew who had vindicated his faith in English; and though he was no match for Joseph Priestley as a controversialist, by the help of books he made a respectable figure in print. A curious elegy in his honour appeared in the *Gentleman's Magazine*. We quote two stanzas :—

> "Though science reared not in his anxious breast,
> Confessions, creeds, nor formularies vext,
> On prophecy's sure grounds he built his rest,
> Nor with their mystic meanings was perplext.
> He took the part benevolent and sincere
> To argue and explain from falsehood clear.
>
> "For to Priestley's philosophic views,
> He cautious answered in his people's name.
> The sceptic turned, nor more among the Jews
> Sought for another argument or claim,
> Nor did the arch demagogue's disloyal train
> From Levi's pen a better chance obtain."

This poetry, as will be seen, is not of a very high class. The author, Lemoine, was neither a Gray, a Cowper, nor a Southey, but he was sincere; and he seems to have really admired David Levi in particular, though he did not experience the same feelings towards the Jews in general. The long intimacy that had existed between the Jewish mechanic and the Christian bookseller, doubtless predisposed the latter to judge the former with a favourable eye. We shall hereafter meet again with Henry Lemoine as a writer on Jewish affairs, who, evidently well intentioned, fell into serious blunders, and who apparently possessing some knowledge concerning the Jews, really frequently misunderstood them.

Among the Jews deserving some notice during the period of which we are writing, that is, the end of last century, we must not omit to mention the name of David Alves Rebello, an eminent member of the Portuguese Congregation. David Alves Rebello was not only a valued member of his own community, where he had filled several offices of honour, but he was an ornament to society of any faith. He was a patron of the fine arts and a benefactor of the poor. He had applied himself to the study of natural history, on which science he left several writings. He was a great admirer of works of art, particularly of coins; and he gathered an elegant, judicious collection of them, as well as of numerous objects of mineralogy, botany, and every other branch of natural history. David Alves Rebello is described by cotemporary writers as having possessed a vigorous and expanded mind, fully equal to grasping successfully with the problems of science. He died in May 1796, at Hackney, where many Portuguese Jews then dwelt; and he bequeathed to his Synagogue a curious legacy of £500, the interest of which was to be devoted to the purchase of certain under-garments to be annually distributed to twelve poor persons of each sex.

Let us now return to the Askenazi Community, and glance once more to the men of note who sprang during the last portion of the eighteenth century from that section of the Jews of London. We shall in due course furnish an account of the Goldsmid family. Of David Levi, the humble and zealous scholar and earnest worker, we have spoken. We will now take a brief glance at two individuals of a very different stamp. The one a clever journalist; the other a famous songster; both Jews, yet neither of whom contributed to the advancement of Judaism.

Lewis Goldsmith was an ambitious young notary who, to acquire some sort of celebrity, published a work entitled "Crimes of Cabinets." In those days it was not safe to write even the truth concerning ministers, for then the greater the truth, was often literally the greater the libel. So Goldsmith the Jew was indicted for libel and sedition, a most unusual occurrence in respect of one of his race, and he sought safety in France.

It was during the time of the first empire, when every man had his price; and the French authorities were not slow in detecting the literary talents of the exile. Soon Goldsmith began to hurl his thunder against the British Cabinet through the columns of the *Argus*, an English journal established in Paris for that purpose.

After a while the French, with the fickleness, proverbially if not always correctly, attributed to their nation, became tired of their protegé, and negotiated with the English Government for the exchange of Goldsmith for some Frenchmen in that Government's hands. Fortunately Goldsmith received timely advice of the negotiations of which he was the object and likely to be the victim, and he forestalled their result by placing himself at once in communication with the English authorities. His offences were not found to be of a very deep dye; he obtained permission to return; duly submitted to a *pro forma* trial for high treason, and was discharged.

The underhand attempts of his late friends greatly enraged Lewis Goldsmith, who started in England the well-known paper called the *Anti-Gallican Monitor*. Then the pliant and versatile journalist turned his keen satire and powers of invective against Napoleon and his court, drawing real or imaginary descriptions of the abuses and excesses perpetrated in those precincts. His inflated periods on this occasion served him to so good a purpose, that Louis XVIII., on his Restoration, at once rewarded the reviler of his enemies by conferring on Lewis Goldsmith a pension for life. We may also mention that a daughter of Lewis Goldsmith became the second Lady Lyndhurst.

In the year 1801, a new singer made his debut at Covent Garden Theatre in the opera of "Chains of the Heart," by Mazzinghi and Riviere. This artist possessed one of the most magnificent and yet one of the sweetest voices ever heard on the stage. He was a short dark man, with restless and intelligent eyes. He was said to be a Jew, and he was called John Braham. John Abrahams, or Braham, was truly born of Jewish parents in the year 1774, and he became an orphan at a tender age. He became early the pupil of Myer Lion, otherwise Leoni, the Synagogue chorister and operatic singer to whom we have already adverted, and who is stated to have been related to young Braham. The future tenor himself as a boy sang in the choir of the Great Synagogue. Subsequently he experienced much kindness from Ephraim Polack, father of Maria Polack, an authoress, and grandfather of Elizabeth Polack, also a writer. Moreover, young Braham enjoyed the protection of Mr Eliason, the eminent merchant and son-in-law of Mr Aaron Goldsmid. At ten years of age the youthful student began singing on the stage, and he successfully delivered the bravura pieces composed for the celebrated Mad. Mara. He played subsequently at Drury Lane, and he resolved to make a continental tour to finish his musical education. In 1798 he visited Paris, and notwithstanding the turmoil of the Revolution, he gave there a number of concerts which attracted considerable crowds. In Italy he studied composition under Isola, and he visited nearly all the principal cities of the Land of Song; in most of which he displayed in public his fine talents. On his return to England he at once became the first operatic performer of the day, and for years he was rivalled on the British stage only by Charles Incledon. This singer had fled to sea in boyhood, and on his return he was taken in hand by Rauzzini, a well-known Italian maestro, who instructed him in music. Incledon was endowed with a splendid voice, but possessed little musical or other culture, and he lacked genius. Nevertheless, the beauty and wonderful compass of his voice made him a dangerous competitor for Braham. The latter represented the romantic or operatic school, while the former shone principally in pure ballad singing. The suffrages of London were divided between the two stars, and their respective merits were canvassed as warmly as in the well-known instance of the differences between Tweedle-de-dum and Tweedle-de-dee. John Braham greatly surpassed Incledon in talents; he became known as a composer, and the musical world is indebted to him for several light operas and songs. Among the latter, the best remembered production is the patriotic air called the "Death of Nelson," which long maintained its popularity. Of Braham it was said in questionable praise that he sang like an angel and spoke like a Jew. It is not believed that he ever formally adopted any kind of Christianity, but there was nothing visible of Judaism with him in his latter days except the ineffaceable stamp imprinted by nature on his countenance. John Braham married, and left several children, one of whom is Frances Countess Waldegrave, now the consort of Lord Carlingford. This greatest of modern English singers, after retiring from the stage, lived in obscurity for many years, and died at an advanced age, we believe in 1856.

We have spoken of the journalist and of the songster, because it is a necessary part of our work to notice eminent or notorious men born within the pale of Judaism, though neither Goldsmith nor Braham in any manner advanced the cause of their race. They were Jews from accident of birth, and not from conviction; and at least in one instance when the forms of the ancient creed became inconvenient and were considered as opposed to worldly advancement, they were, as in other cases, cast off without compunction.

CHAPTER XXX.

FRIENDS AND VINDICATORS OF THE JEWS.

We must yet linger awhile on the latest years of the eighteenth century, for during that period, and during the early years of the present century, many events occurred of direct interest to Judaism. Indeed, we consider that epoch to be one of great moment in Anglo-Jewish history. Judaism seemed to acquire a new life, notwithstanding the desertions from its pale which it has been our duty to chronicle, and which still continued from time to time; and a considerable communal development, as we have already perceived, was unfolding itself in various directions. On future occasions we shall speak of new institutions founded, and of schemes for the amelioration of the Jewish masses proposed or carried out. We will first proceed to treat of the awakened interest and sympathy which were beginning to be felt by thoughtful Englishmen and English women for a long persecuted race.

In the beginning of the nineteenth century, when Napoleon raised his then all-powerful hand to uplift the Jews from the effects of the ill-treatment of ages, and to place them as civilised human beings on terms of equality with the rest of mankind, the inquiring eyes of Europe and of England were turned towards the children of Israel. But even in the preceding decade, between 1790 and 1800, we find signs of freshly stirred-up curiosity concerning Jewish manners and customs, and newly-inspired friendship towards Jews. Jewish Synagogues and cemeteries became the objects of visits from Christians; Jewish merits and demerits were discussed in magazine articles; and Jewish virtues—strange to relate—formed the chords upon which the dramatist played to stir up the hearts of the audience.

In the year 1795, a Christian lady visited the Portuguese

Cemetery at Mile End, with which she appeared to be much gratified. We shall give an extract from her account which is really worthy of note, for it furnishes some curious information. The lady was struck with the sentence from Ecclesiasties, chosen by the Jews, "Then shall the dust return to the earth as it was, and the spirit shall return unto God who gave it," which she considered formed a happy contrast with the French atheistic motto, "La mort est un eternel sommeil." After quoting St Paul, and describing the ceremonies attending a Jewish funeral, our fair writer thus continues: "The dead are interred in rows, without any respect to difference of rank. He who is buried to-day lies next to him that was buried yesterday, whether poor or rich, except a few instances when a husband, wife, or some dear relative purchases the next place to be reserved for himself or herself; nor is there any difference in the coffins. One plain hearse carries all; the more respected they are the more numerous are the train that follow. Those who have been notoriously bad are put into the ground without any ceremony, and I believe put apart from the rest, else the only distinction is the richer having gravestones with Hebrew, Portuguese (or Spanish), and English inscriptions. Some have only one of these languages, many with emblems and devices, such as a hand coming out of the clouds with an axe in the act of hewing down a tree, shedding the water out of a pitcher, or plucking a rose if it is a donzella that lies beneath. On a Mrs Ximenes who died in childbed at the age of sixteen, the emblem is strikingly pathetic. A rose just cropt, a bud remaining over it. 'Oh, spare the bud!' But I could not comprehend that on Sir Sampson Gideon's grave arose a building which appeared to me like a temple divided into compartments, in one of which a man in long robes seems walking in a melancholy manner; in another, a group of figures and a dog; this surprises me as I thought they were not permitted to carve any figures of animals. . . . I must not forget a kind of fountain in which they wash their hands on their return from the ground as a purification: and I am told that the friends and the relatives of the deceased make it a point of tender attention to fill up the grave, which, as such numbers generally attend, is soon performed. Besides the keeper of the place, who lives in a house adjoining, two men constantly sit up every night in a movable watch-box, which wheels over the last grave; this has been done for four or five years, in consequence of their ground being robbed by resurrectionists." Our fair writer's description seems correct in the main, and gives an accurate and pleasing account of the cemetery of the Portuguese Jews. The lady does full justice to the perfect equality that reigns in death among Jews, with whom poor and rich lie side by side without distinction. She falls, however, in error when she alludes to the grave of *Sir* Sampson Gideon. *He* never was interred among the Jews. The Sampson Gideon whose tomb she beheld died untitled. It was his son who was first created a baronet, and then raised to the peerage of Ireland under the style of Lord Eardley, as we have formerly stated. As for the figures she saw over the building which she depicts, they are certainly contrary to Jewish custom. That temple, however, is no longer in existence, for the monument having fallen into a state of decay, the family asked permission of the Synagogue authorities, little more than thirty years ago, to place a new tombstone over the grave of the once great financier. This permission was naturally granted, and the tombstone that had originally covered Sampson Gideon's bones, passed into the possession of his descendants.

Among the friends and advocates of the Jews we must rank a writer who, under the initials of " J. D. I.," espoused in warm and eloquent accents the cause of the Jews, during the same year, viz., 1795. Another writer had addressed a communication to a magazine, in which he repeated a story, found in Matthew Paris, who gravely accused the Jews of killing a Christian child in 1255, for the sake of his blood. Whereupon our author, whose full name we regret we cannot give, answered with an able and glowing defence of the Jews. Want of space and other obvious causes must prevent us from reproducing it *in extenso*, but we shall extract two paragraphs, from which our readers will be able to judge of the whole. " J. D. I.," after lamenting that Dr Tovey, that humane and learned antiquary, should have placed some credence in this legend, founded on such slender basis; and, after rebutting the exceedingly slight evidence adduced in support, thus proceeds:—

"The calumnies which have been spread concerning the descendants of Jews have been numerous, but they have all been like the present one, accompanied with circumstances which in this age destroy their possibility. I shall consume little time in mentioning a few I recollect. Because a king of France happened to be more insane than some of his predecessors, all Jews were expelled from their native country; for the royal lunatic was declared by an archbishop to be so, in consequence of Jewish witchcraft. Because a vagrant, not less insane than this French monarch, proposed exterminating the Turks, the crusaders to begin auspiciously first fleshed their swords among the European Jews; and because these Quixotic expeditions were, as they naturally should be, more destructive to the Jews than to the Turks, half the remaining Jews were massacred on their return. Was there a plague? The waters were poisoned by the Jews! Was there a famine? The harvests were bewitched by the Synagogue! They burnt; they massacred; they tortured, till at length the plague ceased, and the famine was no more: and the consequence was, that murdering Jews was therefore considered as a desirable national expiation. Was a king crowned? the royal ceremony was attended with the splendid destruction of his unhappy subjects, the Jews. . . . It is a great misfortune that the Jewish nation cannot produce one writer to vindicate, with elegance and with truth, their forlorn, their indigent state. The Jews have only found advocates in enlightened Christians, but it is more frequently their misfortune also to receive in silence and resignation the insult of Christians."

Happily, we can truly say now, *nous avons changé tout cela.* The persecution of Jews in civilised states, or at all events in England, is purely a matter of history; and since the days of David Levi, scores of champions from the ranks of Judaism have risen "to vindicate with grace and with truth," the wrongs and sufferings of their brethren.

There is another name which should now be remembered by Jews with that gratitude which unfortunately was not manifested towards its bearer during his life. Richard

Cumberland was the first dramatist who had the courage to make a Jew appeal to the sympathies of the audience. Hitherto in the words of a character in Cumberland's play, whenever playwrights wanted a butt, or a buffoon, or a knave to make sport of, out came a Jew to be baited and buffeted through five long acts for the amusement of all good Christians. Much ingenuity has been exercised in endeavouring to prove that William Shakespeare, in drawing the character of Shylock, desired secretly to justify the Jews. We confess we cannot concur in this opinion. On the contrary, we are heretics enough to believe that Shakespeare represented Shylock not according to nature, but only according to that which nature was popularly believed to be. In other words, he depicted a Jew in conformity with the small knowledge or prejudices of his audience, and he reversed the original story, if he ever had heard of the true version, because he considered, and justly considered, that a cruel, avaricious, and vindictive Jew would impress more and attract an audience better than a philanthropic or benevolent Jew. Richard Cumberland, inferior as he was to William Shakespeare in genius and power, sought to raise and defend an unjustly vilified race; and he ran counter to popular notions to uphold what he believed to be the truth. Instead of depicting the potential villainies of the Jews, he delineated their actual virtues. The "Jew" was first performed in 1794, and was supported by some of the best artists of the day. Sheva the Jew was played by Bannister, "handsome Jack Bannister;" while Jubal, his man, was represented by Suett, an irresistibly droll low comedian. Palmer, one of the greatest "villains" that ever strode on the stage, appeared as Frederick; and the beautiful and celebrated Miss Farren—who subsequently became Countess of Derby—graced the part of Louisa Ratcliff. Sheva the Jew, under the guise of an old hunks of a curmudgeon, conceals the noble heart of a generous philanthropist, who does good by stealth and blushes to find it fame. Under a sordid exterior, Sheva casts his benefactions on the deserving with unsparing hand. A very Harpagon in appearance and manners, he is in reality a Cheeryble in feeling. He starves himself, he pinches his servants, and feeds abundantly the necessitous poor. He succours the son of a Christian merchant unjustly discarded by his father; he saves from want a meritorious youth, and he bestows an ample fortune anonymously on a worthy damsel whose father had helped his escape from Spain; thus enabling the young lady to be honourably recognised as a wife by her father-in-law, the self-righteous Christian merchant. The play was successful enough at the time of its appearance. But the plot is slender, and the language prosy and monotonous. Above all, it lacks the stamp of genius; and thus it happens that whilst audiences flock to hiss at the cruelty and avarice of Shylock, the existence of the beneficent Sheva is scarcely known to the present generation. Still doubtless some good was effected by Cumberland's "Jew" at the period ot its production. It produced a temporary sympathy for Sheva: tears must have been shed by sensitive ladies at the recital of his sorrows, and probably his co-religionists may have inspired kinder thoughts. The "Jew" was not without its imitations, and among these we may mention a piece called the "Jew of Mogador," which is conceived in the same kindly spirit as Cumberland's play. Richard Cumberland, in addition to his drama, again illustrated the sufferings of the Jews, in his description of the wrongs of Abraham Abrahams.

It is much to be regretted that the Jewish nation did not deem it proper to express their gratitude to Cumberland; which is all the more surprising, as the Jews have habitually been most ready to demonstrate their thankfulness towards those who befriended them. The author of the "Jew" felt keenly this neglect. In the memoirs of his own life thus does he express himself on this, to him, sore subject: "The public prints gave the Jews credit for their sensibility in acknowledging my well-intended services; my friends gave me joy of honorary presents, and some even accused me of ingratitude for not making my thanks for their munificence. I will speak plainly on this point. I do most heartily wish they had flattered me with some token, however small, of which I could have said, this is a tribute to my philanthropy, and delivered it to my children as my benevolent father did to me his badge of favour from the citizens of Dublin; but not a word from the lips, not a line did I ever receive from the pen of any Jew, though I have found myself in company with many of their nation ; and in this perhaps the gentlemen are quite right, whilst I had formed expectations that were quite wrong ; for if I have said of them only what they deserve, why should I be thanked ; and if more, much more, than they deserve, can they do a wiser thing than hold their tongue ? "

Richard Cumberland speaks with all the courtesy and dignity of a true gentleman ; which increases our chagrin at his being constrained to give vent to such utterances.

CHAPTER XXXI.

*CONVERSIONIST ATTEMPTS—PRIVILEGE OF PRISONERS
—THE JEWS' HOSPITAL—A BAAL SHEM.*

THE increasing interest felt on behalf of the Jews manifested itself among certain Christians, by an increasing care for the welfare of Jewish souls. According to these persons of peculiar minds, salvation could only be achieved by belief in their own creed; beyond which nothing could be expected except irredeemable perdition. In conformity with these convictions, attempts were made towards the end of last century to convert the Jews on a large scale. No regular society for that purpose had yet been formed, but organised efforts were made to open the eyes of Jews, and to save that stubborn race from the doom of unbelievers. A meeting-house of dissenters in Bury Street opened its portals to the Jews, and efforts were made to attract them within its precincts. A committee of dissenting ministers was appointed to prepare a series of lectures, and a young preacher named Cooper is said to have felt an especial calling for such a mission, and to have gathered crowds to listen to his eloquent accents. The Rev. John Lowe, a Scotch minister, and one of the secretaries of the Missionary Society, drew up a syllabus of subjects for lectures, which were successively delivered by various English and Scotch clergymen. According to the account rendered by one of these preachers, the hall in Bury Street, though large enough to contain 800 to 900 persons, was scantily attended, and not fifty Jews were ever found there at one time. It is represented that some of the principal Jewish merchants were occasionally present at these lectures, but that they seemed incredulous on religious subjects. Cooper, who preached in the fields, is stated to have drawn many Jews who, far from their homes and lost among thousands, were less exposed to observation. But these efforts did not appear to produce any effect—Jews possibly heard these lectures; assuredly they were not converted. We have spoken at length on the subject of Jewish conversions, and we need not revert to the question; we will only observe that conversion societies have seldom, if ever, gained over to Christianity one single Jew of note or position in his own nation. After some years these efforts were relinquished. One of the dissenting ministers, Dr Hunter, who appeared to be more sensible than the rest, declared the undertaking to be fruitless, and he said in his last lecture, " Prophecy did not encourage us as yet to expect the conversion of 1000 Jews in London, and success would have falsified prediction." Dr Hunter also alleged, and the first part of his proposition is correct—" That Jews had not always had before them the amiable and attractive side of Christianity; that they had met with hatred, contempt, and persecution from Christians, and in return hated them and their religion." His concluding remarks deserve reproduction: " Whenever the salvation of Israel is wrought out, you may rest assured it will be at a time and by means of instruments far beyond the power of human sagacity to determine. I have contributed my mite towards the attempt, but under a complete conviction of its total inutility. But so little am I wedded to my own prejudice or opinion, that to live to see the event giving them a flat contradiction, I should consider that as the most blessed event of my life." Oh, that the over-zealous speakers of Exeter Hall could learn a little of the wisdom, moderation, and sincerity of Dr Hunter! and that the pious old ladies and tender-hearted country gentlemen, who are so anxious for the salvation of the Jews, could be prevailed upon to turn their philanthropic attention to the rescue of the numerous heathens who walk in the streets of London, and who know not their right hands from the left! A certain foreign convert, who adopted the name of Frey, exerted himself zealously to induce his former brethren to follow his example, like the fox which had lost its tail. Frey became a Christian clergyman, and to inspire faith in his sincerity, he adopted such extreme views, as to check rather than encourage neophytes; and his own fellow-labourers were constrained to admit that he effected little good in their cause.

Frey was a man of some knowledge in Hebrew, and he wrote a Hebrew lexicon. He addressed a letter to the Jews of which they took no public notice. But a certain Solomon Bennett, a Pole, wrote a reply thereto which was neither a learned nor a well-written production. It was not until some years after the beginning of the present century, that rank and wealth commenced their efforts to win over, not to say purchase, Jews to Christianity; and of these attempts we shall speak in the proper place.

Notwithstanding the improved tone of feeling towards the Jews which was beginning to prevail among the educated part of the population, the general position of that community was by no means more secure, more honourable, or more brilliant than it had been during the preceding half century. They enjoyed neither civil nor political rights. The Alien Act had already pressed somewhat hardly upon them. Again, in July 1798, the Lord Mayor summoned the Wardens of the City Synagogues, to say that the Duke of Portland, one of her Majesty's Secretaries of State, had ordered him to procure a return of all aliens within three weeks, and all Jews not conforming were liable to imprisonment and transportation. The Sephardi authorities took stringent measures to induce all foreign Jews, except those who had become free denizens, to attend in the vestry-room for the purposes of registration. At the same time a meeting of the Honorary Officials of the Ashkenazi Congregations was held at the Anti-Gallican Coffee-house, under the presidency of Mr Abraham Goldsmid, at which it was resolved to register all members, seatholders, past seatholders, and their servants, so as to avoid incurring the penalties of the law.

We are glad, however, to be able to record an example of liberality and good feeling displayed towards the Jews, a few brief years after this occurrence. Mr Abraham Goldsmid and Mr Gabriel I. Brandon, as Presidents of their respective Synagogues, in Duke's Place and Bevis Marks, applied in 1801 to Mr Mainwaring, Chairman of the Commission of Magistrates for the preservation of the peace in the County of Middlesex, praying that Jewish prisoners in Bridewell might be dispensed from work on Sabbaths and festivals. Whereupon Mr Mainwaring desired to be informed of the date of such festivals and the hour of their beginning according to the Jewish ritual. These particulars having been duly furnished, Mr Mainwaring wrote the following courteous communication to Mr de Castro, Secretary to the Portuguese community:

"Sir,—I have received the list of the solemn holidays, transmitted to me by order of the Rulers of the principal Jewish Synagogues, and beg you will present my respectful compliments to these gentlemen, and inform them that I will, as soon as possible, obtain the indulgencies requested for such Jews, as may be so unfortunate as to become prisoners in the gaols under the direction of the magistrates of this county.—I am, &c., W. MAINWARING."

The kind act of this gentleman deserves mention as establishing an official precedent for such exemptions. The same privilege has since been frequently, though not invariably, accorded to Jews in English prisons; where fortunately the number of Jewish prisoners has ordinarily been small, even considering the proportion the Jews bear to the rest of the population.

We have already said that the German Jews were beginning to acquire wealth and position during the last years of the eighteenth century. Men of fortune and public spirit arose among them, and the Goldsmid family shone pre-eminently for their wealth and their munificent generosity.

The want of an asylum for the poor of the German community was beginning to be felt; and in 1795, Messrs Benjamin and Abraham Goldsmid opened for the purpose a list of subscriptions, to which they liberally themselves contributed. In the year 1797, the sum collected amounted to £20,000, which was invested in 3 per cent. stock. The scheme remained in abeyance until 1806, when a meeting of the Jewish subscribers was summoned. We advisedly say of the Jewish subscribers, for a considerable part of this £20,000 had been liberally given by Christians,—by large-hearted men, whose object was purely philanthropic, and who had no desire to meddle in internal Jewish affairs. At that meeting it was resolved to establish an hospital for the reception and support of the aged poor, and for the education and industrious employment of the youth of both sexes. A portion of the funds which served for the foundation of the institution, came from an abortive scheme to establish an hospital for the Jewish sick.

With the funds on hand, which had considerably increased, and which formed a total capital of £30,000 stock, an income of £900 a year was secured. A spacious and convenient building, especially constructed, was opened on the 28th June 1807. It was called the *Neveh Tzedek*—Abode of Righteousness—and it provided for the reception of five aged men, five aged women, ten boys, and eight girls. The new institution proved a success. It was most favourably described in the press of the day; and it has been since steadily extending its scope and its sphere of usefulness. The boys, after a course of proper instruction, were taught a trade in the house, and at the age of twelve or thirteen were bound apprentices to suitable masters. The girls learnt reading, writing, needlework, cooking, and other domestic arts, and were kept in the asylum until fifteen years of age. The aged of both sexes found a refuge under the hospitable roof of the *Neveh Tzedek* in which to spend their declining years, and they remained there until summoned to join the greater number. Among the founders we must not omit to make honourable mention of Mr Joshua Van Oven, who, by his abilities, energies, and activity, contributed to the successful execution of an idea, to the origin of which he was not himself a stranger.

The possession of supernatural powers has been usually attributed to those Jewish doctors who have mastered the secrets of the Kabbala, and the character of a Thaumaturgos is by no means new in Jewish history. A gentleman, popularly invested with those miraculous gifts, made his appearance in London during the latter part of the eighteenth century. This *Baal Shem*, this master of the mode of uttering the Ineffable name; this holder of an extraordinary faculty, which was said to have proved highly valuable to him, was known in everyday life as Dr or Rabbi de Falk. He came from Fürth, where his mother had died in straitened circumstances, and had been buried at the expense of the Congregation: De Falk himself was without means when he reached this country. Whether he owned among his other secrets the grand one of the transmutation of metals, or whether he followed privately some lucrative occupation, like a common mortal, we are unable to state. But by all accounts, soon after his arrival in London, De Falk was seen to be in possession of considerable funds, and one of his first cares was to remit to the Congregation of Fürth the amount of the expenses incurred for his mother's funeral. Usually De Falk was well provided with cash; but occasionally he found himself in absolute need, when he did not disdain to seek advances on his plate from a pawnbroker in Houndsditch. The bolts and bars of the pawnbroker's strong room were insufficient to confine there De Falk's valuables, when he summoned them back to his own closet: but he always honourably acquitted his debt. One day, shortly after having deposited some gold and silver vessels with the pawnbroker, the Kabbalist went to the shop in question, and laying down the duplicate with the sum advanced and exact interest, he told the shopman not to trouble himself for the plate, as it was already in his possession. The incredulity with which this statement was received, changed into absolute dismay, when it was ascertained that De Falk's property had really disappeared, without displacing any of the articles that had surrounded it!

Rabbi de Falk lived in Wellclose Square, where he kept a comfortable establishment. He had there his private Synagogue: and he exercised great benevolence towards the deserving. He is described as a man of universal knowledge, of singular manners, and of wonderful talent, which seemed to command the supernatural agencies of spiritual life. Instances are given of his extraordinary faculties, by respectable witnesses of his day, who evidently placed implicit faith in the stories they related. Dr de Falk was a frequent guest at Aaron Goldsmid's table. One day, it is said, the *Baal Shem* was invited to call on one of Mr Goldsmid's visitors, a gentleman dwelling in the Chapter-house in St Paul's Churchyard, to hold some conversation with him in a friendly manner on philosophical subjects: " When will you come?" asked the gentleman. De Falk took from his pocket a small piece of wax candle, and handing it to his new acquaintance, replied : " Light this, sir, when you get home, and I shall be with you as soon as it goes out." Next morning, the gentleman in question lighted the piece of candle. He watched it closely, expecting it to be consumed soon, and then to see De Falk. In vain. The taper, like the sepulchral lamps of old, burned all day and all night, without the least diminution in its flame. He removed the magic candle into a closet, when he inspected it several times daily, for the space of three weeks. One evening, at last, Dr de Falk arrived in a hackney coach. The host had almost given up all expectation of seeing De Falk, as the taper, shortly before his advent, was still burning as brightly as ever. As soon as mutual civilities were over, the master of the house hastened to look at the candle in the closet. It had disappeared. When he returned, he asked De Falk whether the agent that had removed the candle would bring back the candlestick. "Oh yes," was the reply; "it is now in your kitchen below," which actually proved to be the fact. Once a fire was raging in Duke's Place, and the Synagogue was considered in imminent danger of being destroyed. The advice and assistance of De Falk were solicited: he wrote only four Hebrew letters on the pillars of the door, when the wind immediately changed its quarter, and the fire subsided without committing further damage.

When Dr de Falk made his will, for not all his knowledge could save him from the fate of ordinary mortality, he appointed as his executors Mr Aaron Goldsmid, Mr George Goldsmid, and Mr de Symons. He bequeathed to the Great Synagogue a small legacy of £68, 16s. 4d., and an annual sum of £4, 12s. to whoever fulfilled the functions of Chief Rabbi. To Aaron Goldsmid, De Falk, in token of his friendship, left a sealed packet or box, with strict injunctions that it should be carefully preserved, but not opened. Prosperity to the Goldsmid family would attend obedience to De Falk's behests; while fatal consequences would follow their disregard. Some time after the Kabbalist's death, Aaron Goldsmid, unable to overcome his curiosity, broke the seal of the mysterious packet. On the same day, he was found dead. Near him was the fatal paper, which was covered with hieroglyphics and cabalistic figures.

We need not multiply instances of De Falk's alleged supernatural powers. We must, however, express a regret that his miracles did not assume a higher form. It seems hardly worth while to summon the assistance of the world of spirits, merely to conjure away from a pawnbroker's office some coffee pots and silver dishes. To make a candle burn for weeks is a very purposeless prodigy, unless applicable to the objects of domestic economy. We will not undertake to say whether there is more in heaven or earth than we dream of in our philosophy; whether, as is more likely, De Falk's miracles partook of the nature of the feats performed by Robert Houdin, Professor Anderson, and Dr Lynn; or whether, as is most probable of all, they were ordinary occurrences magnified into wonders by the love of the marvellous and of the supernatural obtaining in the mind of the vulgar. All we have to add with reference to De Falk is, that the poor considered him as a benefactor, and consulted him on every emergency during his life, while they blessed his memory after death for the liberal donations he left, which were dispensed by Mr de Symons, the surviving executor.

CHAPTER XXXII.

THE GOLDSMID FAMILY.

Aaron Goldsmid was a Dutch merchant of means and of good connections, who established himself in this country with his family in 1765. He was the father of eight children, four of whom were sons and four were daughters. The sons grew up and prospered, and wedded wealthy wives from their own community. The eldest son, George Goldsmid, became a partner in his father's firm of Aaron Goldsmid & Son. Asher, the second son, joined Mr Mocatta of Mansell Street, and founded the eminent firm of Mocatta & Goldsmid, who became bullion-brokers to the Bank of England. Originally Mr Goldsmid intended to admit his third son, Benjamin, to a share in the affairs of his house. A serious blow sustained by his firm caused him to alter his plans. He determined that his younger sons, Benjamin and Abraham, should begin an independent business as brokers. The limited capital with which they started, was afterwards increased by a legacy of £15,000, bequeathed to them by an uncle at Amsterdam. For family reasons it was deemed desirable that Benjamin should travel for a few months; and he took this opportunity of visiting some of the principal cities of Europe in company with Mr Joachim, his brother-in-law. In brilliant Paris, in solemn Berlin, in artistic Rome, Benjamin Goldsmid visited his brethren, made himself acquainted with their political condition, with their educational status, and with their material and moral wants. Being of a generous disposition he liberally contributed to the assistance of the Jews abroad, and on his return to England his attention became more easily fixed on the needs of the Jews at home. To all his co-religionists, English and foreign, he always proved open-handed. The death of Aaron Goldsmid occurred suddenly, as we related in the previous chapter. Not many months after he had welcomed back his son Benjamin, the head of the house of Goldsmid divided his fortune equally among his children.

Benjamin Goldsmid was lucky enough to secure the hand of Miss Jessie Solomons, the daughter of Mr Israel L. Solomons of Clapton, an opulent East India merchant, of Dutch extraction. The young lady was a highly-coveted prize, not only for the beauty of her person and the charm of her manner, but because she was reported to be the richest maiden in Israel. The marriage of Benjamin Goldsmid took place as soon after the death of his father as circumstances permitted. The £100,000, brought to Benjamin by his young bride, materially added to the credit of the house; and the increasing operations of the firm of Goldsmid in time attracted the attention of government. Large sums passed through their hands in the purchase and sale of bullion, stocks, navy and exchequer bills, and in negotiating foreign bills of exchange. Their transactions amounted annually to millions, until the extent of their speculations and of their credit, and the liberality of their dispositions, raised them without opposition to the very first place in the Stock Exchange. They were the earliest members of the Stock Exchange, who competed with bankers for national loans. Hitherto, these had been allotted by the Chancellor of the Exchequer to the banking interest, who were wont to form a confederation to keep down the prices. The brothers Goldsmid broke down the monopoly, and the country profited by obtaining more favourable terms. At the same time fortune seemed to follow their every act, and the smiles of the capricious goddess were lavished upon them. Their charity and their beneficence were equal to their wealth, and their liberality was not confined to the poor of their own faith, but was freely afforded to Christians of every denomination. They possessed financial genius of the highest order; they knew a bad name to a bill of exchange as if by instinct. In 1793 when a commercial crisis occurred, as severe as the crisis of 1847, when some of the oldest and most substantial commercial houses in England fell to pieces like houses of cards, Benjamin and Abraham Goldsmid lost only £50! The press of the period faithfully reported their movements, and one day we find recorded a banquet to royalty, the next day an errand of mercy to a prisoner's cell. Their hospitality was unbounded. Their entertainments were on the grandest scale, and were said to have rivalled the fairy glories of the Arabian Nights.

Benjamin Goldsmid, immediately after his marriage, took a tasteful and elegant residence at Stamford Hill; and subsequently he purchased an estate at Roehampton, where he ordered the erection of a princely mansion. Nothing was omitted that could add splendour to this abode of luxury and boundless wealth. Magnificent and costly staircases, vestibules with beautiful and expensive marble pavements, a rich library, a noble dining-room, a choice gallery of paintings, gorgeous drawing-rooms, unique stables, grounds laid out with admirable taste and judgment, and a terrace and lawn, where art and nature seemed to vie with each other to gratify and bewitch the beholder. Such were some of the features of a residence that was compared with Windsor Castle! Brilliant illuminations on public occasions rendered it a fairy palace; and the fête given after the battle of the Nile, is stated to have surpassed in splendour all that had been attempted before in England! Benjamin was a great personal favourite with Pitt, England's celebrated minister. His name, and that of his brother Abraham, were found in all lists of subscriptions for charitable objects. Benjamin Goldsmid was the founder of the Naval Asylum, and for a time the institution was under his management, until the Government adopted it, enlarged it, and rendered it worthy to shelter the children of the sailors of the greatest naval nation in the world. At the anniversary dinner, the Duke of Kent (father of her present Majesty) presided, with Admiral Sir Sydney Smith on his right hand, and Benjamin Goldsmid on his left. Jews and Christians alike freely gave on the occasion, and Benjamin Goldsmid collected £2000 among his friends. Neither did he forget his race and faith. He was a generous donor to the Synagogue funds; and he had an apartment fitted up in his mansion where his household assembled for divine worship, and where was carefully kept a Scroll of the Law. He appropriated a piece of ground to the Chief Rabbi, and he annually presented to him its produce, fine wheat, with which to make Passover cakes. Knowing the low state of education among German Jews in his time, he liberally promoted all schemes likely to raise the mental condition of his co-religionists. He supported all educational movements, and in conjunction with Dr Myers (father of the late Baroness N. M. de Rothschild), he formed a society to assist David Levi in the publication of his works, and he treated Levi in the most generous manner. Unhappily, Benjamin Goldsmid in his later years became afflicted with fits of despondency, for which there was no possible cause. His family do not appear to have felt any serious apprehension. Mischief was brewing nevertheless, and on the 15th April 1808, during an attack of gout, Benjamin Goldsmid took his own life. His mind had evidently become affected, and so certified the jury impannelled for the inquest. Thus perished, at the premature age of fifty-five, the senior partner of one of the wealthiest houses in Europe, a man whose life had presented an unbroken series of successes and triumphs, and who had tasted all the happiness that may fall to the lot of mortals.

Abraham Goldsmid was, if possible, even more popular than his brother Benjamin. His friendly demeanour, his mild, unassuming manner, his extended philanthropy, his ready munificence, were the themes of general conversation. The anecdotes related of his unostentatious charity would almost fill a volume. Now we hear of him saving the humble home of a waiter from the clutches of the bailiffs. Now we see him delicately assisting a single-minded and worthy curate —whose poverty he considered a disgrace to the Church of England—by allotting him a share of a new loan; the letter of allotment being considered a hoax, and thrown aside by the curate, until another post brought a cheque for a large amount realised on the allotment. Another time we find Abraham Goldsmid obtaining the reprieve of a forger; or taking charge of some destitute orphans; or relieving from ruin a distressed officer. He had been united to a Dutch young lady of wealth, and he possessed an establishment at Morden, little inferior in munificence to his brother's residence at Roehampton. It is related that one day King George III., during a drive with Queen Charlotte, alighted from his carriage for a stroll, and stopped to admire some fine trees, enclosed within a gentleman's park. In answer to an inquiry, his Majesty was told that the estate belonged to Abraham Goldsmid the Jew. "What, what, my friend Abraham!" said the King; "I must see it. Go and tell Mr Goldsmid to get some luncheon ready for us, and we shall go to him at once." King George's commands were obeyed, and the vast resources of the household of the great loan-contractor were called into requisition. A sumptuous repast was laid before their Majesties of England. "Farmer George," after having inspected the highly ornamented and beautifully laid-out grounds, was ushered into a handsome and well-proportioned dining hall. Royalty sat down before the well-spread board, while Abraham Goldsmid with his family remained standing like dutiful subjects. "Come, Goldsmid," exclaimed Farmer George, observing this, "if you do not sit down to luncheon I shall stand up too." The King was not a Lucullus, but he loved good cheer, and he seldom enjoyed a repast more than the refection in which, side by side with the financier, he tasted the delicacies of the season.

The death of Benjamin Goldsmid proved a serious blow to Abraham, for the two brothers were tenderly attached to each other. Nevertheless, the latter continued his operations without interruption. In 1810 the houses of Baring and Goldsmid were contractors for the ministerial loan of £14,000,000. Sir Thomas Baring died at this juncture, leaving, it is said, a fortune of £5,000,000. The care of supporting the market fell on the shoulders of Abraham Goldsmid, and the task proved most arduous. A powerful organisation had been formed, which would have required the combined resources of the two houses to overcome. Day by day the price of scrip dropped, and with it dropped the fortunes of Abraham Goldsmid. He held £8,000,000 of stock; he gradually lost all fortitude, and became a prey to despondency.

When the reduction in the price of omnium had reached £65 per thousand, his singularly clear mind became confused, and he appeared restless and disordered. Another circumstance added to his embarrassment. The East India Company had placed Exchequer Bills to the extent of £500,000 in his hands to negotiate. That corporation became alarmed for the safety of their property and claimed its value. The payment was fixed for Friday the 28th September 1810. Abraham Goldsmid was unprepared, and his sensitive and honourable nature made him shrink from facing a disgrace which he exaggerated a thousand times. It has been said, we know not on what authority, that one of his kinsmen hastened to Morden (his residence) on that Friday morning, with the good news that the funds for the East India Company were ready. At all events, it was too late. Abraham Goldsmid was dead!

The news of the calamity produced an unparalleled sensation. The loss of the great loan-contractor was regarded as an event of national importance. Expresses were dispatched to the King and to the Prince of Wales. Consols fell in a few minutes from $66\frac{1}{2}$ to $61\frac{3}{4}$, and omnium from $6\frac{1}{2}$ to $10\frac{3}{4}$ discount. Jobbers met with anxious faces in Capel Court, and merchants attended before their time in the Exchange. Business was suspended; the news of peace or war scarcely caused equal excitement. The public journals teemed with eulogies on a man whose name had been synonymous with charity, with beneficence, with philanthropy. His remains were followed to the grave by weeping and mourning thousands, who, having experienced his generosity and liberality in life, now crowded to honour him in death.

Then for a time the star of the Goldsmid family paled. In later years some members of the family, who had seceded from Judaism, acquired rank and distinction in the service of the East India Company, and one Goldsmid (afterwards a general) fought at Waterloo. It was left to Sir Isaac Lyon Goldsmid, son of Mr Asher Goldsmid, and nephew of Benjamin and Abraham Goldsmid, to revive the glories of his house.

Isaac L. Goldsmid was born in 1778, and received a good education at an English school in Finsbury Square. He became a fluent Latin scholar, and a fair mathematician, while he cultivated at the same time Jewish theology, the higher branches of philosophy, and political science. In due course he was admitted a partner in the firm of Mocatta & Goldsmid, brokers to the Bank of England and the East India Company. This was one of the twelve houses of Jewish brokers then allowed in the city of London. Mr I. L. Goldsmid, as bullion-broker, was by right also a member of the Stock Exchange.

His first speculations were not successful, but subsequently he was more fortunate, and began to amass a vast fortune.

Mr Goldsmid initiated various public undertakings, such as the Croydon and Merstham Railway, which was one of the earliest attempts at railways in England; and he assisted in the establishment of the London Institution and the London Docks.

It was not only towards industrial schemes that his energies were directed. The causes of philanthropy and education enlisted his warmest sympathies. He co-operated with Joseph Lancaster in spreading enlightenment among the masses, and with Mrs Fry in improving the condition of prisoners. The share Mr Goldsmid had in the foundation of the London University and University College are well known. Mr Goldsmid married, in 1804, his cousin Isabel, by whom he became the father of several children. He was much attached to his kindred, and on the downfall of his uncles, he exerted himself strenuously to save the relics of their fortune for their widows and offspring.

As the subject of this sketch grew in wealth, he participated in numerous financial operations, which were mostly connected with Portugal, Brazil, and Turkey. The loans he carried out for these countries were highly successful. He was visited by many foreign political exiles, among whom was Prince Louis Napoleon, albeit the future Emperor of the French did not succeed in enlisting his support. Sir I. L. Goldsmid, after receiving an English baronetcy, was created a Knight of the Tower and Sword of Portugal. Subsequently, the king of that country bestowed upon him the title of Baron da Palmeira, to which a small estate was attached. It is said that Sir I. L. Goldsmid was induced to accept these honours, rather by a desire to vindicate the Jewish name—his race having endured prolonged persecution in Portugal—than by motives of personal ambition.

Sir I. L. Goldsmid, having satisfactorily negotiated two loans for Brazil, was appointed to the financial agency of that empire, which he shared with his friends, Alderman Thompson, M.P., and Messrs T. and W. King. At sixty years of age he retired from business, and was succeeded by his younger son. Sir I. L. Goldsmid then visited France,

Italy, and Germany, for the benefit of his health; and on his return to England he was again drawn into a variety of transactions. He lived until an advanced age, though in his last years he had become childish, and he eventually died in 1859. He was, during his whole life, a strict observing Jew, and the services he rendered to the Jewish cause were of the highest importance. He contributed, to as great a degree as any other individual, to the removal of Jewish disabilities, and his efforts in this direction will receive full justice in due course.

CHAPTER XXXIII.

A SCHEME FOR IMPROVING THE CONDITION OF THE POOR.

How best to relieve the suffering and distress that seem to be the doom of human nature in the present condition of society, without inducing on the part of the poor too great a reliance on the support of the beneficent, is one of those problems, the satisfactory solution of which has baffled human ingenuity. How to cope with pauperism; how to rouse the poor from the slough of despond; how to infuse into them the spirit of hope and the spirit of self-exertion, have been tasks that have taxed to the uttermost the energies and ingenuity of many a philanthropist. If the plague-spots of pauperism, of ignorance, of crime, still eat into the heart of society in our days, after so many noble efforts have been made to grapple with the evils that form hideous blots on our much-vaunted civilisation, the condition will easily be imagined of the lower classes three-quarters of a century since. A vivid picture of that condition is presented by a work on the police of London, emanating from the pen of Patrick Colquhoun, LL.D., an able and philanthropic magistrate, who for many years presided at the Westminster Police Office. The nature of our undertaking prescribes to us the treatment of matters of essentially Jewish interest. We will, therefore, resist the temptation of laying before our readers some remarkable details concerning the poor of London in general, and we will limit ourselves to speaking of the Jewish poor in particular.

We will at once say, that the state of the Jewish indigent at the close of last century was most lamentable—an appalling degree of misery, ignorance, and demoralisation obtained. Even among the Sephardic Jews, with their superior wealth, education, and opportunities, the condition of the poor was highly unsatisfactory. We have it from the pen of an enlightened member of that community, Jacob Abenatar Pimentel, who addressed some letters on this vital question to the authorities of his congregation, that there was a manifest increase of the poor in that period, and that the increase was to be attributed to their own want of industry and sheer idleness. The same gentleman informs us that the poor of his community were averse to hard work; that they only supplied cane strings, barley-sugar, and sweet cakes; that scarcely any mechanics and few domestic servants were found in their ranks; that charities were multiplied *ad infinitum*, and that ruinous establishments were maintained at a heavy expense indiscriminately for the idle, the worthless, and the profligate; that the certainty of being relieved, when suffering the combined miseries of age and poverty, tended to relax the efforts of the humbler classes in early life; that it was better to place them in a position to purchase their own bread rather than to have their bread purchased for them; and, finally, that the poor were little inclined to work, and the authorities, out of mistaken kindness, contributed to pauperise them. These letters of Mr Pimentel seem to have led to nothing beyond an empty vote of thanks to him for his communications! And yet they dealt with most important topics! A wonderful amelioration in the condition of the Jewish poor has doubtless occurred since then; nevertheless, we question whether, even at the present day, the evils complained of by Jacob Abenatar Pimentel, with reference to the mistaken treatment of the poor, have been wholly removed.

The state of the poor among the Sephardim, unsatisfactory as it may have been, was absolute excellence, was supreme goodness, as compared with the vastly inferior general condition of the Askenazi poor. Here we have to deal not only with poverty and idleness; we have to face the lowest depth of destitution, profound ignorance, great demoralisation. The shoals of indigent Jews flocking over from German Ghettos and from Polish villages, without resources, without any other knowledge than that of the exterior forms of their own religion—generally unacquainted with any trade and with the language of this country, found themselves utterly adrift in London, and frequently had to choose between hunger and dishonesty, starvation and petty crime. In a new edition of his work, Mr Colquhoun drew so severe a picture of the malpractices habitually committed by some of the foreign Jewish poor, and painted their sufferings and their general conduct in such gloomy colours, as to attract the attention of some of the most enlightened members of the Askenazim. Mr J. Van Oven, a gentleman who distinguished himself for the eminent services he rendered to the Jewish cause, and for the zeal and ability with which he was always ready to promote the interests of the Jewish race, took up the pen in reply to the strictures of Mr Colquhoun. Under date of the 24th March 1801, Mr Van Oven published a letter addressed to that gentleman, in which he eloquently defended his poorer co-religionists, and propounded the general feature of a scheme for their moral and material improvement. From this source we gather some valuable details on the Jewish poor. Mr Van Oven is able to explain and palliate, though not altogether to deny, the allegations of Mr Colquhoun. "The Jews," says Mr Van Oven, "are refused the privilege of exercising any trade or calling, and they are necessarily driven to the shift of money transactions, which leads to the idea that Jew and usurer are convertible terms. The poor Jews practise petty knavery absolutely for bread. The constrained and deplorable state of these poor gives ground for the continuance of the prejudice against them." He proposed to erect houses of industry and education, with hospitals for the sick, subject to their own ceremonial laws, and to maintain such houses by annual contributions from the sum paid to the general poor-rates by Jewish housekeepers. The whole was to be vested under the management of a properly-elected board. Mr Van Oven thought it an especially favourable moment to moot the question, owing to the presence among the Jews of a man—"who was an honour to his species in general and his nation in particular (Abraham Goldsmid), who united in himself the rare qualities of integrity, generosity, and active benevolence, whose liberality was unbounded, and who had deservedly acquired the love and admiration of all who knew him." As for the general condition of the German Congregations, we gather from Mr Van Oven, through other documents, that the German Jews at that period still possessed the fewest number of rich and the largest number of poor; that the Synagogue in Fenchurch Street comprised a small number of opulent members with very few poor; that the Synagogue in Leadenhall Street, with a sprinkling of rich men, consisted mainly of persons of the middle-class and of poor people; that the Great Synagogue in Duke's Place had the greatest number of all classes, but its poor were altogether unlimited as all strangers were customarily considered as attached to this congregation. The income of the Synagogues was mostly uncertain and fluctuating. The members did not pay, as in the Portuguese Congregation, a fixed rate (finta) and a tax on commercial operations (imposta). They only contributed a rental for their seats, and the offerings made on festivals and on especial occasions, the payment of which there was no means of enforcing. The relief of the poor depended solely on the amount in hand, and was conducted by the overseer at his discretion. No wonder, therefore, that it was totally ineffective.

Mr Colquhoun was a large-minded man, desirous of promoting the welfare of Jew as well as of Christian. A private correspondence ensued between him and J. Van Oven, and these two philanthropic men, of different creeds, learned to respect and esteem each other. Mr Colquhoun drew up the draft of a comprehensive scheme, from the notes furnished him by J. Van Oven. The scheme was discussed by these two gentlemen; it was submitted to and approved by Abraham Goldsmid: it was slightly amended, and eventually Mr Goldsmid placed it in the hands of Mr Addington, the Chancellor of the Exchequer, supported by a petition in its favour. It was proposed, according to this plan, to form a board, consisting of twelve representatives of the German Jews, four representatives of the Portuguese Jews, two aldermen of the City of London, two magistrates for Middlesex, Kent, Essex, and Surrey, and the four presidents of the four City Synagogues, all of whom were to be appointed by the Act of Parliament applied for. This board was to be empowered to purchase land, not to exceed 100 acres, and to erect thereupon the following buildings : 1. An asylum for aged and infirm persons. 2. An hospital for the sick, the maimed, and the diseased. 3. A school for the education of children, and their instruction in mechanical and other useful arts. 4. A workhouse, or institution of industry for vagrant poor, and such as were able but not willing to work for their living.

The Jews were to relieve the parishes they inhabited of all expense for their poor, and the parish was to hand to the Board one-half of the assessment for the relief of the poor contributed by Jews. The Board was to be empowered to levy an assessment from each Synagogue; and if the revenue of the Synagogue should prove insufficient, an individual assessment was to be levied from each member. It was also to possess the power of borrowing up to £10,000. The Board was to inquire into the circumstances of foreign Jews who came over without any evident means of maintenance; and to receive from the several Synagogues all the incomes appropriated to the poor, in order to distribute them.

This scheme, of which we have given the barest outline, would have effected an incalculable amount of good, had it been duly carried out at the time it was proposed. But its very completeness and extended bearing militated against its success, and raised against it strenuous opposition from various quarters. The Great Synagogue certainly regarded it with favour, and appointed a committee, to which was added Mr Van Oven himself, who was one of the medical officers of the Synagogue, to discuss the plan with the committees of the other Synagogues, and forwarded through its secretary to the other congregations copies of the plan and of the resolutions already arrived at on the subject. But De Castro, the secretary to the Portuguese Congregation, hastened to disclaim, on the part of his constituents, any desire to participate in the scheme. The Portuguese Community, he said, already possessed an hospital, an asylum, and a school; and they did not consider themselves justified in altering their political or economical system, which, for upwards of a century, had answered every purpose for which it had been created. The fact is, that the Portuguese Jews, who had already most of the establishments intended to be formed, and who possessed a much larger number of rich men in their body, and a much smaller number of poor in proportion, than any other congregation, would have been considerable losers by the proposed amalgamation. They alleged at the meetings convened in their own vestry to oppose the plan in question, that their charitable institutions had been founded to save their brethren who fled from Spain and Portugal, or who were reduced by misfortunes, and not for the purpose of encouraging German, Dutch, or Polish adventurers;—that they differed greatly from the Germans in ceremonies, customs, and pronunciation, so that they could not read prayers together, and that each community formed a distinct political (not religious) body;—that during the previous fifty years the German Jews, especially the poorer classes, had increased so prodigiously in numbers, that their poor bore no proportion to the Portuguese poor, who were already provided for.

For these and other reasons the Sephardim instructed their attorney to prepare a petition to Parliament in opposition to the petition of the Askenazim, in which the motives were explained at length, why the two sections of the British Jews could not make common cause in the support of their poor. The Portuguese, moreover, dwelt forcibly on their desire to retain their complete autonomy in all respects. Mr Isaac Aguilar and two other representatives of this community waited upon Mr Hobhouse, M.P., who had charge of the Bill, to express the views of their constituents on the introduction into the Bill of a clause excluding altogether the Portuguese Community from the operation of the projected plan.

Thus a union with the Portuguese had to be given up; and the withdrawal of the oldest and still wealthiest congregation in England from the proposed amalgamation scheme proved a serious blow to it. Then the clause asking for half the amount paid by Jews for poor-rates met with disapprobation from high quarters, owing to parochial influence, and had to be abandoned. Finally, the idea of vesting on any body of men the right of coercively taxing the Jewish public, raised a host of enemies to the Bill among the German

Jews themselves. Several pamphlets were written showing the impracticability of the scheme, and Mr Abraham Goldsmid found himself constrained to withdraw the application to Parliament. Mr Van Oven greatly deplored this lame and impotent conclusion: and Mr Colquhoun, who was equally disappointed, thus addressed him in a letter: "You have done your utmost to obtain one of the greatest blessings, moral and political, that could have been conferred on this people. The time must come when the measure must be adopted under perhaps less favourable auspices." The discussion on this scheme, if it did not lead to an immediate practical result, at least aroused the German Jewish Community to a sense of their needs, which have all since been provided for, though at different times, under different forms, and in a manner scarcely verifying Mr Colquhoun's prediction. Mr Van Oven did not altogether renounce his philanthropic designs; and in the Jews' Hospital—to the constitution of which he had materially contributed—he saw the realisation of a small portion, at least, of the extended scheme which he had so ably advocated.

The German Jewish Community of London may indeed look back with pride on the results it has achieved since the beginning of this century. Not only has it provided for the material wants of its poor with a care, with a liberality, with a completeness of detail unapproached by any other race; it has also elevated their spiritual condition until the Jewish poor of all sections of the Jewish Community in London have become equal, if not actually superior, in thrift, in honesty, in sobriety, and in moral and religious condition, to the poor of any other faith or nationality.

CHAPTER XXXIV.

THE GREAT SYNAGOGUE IN THE NINETEENTH CENTURY.

THE history of the principal German Jewish Congregation in London presents few, if any, stirring events since the beginning of the present century. We behold a uniform record of progress in every direction; of progress in wealth, in numbers, in public institutions, in education, in general welfare. The most serious trouble was an occasional difference with the New or with the Hambro' Synagogue. The most startling occurrence was a state visit from Royalty to the Synagogue. The most puzzling dilemma was the election of a Chief Rabbi, or a minister, or a deputy. Legacies were bequeathed by the pious, and the funds of the community were rapidly increasing. As we have often said, the real rock ahead of the Askenazim was the treatment of the poor, especially of the foreign poor. When the narrow parochial spirit predominated, as was too often the case, each Synagogue desired to contribute as little as possible to the relief of the poor. We have seen what the condition of that class was, and in common justice we are bound to observe that to relieve them effectively was indeed a colossal task. In 1804 a conference took place between the delegates of each of the three German City Synagogues, with the view of accomplishing a union between them. The representatives of the Hambro' Synagogue proposed, in addition, the appointment of a committee of seven members from each congregation, to consider the state of the poor. These conferences and committees led to no tangible result, for the inevitable law of self-interest which guides communities, as it does individuals, conduced to a clashing of the apparent interests of the different congregations.

It was only in 1802 that a coolness of long standing

between the New Synagogue and the Great Synagogue had ceased to exist on the auspicious event of the nuptials of Nathan Solomons, the *Rosch* or Principal Member of the New Synagogue, with a daughter of Asher Goldsmid. Mr Solomons was then admitted a member of the Great Synagogue, and eternal amity was declared between the members of the two congregations. This happy concord lasted not quite two years; when the apple of dissension appeared under the shape of a member, who was alleged to have been enticed away from one Synagogue into the other. Mr L. de Symons at this period (1804) suggested an amalgamation of the three Askenazi Synagogues, or at least a fusion of their receipts and expenditures. This proposal was declined by the Hambro' Synagogue, and rejected by the New Synagogue. Happily peace was restored by the (then) new Chief Rabbi of Duke's Place, the Rev. Sol. Hirschel, who attended a meeting of the Synagogue delegates, and desired each congregation to elect representatives empowered to adjust all differences without any further reference to their constituents. A meeting of the representatives so deputed was held under the presidency of the Rev. Sol. Hirschel himself, and it was agreed to continue the *statu quo*, each Synagogue bearing the same share as before of the common burden—that is, the Great Synagogue relieving all the foreign poor in life, and the New Synagogue and the Hambro' Synagogue each affording a small annual contribution to that object; while after death the Great Synagogue was to provide sepulture to two paupers, and the other two Synagogues to one pauper each. This arrangement was the basis of all compacts between the Askenazim congregations; differences of opinion arising only as to the proper sum to be disbursed by each of the smaller Synagogues. It was distinctly stipulated, too, that no Synagogue should accept as member any individual who was member of another. This was considered a point of honour among all Jewish Synagogues in London. So strongly did each congregation resent any infringement of its rights on the part of the others, that once, years after this time, a *Yahid* or member of the Portuguese Congregation, who, on espousing the daughter of a member of the Duke's Place

Synagogue, had permitted the ceremony to be performed by the Rev. Sol. Hirschel, was dismissed summarily from his community, and a serious remonstrance was sent to the German Chief Rabbi.

The treaties between the three German Synagogues were usually made for five or six years, with six months' notice of discontinuation. On the 12th September 1811, the Hambro' Synagogue gave notice of discontinuing the articles of agreement entered into on the 9th March 1805; and the next treaty between the Hambro' and the Great Synagogue was not entered into until March 1815. Then the Hambro' Synagogue covenanted to hand over to the Great Synagogue £125 per annum, and to give interment to six adult foreign poor. Peace being restored between these two congregations, a coolness ensued between Duke's Place and Leadenhall Street. Negotiations between the last two congregations were initiated in 1818; committees met, the most friendly intentions were expressed on both sides, but as neither side would accede to the demands of the other, even in small matters, the negotiations necessarily broke down.

It was not until later times that a complete understanding and perfect union took place between the various German congregations in London. This happy result was partly owing to the exertions of Nathan Meyer Rothschild, as will be seen in its place. In 1808, a contract was entered into between the Westminster Synagogue, in Denmark Court, Strand, and the three German Congregations in the City. According to this treaty, the Westminster Synagogue was allowed to have its separate existence and administration, and as an adequate return for the benefits of the protection of the Great Synagogue, each member was to be considered as member of the Great Synagogue, and to pay annually a small poll tax to the parent congregation.

From statistics of the day we perceive that in April 1804, there were said to be in London 346 places of worship. In six of these establishments the Jews assembled to sing the praise of the Lord of their forefathers; while in six more, the Society of Friends met to wait until they were moved by the Spirit. There were five Synagogues, one Sephardim and three Askenazim in the city, and one of the latter denomination in the Strand. The remaining sixth Jewish House of Worship was a Polish society, gathering in the district which was then the extreme East of London. It should be borne in mind that the German Jews did not lay so much stress on unity as their Portuguese brethren; and they did not think the safety of the community imperilled if a few humble individuals met quietly in some convenient place to perform their devotions.

In the year 1808 several improvements were introduced in the details of internal management in the Great Synagogue. Among others all the salaries of the officials were consolidated and perquisites were abolished; an innovation that was not adopted by the Portuguese until long afterwards. At the same time the property of the Synagogue was augmented in extent by the purchase of an adjoining piece of ground for the sum of £1200, which was raised by an especial loan repayable in six annual instalments. In the same year, Levy Barent Cohen bequeathed £500 to the Synagogue, to be invested in government securities, and to be allowed to accumulate until the 1st January 1823; and then to become available for general congregational purposes. This was the beginning of the Legacy Fund, which received large additions from time to time by similar contributions from the pious. Among other sums willed to this congregation during the first quarter of the nineteenth century, we may mention, £4490, 8s. 1d., from Judah Phillips, of Jamaica, left to trustees for the benefit of his brother and sister to revert after their death to the Synagogue; £3900 from Asher Goldsmid, bequeathed in 1823, for the benefit of the poor; and smaller legacies from B. A. Goldschmidt, of Great St Helen's, and from other benevolent individuals.

The loyalty of the Askenazim was as deep as that of the Sephardim, and they seized every opportunity for its manifestation. In April 1809 the Synagogue in Duke's Place experienced the unusual honour of receiving a state visit from several princes of the blood. Abraham Goldsmid attended personally at a meeting of the Synagogue on the 3d of April, to give notice that the Duke of Cumberland, the Duke of Sussex, and the Duke of Cambridge, intended to assist at a Friday evening service. The Duke of Sussex, it is well known, always displayed much friendship and sympathy for the Jews. On this occasion pompous preparations were made for the reception of these distinguished guests. The Wardens of the day were Messrs Asher Goldsmid, Joseph Cohen, and Moses Samuel. The notice was short, for the visit occurred on Friday evening, the 14th April. The path of the Royal Dukes from their carriages to the entrance of the Synagogue was strewn with flowers; and their advent was hailed with the usual Prayer for the Royal Family—"He who giveth salvation unto kings"—intoned by a well-drilled choir. Some verses, written, we believe, by the late Michael Josephs, were sung; and a few copies printed on silk were distributed to a favoured number. Altogether the celebration is said to have met in the highest degree the approbation of the princely sons of George III.; and the visit of the Royal Dukes still forms a tradition of glory among the older members of the Great Synagogue.

The 25th October 1809 was kept as a jubilee, for George III. had reigned fifty years over these realms. The festival was celebrated according to Jewish customs. The commandments enjoining the remission of debts in the year of jubilee were not forgotten, and the various Jewish Congregations subscribed as far as their means permitted towards the relief and discharge of persons confined for small debts. In the Duke's Place Synagogue, a special service was held at one o'clock in the day. A Hebrew prayer was composed by Dr Hirschel, and translated into English by Joshua Van Oven. An ode, composed for the occasion, was sung by a trained choir; and the ceremony was attended with great solemnity. The Jews participated no less in the sorrows of the Royal family; and on the sad occasion of the death of the Princess Charlotte, special services were performed in all the Synagogues, appropriate sermons were delivered, and the congregations appeared in full mourning.

As the prosperity of this congregation increased, so we find its generosity grow larger and more catholic. The funds of the members of the community were available to meet the calls of public and private charity. Now we find a subscription made to relieve a famine in Sweden; now a collection to diminish the sufferings of English prisoners in France;

at another time contributions are sought in aid of the Waterloo Fund. Irish distress is not forgotten, and on more than one occasion, after the failure of the potato crops, appeals were made by the authorities of the Great Synagogue, on behalf of the hunger-stricken children of Ireland.

The city of London seems to have generally borne a favourable character for liberality, and we hear in 1800, some years after the lease of the ground of the Great Synagogue and buildings expired, that the President of the Congregation, Mr Joseph Cohen, had met with generous treatment from the City Lands' Committee. The lease had really come to an end in 1801, but the congregation experienced great courtesy. The lease was renewed on payment of a fine of £45, and arrears of interest and costs, and it was covenanted that the lease should be renewed every fourteen years from 1815 at a rental of £32 per annum, and on payment of the same fine. It is only at the present time that the tenure of the Great Synagogue has been converted into a freehold.

CHAPTER XXXV.

THE PORTUGUESE SYNAGOGUE IN THE NINETEENTH CENTURY.

THE condition of the oldest Jewish Congregation in London was by no means satisfactory at the beginning of the present century. There was a falling off in the number of members and a proportionate diminution in the congregational income. Its house of prayer was frequented by a scanty number of worshippers. The service was conducted in a slovenly, unimpressive manner; decorum was little regarded; choral music was not known; and a general indifferentism seemed to reign in the community. The aspect of affairs appeared so grave in the year 1802 that an inquiry into the ecclesiastical state of the community was instituted. The Council of Wardens had strenuously recommended this step, otherwise said they, "In this Kahal (congregation), which had shone brilliantly for more than a century as one of the principal in Europe, the study of the law will be entirely lost, and the Kahal will become an object of contempt and ridicule." The gentlemen to whom this delicate investigation was entrusted were Messrs Jacob Samuda, Joseph Sasportas, Gabriel Israel Brandon, Jacob Aboab Osorio, and Jacob Mocatta. Their report was presented in January 1803. It recommended that a Haham (Doctor of Divinity) or Rabbi should be appointed as the spiritual guide of the congregation; that the Committee of the Heshaim (charity schools) should revise their laws and take measures to effectively promote the education of the children; and that the Medrash (Religious College) should be better regulated, so that members of the congregation might be induced to send their children for religious instruction to a Yeshiba or school to be established in connection therewith.

Since the death of Haham D'Azevedo the Portuguese Community had been without a pastor, and the loss of Rabbi Hasdai Almosnino, the Chief of the Beth Din, had left the congregation destitute of able expounders of the Jewish law. It was resolved to appoint a Haham without further delay. The requirements of the congregation having been made known, two applications for the vacant office were presented, and the selection fell on Rabbi Raphael Meldola of Leghorn. Of the qualifications of this gentleman we shall speak more fully hereafter. For the present we will merely say that he was nominated on the 7th October 1804; that ample provision was made to enable him to fulfil his functions worthily; that a residence was chosen for him and appropriately furnished; and that all honour was paid to him on his arrival in this country.

The Board of Shechita, a body of gentlemen deputed by the various London Synagogues to superintend arrangements for slaughtering animals and inspecting the carcases for sanitary purposes, according to the Mosaic law, was constituted, as we have already stated, in the year 1805. This was a great improvement on the former faulty and incomplete mode of supplying meat suitable for Jews; and not only much inconvenience and annoyance to the public and to the Synagogues were thus saved, but an absolute profit accrued after payment of all expenses. At the end of the first year a surplus of £397, 7s. 9d. was on hand, and each Synagogue was credited with the fourth part of that sum, which was invested in consols. The net produce increased in subsequent years, and to the present day it continues to be equally distributed between the Portuguese Congregation and the three German Synagogues in the city.

In 1807 the Bevis Marks Synagogue furnished a minister to the Portuguese Congregation of Charlestown, South Carolina, in the person of Benjamin Cohen D'Azevedo, son of their former rabbi. The South Carolinians, who had trumpeted forth their wants in high sounding language, and had dwelt on their potential liberality and generosity in terms which at all events had not the merit of modesty, showed scant courtesy to the nominee of the parent Synagogue in London, or to that Synagogue itself. They sent back Benjamin C.

D'Azevedo without assigning any plausible cause. This line of conduct stung to the quick the Portuguese pride of the rulers of Bevis Marks, who resented it in no measured words, and took the returned minister into their service as teacher.

The new Haham was a man of active temperament, and he repeatedly declared that he had accepted the post he occupied, to *act* and not merely to *speak*. He addressed a communication to the Mahamad, urging that body to take stringent measures to prevent the children of the poor from attending certain schools opened in the neighbourhood for conversionist purposes, and wherein tracts were distributed. In July 1802 he joined Dr Hirschel in a declaration referring to the maintenance of the sanctity of the Sabbath.

At the end of 1808, the Sephardic Synagogue found itself short of funds. There was a narrower number of members to offer, and the offerings themselves were smaller; moreover the *imposta* (tax on commercial transactions on commission) was falling into desuetude. It was resolved to summon a meeting of members. The meeting was convened for the 18th January 1809, and was carried out with great solemnity. It was held in the Synagogue itself; and only the members who were not indebted to the *Zedaka* (poor fund) were admitted. At 11 o'clock the doors of the Synagogue were closed, no one was allowed to enter or to leave, and the keys of the doors were deposited with the president, who stood before the reading-desk. Before the affairs of the congregation were discussed, some psalms were chanted and a prayer was recited. In our present matter-of-fact days, when reason often holds the place of faith, when doubt is substituted for reverence, and when speed rather than dignity characterises the actions of our lives, our readers may well feel surprised at so many formalities accompanying, and so much importance being attached to, a mere Synagogue meeting. It is certain that on the occasion in question, the members present were deeply impressed with the momentous character of the proceedings. The president made an opening speech; and it was resolved to grant power to the elders to increase the *finta* from £900 to £1400 per annum. No Yahid (or member) was to be called upon to contribute more than 4 per cent. of the total amount of the *finta*, nor less than 10s. per annum.

The impost was reduced to 6d. per £100. Other provisions of minor consequence were made in addition; and a small sum was ordered to be sold out of the funds to provide for immediate urgencies. At the same time, it was resolved that no *Minyan* (congregation for prayer) should be permitted to assemble within six miles of the Synagogue, instead of within four miles, as was formerly the case.

The finances of the Synagogue, under skilful management, soon recovered their balance; gentle pressure was laid on members who were in arrears in their accounts. Some of the defaulters settled; others undertook to settle them as soon as circumstances permitted, and only a few allowed their names to be posted up on the doors of the Synagogue. It was not found necessary to call for more than £1200 of the £1400 voted for *finta;* and a year or two afterwards we find that the deficit had disappeared.

In 1809, Joseph Barrow died, and bequeathed to the wardens of the Portuguese Synagogue and their successors a sum of £2000, to build almshouses for the residence of respectable indigent families. The sum was invested in consols; and it was not until 1815 that a suitable piece of ground was found and purchased, and the beneficent intentions of the donor were begun to be carried out. In 1813 the funds of the Synagogue were considerably increased by the death of Abraham Lopes Pereira, of Hackney. This gentleman left £500 to the Synagogue wardens for the benefit of the poor; £100 to the congregational hospital; and several other legacies to charitable institutions. He bore in mind that cold chills the limbs of Christians as well as of Jews, and he gave to the churchwardens of his parish in Hackney £200, the interest of which was to be annually expended in furnishing coals to the needy. Finally, he willed the residue of his estate to the wardens of the Portuguese Synagogue for the benefit of the poor. Such residue amounted to between twelve and fourteen thousand pounds, and formed a noble addition to the capital of the community.

In the beginning of the century, the house of Alexander Lindo, engaged in the West India trade, enjoyed great repute for wealth and integrity. It had embarked in extensive transactions in connection with the French Government; and trusting to the faith of the First Consul, it was induced to enter into large contracts, and to effect immense shipments to the French West India islands. General Leclerc (the beloved of Hortense Beauharnais, stepdaughter of Napoleon, and afterwards Queen of Holland) then commanded the French forces at that time. He gave in payment to the representative of Alexander Lindo, a bill for the sum of £260,000 on his Government. This draft, for an amount that must in those days have been considered a vast sum, was dishonoured on the frivolous pretext that the bill had been issued at a discount, and that full value had not been given for it. This unexpected check seriously affected the house of Alexander Lindo, who had every reason to consider himself very ill treated by the French Government. The celebrated General Rochambeau, who succeeded Leclerc, protested in the strongest language against the conduct of the Government. He gave the lie direct to the statements made by the Minister of Marine to the First Consul, and declared that the bills given in payment by General Leclerc and himself had been perfectly correct and against proper value. We are unable to state whether the representations of the General had any effect, and whether Lindo came to his own again. Certain it is, that his firm never regained its former position, and that the unjust and arbitrary act of the consular Government brought one of the most respected members of the Sephardim Congregation to the verge of ruin. Alexander Lindo was one of the few remaining representatives of that series of merchant princes who once had flourished among the Portuguese Jews. The Ricardos, the Ximenes, the Rodrigues Lopes, the Jessurun Alvares, the Levys, were verging towards another church, and now a calamity fell on the head of one of the numbered faithful. Alexander Lindo was a zealous Jew; he took great interest in the affairs of the congregation; he had passed through its various dignities until he became president; and he was one of the largest contributors to its funds. For many years his affairs remained unsettled. He died in 1818, and left a legacy to the Synagogue, but his executors were unable to pay it at the time, for his estates had been placed under the control of the Court of Chancery.

CHAPTER XXXVI.

JEWISH VOLUNTEERS—WRITERS ON THE JEWS.

MARTIAL ardour is not a quality usually ascribed to Jews. Nay, sneers have not been wanting on the assumed want of bravery on the part of Jews. It is possible, and even probable, that the oppression of ages may have somewhat broken the spirit of the descendants of one of the most belligerent of ancient races. But as soon as they are, we will not say placed on an equality with their fellow-citizens, but even treated with some toleration, and allowed to hold a stake in their fatherland, they come forward and are ready to live and die for their country. Witness in our day the remarkable spectacle of sons of Israel reciting their prayers on the Day of Atonement in the ranks of the German Army, to the accompaniment of the roar of the guns of the maiden fortress of Metz. Witness the sight of Frenchmen of the Jewish religion falling sword in hand *pour la belle France* in the plains of Champagne, or within sight of the forts of beleaguered Paris. Witness the numerous Jews of Italy who many times shed their blood in the cause of Italian unity. Witness in the beginning of the present century the Jews who, serving under the banners of the greatest conqueror of modern times, left their bones to char beneath the torrid sun of Spain, or to bleach on the snow-clad steppes of Russia.

Happily, England, since the return of the Jews to its hospitable shores under the Commonwealth and Restoration, has never been under the necessity of defending itself against a foreign invader on its own soil. But whenever a danger real or supposed arose, the Jew came forward ready to bear his full share of hardship and danger. In the autumn of the year 1803 England was in a commotion. The Treaty of Amiens had not stopped the career of the " Corsican

Usurper," and war with France had been again declared. Regular troops were being raised, militiamen were being drilled, and volunteers freely flocked to the standard. Bellona sounded her shrill trumpet from Land's End to John o'Groats. On the 19th October, London wore the appearance of a Sunday. A fast was strictly observed, and the shops were closed. A number of volunteer corps paraded the city, and ten regiments attended divine service, filling every principal church. The corps who had not already taken the oath did so on that day. Three hundred of the most respectable individuals of the Jewish persuasion took the oaths to Government on that occasion. A contemporary publication states that " By an order from their High Priest they were prohibited from attending in our churches during the time of Divine Service. The High Priest, however, expressed his highest concurrence to their taking the oaths of fidelity and allegiance to our king and country. Those gentlemen accordingly took the oaths, either upon the drilling grounds of their respective corps, or in the vestry-room of the churches, as circumstances required. They were sworn upon the Book of Leviticus instead of the New Testament.

On the 26th October a great burst of loyalty was displayed by the armed citizens of London, who were desirous of showing their sovereign that they were ready to shed their blood in defence of their country. A general review of volunteers was witnessed in Hyde Park, by an enthusiastic assemblage of upwards of 200,000 spectators. The King, accompanied by the French princes, Monsieur, the Prince of Condé, the Duke of Bourbon and the Duke of Berry, attended by the celebrated General Dumouriez, rode before the ranks amid repeated cheers. Several hundred Jews were present among the volunteers. His Majesty on subsequent occasions reviewed the different corps separately. Once when the King was inspecting an East-end regiment in which the Jewish element predominated, he is said to have expressed some amused surprise on hearing from the roll-call some of the volunteers designated by names usually borne by familiar quadrupeds, such as Fox, Wolf, Bear, and Lyon.

We have repeatedly noticed the loyalty of the Jews, and the attachment and devotion they have invariably displayed towards the governments of all countries,—without regard to their form—where they have met with common toleration and ordinary justice. In England they have ever been ready, as circumstances occurred, to pray for the recovery of a sick monarch, to offer thanks for his escape from the bullet or the knife of the assassin, to rejoice at his marriage, or mourn at his death. At different times during the reign of George III., the Jews returned thanks in the Synagogues for the King's recovery, even before the church prayers were ordered by the Government; though in this they were kept in countenance by the Dissenters. During the severe illness of the present Prince of Wales, prayers were daily offered in several of the London Synagogues for his recovery, to Him who sends salvation unto kings. Indeed, the first prayer raised for his restoration to health was in a Jewish Synagogue; and when the Angel of Death, which had so long hovered over his threshold, sheathed his sword and passed away, the Jews were the first to sing a Song of Thanksgiving to God.

At the period of which we are speaking, a simple and yet most important action was performed by a Jew, which does not appear to have been sufficiently known, or to have met with public recognition. On the 15th of May 1800, George III. had two narrow escapes from being killed. On the morning of that day, when reviewing the Grenadier Guards, a bullet struck and wounded a gentleman who was standing not twenty yards from the King. At first it was considered that this was the result of an attempt on the King's life, though subsequently the event was attributed to accident. In the evening "Farmer George" went to Drury Lane Theatre to see a comedy by Colley Cibber, and crowds flocked thither to cheer the popular monarch. While the King was bowing his thanks from the royal box, a man named Hadfield rose from the front row of the pit and fired a horse-pistol point blank at the King. Two slugs passed over George III.'s head and effected a lodgment in the wainscot of the box. The King never lost his self-possession, and instead of retiring as he was entreated to do by the Earl of Salisbury, his Lord Chamberlain, and others of his retinue, he with great composure looked round the house and ordered the performance to commence. These are facts with which all readers of history are acquainted. But probably they are not aware that Hadfield, the ex-soldier and lunatic who fired at the King, missed his aim because some man near him struck his arm while in the act of pulling the trigger. This individual was a Jew named Dyte, and to him in all likelihood the country owed the King's life. Dyte was the father of the late Henry Dyte, formerly Honorary Secretary to the Blind Society, and the grandfather of D. H. Dyte, Surgeon to the Jewish Board of Guardians. It is stated that Dyte asked as his sole reward the "patent" of selling opera tickets, then a monopoly at the Royal disposal; and we presume he obtained from King George's generosity this very modest recompense. The Jews in those days seldom entertained very ambitious feelings, and their desires and hopes were not permitted by circumstances to assume a very high flight.

In the beginning of the nineteenth century we find considerable attention devoted to the Jews by the press. The history, creed, habits, and language of the children of Israel formed the theme of many an essay or article in English periodical literature. In a single number of a monthly magazine published in 1810, we find no fewer than seven papers on the subject of the Jews. Some of these lucubrations treated of the spiritual condition of the Jews, principally lamenting their misguided obstinacy in questions of faith. Others spoke of mere temporal matters. From these writings we glean much curious information on the state of the Jews in England at that period. Among the persons who displayed great interest in Jewish affairs, we may name Henry Lemoine, whom we have already mentioned as the author of an elegy on David Levi. Henry Lemoine had been a bookseller in Bishopsgate Churchyard, until his business failing, he gained a precarious subsistence by composing verse and prose for the magazines. Shortly before his death Henry Lemoine obtained hospitable shelter under the roof of a benevolent Jew, who, finding him in sore distress, generously secured him from want in his last days. Henry Lemoine had become intimate with David Levi, to whom he furnished books; and he wrote a short biography of Abraham Goldsmid. Thus he ought to have been well conversant with

Jewish affairs, which, however, he did not prove himself to be. He conceived an opinion far from favourable on the attainments of the Jews and on their general condition in the country. According to him, they were too much under the control of their ecclesiastical authorities and Synagogue wardens. The Synagogue laws were too stringent, and the Synagogue elders too high-handed. As the Jews agreed to submit their differences to their authorities, many arbitrary decisions were arrived at, which were not always found legal by courts of law. The Jews were generally ignorant on most subjects; even those connected with their own form of worship. What they knew of the Pentateuch, or of their prayers, was derived from collateral English translations printed with the original Hebrew; with the Talmud and rabbinical writings they were utterly unacquainted. They were born and bred to commercial transactions; their knowledge was confined to such topics, and all their leisure was spent in the amusements of the town, visiting or walking, but always with an eye to business. Learned English Jews were rare, albeit there were a few such living, who were an ornament to society. The foreign Jews, German, Dutch, or Portuguese, were more cultivated. No absolute agreement had been made between the Jewish Synagogues to maintain their poor; but as the rich were always at hand, the poor did not perish of want. From the few trades the Jews followed, their industry and sobriety must have been great indeed to enable them to live. As their diet and ceremonies precluded them in a great measure from learning trades, they became dealers. Their capitals were small. He (Lemoine) did not think there were thirty members of the Great Synagogue, twenty members of the Fenchurch Street Synagogue, and six of the New Synagogue, who possessed above £5000 to £6000. He excepted the Portuguese Jews, some of whom had brought large fortunes into this country. He considered the Jews, as a rule, a poor race of people, whose religious and ceremonial laws had always placed an insuperable obstacle to their rising beyond a certain sphere in this state of existence.

We are unable to state how much truth there was in this picture of the Jews of the day; certain it is that it was emphatically contradicted by both Jews and Christians. A writer named Atkins, who had composed a History of the Modern Jews in a very kindly spirit, and dedicated it to Abraham Goldsmid, altogether demurred to the opinions and statements of Henry Lemoine. He took up the cudgels on behalf of the Jews, and expressed a very different view on their state from that entertained by Lemoine. He said there were numerous respectable artisans of every description among them, but chiefly in the jewellery and gold and silver trinket department. He believed that the word "jewel" had been derived from Jew, as they were probably the first people who introduced such ornaments into use, and who were then considerable dealers in jewels in the rough and manufactured states. With all deference to Mr Atkins, we do not agree with his derivation of the term jewel, which we think is probably derived from the Italian *giojello*. The Florentine and Venetian artificers of the Middle Ages were celebrated far and wide for their cunning in the manipulation of the precious metals, and were perhaps the founders of modern jewellery. With reference to the Jews, Atkins considered that, notwithstanding the strictness with which most of them kept their Sabbath, they were, by unremitting diligence and constant attention, at least as successful as their Christian neighbours who worked another day in the week. Altogether, Atkins entertained a much higher opinion than Lemoine concerning the wealth, as well as the intellectual attainments, of the Jews.

Among the writers who displayed a warm sympathy for the Israelites, at the period of which we are speaking, we must mention Thomas Witherby and William Hamilton Reid.

The former was a retired bookseller, and had always manifested a sincere friendship for the Jews. His opinion concerning the Jewish religion may be gathered from the following extract from a letter addressed by him to Mr Joshua Van Oven, with whom he occasionally corresponded : " The Roman religion has tended to persecute both your nation and those Christians who are more friendly to you, because we read your Scriptures as well as our own. The Mohammedan religion, instead of tending to this object, compels a uniformity of creed by the sword. The Jewish is the foundation of all true religion, and we can conceive that the Christian is the same being founded thereon." Whatever may be thought of Witherby's theology, there can be no question as to his kindness towards the children of Israel. In 1810, and the following year, he repeatedly took up the pen in defence of the Jews, in the public press, against the attacks of intolerant fanaticism on the one hand, and against the wiles of the conversionists on the other. According to the theory of some men, their own religious belief is faith; the religious belief of their neighbours is superstition. Witherby was not of that class of men; he was liberal towards all—even the conversionists against whom, as a class, he entertained special aversion. Speaking of the manners of the Jews, he mildly says that in some respects they differ from those of Christians. He did not think the Jewish mode of worship so solemn as that of Christians; and in mentioning to a Jew what he deemed a deviation from seriousness in the middle of prayers, he received the following reply: "Ours is not a melancholy religion."

William Hamilton Reid was a gentleman of some literary attainments, and he had produced several historical works which had met with fair success. Among others he had published a book called "The New Sanhedrin and the causes and consequences of the French Emperor's conduct towards the Jews." The work was written in a most fair and impartial spirit, but he had been a considerable loser by its issue. We will quote his own words with reference to his relations with the Jews: "Nevertheless, the attention I have since received from a few enlightened individuals of the Jewish persuasion in this metropolis, with whom I have had the happiness of being acquainted, I look upon as a source of the purest gratification, particularly in being a witness of their integrity as men, their industry and ingenuity as mechanics and artists, and of their gratitude in general to Christians who do not persecute them with their ill-timed importunities about conversion and repentance, while so many there are of our own people who stand more in need of these changes themselves." On another occasion William Hamilton Reid says, that the antipathies of Jews to Christians were fast wearing away, that the former condemned no one for their faith, and did not wish to make any converts, and only required of their fellow-subjects to be suffered to enjoy in peace that liberty of conscience which Government and the Church of England liberally allowed them. We are also told, by the same authority, that the sermons of Dr Hirschel frequently dwelt on the duties of universal toleration; that many of the wealthy Jews were found among the subscribers to the Christian charitable foundations, and that in return many Christian names appeared among the list of donors to the new Jewish Hospital in Mile-End. These Christians, we are assured, did not require the least interference in the management or education of the Jewish children there, and had no connection whatever with the London Society, or with the missionaries who preached in the Jews' Chapel, near Spitalfields.

Among all these discussions on Jewish affairs only one Jewish writer makes his appearance in print. He adopted the signature of "An Unconverted Jew and Englishman." According to his statement, William Hamilton Reid was the most accurate exponent of facts referring to the Jews, and Henry Lemoine the least correct. Indeed, the assertions of the latter are said to be full of errors. The Jews possessed five Synagogues in London, each with its own code of regulations, which interfered no more with the laws of the country than the rules of an Oddfellows' club interfere with the penal code. Each Synagogue had its independent code. Jews in country cities governed themselves without any orders from the London vestries. The poor were amply provided for, and upward of thirty societies existed for the relief of their wants. All those Jews whose circumstances permitted it subscribed liberally to Christian institutions, and at the same time they acknowledged in return with heartfelt gratitude the liberal donations of many worthy Christians to the new Hospital.

CHAPTER XXXVII.

RISE OF THE LONDON SOCIETY—THE DUKE OF SUSSEX—A WEDDING AND A MURDER—A NOBLE-HEARTED JEW.

WE have seen in our previous chapter that the press, that mighty engine, had eagerly canvassed the affairs, status, and aspirations of the Jews in this country, and that many Englishmen of eminence and learning had turned their eyes towards the Jews with curiosity, if not with interest. But it was not merely the worldly position of the Jews that called for consideration from the would-be benevolent. The spiritual condition of the children of Israel, even more than their material welfare, seemed to engross their attention and trouble them sorely. Indeed, some Christians, possibly well-meaning and assuredly ill-judging, insisted on saving the souls of the Jews from everlasting perdition, under cover of an attempt to relieve their bodily wants. These efforts, which formerly had been of a desultory nature, now became regularly organised and controlled by a paid staff. In 1808 a committee of gentlemen who professed great interest in the Jews, founded a society for the ostensible purpose of "visiting and relieving the sick and distressed, and instructing the ignorant, especially such as are of the Jewish nation." At first, indeed, the association, which had been formed on dissenting principles, did not prosper. Frey, a convert of whom we have already spoken, was one of its most zealous instruments, though his ill-directed, fiery enthusiasm, did little good to the cause he advocated. The society was subsequently reconstituted on Church of England principles, and was termed the "London Society for promoting Christianity among the Jews." Wealth and rank were gathered within its fold, and men of title acted as its honorary managers. Still the corporation was heavily in debt—it is said to the extent of £14,000—when Louis Way, a gentleman of large means, and a mistaken philanthropist, endowed it with a considerable fortune. On the 7th April 1813, the Duke of Kent, father to the Queen, laid the foundation-stone of what was called the *Episcopal Jews'* Chapel in Cambridge Heath, Bethnal Green. We must, however, render the Duke the justice of saying, that he expressed at the time his high sense of respect for the Jews, naming especially Benjamin Goldsmid in tones of warm eulogy; that he strenuously disclaimed any intention of proselytising among the Jews; and that when he discovered the line of conduct followed by the London Society, he declined to hold any further connection with that corporation.

The assistance of Mr Louis Way enabled the London Society to satisfy its liabilities, and left it ample funds with which to pursue its glorious chase after souls. The proceedings of this society have been, as a rule, of the most unscrupulous nature in carrying out its objects, and they have met with merited censure at the hands of many right-thinking members of the Church of England. Thomas Witherby strongly animadverted against the ill-advised and unprincipled schemes of the conversionists; and in a letter he addressed to the Rev. Christopher Wordsworth, D.D., we gather that this truly Christian clergyman denounced these practices with as much severity as Witherby himself. Indeed, the London Society was not a popular institution; and its *modus operandi* was held up to public obloquy on frequent occasions in the public press, from the time of its establishment until about 1830. Soon after its formation an attempt was made to raise a fund to advance loans to Jews, who might be induced to intermarry with Christians. Subsequently to punish the Jews for their obduracy, it was proposed to translate a book called *Toledoth Jesu*, the "Generations of Jesus," a work possessing no authoritative character among the Jews, but which is said to contain some passages inimical to Christianity; thus stimulating popular prejudice against the Jews. The first of these schemes was held up to public ridicule; the second to public execration. Neither was carried out; for however prejudiced and intolerant an Englishman may be, there is usually in his composition a sense of honour and justice, that prevents him from having recourse to unfair, not to say nefarious, practices even to accomplish a favourite object. Strong indignation was expressed from many quarters against such and similar measures; and honest Thomas Witherby emphatically stated "his hope that the insiduous policy of the London Society will expose them to that contempt to which the meanness of their measures so justly devotes them." Nevertheless, such were the blindness and credulity of the public, that the income of the London Society steadily increased, and in 1828 reached the sum of £14,000. In that year the number of converts secured consisted of two adults and eighteen to twenty children, rendering the cost of persuading a human being to embrace Christianity at between £500 to £600. At this period the London Society solicited further subscriptions to enable them to award an annuity to every neophyte; which modest demand called forth expressions of unqualified anger from the press. Journalists complained of the gross injustice, when the country was over-burdened with debt and eaten up by pauperism, of taking away charitable donations from worthy Christians to bestow them upon unworthy apostates. Such, however, is the maxim to the present day of those gentlemen who parade, on the platform of Exeter Hall, their benevolence and their lack of discrimination, their love for the Jews, and their aversion to Judaism.

The Jews may esteem themselves fortunate in having succeeded in securing the friendship and protection of several members of the reigning family. The Duke of Kent, as we have already seen, after passing a high eulogy on the Goldsmid family in particular, and on the Jews in general, ceased to countenance the London Society when he discovered its true colours. The kindliness evinced by his royal brother, the Duke of Sussex, is well known to many living members of the Jewish community. The Duke of Sussex displayed in many ways his sympathy and good feeling for the Jews. He became the patron of the Jews' Hospital in 1813, at the prayer of that zealous worker, Joshua Van Oven, and he regularly presided at the anniversary banquets of that institution. His Royal Highness studied Hebrew under the Rev. Solomon Lyon of Cambridge, and a Mr Levy of London, and opened his doors to Jews with great affability. It is even said that the Duke was an honoured visitant to Jewish households. He read daily portions of the Bible in the grand old language in which it was originally written; and manifested the greatest interest in the progress of Jewish education and subsequently of Jewish emancipation.

A Jewish wedding at the present day is an event which, however interesting to the parties immediately concerned, is not likely to draw the attention of the British public. Such was not the case in 1810, when Jewish ceremonies were an object of especial curiosity. Indeed, one of the magazines of the period thought it worth its while to favour its readers with a circumstantial account of the nuptials of Mr Jonas Lazarus with the beautiful and accomplished Miss Rosceia Nathan, daughter of Mr M. I. Nathan of Godmanchester, Huntingdonshire. The details of the happy event are fully related, and we learn, among other things, that the ceremony was performed under a canopy in the garden of the residence of the bride's father; that the bridegroom was preceded to the presence of the bride by a band of music playing a grand martial air; and that four green tapers were kept burning during the celebration. In our days martial strains and green tapers are no longer considered as necessary adjuncts to the solemnity of the scene, or indispensable to the happiness of the newly-married couple, but otherwise the ceremonies followed on those auspicious occasions have undergone no change.

From a marriage to a murder, from the shedding of wine to the shedding of blood, there seems to be a long distance. Yet deeds of violence and festive gatherings, joy and sorrow, intermingle with each other during every period of our existence. A clergyman from a wedding proceeds to a funeral, and the same column of a newspaper chronicles a birth and a death. In 1812 a man named Wyatt of Fowey was tried at Launceston assizes for the murder of a Jew called Isaiah Falk Vallentine. Wyatt, who kept a public-house at Fowey, had been intimate with his victim, whom he invited to Fowey, on the plea of having some buttons or guineas to sell. Wyatt, under the plea of leading Vallentine to meet the sellers of the coins, conducted him along a quay whence he threw him into the water, suffocated him, and then robbed him of £260, which the dead man had on his person. Wyatt was found guilty on circumstantial evidence, and condemned to death. A curious point of law was raised on this trial. In those days the law required capital punishment to be inflicted within forty-eight hours of the judge's sentence. Murderers were usually tried on Friday and their execution —if convicted—was fixed for Monday, to give them the benefit of Sunday, which is a *dies non*. On this occasion the murderer was brought up on Thursday, instead of Friday, to receive sentence. On the justice presiding in court discovering his error, he sentenced the prisoner again on the Friday. But a doubt arose as to the legality of the sentence; the prisoner was respited; the opinions of the judges *in banco* were taken, and the law was not carried into effect for some time.

The following story is related by a Christian, an officer in the navy, who probably entertained the prejudices of the day against a Jew, or at all events who regarded the latter with no especial favour. An Israelite, named Jacob von Helbert, engaged a passage for himself and Moses Levy, his servant, on board the good ship *Pelham*, Captain Wells, bound for Bombay. Von Helbert, being strict in his religious observances, engaged the captain in a bond to supply him with meat killed according to Jewish usages, or in default thereof to furnish him with a fowl daily for his (Von Helbert's) subsistence. It seems that Moses Levy slaughtered the sheep for the captain's table; but after a time the meat would turn out with provoking frequency unfit for Jewish food. It came to be a common, if not choice joke on the part of the captain to say, "Well, Moses, is it a New Testament or an Old Testament sheep to-day?" The reply very frequently was: "That cannot do for my master, sir." "Your master is very unfortunate in a servant," would be the captain's rejoinder; "had you not come on board the *Pelham*, Moses, Jacob Von Helbert would have adopted a Christian's opinion about meats long ago." Then the servant would bow and the master remain silent. The voyage was long and tedious, but like all other things it came to an end. And now came the explanation of the mystery. Among the passengers there was a lady, young, fair, and alone. The captain, taking advantage of her unprotected condition, addressed to her words of, we will not desecrate the term love, but say of coarse passion. Miss Black declined his overtures with contempt, and refused to sit at table with him. The captain tried to starve her into compliance, and ordered that no food should be supplied to Miss Black. *Jacob Von Helbert sent the lady half every fowl he received*, and the meat had been said to turn out *terefa*, or unfit for Jewish food, so that the lady might not perish of want. Such an act of kindness exalted the Jewish character. Hunger was nobly borne to save an exposed, insulted woman from the machinations of a sensual despot. A degree of self-abnegation was practised, not often displayed on behalf of a total stranger.

CHAPTER XXXVIII.

THE CASE OF HARPER'S CHARITY—THE LAWS OF THE GREAT SYNAGOGUE—UNION OF THE CITY ASKENAZIM CONGREGATIONS—IRREGULAR MARRIAGES.

A CURIOUS case occurred in 1817, illustrating the manner in which the Jews on some occasions were regarded by the law. A certain bequest for purposes of charity had been devised by an inhabitant of Bedford, named Harper, to the parishioners of that town. Hitherto the Jews had participated in the division of the fund in question, when suddenly it was discovered that a Jew was not a "parishioner." The Jews of Bedford resolved to lay the case before the Lord Chancellor, and they addressed themselves in the first instance to the authorities of the Great Synagogue. The vestry of that congregation at once appointed a committee to investigate the subject, and sought the co-operation of the other Synagogues in London. The Hambro' Synagogue and the Sephardi Synagogue declined to entertain the matter, referring it to the Board of Deputies, while the New Synagogue heartily took it up, and voted a sum of money for legal expenses. The opinions of several eminent counsel were asked, and they seemed to have been favourable to the Jews. Mr Samuel Samuel, the chairman of the committee, bestirred himself with much zeal; consultations were held with Sir Samuel Romilly, and the case was laid before the Lord Chancellor. It was not until the year 1820 that the highest legal functionary in the country decided that a Jew was not a parishioner; and all that the two Synagogues could do was to pay cheerfully the heavy law costs incurred. In after years the efforts of Mr Lissack of Bedford culminated in obtaining a recognition of the rights of Jewish townspeople to the advantages of Harper's foundation.

T

The absence of decorum in public worship, which formerly too often marked Jewish devotions, did not fail to attract at various periods the attention of pious and enlightened Jews. In May 1821 a petition, signed by several of the principal members of the Great Synagogue, among whom we find the name of Goldsmid, set forth forcibly the evils of the prolonged Meshabirach. The petitioners, in entreating the committee to shorten the Meshabirach (complimentary money offerings), alleged that " it is pitiful to behold how indecently our solemn prayers are hurried on, particularly during the sacred holidays, in order to allow time for a system of finance, which, however beneficial in its operation, is certainly inconsistent with decorum and public order." The interruption to public worship, caused by a serious and growing evil, was clearly pointed out to the ruling powers, who nevertheless deferred the consideration of the memorial. After several adjournments it was eventually decided "that, from the manifold distresses of the poor and the consequent claims, it was inexpedient to hazard any experiment by which the revenue was likely to be diminished." One great step in advance towards the abolition of these sources of indecorum was taken by the Hambro' Synagogue in 1832, when that congregation, on the proposal of Mr Abraham Henry, its treasurer and one of its most intelligent members, abolished the sale of the *Mitzvoth* (honorary offices during services). The example was sooner or later followed by all other London Synagogues; but the abrogation of the Meshabirach has not yet been entirely effected in any Jewish place of worship except the West London Synagogue of British Jews. The evil has doubtless been much reduced since the accession to office of the present Chief Rabbi; but money offerings still continue to be publicly proclaimed during the service in all London Synagogues, except in the one last mentioned, to the grave disturbance of the solemnity of prayer. The exigencies of financial wants doubtless form a barrier to the suppression of this indecorous and irreligious practice. We entertain, nevertheless, the utopian belief that at a future period, more or less distant, a substitute will be discovered for this objectionable means of raising Synagogue revenue.

In November 1819, a committee was appointed by the vestry of the Great Synagogue to consolidate, revise, and reform the laws of that congregation, and to record them in Hebrew and English. This committee, of which Mr Joshua Van Oven and Mr Hyman Cohen were members, performed its delicate task carefully and conscientiously. The Synagogue laws were then written in that mongrel dialect called Jewish German, which was neither Hebrew nor German; which was read by few and understood by fewer still. The labours of the committee occupied some years, and their report was not delivered to the constituent body until the 28th February 1825. The laws then had been framed and classified; they had been translated into English and subsequently rendered into pure Hebrew. They were adopted after due discussion by the vestry of the Great Synagogue; they were printed and circulated, and they remained in force for the lifetime of a generation. In November 1854 it was considered that a modification and revision of the then existing code was needed, and a sub-committee was elected for that purpose. It may be noted that Dr Barnard Van Oven, the able and zealous son of an able and zealous father, Joshua Van Oven, was appointed chairman of the sub-committee. The report of the sub-committee with the amended code of laws was presented on the 16th March 1858, and the sub-committee, before closing their report, recorded their grateful appreciation of the services of their chairman. The revised code was submitted to the consideration of the vestry, and underwent the most careful and minute consideration of that body, during a period of nearly three years. Before it was finally adopted it was laid before a conjoint body, consisting of the vestry and of forty-two members of the congregation, and finally the parts relating to religious matters were submitted to the Chief Rabbi, the Rev. Dr Adler. This code of laws, which is the one now in operation, was framed to meet the requirements of the epoch, maintaining intact at the same time those principles which had always governed the community.

The good understanding between the Askenazi Synagogues was subject to frequent interruptions, usually on the old score of the relief of the foreign poor, and occasionally on the ground of a member being surreptitiously taken by one Synagogue from another. Treaties were made between the Great Synagogue and the two sister Synagogues, which in due course were infringed or lapsed; and, as a rule, no one was ever to blame whenever any irregularity happened. It would be useless and uninteresting to our readers to render a detailed account of these differences; to state the number of meetings in which the representatives of one Synagogue met the representatives of the others; or to give extracts from the voluminous correspondence that passed between the secretary of the Duke's Place Synagogue and the secretaries of the New and the Hambro' Synagogues. The first germs of a complete union between the three German congregations were due to the good offices of Mr N. M. Rothschild, whose mediation was accepted in September 1824, in a discussion between the Great Synagogue and the New Synagogue. A meeting of the representatives of these two Synagogues, and of those of the Hambro' Synagogue, was held at Mr Rothschild's residence in May 1825. Though no final arrangement was concluded then between the three Synagogues, the proposals made at that conference served afterwards as a basis for negotiations, which ultimately resulted in a permanent and complete union of the three German city congregations under one ecclesiastical head. The Great Synagogue still continued to be, as it always remained, the leading Askenazi community in the United Kingdom, to which proud position it is justly entitled, by the superior numbers, wealth, and influence of its members. The funds of this Synagogue had rapidly increased since the commencement of the present century; and in July of the year 1828, its invested capital amounted to upwards of £28,000. Mr Rothschild again placed his mansion and his good services at the disposal of the representatives of the three German Synagogues at this period (July 1828); but for various causes, though an understanding was established between the Synagogues, no definite treaty was signed at the time. In April 1834, when differences threatened to arise between the Duke's Place Synagogue and the New Synagogue on the question of burials, it was considered advisable to end this state of uncertainty. Delegates were appointed by these

Synagogues and by the Hambro' Synagogue, and in July 1835, a convention was signed by the delegates, subject to the ratification of their constituents. This was fortunately given in due course, and then Mr Rothschild's good work was crowned. The convention between the Synagogues was based on fair and equitable terms. It provided that the foreign poor should be interred—one-half of their number by the Great Synagogue, and one-quarter by each of the other two Synagogues; that the cost of relieving the stranger poor should be defrayed in the same proportion; that the amount received from the Polish Synagogue in Gun Yard should be divided in the same ratio, as well as the profit that might accrue from the receipts for the burial of strangers. It was also agreed that all flour for Passover should be purchased conjointly; that a committee of arbitration should be annually appointed, consisting of three members from the Great Synagogue and two members from each of the other two Synagogues, to adjust any diversities of opinion that might arise between the Synagogues; that monthly statements should be exchanged by the Synagogues; that each overseer of the poor should be appointed at a common charge. In our days various services to the poor are rendered expeditiously, efficiently, and completely by the Board of Guardians, which affords the greatest obtainable amount of good to the indigent at apparently the lowest practicable cost.

In the year 1825 the attention of Dr Hirschel, the Chief Rabbi of the German Jews, was directed towards a marriage performed by a Pole, named Solomon Bennett, which Dr Hirschel and the Haham of the Portuguese Jews considered irregular according to Jewish custom, and they united in reprimanding the officiator. Unfortunately, marriages of this nature, styled *kedushim* by the Sephardim and *mekedisch* by the Askenazim, had been frequent among the members of both congregations. Some of these indeed perpetrated the worst evils of Fleet marriages. Any designing man might entrap an artless girl into forfeiting her freedom. These unions were as simple and easy as Scotch marriages, and the reader will easy imagine what incalculable evils they might originate. We have already spoken at length on Jewish marriages, and we will only revert briefly to the subject. Not unfrequently it happened that a scheming, unprincipled man, having given to some girl of reputable parentage the title of wife, allowed her to return home to her father. The matter would soon be brought to the knowledge of the wardens, who would take the opinion of the Beth Din, on the validity of the marriage. If pronounced valid, the speculating husband coolly asked a good round sum of the father, to agree to the formalities requisite to release the maiden wife. Of course it often occurred that the husband was truly attached to his bride; and that this form of marriage was adopted through a disparity of condition, or other similar cause, and then other evils would ensue. To render such unions more difficult, if not impossible, the committee of the Great Synagogue ordered that seven or eight days before the solemnisation of a marriage, the names of the parties intending to marry should be notified in Hebrew and English on a tablet placed in a conspicuous spot in the Synagogue. This rule, however, does not appear to have been strictly adhered to. Among the Portuguese, the Mahamad (vestry) had always constituted a court of marriage and divorce; and, subject to the religious opinion of the Beth Din, they made and unmade wives with a speed and ease that Sir Cresswell Cresswell never equalled, and Sir James Wyld would have regarded with astonishment. The five gentlemen composing the Mahamad decided the fate of the couples brought before them. We recollect one instance in which a husband, having prayed for a divorce against his wife, apparently on valid grounds, the matter was put to the vote, and the question was decided against the husband by the hesitating vote of the President. It seems rather hard for any one to be inflicted for life with an uncongenial or offending partner, purely on account of a president's casting vote.

CHAPTER XXXIX.

ISAAC D'ISRAELI AND HIS FAMILY.

In the beginning of the present century, several families of note among the Jews of Portuguese descent abandoned the faith taught by Moses, to follow the precepts of Jesus of Nazareth, or to speak with strict accuracy, to obey the dictates of St Paul. In most of these instances the change was evidently a matter of pure personal convenience.

The greatest loss to Judaism, at least from an intellectual point of view, was unquestionably the secession of Isaac D'Israeli. How his ancestors had abandoned the Spanish Peninsula, sought refuge in Venice, and assumed the name of D'Israeli—an appellation never before borne by Jews—is a "twice-told tale," well known to most of our readers. Under the shelter of the Lion of St Mark, the family of D'Israeli followed commercial pursuits and prospered. For two centuries they flourished as merchants, protected by the "Queen of the Adriatic." In the year 1747 the then representative of the lineage despatched his younger son, Benjamin, to a country where a settled dynasty reigned, and where public opinion was presumed to be in favour of freedom of conscience. Benjamin D'Israeli fixed his residence in England, and in time became the father of Isaac D'Israeli. Benjamin D'Israeli appears to have acquired affluence by trade. He did not take great interest in Synagogal matters, and indeed, like some of the Italian Jews who, tempted by the comparative liberality of English institutions, had quitted the azure skies of Italy for the dusky yellow of London fogs, he was somewhat lax in his observances. But he contributed liberally to the support of the Synagogue, and his donations increased according to his means. His finta (Synagogue tax), which was assessed at first at 10s. per annum, gradually was augmented until it reached in 1813, £22, 13s. 4d. Benjamin D'Israeli only, served once a minor office in the Synagogue, that of Inspector of Hes-Haim, or the charity school. That was in 1782, and from the fact of his not being appointed to any other honorary post, it seems that he did not display much zeal in his superintendence over the unruly charity boys. Isaac D'Israeli, his son, was a student and a writer, and mixed little with the world. He was born in 1766, and married Maria Basevi, the sister of Joshua or George Basevi. He was the father of four children, one daughter and three sons, who were in their childhood brought up, at least nominally, as Jews. Indeed, the boys were all initiated in the covenant of Abraham. Isaac D'Israeli was not a frequenter of the Synagogue; and, albeit he paid regularly his finta of £10 per annum, and a few guineas more for charitable subscriptions, he entirely abstained from any close connection with his community. On October 3, 1813, he was elected Parnass or warden of the Bevis Marks Synagogue. This office he declined, and he wrote to that effect to the Mahamad (Wardens), dating his letter from King's Road, Bedford Row. Isaac D'Israeli expressed surprise that at so late a period of life he should have been so elected; he thought that had their choice been worth a moment's consideration, they must have been aware of its singular impropriety, and he concluded by saying: "I am willing to contribute, so far as my limited means permit, to your annual subscriptions, but assuredly without interference in your interior concerns." No notice was taken of this communication, and the author of "Curiosities of Literature" was fined £40. The secretary of the Synagogue sent Mr D'Israeli a summons to a meeting, which the latter returned under date of the 26th October, attributing the occurrence to a mistake, and concluded by saying, "I mentioned the terms on which alone I could allow myself to be considered in any way connected with your society." The reply to this remonstrance was a letter from the secretary, J. de Castro, enclosing copy of a resolution in Portuguese, passed by the elders, to the effect that Mr D'Israeli's election was in accordance with the Ascamoth or laws of the congregation.

The observations of Mr D'Israeli made no impression on the Elders, and the only reply vouchsafed to him was *non possumus*.

Isaac D'Israeli addressed a highly interesting letter to the authorities of the Synagogue, which, as expressing the views on modern Jewish worship of so eminent a man, deserves to be laid before our readers.

This letter, which, we believe, has never before seen the light, was couched in the following terms :—

"You are pleased to inform me that my election of Parnass is in strict conformity with your laws. Were I to agree to this it would not alter the utter impropriety of the choice. Whatever may be the laws, the spirit of the laws must depend on their wise administration.

"A person who has lived out of the sphere of your observation, of retired habits of life, who can never unite in your public worship, because as now conducted it disturbs instead of exciting religious emotions, a circumstance of general acknowledgment, who has only tolerated some part of your ritual, willing to concede all he can in those matters which he holds to be indifferent; such a man, with but a moderate portion of honour and understanding, never can accept the solemn functions of an elder of your congregation, and involve his life and distract his business pursuits not in temporary but permanent duties always repulsive to his feelings.

"I lament the occasion which drives me, with so many others, out of the pale of your jurisdiction. The larger portion of your society bears a close resemblance to the tribe of Ephraim, whom Hosea curiously describes, chap. vii. 8, 'Ephraim hath mixed himself among the people! Ephraim is a cake not turned!' That is a cake upon the hearth, baked on one side, and raw on the other, partly Jew, and partly Gentile! Why have you so many Ephraimites? The cause of this defection is worthy of your inquiry. Gentlemen, allow me to add, that whenever the governed are unruly, some defect will be discovered in the governors. Even the government of a small sect can only be safely conducted by enlightened principles, and must accommodate itself with practical wisdom to existing circumstances, but above all with a tender regard to the injured feelings of its scattered members. Something like the domestic affections should knit us all together—a society existing on the voluntary aid of its members is naturally in a feeble state, and if it invests itself with arbitrary power, a blind precipitation in a weak body can only tend to self-destruction. Many of your members are already lost; many you are losing! Even those whose tempers and feelings would still cling to you, are gradually seceding.

"But against all this you are perpetually pleading your existing laws, which you would enforce on all the brethren alike!

"It is of these obsolete laws so many complain. They were adapted by fugitives to their peculiar situation, quite distinct from our own, and as foreign to us as the language in which they are written. Some of you boast that your laws are much as they were a century ago! You have laws to regulate what has ceased to exist; you have laws which, through the change of human events, prove to be new impediments to the very purposes of the institution, and for the new circumstances which have arisen, you are without laws.

"Such, gentlemen, is my case; invincible obstacles exist against my becoming one of your elders, motives of honour and conscience! If you will not retain a zealous friend, and one who has long had you in his thoughts, my last resource is to desire my name to be withdrawn from your society.

"It remains for you, gentlemen, to set a noble example of dignity and political wisdom. Let the award of the Mahamad be revised because they have erred in the choice of a fitting person to become a Parnass.

"At all events you have my warm wishes for happier days. Do not shut out the general improvement of the age. Make your schools flourish, and remember that you have had universities ere now; a society has only to make itself respectable in these times to draw to itself the public esteem. Believe me I have not come like Sanballat the Horonite, who with bitter derision impeded Nehemiah in his zealous labour of rebuilding the walls of the Holy City, scoffing at him for receiving the stones out of the heaps of the rubbish (Neh. iv. 2).—I am, gentlemen, with due respect, yours,   ISAAC D'ISRAELI.

"6 KING'S ROAD, BEDFORD ROW,
    Dec. 3, 1813."

Mr D'Israeli, it will be perceived, did not write as if he were a strict orthodox Jew; but he showed a strong feeling for his race and a desire to remain connected with the Jewish body, provided such connection could be continued in a manner in accordance with his views. The author of the "Curiosities of Literature" had been brought up from childhood aloof from his own co-religionists, and his course of reading and literary studies had not tended to impress him with sufficient reverence for the ceremonial laws of the Jews.

He had no desire to quit Judaism for Christianity; but he wished to follow only that portion of Judaism which coincided with certain facile opinions he entertained.

It must at the same time be admitted that the authorities of the ancient Portuguese Congregation, and for that matter the authorities of other Jewish Congregations too, did nothing to keep those of their brethren who had any tendency to waver from their old creed. As we have before asserted, the rigidity with which certain congregational laws or regulations that might advantageously have been modified were enforced; the unwillingness to grant any concession to the desires or views of individual members; and the indecorous, slovenly, and unattractive manner in which Synagogue services were too often conducted, caused, or at all events hastened, the secession of many an old family from the faith of Israel.

The elders did not show any disposition to yield to D'Israeli's requests. They merely instructed their secretary, through the Mahamad, to write to Mr D'Israeli "that in accordance with the present laws, it is not possible to grant him the exemptions he desires."

In the month of March following (1814), Isaac D'Israeli received his Synagogue account, in which he was debited with the usual fine for non-acceptance of office. This he repudiated, but he expressed his willingness to discharge his regular finta. The question appears to have remained thus pending until March 1817, when the author of "The Amenities of Literature" received new accounts and summonses to attend meetings. These proceedings irritated him, and he wrote to the Mahamad (Wardens), regretting that he had not been "suffered to remain in quiet as a useful contributing member, although otherwise unfitted to deliberate in their councils." He concluded by saying: "I have patiently sought for protection against the absurd choice of two or three injudicious individuals, but I find that you as a body sanction what your own laws will not allow. I am not a fit member of your society, and I certainly am an aggrieved one. I must now close all future correspondence, and I am under the painful necessity of insisting that my name be erased from the list of your members as yehidim (acknowledged members) of the Synagogue.—I am, &c., I. D'ISRAELI."

His resignation was followed by that of his brother-in-law, Joshua or George Basevi, the well-known architect.

In May, in the same year, Sarah, widow of Benjamin D'Israeli, obtained the permission of the Mahamad to place a new tombstone on her husband's grave. In 1821 Isaac D'Israeli applied to the secretary of the Portuguese Congregation for the certificates of birth of himself and family. There was some hesitation in complying with this request, owing to the indebtedness to the Synagogue of Mr D'Israeli. But an arrangement was arrived at, through the intervention of Ephraim Lindo, by which the Mahamad agreed to receive as full payment, the amount of the finta and offerings due by D'Israeli up to 1817, waiving the remainder of their claim for fines. On Ephraim Lindo handing over to the secretary the sum of £40, 17s, on account of D'Israeli, the resignation of the latter was accepted, and the required certificates were furnished him. Mrs Isaac D'Israeli, who was born in December 1755, gave birth to her only daughter, Sarah D'Israeli, in December 1802, while her eldest son, the Right Hon. Benjamin D'Israeli, saw the light on the 21st December 1804. The present Premier of England thus proves older than he is usually said to be. His two younger brothers were respectively born, Ralph D'Israeli in 1809, and James D'Israeli in 1813, and they were all initiated into the covenant of Abraham.*

At this period ended the connection between the D'Israeli family and the Synagogue; a connection that might never have been severed, had the authorities of the Sephardi Congregation displayed more judgment and tact in their dealings with Isaac D'Israeli.

We have spoken of this gifted family when they belonged to the Jewish communion. Of the literary career of Isaac D'Israeli, the talented father, and of the literary and political career of Benjamin D'Israeli, the still more highly endowed son, it is not our province to speak. Isaac D'Israeli

---

* It may be interesting to our Jewish readers to learn that the gentleman who performed the initiatory rite on the present Premier of England was a relative of his mother, the late David Abarbanel Lindo, an influential member of the Spanish and Portuguese Congregation, and a merchant of high commercial standing.

in his "Curiosities of Literature," suggests some work recording "a history of events which have not happened." He speculates on what might have occurred if Charles II. had not been defeated at Worcester ; if Charles Martel had not routed the Saracens at Tours, and the Mohammedan rule had been established in Europe; if Martin Luther had not been too much terrified at the threats of Cardinal San Sisto to renounce his errors, which at one time he was disposed to do, had he received some preferment. As the author himself says, it is often that the fortunes of men and of nations revolve on a single event. A fair ground for speculation may be formed as to the potential history of Benjamin D'Israeli, had the few gentlemen who ruled over the Portuguese Community in 1814 resolved to conciliate the good will of Isaac D'Israeli. It was only a question of two or three votes. Benjamin D'Israeli might in that case have been a brilliant man of letters, a successful lawyer, a rising member of Parliament. In all human probability he would not, whilst we write, be guiding the destinies of England.

CHAPTER XL.

*J. KING AND JEWISH WORSHIP—SIR MAURICE XIMENES—
MORDECAI RODRIGUEZ LOPEZ.*

THE sincere love we bear for a dear friend or relative, the deep devotion we feel for the faith in which we have been born and in the traditions of which we have been nurtured, do not prevent us from acknowledging the faults of the one, or from observing the blemishes that may have crept into the forms of the other. Without going so far as to admit the entire justice of I. D'Israeli's strictures on the authorities of the Bevis Marks Synagogue, we find much in his remarks on the religious condition of that community, that should have been received with far greater attention and consideration than were vouchsafed to his words.

The Jews must acknowledge it, however harshly the admission may grate on their ears. The mode of worship as conducted in Jewish Synagogues in the early part of the nineteenth century, did not satisfy either the minds or the hearts of many sincere and conscientious Jews. Aged living witnesses confirm verbally, what men now dead had written. Thoughtful and earnest Jews keenly felt the abuses that shocked their sense of religious decorum, and vainly endeavoured to remedy the crying evils that throve almost unchecked before their eyes. In 1812 J. King, a member of the Portuguese Congregation, addressed several communications to the wardens of that community, wherein he repeatedly stated that his absence from Synagogue for many years was because "it was not a place of devotion, and prayers could be better said in the closet." He observed "with grief and astonishment how little the Synagogue was attended, how indecent was the conduct of those that did attend, and how extremely uneducated and disorderly were the charity boys." He offered to contribute to the better instruction of these children, so that they should no longer distress people's ears by discordant noises. He complained that the house of prayer was converted into an exchange or mart for the discussion of news or carrying out of commercial transactions. He strongly recommended reform in these respects, and concluded by placing his purse and his person at the service of the congregation. His allegations unfortunately only confirm pictures drawn by higher hands, as to the truth of which we can entertain no reasonable doubt. Mr King's proposals were coldly received; they were deferred consideration until he wrote again and again urging the Mahamad to make some alterations to avoid a schism. Eventually, King's services not being accepted and his advice not being followed, he returned to his retirement from his own community. Nevertheless King lived and died a Jew. Belonging to a middle-class family in his congregation, Rey, for such was his original name, was fortunate enough to win the affections of an Irish Catholic lady of rank and fortune, whom he married. King, who had anglicised his pseudonym, being thus possessed of a wealthy and influential wife, might, had he consented to embrace Christianity, have aspired to some high post. But he strenuously resisted his wife's solicitations and the temptations to which he was exposed. He did not deviate from the old faith. On the contrary, he proved himself attached to its tenets. He was deaf to the pleas of conjugal love, and to the calls of ambition; and he even edited and published at his own expense David Levi's Dissertation on the Prophets. He died in 1824, bequeathing a small legacy to the Synagogue.

Among the defections of note from Judaism, which occurred during the first quarter of the century, in addition to the withdrawal of Isaac D'Israeli, we will mention the cases of the families of Ximenes, Rodriguez Lopez, and Uzzielli. Moses Ximenes was an ambitious and rich man, indifferent in religious matters, eager for worldly honours. In 1802 he had been elected to office in the Synagogue, which he declined to accept. Having been fined for non-attendance, according to custom, he desired to retire from the community, deputing his friend, Mr Uzzielli, to pay what was due to the

Synagogue. Uzzielli adopted Christianity, and became the founder of the family of that name, several members of whom have since become well-known financiers. Moses, otherwise Captain, Ximenes did not leave his community in real or affected anger like some other neophytes. On the contrary, he embraced his new faith while expressing the most friendly feelings towards the professors of the old faith; and in his parting communication, he thus wrote to the Mahamad of the Portuguese Synagogue:—"I shall always be ready to cheerfully contribute to any of those charities that do so much honour to your heads and hearts, and in which no body of people are so praiseworthy as yourself." We have here at least the not common spectacle of an apostate, who does not revile and vilify his former co-religionists or their institutions. Ximenes was knighted; and Sir Maurice Ximenes became high sheriff and magistrate of his county, and died apparently a prosperous man.

Mordecai Rodriguez Lopez was descended from an ancient Sephardi stock, whose name we have met already, who flourished in the world of finance, and who realised fortunes in foreign trade. Mordecai Rodriguez Lopez dwelt in Clapham, and had wedded Rebecca, daughter of Menasseh Pereira of Jamaica, by whom he had a son, Menasseh Lopez, who was born in that island in 1755. The elder Lopez, after a residence in the West Indies, returned to England an opulent man. He conformed outwardly to the rites of Judaism for many years, and served the usual Synagogue offices. Towards the end of the 18th century his attendance and that of his son at the house of prayer, slackened; rumours as to his orthodoxy arose, and a letter to the following effect, dated 11th July 1802, did not cause much surprise to the Mahamad, to whom it was addressed:—"A recent circumstance in regard to my future situation, which will very soon appear, makes it incompatible to my remaining any longer a yahid or member of the congregation, and I have desired my friend, Mr Moses Lindo, junr., to apprise you of my intention and to pay my account with the Synagogue." In concluding his communication, Mordecai Rodriguez Lopez, like Moses Ximenes, expressed the best wishes for the welfare of his late brethren, and, moreover, he stated that he had instructed Moses Lindo, junr., to present the Synagogue with £150 for the zedaka or charity fund. The "recent circumstance" adverted to by Lopez was evidently his conversion and that of his son to the recognised religion of the State. The change in the theological opinions of Mordecai and of Menasseh Lopez happened by a singular coincidence to manifest itself at the time of a general election, and the fact was immediately followed by the return of Menasseh as member for New Romney. Menasseh Lopez was created a baronet in 1805, with remainder to his nephew, Ralph Franco. In the next election, Sir Menasseh secured a seat for Barnstaple, for which borough he was again re-elected in 1818. Curious to say, we find that an attorney, named Dance, who had insulted Sir Menasseh Lopez, incorrectly described as "a Jew baronet," was condemned to twelve months imprisonment, and to be struck off the rolls. On the 18th March 1819, the "Jew baronet" was found guilty at the Exeter Assize of having bribed the electors of the borough of Grampound to secure his election, and sentence was deferred. On the 13th November he was again prosecuted for a similar offence, and convicted, and he received sentence in the Court of Queen's Bench. He was condemned for the first offence to be imprisoned for twenty-one months in Exeter Jail, and to pay to the King a fine of £10,000, and for the second infraction of the law, which had been committed in Devonshire, he was sentenced to a further confinement of three months and another fine of £2000. Notwithstanding these untoward circumstances, Sir Menasseh Massey Lopez was once more returned to Parliament, and this time he was chosen as a fit representative for the immaculate borough of Westbury. In 1826 he resigned to make room for Sir Robert Peel, who had been ejected from the Protestant University of Oxford, on account of his public conduct on the question of Catholic emancipation. Sir Menasseh married the daughter of Mr John Yeates of Monmouth, and his only child, Esther, died in 1819, when twenty-four years old. Sir Menasseh Massey Lopez, Bart., died at an advanced age in 1831, at Maristow House. He was then fulfilling the functions of Recorder of Westbury, in addition to being a magistrate for two counties. He was succeeded by his nephew, Ralph Franco, who became Sir Ralph Lopes, Bart., the last letter in the name being softened into S. The landed and personal property bequeathed by the first baronet was estimated at upwards of £800,000. Sir Massey Lopes, one of the present Lords of the Admiralty, is the son of Sir Ralph Lopes, Bart., otherwise Ralph Franco. It is worthy of remark that Sir Massey Lopes, the son of a Jew, holds a place in the present Conservative administration, which is headed by the son of another Jew, himself born within the pale of Judaism.

It may be observed that few of those gentlemen who so easily renounced their old creed had been a frequent or regular attendant at Synagogue. Nobody suddenly becomes very wicked, says the old Latin adage, or, we may add, very good either. Few men who are zealous and sincere followers of one religion readily embrace another religion, without even going through the form of an inquiry. The Jews who abandoned Judaism in the early part of this century, had long been lax in their observances. Indifference to form leads to indifference to principle, and convenience points to a change which can do no worldly harm, and may conduce to a great many very material advantages.

Judaism has shown itself to be possessed of far greater vitality than it got credit for from Isaac D'Israeli. Some families of eminence did doubtless lapse from Judaism in his time; and we have at different periods thoroughly inquired into the subject of conversions to Christianity. But the enjoyment by Jews of civil and political freedom, the introduction of wholesome improvements in the performance of Jewish religious services, the spread of enlightenment and education among the Jews, and various other causes have long obviated any temptation for Jews to forsake their old religion.

To abandon one's faith is no longer regarded as a passport to good society, or as a preliminary to entrance into public life. Apostasy is not considered by right-minded Christians as a title to their confidence, and a conscientious Jew may aspire to serve his country and to rise to high dignity, and still remain an open and zealous believer in the Lord of Israel.

CHAPTER XLI.

A CHIEF RABBI AND A HAHAM.

A SPIRITUAL pastor must always exercise great influence over his flock, and the Rev. Solomon Hirschel undoubtedly possessed great authority over the Askenazim of London. The Rev. Solomon Hirschel, as our readers may recollect, was born in England, and was the son of a former rabbi of the Duke's Place Synagogue, Rabbi Hirsch. The future head of the German Community of London was educated in Germany and in Poland, where the public schools being closed against him, he devoted himself to the study of Jewish theology. Solomon Hirschel possessed a clear understanding, keen humour, and sound judgment, and he acquired a correct and pure style of Hebrew composition. Mathematics formed a favourite pursuit of his. This science, by its ingenuity and by the facility with which it can be acquired in solitary research, had always been a favourite study of the rabbis.

According to the custom obtaining in his day among the Jews of Poland, Solomon Hirschel married at the early age of seventeen. For nine years he occupied the Rabbinical Chair of Prenzlau, in Prussia. In 1802, when forty years old, he was called to preside over the Synagogue in Duke's Place; but gradually his jurisdiction was extended over all the Jews of Askenazi Minhag or rite in London, and indeed in England.

With this appointment began a new and important phase of the life of the Rev. Solomon Hirschel. The period of his administration deserves a conspicuous place in the annals of the English Jews. It was during this period that the scattered elements formed by the English Jews were gathered into one compact mass, and that the Spanish and Portuguese Jews and the German Jews, who were formerly spoken of as two distinct "nations," became closely connected together as members of the same ancient race and followers of the same ancient creed. It was during this time that monuments were established, demonstrating to posterity the munificent charity of the English Jews towards their poorer brethren. It was at this epoch that the Jews' Hospital, the Jews' Free School, and several useful institutions were founded. During this period the ever memorable mission to the East was performed by Sir Moses Montefiore; and, we must add, it was at this period that the unfortunate schism took place, which separated some of the best members of the old congregations from their early associations and former brethren. The Rev. Solomon Hirschel had seen the communities which he guided increase in number, in wealth, and in enlightenment. Nevertheless his life was not without its bitterness. In his earlier days he is said to have been disturbed by family troubles, while in old age the dissensions prevailing in his congregations sorely vexed his spirit.

Considerable dissatisfaction had manifested itself principally with liturgical forms. Though the Rev. Solomon Hirschel represented the spirit of a bygone age, he is said by those who knew him best to have possessed a tolerant and equitable disposition. Had the secession movement occurred a few years earlier, it is believed that the pious rabbi by his prudence and energy might have averted the unhappy consequences which followed, and that by counselling opportune and moderate reforms, only two communities of Jews might yet exist in Great Britain. But it happened otherwise. The Rev. Solomon Hirschel, broken in mind and body and weighed with years, was unequal to the emergency. Fasting and other privations had told on his powerful frame. At one period he never ate meat except on Sabbaths; at another period he fasted altogether during the whole of every Monday and Thursday, and only medical prohibition prevented him from fasting on such days to the last moment of his life. Two severe accidents confined him to his chamber for some months before his death. He died on the 31st October 1842, when he had reached the advanced age of eighty-one.

The Rev. S. Hirschel was an uncompromising foe to conversionists; but he was mild in manner and desirous of avoiding religious controversies with non-Jews; and especially careful not to give offence to Christians. Once indeed he strongly remonstrated against some unseemly and ill-judged expressions on the part of some members of a debating club which styled itself the Philo-Judæan Society, and which consisted mainly of Jewish young men. Above all, the learned rabbi loved peace and hated public polemics, invariably checking intemperance of expression. He left a family of four sons and four daughters, to whom he bequeathed his savings, said to amount to £13,000 or £14,000. His property was sold at public auction by the well-known George Robins, who treated the objects of Jewish worship, the use of which was unknown to him, with great respect and good feeling. The excellent library which the Rev. S. Hirschel had gathered was purchased for the Beth Hamedrash, and some of his flock eagerly bought as keepsakes the articles he familiarly employed in domestic worship.

The late rabbi was a man of commanding presence and tall stature. He had a lofty forehead and a keen eye, and his countenance is described as having a benignant and intellectual expression. His appearance abroad inspired reverence, and most persons in the streets touched their hats and made way for the High Priest of the Jews, as they styled him. Two or three portraits of him are extant, the best being that seen in the vestry of Duke's Place. The Rev. S. Hirschel was wont to rise at early dawn, rarely retiring until midnight, and occupying every available moment in his engrossing theological studies. He was endowed with a remarkably quick perception of character; and to him was attributed a ready wit. The manuscripts he left behind are said to be richly garnished with humorous sayings.

The funeral of the late Chief Rabbi, which was celebrated on 2d November 1842, presented an imposing spectacle. His body was brought from his residence in Bury Street to the Duke's Place Synagogue by twenty-four bearers, one of whom was Sir Moses Montefiore. The bier was placed before the ark, which was covered with black cloth. The numerous windows were darkened, the Synagogue was illuminated with wax tapers, and the whole arrangements had a sombre and impressive effect. The service was read by the Rev. S. Ascher, and then a procession was formed to accompany the mortal remains of the Chief Rabbi to the German Jews' Cemetery in North Street, Mile End. The procession comprised upwards of a hundred plain carriages, for mourning coaches had been eschewed by the directions of the deceased. Deputations from all the Synagogues and all the Jewish schools in London attended the funeral, and the scene at the burial-ground was most solemn and striking. Several brown paper packets, sealed with wax and containing papers and documents, were thrown into the grave by order of the deceased. The shops of Jewish tradesmen remained closed until after the conclusion of the funeral ceremony, which lasted from ten until three o'clock. A medal was struck in commemoration of the late Chief Rabbi, displaying an emblematic device with inscriptions in Hebrew.

Shortly after the Duke's Place Synagogue, which had been for many years without a spiritual guide, had resolved to elect a chief rabbi, the Portuguese Community, who had found themselves in precisely the same position, determined to supply a similar want. Our readers are already aware that the Rev. Raphael Meldola was appointed in 1805 Haham of the Sephardi Congregation, and that he fulfilled his functions with zeal, if not always with the tact and discretion desirable in a man occupying his responsible post. The learned Haham was born at Leghorn in 1754. He was the son of Haham Moses Meldola, formerly Professor of Oriental Languages at the University of Paris, and whose literary writings are to be found in the works "Tosaphot Rekem," "Mahamar Mordecai," &c. His ancestors had been great rabbis and men of erudition for many generations; his grandfather had been Haham at Pisa, and then had been called to France, while his uncle became Rabbi of the ancient and important Congregation of Amsterdam. Haham Raphael Meldola himself became an accomplished theologian and philosopher. After a regular course of studies, he was admitted member of the first rabbinical university at the age of fifteen; and in 1803 he received the title of Rab, and was appointed a judge to try causes among his own people, as was customary in Italy. At an early age he published a work called "Korban Minha," a literary comment on and explanation of the service of the High Priest read in Synagogue on Kipur day. In 1796 he brought out a rabbinical work entitled "Hupat Hatanim," which is said to display great mathematical as well as talmudical knowledge. He moreover left ten MS. works, one of which was published by his son, the Rev. David Meldola, and was entitled "Hezek Hemunah, Faith Strengthened." This forms a complete exposition of the Jewish doctrines, rites, and belief, in the form of dialogues in pure Hebrew with an English version.

Haham Meldola was humble in manner and unpretending in deportment. Some infirmity of temper, however, brought him into occasional collisions with the Synagogue authorities or officials, to the detriment of the dignity of his office. He was a kind-hearted man, ever ready to lend a willing ear to tales of distress and to do his uttermost to procure assistance for those who really deserved it. Haham Meldola died in June 1828, at the age of seventy-four, and was interred in the old burial-ground by the side of Rabbi Nieto at his especial desire. Truly there was this resemblance between those two learned rabbis, that both were natives of Italy, both had prosecuted their studies at Leghorn, both had been appointed chiefs of the same college, had been called to London, had acquired considerable fame for learning, and both died at about the same age.

The Rev. Solomon Hirschel and Haham Meldola laboured under the disadvantage of being called upon to direct spiritually congregations with the language of which they were more or less unacquainted. The Rev. Solomon Hirschel, though an Englishman by birth, had been brought up abroad, and like Haham Meldola, he never succeeded in mastering the tongue in which Shakespeare and Milton wrote. Pulpit instruction did not form a recognised part of the service in those days, and the exhortations which those reverend gentlemen, at rare intervals like angel's visits, addressed to their flocks, fell on unprepared soil. The strange German speech of the Rev. Solomon Hirschel, and the very questionable Spanish in which Haham Meldola gave his religious instruction to his congregants, were necessarily only understood by a small minority of them. The Jews of German and Spanish or Portuguese origin have ordinarily adopted the language of this country as their own, at all events in the second generation; and thus it happened that the reverend preachers directed their homilies to nearly empty benches.

The Jews have now changed all this. Religious sermons form in nearly all Synagogues an acknowledged portion of the services; and the Jews of all sections of the community may consider themselves as extremely fortunate in having secured the benefit of the presence of lecturers eloquent and learned, who impart to their respective congregations the fruit of their studies and meditations in pure English.

CHAPTER XLII.

JEWISH WORTHIES — THE REV. SOLOMON LYON — EMMA LYON—MICHAEL JOSEPHS—ARTHUR LUMLEY DAVIDS.

THOUGH the Jews of England have not been so prolific in producing great names in literature as their Continental brethren, they can show, nevertheless, a fair number of scholars, linguists, and men of letters, of such extended knowledge and varied talents as would reflect credit on any community. It must be owned that English Jews have never displayed any especial predilection for literature. They have not risen to high rank in journalism, and they do not influence or guide the opinion of an important section of the community. Their literary reviews do not decide the fate of a new book; they do not draw the tears or raise the smiles of crowded audiences before the curtain, by the invention of heart-stirring plots, or by the creation of original types of character; and with, perhaps, one single exception, they do not enchain the attention of thousands of readers of fiction to the fortunes of the puppets of their imagination, through the customary three volumes. The few names at the head of this chapter, and the far greater number who have distinguished themselves since, clearly prove that it is not the lack of any natural gift which prevents the Jew from achieving success in the pursuit of literature. The prospect of speedy wealth in the Stock Exchange, or the ambition of vying with the merchant princes of England, undoubtedly exercises an alluring influence in this century, when the sovereign sway of gold becomes daily more and more apparent and irresistible. Moreover, the bar, music, and painting, have attracted the greater part of such Jewish talent and energies as have not been monopolised by commercial or financial occupations. Few Jews have devoted themselves heart and soul to the pursuit of literature.

Among the learned Jews at the beginning of this century, we must not omit to mention the Rev. Solomon Lyon of Cambridge. This gentleman was a scholar of considerable attainments. He was educated at the University of Prague, and he settled in this country in the latter part of last century. He established the first Jewish boarding-school in England, and became a registered tutor at the University of Cambridge. He taught Hebrew to several persons of social distinction, among whom may be named the Duke of Sussex, the present Duke of Wellington, Charles Poulett Thompson, Colonel Thompson, the Corn Law reformer, Dr Mansell, Bishop of Gloucester, and many others. He wrote a Hebrew Grammar and several erudite treatises. He was himself an able man, and he associated with men of ability. From him descended a gifted family. His daughter, Miss Emma Lyon, was an accomplished poetess, and those who had the privilege of knowing her personally, are aware that she was as estimable and kind-hearted as she was intellectual and well educated. This lady was the first Jewish Englishwoman who was an authoress. She received an unusually good education for her days; her father's position and connections at the University of Cambridge affording her exceptional advantages of this nature. Miss Emma Lyon published a volume of poems in 1812, which proved highly successful, and met with a very favourable reception from the reviewers of the period. After her marriage with Mr Abraham Henry, this lady continued to write occasional poems, which were recited at public institutions, such as the Jews' Hospital, Jews' Free School, Society of Friends for Foreigners in Distress, &c. Among Mrs Henry's children, we may name the late able and accomplished editor of the *Jewish Chronicle*, a gentleman who was as much esteemed in his community for his talents as for his largeness of heart and modesty of disposition.

Many of our readers will doubtless recollect the venerable figure of the late Michael Josephs. He rendered great service to Anglo-Jewish literature, and no Anglo-Jewish history would be complete without a glance at his life and at his works. Michael, or as sometimes he styled himself Myer, Josephs, was born in Königsberg in 1763, and he came to London when a youth of sixteen. The great intellectual movement led by Mendelssohn in Germany had begun at that time, and he came to England inspired by it. The movement would have spread to England had a favourable field for literary culture and a love for Hebrew literature existed here. Michael Josephs brought with him great knowledge of the Holy Scriptures, and much aptitude for Hebrew writing. He had the gift of making happy epigrams; and ingenious turns in prose and in verse characterised all his literary works. Many of his epigrams and poems are scattered in different journals; and many are dispersed in manuscript partly among his own papers, and partly in the letters he addressed to his friends. He composed for many years the Hebrew ode recited at the anniversary banquet of the Free School. The fugitive pieces he wrote may be numbered by the score, and these will always be read with pleasure by all who understand and appreciate Hebrew literature. Probably his fame as a Hebrew scholar rests more solidly on his Hebrew and English Lexicon, a work of great utility, and which displays real scholarship and mastery over the sacred tongue.

Michael Josephs took an active part in all the movements tending to the advancement of progress and enlightenment among his co-religionists. He participated in 1830 in the foundation of the Hebrew Literary Society for the cultivation of the sacred language, a society which came to an untimely end in less than two years. It is said that he was frequently consulted by the Chief Rabbi, the Rev. Dr Hirschel, on questions connected with Hebrew composition; an art of which Michael Josephs was complete master. He also was the first to suggest the necessity of replying to "M'Caul's Old Paths;" a work which has been since answered, though perhaps not so completely as might be desired. Michael Josephs was a merchant by profession; and he graced his leisure hours by the pursuit of those studies for which his education and tastes had so well fitted him. In his religious views he belonged to that happy medium, which it is to be lamented is not found oftener among men of intelligence. He was not one of those who consider the slightest infraction of the minutest observance as a mortal sin; nor did he hold with those who completely disregard the ceremonial law of Moses. He was a wise and prudent man, and he would often familiarly say, like Socrates, "Let us sacrifice a cock to Æsculapius."

Mr Josephs had a true love for his fellow-creatures. Charitable himself, he was the cause of charity in others. From the esteem he enjoyed in his community, it was easy for him to gather important sums for deserving objects. In his literary labours he was indefatigable; and to literary aspirants from Germany he proved little less than a providence. His purse and his advice were at their service, and he never abandoned them until their object, so far as it was attainable, was accomplished. In his last years Michael Josephs lived in retirement, surrounded by three of his sons who cheered his last days. He died in 1849, having reached the patriarchal age of eighty-six. He was deeply regretted by the rich and by the poor; and especially by men of letters. The void his death left in the community was not easily filled. Zealous workers among the Jews in the cause of charity have always been plentiful; zealous workers in the cause of Jewish literature have been found, though not so numerous. Men who have worked, at the same time, to elevate the Jews spiritually and to ameliorate their physical condition, have not been numerous, and Michael Josephs may justly claim to rank among them.

The dispensations of Providence are at times strangely incomprehensible. A thunderbolt falls. The old worn-out decayed trunk, leafless, branchless, with scarcely any vitality, is spared, and a young vigorous sapling, hardly finished growing, with all the elements of a fresh robust life before it, is stricken to the earth. A pestilence arises. The aged invalid who for years has been tottering on the verge of the grave, to whom existence is no longer aught but a prolongation of pain, who longs to lie down and die that he may rest from the weary pilgrimage which has proved to him nought but vexation of the spirit and suffering of the flesh; he escapes unscathed. The youth whose career opens with brilliant prospects: who is endowed by the gifts of nature, whose bright genius raises the highest hope as to his future career, whose path seems strewed with flowers, is inexorably snatched from our midst by the merciless angel of death. The blooming young bride perishes and the wrinkled old beldame survives; why or wherefore our limited intelligence cannot fathom. Arthur Lumley Davids, like Numa Hartog and like Philoxene Luzzatto, the prodigiously learned son of the great Hebraist, Professor Luzzatto of Padua, lived indeed but a short span of time. Arthur Lumley Davids was born in the year 1811, and he died in July 1832, ere he had reached his twenty-first birthday. Before he was twenty, this wonderful young man had delivered a lecture in the presence of the "Society for the Cultivation of Hebrew Literature" on the Philosophy of the Jews, a lecture replete with deep learning and profound research. Before he reached to the years of manhood, before he was called away from his family, he had written a Grammar of the Turkish language, with a preliminary discourse on the language and literature of the Turkish nation, &c.; a work which called forth from the most competent judges of the subject the most unqualified praise. The "Literary Gazette," the arbiter of literary merit in those days, expressed itself on the subject in the following terms: "We are informed that the author of this volume has not yet completed his twenty-first year; and if we were disposed to think very highly indeed of the learning and research which it displays, even had they marked the labours of grey hairs, how much more must we prize and estimate them when we learn that the extraordinary effort proceeds from the verge of boyhood." Happily this great work was honoured with the applause of the monarch the language of whose people it illustrates; and it secured to its author immortal fame.

Davids, in the few years of his life, had acquired a fund of knowledge so extensive and so varied, that were age reckoned by the amount of learning attained, he must have reached a patriarchal old age. Had he been spared to his co-religionists and to the world at large, a mind so ardent, so stored with erudition, and so endowed with zeal and perseverance, would undoubtedly have amply realised the glorious promise of youth. Providence had decreed otherwise. Davids had been bred to the law, and was possessed of a competent fortune. Within a few weeks of that epoch of life which would have rendered him his own master, in the midst of his pure and lofty aspirations, he became a victim to the new pestilence that was then spreading its ravages over every country in Europe. Like so many other men of genius, the mind seemed to be too powerful for the slender body. Exhausted by nightly vigils and incessant labour, his corporeal strength was insufficient to withstand the violent attack of cholera with which he was seized on the night of the 17th July 1832. He suffered in silence to avoid alarming his mother, and when medical assistance became available, it was, alas! too late. His pure spirit fled to its Creator. To the sorrow of his broken-hearted mother we need not advert here. Nothing could console her; not even the generous testimonial of Sultan Mahmoud II., who presented to Mrs Davids a splendid diamond ring, accompanied by a letter expressing his high approbation of the work dedicated to him, and his deep regret at the author's premature death.

In Arthur Lumley Davids the Jews of his day lost one of their brightest ornaments. His noble efforts contributed to vindicate Jewish fame from the unjust reproaches which the prejudice of ages had heaped upon it. He gave a glorious example to the youths of Israel, and no doubt the good seed has borne good fruit. Albeit there has been only one Numa Hartog, it is impossible to say what amount of honest emulation and good work the memory of Davids may have induced.

CHAPTER XLIII.

THE JEWS IN HAMBURG AND IN LISBON—THE SHAARE TICVA SCHOOL—AN UNLAWFUL MINYAN—GIFTS TO THE SEPHARDI SYNAGOGUE.

ALBEIT the Portuguese Jewish Community of London had ceased in the second decade of the present century to be the wealthiest and most important Jewish body in this country, it still remained an influential and opulent congregation, able and willing to stretch forth a helping hand to its distressed brethren abroad. Napoleon Bonaparte was approaching his downfall, and his lieutenants were making a desperate resistance to a coalesced Europe. The French were shut up in Hamburg among other places, and as their provisions were diminishing, their authorities ordered the expulsion of non-combatants. Numbers of poor Jews precipitately quitted Hamburg and sought refuge in Altona, utterly unprovided with the barest necessities of life. Sick women and starving children indeed formed a heartrending spectacle. A committee was constituted by the Jews of Altona; and as many of the fugitives were of Spanish and Portuguese origin, application for assistance was made to the Bevis Marks Synagogue. A grant was at once allotted to their suffering co-religionists, by the elders of that congregation, who assembled especially for the purpose. Several sums of money were remitted to Altona, and doubtless many Jews were saved from the pangs of starvation, or from the poisoned breath of typhus fever. In the course of the correspondence between the authorities of Bevis Marks and the chiefs of the Hamburg Congregation, it transpired that the latter body was, or claimed to be, the oldest Spanish and Portuguese Community in the world. It was stated that at this period (1814) this congregation had been in existence for over 400 years. We think, however, that the Jews of Leghorn may claim at least as ancient a foundation for their congregation, which dates back over four centuries.

In 1816 the Mahamad of the Sephardi Congregation were informed that the barriers of intolerance were broken down in Portugal, and that the government of that country had permitted the Jews of Lisbon to profess openly their ancient faith. Lusitania, less intolerant and bigoted than the land of the Cid Campeador, did not consider that the peaceful existence of a few Jews within its bosom would imperil the national safety of the State or its national religion. Hitherto such Jews as might happen to die in Lisbon, were interred in the English cemetery. At this period it was resolved to purchase a piece of land for a burial-ground, and the Portuguese Jews of London contributed a small sum to that pious object. The number of Jews dwelling at that time in the capital of Portugal seems to have been very limited, and it appears that it did not increase with any great rapidity when they were allowed to constitute themselves into a congregation. On the other hand, the descendants of Jews, who to save their lives adopted Catholicism, formed a not inconsiderable part of the population. Jewish blood runs through the veins of some of the noblest families of Portugal, and the saying of that enlightened minister, the Marquis de Pombal, to King José I., has often been quoted. When the King expressed a desire that those individuals whose ancestors had been Jews should wear yellow hats, the minister brought two such hats to the king, observing that one was for his Majesty and the other for himself.

The Portuguese language had constituted for more than a century and a half, the official language of the Jewish Community of Bevis Marks. In the beginning of this century that tongue had fallen into desuetude, and was only understood by some of the foreign Israelites who settled in London. In February 1819, it was resolved to adopt the plan of keeping the minutes of all proceedings in the English instead of the Portuguese language; and a month afterwards a committee was appointed, of which Mr David Brandon was chairman, to translate the Askamoth (laws) of the congregation from the tongue of Camoens to that of Shakespeare.

The task was creditably performed; and since that period members of the congregation could no longer plead that they were unacquainted with the laws regulating their community, because they were written in a foreign language.

In 1821 Mr de Castro, the secretary of the Synagogue, died. In August of that year his successor was elected in the person of Mr Solomon Almosnino, the well-known and esteemed gentleman who for more than half a century has served his community most zealously and efficiently, gaining the respect of all with whom he has come in contact.

The state of the education of the Jewish poor remained in an unsatisfactory condition, notwithstanding the frequent changes and reforms introduced into the management of the communal schools. To increase and improve English instruction a grant of £40 per annum, from the legacy of £5000 left by Moses Lamego in 1757, was allotted for the payment of an English master to the school of "Heshaim," in addition to the interest of £1000 in consols. A committee to inquire into the state of the educational institutions of the congregation having been appointed early in 1821, the result of its labours became known towards the close of the year. The recommendations of the committee were acted upon. The schools that had existed until then under the direction of Heshaim were abolished. A society was established in their place under the name of *Shaare Ticva* (Gates of Hope), for the support of a Spanish and Portuguese Jews' Charity School, for the education of poor youths in the principles of the Jewish religion. The same sums as before were placed at the disposal of the governors of the institution. For the last generation the zeal and efficiency displayed by the various masters and managers have raised considerably the standard of education; and those schools have now become equal to any others of the same class and appertaining to any sect in the country.

It is a trite saying that small causes frequently lead to great events. Had Grouchy not lost his way on his march to the field of Waterloo, he would have arrived there before Blücher, and Napoleon Bonaparte might have died on the throne of France. Had Louis Philippe not forbidden a few opposition deputies to dine at a public banquet, his grandson might now be King of France. And to speak of comparatively small events, had not a certain narrow and exclusive spirit reigned in Bevis Marks, the schism that caused so much pain in the Jewish Community thirty-three years ago might probably never have occurred. The first circumstance that sowed the seed of dissension among the Sephardim in London took place in the year 1822. A foreign gentleman of good family, and of extremely orthodox principles, who was settled in England, took occasion on the initiation of a son into the covenant of Abraham, to receive a number of friends at his house to read prayers during the first night of Pentecost. This custom is very generally observed abroad, and is by some families practised in London to the present day. On the following morning the prayers allotted to that festival were recited with *Minyan*. The event created a great stir. The first, the fundamental law of the congregation, which sternly prohibited the meeting of ten or more Jews for the celebration of prayers in any locality within a certain radius from the Bevis Marks Synagogue, had been infringed. The offenders, twelve in number, were summoned before the Mahamad, and were placed on their trial. A number of witnesses were examined and cross-examined. The opinions of the Haham and the Beth Din were taken. The principal offenders did not appear in defence; the minor delinquents alleged various pleas in extenuation. All the transgressors were found guilty, and various penalties were inflicted upon them. The gentleman at whose house had occurred the unlawful proceeding of chanting prayers with *Minyan*, and his father and another relative, were deprived of their seats in Synagogue, their names were erased from the list of *Yehidim*, they were relegated to certain places at the back of the *Theba* (reading-desk), disqualified from being called up to the law, declared ineligible for two years for any pious duties, and finally fines of £40 and £20 respectively were inflicted upon them. Minor penalties varying in degree were laid on the other transgressors, all of whom were foreigners, and some making only transient sojourns in England. The condemnations were read in Synagogue, and much unpleasantness ensued. One of the parties implicated attended Synagogue, and on being removed from his former seat, he commenced an action at law against the Synagogue authorities, which after a short time was abandoned. The matter remained in abeyance until November 1825, when the death occurred of the mother of the gentleman at whose house the *Berith* had taken place. The lady's husband and son then expressed a desire to return to the Synagogue, and offered to pay the fines which had been imposed upon them; and those others who had shared in their condemnations, and who were still in England, manifested a similar wish. The gentlemen in question were re-elected as *Yehidim*; they duly performed the necessary ceremonies to purge themselves from ecclesiastical censure; their fines were remitted, and they became useful members of the congregation. But the bitterness of their punishment they never forgot. When years afterwards other members of the community asked for the privilege of erecting a place of worship nearer to their own homes than the ancient building in the city, the same men, actuated by a sense of a former wrong, strenuously opposed any concession to others, of that which had been refused to them. They had been treated harshly, as they considered; and by a strange code of justice, they determined to revenge themselves by inflicting harsh treatment upon others. We shall enter more fully into this subject in its proper place.

The financial position of the Bevis Marks Synagogue was, generally speaking, favourable. Albeit the impost formerly levied on the transactions effected by the members had gradually been abandoned, and the finta was sometimes in arrears, so many pious legacies had been left to the Synagogue that its funds were continually increasing. Without mentioning the numerous small sums bequeathed to the congregation, we will only record some of the larger gifts presented at this period. Among these we may mention a legacy from Mr Samuel Bensaken of Philadelphia, and the residue of his estate, which produced £1218, 17s. 11d.; a donation by the illustrious philanthropist, Sir Moses Montefiore, in the year 1823, of an estate of thirteen houses in Cock Court, Jewry Street, the rent arising from which was to be invested in the three per cent. consols for five years to form a repairing fund, and then the dwellings were to be occupied by deserving poor as almshouses: and finally, the

Lara gift, which was handed over to the Synagogue in June 1826. According to this generous contract, Mr Lara of Canterbury assigned at once as a fund to several trustees an annual revenue of £647, 4s. per annum, which was to be paid to him during his life-time; after his death £500 a year was to be allowed to Mrs Lara, and at her demise the sum of £550 per annum to be appropriated to the following philanthropic objects: (1.) £150 per annum to be applied to the education and maintenance of two Portuguese boys, who were to be instructed in higher studies so as to fit them for the clerical offices of the congregation. (2.) £70 per annum to be allotted to the support of three invalids in the hospital called Beth Holim, and £40 per annum to the clothing of twenty poor girls of the congregation. (3.) £50 per annum to be expended in assisting ten poor lying-in women at their own homes. (4.) £100 to be given annually as a dower to a Portuguese Jewish woman, married for not more than a year to a Portuguese Jew. (5.) £70 a year to be awarded to the Hebra (burial society) to abolish the use of calico shrouds and to replace them by linen. (6.) £70 per annum to be given for the establishment of a dispensary for the poor near the Synagogue. The surplus was to accumulate and to be applied, part to existing institutions and part to the support of the aged poor, either at the hospital or asylum called Beth Holim, or in some other especial establishment.

This represents an extended range of benevolence, and doubtless Mr Lara's dispositions effect a great deal of good, benefiting as they are intended to do various classes. Mrs Lara survived her husband for many years; and during her life-time she made several important gifts of money to the Synagogue.

CHAPTER XLIV.

MOVEMENTS IN THE PORTUGUESE CONGREGATION—PARTIES IN THAT COMMUNITY — PROGRESS OF THE SEPHARDIM— SIR MOSES MONTEFIORE.

As the century advanced, cordiality became more apparent in the relations between the ancient Sephardi Synagogue and the more modern Ashkenazi Congregations. The suspicious, doubtful manner in which German Jews had been regarded in Bevis Marks, had long given way to a more brotherly feeling. Family ties had multiplied between the Jews of Spanish or Portuguese, and the Jews of German or Polish descent. It was not, however, until 1825 that a German was allowed in the Portuguese Synagogue to be called up to the Law or hold a *mitzvah;* these privileges until that period had been denied to the members of his community. In September 1826, the ministers of the Bevis Marks Synagogue, on the invitation of Mr A. Kisch, were permitted to attend the consecration of the new Westminster Synagogue in Denmark Court, and to take part in the celebration of the service. In 1834, whilst the New Synagogue in Leadenhall Street was undergoing repairs, the *Shaare Tieva* school-room was placed at the disposal of the members of that congregation for the purpose of reciting prayers during the New Year Holidays. This simple act of courtesy did much towards establishing warm relations between the two communities of Jews in England.

After the death of Haham Meldola in 1828, the state of public feeling among Portuguese Jews on questions connected with public worship seems to have been of an unsatisfactory and unsettled nature: so much so, that on the 4th December 1828, a Committee of Elders was appointed to inquire into the best means of raising altogether the tone of public services, infusing therein greater decorum and devotion. Mr Moses Mocatta, the President of the Congregation, in his charge at the close of the Session of the Elders in the same year, adverted to the uneasy state of feeling obtaining among the members of the congregation, and deeply regretted that party sentiment ran high in the community, and that an unfortunate opinion had gained ground among the *Yehidim*, that men and not measures influenced votes, and that all proposals were accepted or rejected purely from party considerations. Mr Moses Mocatta, in wise and conciliatory language, deprecated that party spirit should predominate in so small a community. He lamented that gentlemen who considered themselves aggrieved should take the law in their own hands by curtailing their offerings. Finally, he concluded by some excellent advice to his brethren, recommending them " to restore, by forgetting supposed injuries and disappointed results, that brotherly love and good understanding which, until recently, were ever implanted in our breasts."

We are unable to say what effect these prudent and well-intentioned words had on the community. The speaker little foresaw that years afterwards his own name would raise a whirlwind in the assembly over which he was then presiding. Human passions and failings reign alike in the council of a small sect and in the parliament of a great nation; and doubtless by the time the Greek Kalends shall have arrived, we may expect perfect unanimity, concord, and unselfishness in all assemblages of men.

The report of the Committee for the Promotion of Religious Worship was delivered. That document contained a number of recommendations which were adopted by the elders. It was resolved that the children of the *Shaare Ticva* and Orphan Schools should be taught to chant; that the wardens themselves should attend Synagogue as often as possible; that they should abstain from conversation, and give a good example to the congregation by not stirring from their seats until the end of the service. Certain alterations in the mode of reading prayers were suggested, so as to save time, and the *Mahamad* was directed to take measures to abridge the length of the service, as far as practicable. The importance of the study of the Hebrew language was strongly impressed on fathers of families. All proclamations in the Synagogue were to be made in the English language. Moral and religious discourses were deemed essential to the welfare of the congregation; an English sermon was to be delivered every Saturday afternoon, and its text to be taken from Scripture. Every sermon before delivery was to be submitted to a committee of three elders, who were to examine the MS. to see that nothing was contained therein opposed to Jewish doctrines or hostile to the institutions of the country. A committee was appointed at the same time to investigate the state of the Medrash (Theological College). This step in due course led to a thorough reform of that institution with the introduction of more stringent regulations as to its discipline.

There were few persons capable of acting as preachers in those days either in the Portuguese or in the German Community, a state of things strongly contrasting with what obtains now, when highly qualified gentlemen abound. The Rev. D. A. de Sola, one of the ministers of the Synagogue, was the first gentleman who offered himself, and he was accepted as public instructor. He preached for some years, giving great satisfaction to his flock; but the practice of delivering sermons was subsequently abandoned in this congregation, and was not resumed as a regular institution until more recent times.

As the union of the two branches of the Jewish race in England became closer, they joined together in various undertakings of common advantage. When London was visited in February 1832 by a new and mysterious disease, the cholera morbus, the principal Jewish Synagogues took stringent measures to preserve their poor against the attacks of that pestilence. Visiting committees were established by the Bevis Marks Synagogue and by the three city German Synagogues, which worked harmoniously together. In the Portuguese Synagogue a sum of £500 was placed at the disposal of the *Mahamad* from the legacy fund; subscriptions were raised; visiting committees established; bedding, blankets, sheets, and under garments were distributed to the poor; and such articles of personal apparel as had been pledged were redeemed, and returned to their owners. The other Synagogues displayed equal activity; and the Jews of London suffered much less, in proportion, from the visitation of the Asiatic pestilence than their Christian countrymen.

The Portuguese Congregation also bore its fair share of the expenses entailed upon the Jews by their prolonged struggles to obtain from the Legislature of the country a recognition of their civil and political rights.

At one time the Bevis Marks Synagogue was threatened with an invasion, which filled its members with indescribable alarm. The shrill shrieks of steam engines, and the thunder of railway trains, might have startled the ears of worshippers in the Portuguese Synagogue had the Blackwall Railway Bill obtained the sanction of Parliament. It was proposed by the promoters of that Bill to take possession of the almshouses, school premises, and readers' residences in Heneage Lane, and to run their line a few feet below the surface of the ground, and within five yards from the Synagogue itself. A petition was prepared in opposition by the Synagogue authorities, and it was presented to Parliament by Mr Crawford, a city member. Fortunately, the Bill was defeated in the Legislature, and the Jews were not disturbed in their devotions by the piercing whistle of one of the most important instruments of modern civilisation.

On the death of King William IV., in 1837, special funeral services were performed in all Jewish Synagogues, which were draped in black. At Bevis Marks, Mr Abraham Alexander Lindo volunteered to preach a discourse. This gentleman, in 1839, wrote a pamphlet entitled, "A Word in Season," and he expressed a desire to continue the subject. The *Mahamad* observed to him that they had seen his publication, which had been issued without their sanction, and they cautioned him against repeating the offence, lest he fall under penalties. Free thought and a free press were not understood in those days. No books touching on religion could be published by a member of the Synagogue, without the permission of the Wardens. Even the useful almanac, compiled by the late Mr E. H. Lindo, was not allowed to mark the course of time and the return of Jewish festivals without repeated applications of the author to the custodians of Sephardi orthodoxy.

In that year (1839) the boys who had assisted the readers in chanting prayers were formed into a permanent choir, which was placed under the direction of Mr Moss. At the same period was founded the Infant School, which affords education to female children of the poor; and an outfit for the girls was provided by private subscription.

The Portuguese Community at this epoch, limited as it was in numbers, was far from being homogeneous in its religious views. A party of gentlemen existed who appeared desirous of introducing important modifications in Jewish religious observances; while another party insisted on the intact maintenance of the traditional practices of Judaism. The former party was composed of some of the descendants of ancient families long settled in this country; whilst the latter, which was far more numerous, was to a great extent recruited from foreigners from the extreme south of Europe, or from the continents of Asia or Africa. The movement into which the first section of Congregants entered will be duly recorded in its proper place. At present we will only relate that a portion of the most orthodox members of the Congregation formed themselves into a society styling themselves "Shomeré Meshmeret Hakkodesh" (Preservers of Sacred Institutions), with the object of upholding and preserving the Jewish faith as handed down, and of preventing innovation or alteration in any of its recognised forms, unless sanctioned by properly-constituted religious authorities. These individuals displayed more ardour than discretion. It is difficult to estimate the amount of mischief that may be committed by excess of zeal. So this association was not approved of by the moderate members of the community, who endeavoured to hold a balance between the two extremes.

The authorities readily recognised that it would cause more harm than good, and that it would tend to fan into a flame any unpleasant feeling that unhappily might exist among different sections of the Congregation. Such gentlemen as had taken part in it were recommended to dissolve the society, and as this was not done at once, the Wardens adopted more stringent measures, and gave forth a notice that members of the association of "Preservers of Sacred Institutions" would not be eligible for any office in the Congregation, or as members of any committee, so long as they remained members of such society. This resolution was rescinded soon afterwards, on the solemn assurance of the individuals in question that the association was no longer in existence.

In May 1839 the condition of affairs appears to have been far from satisfactory; for it was deemed advisable to elect another committee, consisting of five Elders and the Wardens, "to take into especial consideration the condition of the ecclesiastical department of the Congregation and the state of the Beth Hamedrash, so as to better promote the religious instruction and general welfare of the Congregation." Unfortunately, these well-meaning efforts were quite unavailing to stem the running waters that had sprung up in the midst of the community. The conflicting ideas of different members of the oldest Synagogue in London could not be reconciled, the most painful episode in modern Anglo-Jewish History occurred, and brothers were separated from brothers, and friends from their dearest friends.

From the date of this schism within its bosom—the bitterness of which has long since died away—the Spanish and Portuguese Jewish Community has followed the even tenor of its peaceful career and material prosperity, which the secession of some of its *Yehidim* only temporarily diminished. The Sephardim, like the Ashkenazim, have worked hard in the cause of education and in the advancement of the welfare of the Jewish race at home and abroad. They bore their full part in the various movements for the promotion of the civil and political rights of the Jews in England; and they contributed to all missions intended for the relief of their distressed co-religionists scattered throughout the globe. Finally, the Jews of Spanish and Portuguese descent possess an especial source of pride; for from their community has arisen the noblest figure in Israel, whose extended beneficence is catholic and widespread; who, with a deep-rooted attachment to his own race, has devoted the greater part of a long life to the relief of suffering humanity; and whose goodness and charity are resplendent wherever the sun shines—we mean the pre-eminent philanthropist, Sir Moses Montefiore.

Here we feel greatly tempted to descant on that wonderful combination of virtues which has produced a long series of almost heroic deeds of benevolence, and to linger on the beauties of a life unique among our cotemporaries. We feel the more impelled to dilate upon the merits of such a man and such a Jew as Sir Moses Montefiore, as we encounter his name in the Jewish history of the last half century at every turn. Wherever charity extends its hands to help the poor, or philanthropy exerts its powers to benefit mankind, or human tenderness hastens to the rescue of the oppressed and the persecuted—in all such situations we find the figure of Sir Moses Montefiore foremost in the canvas of cotemporary Jewish history. But forcible reasons deter us from the gratification of such a desire. Our powers, in the first place, would utterly fail in rendering adequate justice to so great a subject; and not all that any writer could say, be he the lowliest or the highest in the land, could add to his fame or increase the glory of his reputation. It were impossible to gild fine gold, or to add perfume to the lily. Other motives of a more private nature would prevent us from following our inclinations, while our plan would scarcely admit of an extended discourse on one theme only, however lofty it might be. Finally, we confess we much admire the rabbinical maxim, which advises us never to praise a man in his presence, a maxim which was wisely and practically adopted by the ancient Greeks in not erecting statues to their heroes in their life-time. A statue to Sir Moses Montefiore is already raised in the hearts of all his kindred and race throughout the world.

CHAPTER XLV.

NEW ASHKENAZI INSTITUTIONS—SYNAGOGUE LIBERALITY.

THE annals of the Ashkenazi Community in London during the second quarter of the present century, though scarcely very eventful, offer an unbroken record of increasing prosperity and influence, and of advancing social and political importance. A great number of educational and charitable institutions were founded since the hot days of June, when the plains of Waterloo witnessed the downfall of the greatest conqueror of modern ages. First we have the Free School, which was established in the memorable year 1815, to instruct six hundred boys and three hundred girls, and which is at present the largest and one of the best organised institutions of the kind in the United Kingdom. To clothe the naked and feed the hungry are maxims strictly practised among the Jews, and a variety of associations have been called into existence for those purposes. In 1818, some charitable members of the more ornamental half of the human race, under the title of the "Ladies' Benevolent Society," undertook to clothe half-yearly poor Jewish girls between the ages of eight and fourteen. In 1820 was founded the Western Institution for educating, clothing, and apprenticing indigent Jewish boys. In 1821, other benevolent individuals joined together for the same philanthropic objects, and formed the Westminster Benevolent Institution. In the same year a New Synagogue was opened in Brewer Street, the Congregation of which was partly drawn from the members of the Westminster Synagogue. In 1824, the Society for the Relief of the Indigent Poor began to allow 5s. per week to necessitous widows; and in 1828 the Western Jewish Philanthropic Institution commenced to grant loans not exceeding £5, and gifts not exceeding £2, to cheer the needy during the Jewish festivals.

That most excellent institution, the Jews' Orphan Asylum, for the education, maintenance, clothing, and apprenticing of male and female orphans, was opened in 1851. Many other charities were created to benefit the poor in various ways, and which it would be tedious to mention here. We will only advert to the erection in 1838, by Mr A. L. Moses of Aldgate, at his sole expense, of twelve commodious and handsomely-constructed almshouses for the use of as many respectable poor females of the German Congregation, as an act of true liberality and philanthropy.

The London Hospital for many years has been a source of signal advantage to the Jewish poor. The calls on the services of that establishment were so great in former times, that in February 1828 it was found advisable to recommend that Jewish governors of the hospital should leave blank admissions for the hospital, to be distributed to the Jewish poor when needful by the Secretary of the Great Synagogue.

Due honour must be given to the Great Synagogue for the liberality and generosity with which it has almost without exception treated its officials, high and low. The enumeration of the loans and grants made to meritorious officers of that Congregation would fill a dozen pages. We will merely adduce an instance as an illustration. In 1829, the Reader of the Synagogue, Mr D. Elias, fell into ill-health, and six months' leave of absence was granted to him. Mr Elias, it seems, was subject to a pulmonary complaint, and two physicians, Dr Barnard Van Oven (son of Mr Joshua Van Oven) and Dr Robertson, certified that by continuing his profession he would endanger his existence. At the expiration of his leave of absence the unfortunate minister felt himself constrained to tender his resignation. His engagement was only for three years. Nevertheless, the Vestry of the Synagogue presented Mr Elias, over and above the salary due to him, with the sum of £200. They handed him in addition a further sum for his travelling expenses; they allowed his wife to continue to reside for a certain time, rent free, in the house allotted to him; and on her departure to join her husband, who was a foreigner, and who had returned to his native country, they bestowed upon her another gratuity. Readers, choristers, beadles, and watchmen, all equally partook of the liberality of the Synagogue. They were not its only recipients. Occasional assistance was given to decayed members. To a gentleman who was once a President of the Congregation and had fallen into temporary difficulties a loan of £100 was awarded.

On the retirement of Mr Elias from the post of Reader, the vacancy was not filled up for some time. Many applications for the post came from different parts of the Continent, not only from Germany and Holland, but from Dijon and Besançon in France, as well as from Brussels. Several of the candidates came over to this country, were tried and found wanting. It was not until the 20th May 1832, that the election took place, when the choice fell on Mr Simon Ascher of Gröningen, whose melodious voice is well remembered by many Jewish readers. We need hardly say that the disappointed candidates were not sent away empty-handed.

In November 1831, when the approach of the cholera morbus was producing a general sense of alarm in this country, Mr Charles Pearson, Chairman of the City Board of Health, addressed a letter to the Wardens of the Great Synagogue, recommending them to put their house in order in good time. Mr Pearson pointed out the dangers resulting from the congregation of dealers in old clothes who assembled in Cutler Street, and brought together a great accumulation of filth, which was most injurious to the public health. Unfortunately, the Wardens do not seem to have been able to remedy this evil thoroughly, for they were afraid of depriving of their living a body of industrious men who had no other resource than this trade. The Great Synagogue, in conjunction with the Portuguese Synagogue, as we have said in a former chapter, took many precautions to diminish the consequences of the dreaded visitation, and with very fair success. We must not omit to relate that the Board of Health of the Parish of St Botolph behaved very liberally to the Jews, and passed several measures conceived in a friendly spirit. The Board called upon the surgeons of the different Jewish Synagogues to attend professionally all Jews and Jewesses who preferred being under their care. They granted to them the use of the Cholera Hospital for the purpose, and they engaged the services of a Jewish nurse. They gave notice at the outbreak of the disorder to all poor Jews residing in the parish, that they would be admitted to the hospital on the certificate of their own (Jewish) surgeons. These acts of kindness were duly appreciated by the Jews, and their gratitude was warmly expressed by the Synagogues.

The Duke's Place Synagogue, as the representative of the German Jews in London, was in the continual receipt of appeals from their co-religionists from all quarters of the globe. If there was a fire in Constantinople, an earthquake in the West Indies, a famine in Poland, a prayer for help would certainly reach Duke's Place. In 1832, an application came from Mr Rothschild on behalf of the community of the island St Thomas, for assistance in building a Synagogue. A sum of £20 was granted, and a deputation waited on the great financier with the cheque. Mr Rothschild declined to accept the cheque, and bade the deputation authorise Mr Wolff, the President of the Congregation of St Thomas, to draw on him (Mr Rothschild) for the amount, with an addition of £10, 10s. which he would give on his own account.

In 1834, the Great Synagogue several times narrowly escaped destruction. Three distinct fires took place in that building within the course of a few months, all arising apparently from the defective and dangerous construction of the stoves employed to heat the Synagogue.

The danger was considered so great that there was some difficulty in renewing the insurances. The Globe and Alliance Offices declined to continue the risk, except at an additional premium and unless some further alterations were made. Eventually the Sun Fire Office accepted the insurance on condition that the stoves were enclosed. That arrangement was duly carried out, and happily the Great Synagogue has stood ever since safe and unscathed, the building being now heated by means of hot water pipes.

The Jews were for ages debarred from many rights and privileges; but it may not be generally known that the possession of some of these could not be purchased even by apostasy. The question of the privileges of baptized Jews was tried before the Court of Aldermen on the 4th March 1828. The Jews were excluded from the advantages of citizenship in the city of London. Certain individuals named Saul prayed to be allowed to carry on business in the city. These persons, born of Jewish parentage, had been initiated into Judaism at their birth, but from their infancy they had been brought up in the Protestant faith. In the year 1785, the Court of Aldermen had made a standing order that baptized Jews should not be admitted to the freedom of the city. The reason alleged for this resolution was a fear lest a number of Jews of indifferent character should accept baptism, and set up in business to the detriment of good and real Christians. Upon the strength of this order all succeeding courts had rejected the applications of individuals who had renounced the forms, customs, and opinions of the Jews. On the occasion in question several members of the Court, especially Aldermen Wood, Waithman, and Sir Peter Laurie, encouraged the applicants. Mr Law argued the question on behalf of the petitioners. He stated that the petitioners never had been Jews. They had been baptized in 1803, but he defied the Court to prove that they had been Jews before that period. He adverted to the case of Galindo, which had been tried in 1783, when the Recorder and the Common Sergeant had both agreed that baptism was a sufficient renunciation of Judaism, but Mr Nugent, the Common Sergeant, had placed before the Court, as a matter of expediency, that there might be so many applications even from persons of the lowest sort, that they might be attended by great inconvenience to the public. After some discussion the Court granted the prayer of the petitioners; the order was rescinded, and Messrs Saul were received as freemen of the city of London. What changes indeed have arisen in less than half a century! In the wealthiest city of the world, where even converted Jews were not admitted to citizenship, we have witnessed two Jews dispense justice as its chief magistrates!

Another curious point of law, in which Jews are concerned, was raised in the following year in the Sheriff Court, Guildhall. A trial took place in that Court in July 1829, for the recovery of the price of a horse found unsound, when a verdict for the defendant was entered. It was moved, on behalf of the plaintiff, that the verdict be set aside, upon the ground that John Salmon, an Israelite and one of the jury, was sworn on the New Testament, though he was of the Jewish religion. Salmon had stood in the box with other jurymen as Christians, and he did not put on his hat or observe any of the ceremonies followed by Jewish people in taking oaths. It was urged that this mode of swearing was not binding upon a Jew to the value of a straw, and that the verdict ought to be set aside, as being in reality the verdict of eleven instead of twelve men. Affidavits proving that Salmon was a Jew were put in. The application was opposed, purely on technical grounds. Mr Sergeant Arabin ruled that the affidavits were not strong enough to sanction a disturbance of the verdict, and the application was refused.

Doubtless no sincere and observing Israelite would consent to be sworn except according to Jewish custom with his hat on, and on the Old Testament; but what value may be attached to the oath of a Jew taken on a book which he does not hold sacred, is a question for his own conscience. Moreover, we are informed that a Jew who takes the oath on a book in the contents of which he does not believe, and which therefore may not be binding on his conscience, is guilty of contempt of court.

CHAPTER XLVI.

TESTIMONIAL TO SIR MOSES MONTEFIORE—SYNAGOGUE IMPROVEMENTS.

In 1840, when the eminent philanthropist, Sir Moses Montefiore, undertook his noble mission to Damascus, to save his suffering co-religionists from the tortures inflicted upon them by fanaticism and superstition, the members of the Great Synagogue contributed to the subscription raised to defray part of the expenses of that memorable journey. The history of that glorious mission we shall relate in a separate chapter. Here we shall merely record that a suitable welcome was given to the champion of Israel, on his return from the self-imposed task which he had so successfully accomplished. At the suggestion of the Mahamad of the Sephardim, sub-committees were appointed in December 1840, by the three city Synagogues of the "Germans," in conjunction with the Westminster Synagogue, to consider what measures ought to be adopted by their several congregations on the return of Sir Moses Montefiore. The celebrations took place with great solemnity in the Portuguese Synagogue on the 8th March 1841, and in the German Synagogues on the 13th March. On those occasions thanksgivings were offered up in the several Synagogues to Almighty God for His infinite mercy to His people Israel, in causing their accused brethren in the East to be delivered from unjust and cruel persecutions. Sir Moses and Lady Montefiore were present at the Bevis Marks Synagogue and the Great Synagogue respectively: and the chief men among the Jews gathered to do honour to the illustrious philanthropist and to the accomplished partner of his beneficent labours.

The amount subscribed by the Jews towards the cost of the journey to the East amounted to £6774. The sum disbursed exceeded the sum collected. But as Sir Moses Montefiore generously insisted on bearing himself a part of the expenditure to the extent of £2200, a surplus remained of nearly one-fifth, which the trustees resolved to return to the original contributors.

It has always been a weakness with Englishmen to embody the expression of their gratitude in so many ounces of solid silver. As a mark of gratitude to Sir Moses Montefiore for his great services to his community, a very handsome testimonial was presented to him on the 27th February 1843. This testimonial consisted of a splendid silver ornament in the form of a miniature monument, three and a half feet high, of great weight, and covering a large quadrangular base. It was surmounted by several figures, the most prominent of which was David Conquering the Lion. It was designed by Sir G. Hayter, sculptured by E. Bailey, R.A., and executed by Mortimer and Hunt of Bond Street. The inscription stated that it was presented to Sir Moses by a large number of his Jewish brethren in the United Kindgom, Jamaica, Barbadoes, and Gibraltar, in commemoration of the many personal sacrifices endured, and the philanthropy displayed, by him and Lady Montefiore during his mission to the East.

The Jews of Germany were not behind their English brethren in expressing their admiration and respect for Sir Moses Montefiore. They offered to him an elegant album, folio-sized and of double width, bound in maroon velvet, and framed in gilded bronze. Appropriate paintings appeared on each cover, and every page was ornamented with a border engraved with tasteful and suitable emblematic devices. The album contained an eloquent address signed by Dr Philippsohn and by 1490 other persons, including many names distinguished in literature and art.

In May 1841 the first effort at organising a regular choir was made in the Great Synagogue. Formerly the only approach to a choir in German Synagogues consisted of two persons who aided the hazan or precentor, one being called the singer and the other the bass. But the propriety of having an organised choir being admitted, Mr Simon Ascher selected several youths to undergo training for the purpose, and Mr Julius Mombach was appointed to instruct them in singing. Mr Mombach has been for many years an able composer of sacred melodies, and the choir of the Great Synagogue has been formed and maintained in its present state of high efficiency mainly by his exertions.

At the same time it was resolved to obtain, if practicable, pulpit instruction in English. In reply to some advertisements seeking the services of a preacher competent to deliver sermons in the English language, Mr D. M. Isaacs appeared as a candidate. Mr Isaacs had been one of the earliest preachers in the English language. He had already officiated for some years as minister in Liverpool and elsewhere. He had not long before been invited to preach in the Duke's Place Synagogue on the occasion of Sir Moses Montefiore's return from the East. Mr Isaacs was not elected, and the Great Synagogue remained without religious discourses. The reverend gentleman has since been pastor at Liverpool and Manchester, where he has obtained a reputation for scholarship and eloquence. Though he is not an Englishman, his accent and fluent acquaintance with the English language would proclaim him of English birth.

The secession of some members of the orthodox congregations did not affect the German Community as much as it temporarily affected the Portuguese Community. The vast numbers of the Ashkenazim and their great wealth could not be influenced by the loss of a few individuals, however greatly their departure from orthodox Judaism may have been regretted. Since the days of the Reform movement, the development and increase of the German Jews in London has been as astonishing as their progress has been uninterrupted. New schools have been founded, new and sumptuous places of worship have been opened, new charities have been established; and in every quarter we perceive signs of commercial and communal activity, prosperity, and enlightenment.

CHAPTER XLVII.

SIMON SOLOMON—ISAAC GOMES SERRA—ABRAHAM MONTE-FIORE—NATHAN MEYER ROTHSCHILD.

WE have hitherto endeavoured to bestow our humble meed of praise upon those individuals who have raised the name of Jew, or who have contributed to the advancement of Judaism. We shall continue to glance at the career of those Jews who distinguished themselves during the first half of the nineteenth century for their virtues, their conspicuous abilities, or their attainment of high position. Should we omit to give due place in our list of worthies to any deserving personage, we trust the reader will attribute such omission to the imperfection ordinarily attending human undertakings, rather than to any wilful exclusion on our part. At present we shall speak of the men whose names head this chapter, and whose claims to the respect or admiration of the world are based on widely different grounds.

The name of Simon Solomon is probably new to our readers. Simon Solomon was not an eminent financier, a successful writer, or a brilliant scholar. He was merely a truly good and pious man. His lines were not cast in pleasant places, for his lot was lowly. Born in Lissa in Polish Prussia, he immigrated in early youth into this country, where he followed the trade of fancy boxmaker. Simon Solomon was not an illiterate man: he was proficient in Hebrew and rabbinical literature, and he was well acquainted with French and German. Possessed of persevering, industrious habits, he was able not only to provide for a large family and to contribute to the necessities of his own community, of which he was a conscientious member, but also to fulfil what he considered his duty, in relieving his Christian neighbours in such a manner as to ensure the admiration and esteem of all who knew him. Apart from his private charities, he was one of the first founders of the Clerkenwell Philanthropic Society, to which he and his family liberally contributed, and he was chosen in conjunction with others, the winter before his death, to dispense bread and coals. Precluded by his religious scruples from accepting the refreshments which were offered to him during his rounds, he underwent many privations. He was nevertheless so ardent and cheerful in the performance of these duties, that the poor in his presence always seemed to forget their poverty, and hence, like Job, the blessing of "those that were ready to perish" often came to him, and he literally made the "widow's heart dance for joy." Simon Solomon died suddenly in 1817, at the age of sixty-nine. He was interred hastily, to the sorrow of his neighbours, many of whom were unable to pay their last mark of respect to his remains, which were hurried to the cemetery at Ducking Pond Row, ere the recipients of his bounty were aware that they would meet his kindly eyes no more. Simon Solomon by his unwearied beneficence did much to dispel the prejudices existing against Jews, especially among the lower and middle classes. He was strictly Jewish in his belief, and always averse to the attempts of those who professionally aim at the conversion of Jews; but he had no objection to an attendance upon Christian worship for the sake of doing good. He broke a lance with converted missionaries, and he published an animated letter to the Rev. C. Frey, on the subject of his conduct with respect to the Jewish proselytes made by the London Society.

Isaac Gomes Serra was a different type of a noble-minded Jew. He was the last descendant of an ancient Portuguese family, and he died in 1818. He united to a courteous and dignified bearing true piety and sincere philanthropy. He inherited a considerable fortune, and after having pursued for some years a commercial career, he retired, and resided in a handsome dwelling in King's Road, Bedford Row; a situation greatly coveted in those days. Isaac Gomes Serra, albeit a zealous and devout Jew, was very popular among Christians. In the Synagogue he served all the offices filled by laymen. In his later days he devoted his time and attention almost exclusively to beneficence. He not only gave freely to the schools of his own race, but his fortune and generosity permitted him to bestow time and funds in the management and support of charities based on the established Church of the country. He was an active member of the committees of the City of London Lying-in Hospital, and of the workhouse of his parish, St Andrew, Holborn. He was also an assiduous member of the committee of the Small-pox Hospital, and was liberal in his subscriptions to many other charitable institutions. His conciliatory manners and urbane address ensured him polite attention at those meetings of which a Jew formed part for the first time. He is described by a Christian writer of the day in these words: "In temper placid and serene but just, in character respectable, in age venerable; as a Jew he was conscientiously strict; as a member of society, upright, benevolent, and honourable." Let us hope that many Jews of the present day may have earned similar praise!

In 1824 the Portuguese Community of Bevis Marks lost another eminent member in the person of Abraham Montefiore. This gentleman, well known for his benevolence and kindly character as well as for his great wealth, was a leading member of the Stock Exchange. He had been to Cannes for the re-establishment of his health, and he died in the prime of life, on his way home, leaving two sons and two daughters. Mr Abraham Montefiore, who was greatly esteemed, was the brother of Sir Moses Montefiore, and he had married, as his second wife, Henrietta, sister of Mr N. M. Rothschild. Mr Montefiore was buried in the Portuguese cemetery at Mile End, and Dr Hirschel performed the funeral rites. The elder of the two sons of this gentleman is the present President of the Jewish Board of Deputies. His second son is President of two of the most important institutions of the Sephardi Community, the Hospital and the Congregational Schools. One daughter, Mrs H. Montefiore, was an authoress of distinction; another daughter is the wife of Sir Anthony de Rothschild.

The name of Nathan Meyer Rothschild is as familiar to the Hebrew public as household words. We shall not repeat here the history of the rise of the Rothschild family, which has become as popular a story as the legend of Alfred burning the cakes, or of William Tell transfixing the apple on his son's head. Nevertheless, in modern Anglo-Jewish history an honourable place must be given to a family which not only has attained unparalleled wealth and financial pre-eminence, but which has become famous for its unbounded munificent and almost unrestricted charity. We cannot pass over the subject without offering a few remarks. Nathan Meyer Rothschild came over from Frankfort to England in 1800, when he acted for his father in the purchase of Manchester goods. It was not until the breaking out of the war with Spain, in 1808, that his extraordinary means, which were displayed in making the remittances for the English army, became apparent to the mercantile world. Through the agency of his father, large sums were placed to his credit. Gradually his financial transactions pervaded the whole of the continent, and exercised more or less influence on monetary affairs of every description. No operations on equal scale had existed in Europe previous to his time. Sampson Gideon and Benjamin and Abraham Goldsmid, were puny speculators in comparison with N. M. Rothschild. The latter operator and his brothers participated in most of the great financial affairs of Austria, of France, of England, and of nearly every other country. Nathan Meyer Rothschild was considered the head of the firm, though really not the eldest brother in his family. In addition to the essential co-operation of his relatives, he had agencies in almost every important city in the old or the new world, in all of which, under his directions, extensive operations of various kinds were carried out. Mr Rothschild's loan contracts were not uniformly successful in the first instance. He was at the outset exposed to severe reverses which would have proved fatal to houses of inferior means. One of those reverses was connected with a loan of Exchequer bills in a $3\frac{1}{2}$ per cent. stock, the first of that denomination introduced into the English market; he is said to have lost thereby £500,000. This loan was a project of the then Chancellor of the Exchequer, the Right Honourable Nicholas Vansittart, afterwards Lord Bexley. Another event by which he would have been exposed to great danger was the conversion of

French rentes projected by M. de Villèle, the French Minister. Fortunately for Mr Rothschild the measure was lost by a single vote in the Paris Chamber of Peers; had it been carried, the convulsion that shortly followed in the money markets of Europe would probably have proved fatal to his position, notwithstanding all his vast resources. Another perilous contract was the four per cent. loan made with M. de Polignac, previous to the celebrated three days of July 1830, which heralded the fall of the Bourbons in France. The stock went down twenty to thirty per cent.; but luckily for Mr Rothschild the greater part of the loan had been distributed among the subscribers who suffered more or less severely.

The great financier's success in loans made it a matter of rivalry with all those states which wanted to borrow money to obtain his co-operation. He uniformly refused to enter into any such contracts for Spain and the American Republics, formerly its colonies; but whether his conduct was actuated by mere worldly prudence, or from a disinclination to assist a race which had maltreated his own, and banished it from the Iberian peninsula, we are unable to say.

Mr Rothschild's operations in bullion and foreign exchanges were nearly as considerable as his loan contracts. He never hesitated for a moment in fixing the rate either as a taker or as a drawer of bills on any part of the world. Notwithstanding the immense transactions into which he entered every foreign post day, and that he never took note of them, he could dictate the whole on his return home to his clerks with the most perfect accuracy. He is said to have been very liberal in his dealings; and many merchants whose bills were declined in other quarters found ready assistance from him. His judgment was proved to be correct, by the very small amount of loss which he incurred in such liberality. His attachment for and confidence in his wife (a daughter of L. B. Cohen, and a sister of Lady Montefiore) were unbounded, and he proved them by entrusting to her the administration of his will and the distribution of suitable legacies to numerous charities. For some weeks before his death he was ill at Frankfort, where he had been attended by Professor Chelcus of Heidelberg. He died at Frankfort, in 1836, at the age of sixty. He was, perhaps, the greatest financial genius that this century has seen; and his demise caused a great tumult, such as followed the death of Abraham Goldsmid. The timid were greatly alarmed. They said it was impossible to foresee what difficulties might arise on the withdrawal of the ability with which the foreign exchanges had been managed. Mr Rothschild had prided himself on the dexterity with which he distributed his immense resources, so that no operation of his should long abstract bullion from the bank. No catastrophes, however, occurred in the bourses of Europe after the death of the autocrat of the Exchange; and the affairs of the world in general, and of his firm in particular, proceeded as evenly and as quietly as if he had been at the helm to direct the ship to port.

The body of Mr Rothschild was brought to England on the 4th of August 1836, and was conveyed to his house in St Swithin's Lane. The funeral took place on Monday, the 8th of August; the remains were removed in a hearse drawn by six horses, and were followed by thirty-six mourning coaches and forty-one private carriages. Among these were the carriages of the Austrian, Russian, Prussian, and Neapolitan Ambassadors, of Lord Stewart, Lord Dinorben, Lord Maryborough, and the Lord Mayor, Sheriffs, and Aldermen of the city of London. When the procession reached Whitechapel Church, the children belonging to the Jews' Free School and Orphan Asylum joined in the *cortége*, which proceeded until the hearse drew up at the north entrance of the then burial-ground of the Great Synagogue. The Rev. Mr Ascher performed the service, and the Rev. Sol. Hirschel delivered in English an eloquent and fervent address, in which he expatiated on the beneficence of the deceased, who, in addition to his public subscriptions to nearly every Jewish and Christian charity, had placed many thousands of pounds in the hands of his relict to be distributed among the poor.

CHAPTER XLVIII.

BLOOD ACCUSATIONS IN THE EAST—MISSION OF SIR MOSES MONTEFIORE.

IN the spring of 1840, the Jews of Europe were startled by rumours of two cruel persecutions in the East, of which their brethren were the victims. Tales of false accusations and infamous aspersions against the unhappy Jews, of tortures and imprisonment to which respectable fathers of families were subjected, of odious calumnies propagated and vehemently supported by persons who ought to have known better, reached London and Paris. The reports gradually gained a tangible form, and the harrowing details—ascertained to be true—stirred the hearts of all Jews from the banks of the Danube to the banks of the Thames, and raised the indignation alike of Jew and of Christian.

This was the story: Father Thomas, an Italian priest, who exercised at Damascus the profession of physician, and who visited the houses of Catholics, Armenians, and Jews, for the purposes of vaccination, disappeared with his servant on the 1st of Adar. On the following day, a number of so-called Christians crowded to the Jewish quarter, and seizing upon an unhappy barber, they dragged him before the Pasha. The infuriated mob shouted that the Jews had murdered Father Thomas to employ his blood in their superstitious rites, and the Pasha, to calm the rioters, ordered five hundred blows to be administered to the wretched barber. This miserable creature, on being urged to confess, yielding to intolerable physical pain, accused some members of the families of Farhi and Arari, and several other Jews, of having offered him three hundred piastres to kill the padre. Under unbearable torture, he gasped out that as the Passover holidays were approaching, they required human blood with which to knead their cakes. The prisoner at the same time maintained that he had refused to lend an ear to these instigations, and that he had informed the priest of the danger he incurred. The Pasha ordered the arrest of the individuals inculpated, six of whom were seized; and the remainder saved themselves by timely flight. All the prisoners were submitted to the "question," and endured some of the most excruciating tortures that the devilish ingenuity of semi-barbarians could invent. They were flogged. They were soaked with their clothes for hours at a stretch in cold water. Their eyes were punctured. They were made to stand upright for three days without being permitted the slightest support, and when their wearied bodies fell down, they were aroused by the prick of the soldiers' bayonets. They were dragged by the ear until their blood gushed. Fire was set to their beards till their faces were singed, and candles were held under their noses so that the flames burnt their nostrils. Fire, water, and iron were used to extort admission of guilt from the unhappy Jews; and when all these means failed, moral torture was employed. The Pasha carried the children of one of the prisoners to a dungeon, and fed them—or rather starved them—on bread and water, and forbade the mother from visiting them, hoping to tear from the heart of the wretched father a confession which no amount of physical pain could extort.

In vain the poor Jews appealed to their sacred writings, which stringently prohibit the shedding of human blood. A courageous man, who boldly came forward and stated that the Christians themselves must have put to death the padre, perished under the bastinado. Some dwellings inhabited by Jews were demolished to seek the bodies of the missing friar and his servant, which, as may be expected, were not found. Upon this, fresh cruelties were heaped on the prisoners. It is not surprising that, under such combinations of horrors, several of the incriminated Jews should at last have allowed a frantic confession of guilt to escape their lips. Witches and wizards, it is well known, not so many centuries ago, and in England too, were wont, under the persuasive arguments of fire and steel, to admit the commission of utterly impossible deeds of darkness. So some of the mangled and bleeding Jews said that they had given a bottle containing some of the blood of the padre to Moses Abulafia, who in his turn, after receiving a thousand blows, and hardly knowing what he was uttering, stammered out that he had hidden the blood in a certain closet. Abulafia was carried on the backs of four men to the closet indicated by him, where naturally no traces of blood were discovered. On the other hand, what was of much more value to the Pasha was perceived, that is, a considerable sum of money, which was promptly appropriated to his own uses by that functionary. As to Abulafia, he saved his life by embracing the Turkish religion. A wise individual ascertained, through his knowledge of the stars, that the imprisoned Jews had murdered Father Thomas, and that some other Jews had killed the servant; upon which six other unfortunate Israelites were arrested and thrown into prison. Damascus became so unsafe for Jews, that an Israelite, who served the office of treasurer to the Pasha, was constrained to adopt the faith of Islam in self-preservation; and few Jews durst venture into the street.

While this tragedy was being enacted in Damascus, a no less serious occurrence happened in Rhodes. In that island a Greek boy, ten years of age, having disappeared, a rumour at once spread that the Jews had killed him. Strange logic, indeed! A Christian child was missing, *ergo* the Jews must have assassinated him. The Consuls of the European powers proceeded in a body to the residence of the Pasha, and demanded justice against the Jews. The British Consul, Mr Wilkinson, and his son, were among the bitterest denunciators of the hunted Jews. The Austrian Consul alone had the courage of defending the unhappy descendants of Abraham against the unfounded and infamous accusation. Two Greek women charged the Jews with this crime. To the shame of civilisation, and the utter disgrace of so-called Christianity, the Consuls subjected one of the Jews to the bastinado. They burned his flesh with red-hot irons, and dislocated his bones on the rack, until praying for a death that would not come, the unfortunate victim named at random several other Jews as his accomplices. These were even in their turn seized and put to the rack, until they also prayed to their God to release them speedily from their sufferings. Christians went round to the Jewish quarter in the dark, endeavouring secretly to introduce dead bodies of Christians into Jewish houses to incriminate the latter, and Jews were not permitted to leave their quarter.

A thrill of horror and of compassion moved the Jews of Western Europe on hearing these recitals, which were duly attested by trustworthy and impartial witnesses. Urgent prayers for assistance reached the ears of Sir Moses Montefiore; and the noble-minded philanthropist, before whom the cause of his brethren was never pleaded in vain, at once took up arms in their favour. A meeting was held, on the 21st April 1840, at the residence of Sir Moses Montefiore, Grosvenor Gate, Park Lane, in which were present not only the members of the London Committee of Deputies of the British Jews, but such other eminent men as Isaac L. Goldsmid, Isaac Cohen, David Salomons, A. A. Goldsmid, Drs Loëwe and Barnard Van Oven, and several of the most distinguished members of the Portuguese Community. Monsieur Crémieux, the Vice-President of the Consistoire Central of the French Jews and present President of the Alliance Israelite Universelle, also attended to represent the Jews of France. Translations of various communications from the East, addressed to Messrs Rothschild and Sir Moses Montefiore, and giving minute details of the sufferings of the unhappy Jews of Damascus and of Rhodes, were read, and produced a profound and painful sensation. A letter was also read from the Rev. Sol. Hirschel, the Chief Rabbi, solemnly repudiating such charges, and declaring them to be false and malicious; for so great is the horror evinced by the Jewish law at the shedding of blood, that the slightest admixture of blood, even that of animals, would pollute the common food of man; still more would human blood desecrate and render abominable a religious rite. A series of resolutions were adopted expressing the concern, disgust, and horror of the meeting at such unfounded and cruel accusations against their brethren in the East, and against the barbarous tortures inflicted upon them; entreating the governments of England, France, and Austria to take up the cause of the unhappy Jews; and appointing a deputation to wait on Lord Palmerston (who was at the time Her

Majesty's Secretary for Foreign Affairs), which comprised Sir Moses Montefiore, Baron de Rothschild, Sir I. L. Goldsmid, David Salomons, Mr A. A. Goldsmid, and Mr F. H. Goldsmid.

Lord Palmerston received the deputation at the Foreign Office with the greatest urbanity and kindness, expressing his abhorrence of the cruel persecution of which the Jews were the objects in the East, and his surprise that the calumny should have met with the slightest credence. He assured the deputation that the influence of the British Government would be exerted on behalf of the Jews, and that he would give instructions to Colonel Hodges at Alexandria, and to Lord Ponsonby at Constantinople, to direct them to use every effort to prevent a continuance of such inhuman and undeserved treatment.

The same deputation then waited on the Austrian Ambassador, who was absent, and on M. Guizot, the French Ambassador. M. Guizot gave fair words, which were not borne out by the deeds of his chief in Paris, M. Thiers, the minister of Louis Philippe. France, the country which boasts of being the leader of civilisation, acted on this occasion as the champion of ignorance, fanaticism, and savage superstition. Count Ratti Menton, the French Consul at Damascus, was one of the most active persecutors of the wretched Jews. He had lived in Spain for some years, and had imbibed a blind hatred against the Jews. Though the French Government sent M. de Melvoires to inquire into the conduct of M. Ratti Menton, the latter was fully exonerated, and M. de Melvoires was appointed French Consul at Beirout. In fact, as M. Crémieux said, "Nous avons la France contre nous." France had then ambitious dreams in the East, and supported the rebellious policy of Mehemet Ali against his Suzerain the Sultan of Turkey. Mehemet Ali had possessed himself of Syria, which was occupied by his troops. But England, Russia, Austria, and Prussia sided with Turkey, and a very complicated Eastern question was arising at this period, and threatening serious consequences.

The English Press at large almost unanimously reprobated the conduct of the accusers and persecutors of the Jews, and expressed their belief in the complete innocence of the calumniated Israelites. We may also honourably mention the *Malta Times*, which warmly espoused the cause of the tortured Jews, and strenuously maintained their innocence. The English nation, which as a rule is always ready to sympathise with the weak and oppressed, showed in an unmistakable manner their compassion for the Jews. The Lord Mayor convened a meeting at the Mansion House for the purpose of expressing the sympathy of the citizens of London with the Jews of Damascus, and their detestation of the atrocious calumnies which had been circulated against them. Mr Alderman Thompson presided until the arrival of the Lord Mayor, Sir Chapman Marshall. Many friends of justice, humanity, and toleration met together, albeit of different political parties; and such men as Mr J. A. Smith, M.P.; Sir Denham Norreys, M.P.; Mr James Morrison, M.P.; Mr W. Attwood, M.P.; Dr Bowring, Mr Martin Smith, M.P.; Mr S. Gurney, Lord Howden, Hon. and Rev. Baptist Noel, Sir C. Forbes, Thomas Campbell the poet, Mr David Wire, Mr John Masterman, Mr John Dillon, and the "great liberator," Daniel O'Connell, with one voice declared emphatically their utter disbelief of the odious calumnies spread against the Jews. A statement from the Rev. Mr Pieritz, a Jewish convert who had become a Christian clergyman, bore witness to the sufferings of the unfortunate Jews, and strongly confirmed the great aversion of his former co-religionists to the taste of the blood of animals. Several eloquent speeches were made, and were followed by a number of appropriate resolutions setting forth in forcible terms the commiseration felt by all true Christians for the poor persecuted Jews of Damascus and Rhodes; their abhorrence at the use of torture; their disbelief in the confessions thereby obtained; and their deep regret that in this enlightened age a persecution should have arisen against their Jewish brethren, originating in ignorance, and inflamed by bigotry. Finally, the gratification of the meeting was manifested on perceiving that many persons of distinguished rank, as well as the Government, had testified their willingness to uphold and support the cause of suffering humanity.

The sympathy of their fellow-citizens greatly encouraged the Jews of England in their exertions. A subscription to defray the expenses of a mission to the East was actively being raised. The Sephardi Congregation handsomely gave £500 from their fund of *cautivos*; other Synagogues offered according to their means. Contributions came in not only from the London Synagogues, but from several continental congregations; and from Hamburg to Leghorn funds were collected for the defence of the unhappy Jews of Damascus and Rhodes. Meetings of Jews took place for the same purpose, even in America and the West Indies. In New York, Philadelphia, St Thomas, and Jamaica, the Jews showed to the best of their power that they had not forgotten their persecuted and tortured brethren in the far East.

The Board of Deputies, as the political representative of the Jewish community in England, took the lead in action. At a public meeting held on June 15, 1840, in which there were present not only the Deputies, but the principal ecclesiastical authorities and many of the most influential members of the London Jewish Congregations, it was resolved to send a mission to Mehemet Ali, to intercede on behalf of the Jews of Damascus. The whole community unanimously pointed to one man. Who so zealous, so philanthropic, so earnest, so able and courteous, as Sir Moses Montefiore? To Sir Moses Montefiore, who was President of the Board of Deputies, was entrusted the important task of representing the British Jews, while M. Crémieux accompanied him as the envoy of the French Jews. The subscriptions raised were intended to defray the expenses of, and to remunerate, those who accompanied Sir Moses Montefiore in his errand of mercy. Sir Moses Montefiore, always ready to sacrifice his comfort and to imperil his valuable life in the service of his brethren, accepted the honourable, and what to any one else would have been the onerous, mission. M. Crémieux failed in obtaining the recommendations he had expected from the French Government, and it was then agreed that Sir Moses Montefiore should be the recognised head of the mission, and that M. Crémieux should act as his counsel under his direction, and in conjunction with Mr Wire. Mr H. de Castro was appointed President of the Board of Deputies in the absence of Sir Moses Montefiore, and a Committee of Correspondence was elected from the members of that body.

 Sir Moses Montefiore, accompanied by his estimable consort, Lady Montefiore, by Mr Wire and Dr Loëwe, left London on the 7th July 1840. In Paris, his party was increased by the additions of M. Crémieux and Dr Madden. Sir Moses Montefiore proceeded to Malta *viâ* Marseilles and Leghorn. He had the satisfaction of being able to advise from the very beginning of the journey, that the imprisoned Jews of Rhodes had been released after being honourably acquitted, and that they had commenced proceedings against their persecutors. At Leghorn, the accounts received from Syria by Sir Moses were very discouraging. That province was in open revolt against the rule of Mehemet Ali; Suleyman Pasha, one of the Viceroy's generals, had been attacked and taken prisoner, and Beirout was blockaded. The dangers of the expedition were pointed out to Sir Moses Montefiore. He declined to return without having achieved success, and he resolved to proceed forward at all risks, rather than desert his unhappy brethren. In pursuance with this noble resolution the Jewish mission proceeded to Malta. In the same packet in which they sailed, were the correspondents of the *Times* and the *Morning Chronicle*, who went to seek information on the question of the Jews of Damascus. Sir Moses Montefiore and his party arrived at Malta on the 27th July, when hearing that the insurrection in Syria was on the point of being quelled, they continued their voyage to Alexandria.

 On his arrival at Alexandria, Sir Moses Montefiore delivered his despatches to Colonel Hodges, the English Consul-General, who promised to procure him an interview with the Viceroy. At the same time all the foreign Consuls, with the exception of the French Consul, offered their support to Sir Moses Montefiore. Mehemet Ali received the members of the Jewish Mission very courteously, and said he would consider the petition which they presented to him. The petition asked for permission for Sir Moses and his party to proceed to Damascus to obtain evidence on behalf of the imprisoned Jews, with leave to see and interrogate the prisoners, and for absolute personal safety for the members of the Mission and for all persons giving evidence. A second and a third interview followed between the successor of the Pharaohs and the champion of the Jews. The Viceroy said he was too much occupied to decide on the question; but on being pressed he agreed to give orders for the better treatment of the prisoners. Sir Moses Montefiore placed himself in communication with Mr Werry, the British Consul at Damascus, who, in conjunction with Mr Merlato, the Austrian Consul, had endeavoured to alleviate the miseries of the Jews, and to defend them against the rabid Hebræophobia of M. Ratti Menton. Sir Moses had the satisfaction of receiving from Mr Werry a detailed account of the improved condition of the remaining incarcerated Israelites, three of them having died under torture. But the political situation in Egypt was becoming serious. England, Russia, Prussia, and Austria insisted on the recognition by the Viceroy of the Suzerainty of the Porte, and on his abandoning Syria. France encouraged the ambitious designs of Mehemet Ali. The four powers despatched an ultimatum to the Viceroy requiring an immediate decision. War seemed imminent, and Sir Moses Montefiore was preparing to depart from Alexandria. Mehemet Ali rejected the terms offered by the four powers; and these, like the Sybil, who destroyed each time one of her books asking the same price for the remainder, sent back another ultimatum less favourable to Mehemet Ali.

The French Government, while countenancing Mehemet Ali in his resistance to allied Europe, opposed strenuously the rendering simple justice to the Jews of Damascus. Monsieur Thiers declined to furnish Monsieur Crémieux with letters to the French Consul at Alexandria, and the conduct of Count Ratti Menton was sanctioned by his superiors in Paris. A strange decree of Providence was that which rendered many years afterwards M. Crémieux and M. Thiers —the former the advocate who was a suppliant on behalf of his oppressed brethren, and the latter the minister who refused to grant his prayer—colleagues in the same government of their conquered and humiliated country!

The position of Mehemet Ali was becoming complicated,

and he determined to get rid of one cause of embarrassment. Mr Briggs, an English merchant, who had taken much interest in the fate of the Damascus Jews, waited on Sir Moses Montefiore, and informed him that the Viceroy had expressed an inclination to release the prisoners, provided the whole matter were allowed to fall into oblivion. Now Sir Moses Montefiore, with great courage and patriotism, had demanded not merely the release of the Jews, but a new trial, to enable them to clear their character even from suspicion. He justly required the complete vindication and rehabilitation of his co-religionists. On considering the perturbed political state of the country, Sir Moses Montefiore agreed to waive his demands for a new trial and for compensation, provided Mehemet Ali discharged at once the prisoners and declared in his Firman his complete conviction of their innocence. The Viceroy was also to give his permission for those who had fled to return to their homes, and to express his desire that for the future the Jews should live unmolested in his dominions. At the suggestion of Mr Briggs, these conditions were embodied in a memorial to be presented to His Highness the Viceroy, to which were appended copies of Bulls from different Popes, acquitting the Jews of the charge of using blood in their ceremonies; a Firman of the Porte to the same effect; an account of the proceedings at Rhodes against the Jews, and of their acquittal by the Courts of Constantinople, together with some other documents. These documents were not presented to His Highness, for on their being privately submitted to an Effendi, one of his councillors, it was recommended to refrain from so doing, as it was not considered that Mehemet Ali would comply with the requests therein contained.

Then Sir Moses Montefiore resolved to apply for a simple discharge of the prisoners. A petition for that purpose was drawn up, signed by himself, by M. Crémieux, and by ten foreign consuls. Mehemet Ali offered the discharge of the prisoners as an act of grace, which Sir Moses Montefiore declined to accept. Eventually, the discharge was obtained as an act of justice. The demands of Sir Moses Montefiore were in point of fact substantially if not formally conceded. The imprisoned Jews were liberated. The fugitive Jews were permitted to return to their homes unmolested. An order of general protection to the Jews was given. A Firman permitting the members of the Jewish Mission to proceed to Damascus was granted. And the Viceroy personally assured Sir Moses Montefiore of his complete disbelief of the calumnies directed against the Jews. The head of the mission was strongly dissuaded from going to Damascus, owing to the fanaticism of the nominal Christians; and Mehemet Ali himself pointing out the dangers of the journey, the expedition had to be abandoned. An authenticated copy of the order of release was forwarded to Damascus, and the British Consul was requested to see that the mandate was promptly carried out.

The Mussulman inhabitants of Damascus manifested their extreme satisfaction at the discharge of the prisoners; and on the return of the latter to their distressed families, the greater part of the Mohammedan merchants hastened to pay to them visits of condolence, and to express cordially the pleasure felt at their liberation. Count Ratti Menton, when he heard of the order, stormed and raved, and endeavoured to oppose its execution; and to our regret we must record that the Christian population slunk silently and moodily about the streets of Damascus as if a calamity had befallen them. These unhappy Christians had forgotten, if they had ever known, the dearest and most sacred precepts of their own religion.

The Jewish Mission sent a letter of thanks to the Viceroy, drawn up in the Turkish language by Dr Loëwe, and it was received by His Highness before their departure. Mehemet Ali appeared much gratified on hearing the joy experienced by his Mussulman subjects at the happy termination of the sufferings of their Jewish fellow-subjects; and Sir Moses Montefiore and he parted under mutually favourable impressions.

Sir Moses Montefiore, not satisfied with obtaining such noble results, and impelled by an unconquerable love for his race, and by indefatigable philanthropy, decided on extending his journey to Constantinople. In the capital of the Turkish Empire, Sir Moses Montefiore was courteously received by Reschid Pasha, the Grand Vizier, and by the

Sultan himself, and he succeeded in obtaining the celebrated Hatti Homayoun or Firman, in which the Chief of the Faithful declared his perfect conviction of the innocence of the Jews against the accusations of which they had been the victims; and he granted them the same protection, rights, and privileges as were accorded to other races in his dominions.

These are the glorious achievements of that memorable mission; when by a wonderful combination of qualities on the part of Sir Moses Montefiore, and by the zeal and abilities of the gentlemen who accompanied him, nine persons were saved from a lingering and cruel death. Moreover the position of the Jews in the East was materially raised; despotic Pashas were taught that enlightened humanity knows no distinction of clime or of creed; and the Sultan by his own sign manual decreed the civil rights of the Jews, and established their equality before the law to other classes of his subjects.

CHAPTER XLIX.

SOME MORE JEWISH AUTHORS

THE Jews of a former generation may not have reached to the very foremost rank in literature; but many of them assuredly performed meritorious work and attained honourable places among Jewish and among English *litterateurs*. We do not profess to mention the name of every British Israelite who entered into the thorny path of literature; our object being to offer a few remarks on those whose productions have acquired most fame, or who appear to deserve especial commendation.

Many of our readers will probably recollect the modest figure of the Rev. D. A. de Sola, the senior minister of the Spanish and Portuguese Congregation. Mr D. de Sola, from his unassuming presence and manners, was not generally known to possess the learning and abilities which he undoubtedly displayed in his numerous works. He was descended from an ancient family which emigrated from Spain in 1492 and settled in Holland—a family which seems to have given birth to many scholars of eminence. Isaac de Sola distinguished himself as a preacher in London, between 1690 and 1700, and his remains were interred in the Sephardi cemetery in 1735, while Dr Benjamin de Sola, Court Physician to William V., Prince of Orange, and Stadthouder of Holland, was a practitioner of great repute at the Hague. David Aaron de Sola was born on the 26th December 1796, at Amsterdam, and he was the son of highly educated parents. His uncle, the said Dr Benjamin de Sola, was desirous of training young David to the medical profession, but the future minister preferred to devote himself exclusively to his favourite theology and Hebrew literature. He was admitted a student in the Medrash at the early age of eleven, and continued his attendance there for nine years; during which time he was promoted through all the five degrees up to the highest. He became well versed in the superior branches of Jewish theology, and also gained a good knowledge of secular literature. At the same time he learnt several modern languages, and wrote fluently in English, German, and Dutch, in addition to Hebrew.

When the Sephardi Congregation of London desired the services of a second *Hazan* or minister—the Rev. Isaac Almosnino being then the first—D. A. de Sola came to London and became a candidate for the vacant post. He was duly elected, and though the position was not very brilliant, the young minister entered eagerly and zealously in his new career, hoping to be able to raise his office by his unwearied exertions. Having become united in marriage to the eldest daughter of Haham Meldola, he devoted himself to a more profound study of the English language. The Rev. D. A. de Sola's contributions to Jewish literature are too numerous to be mentioned here, and we can only advert to a few of the most important. His first published work was entitled "The Blessings," with an introductory essay on Thanksgiving. The subject and plan of the book originated with Sir Moses Montefiore, to whom Mr de Sola acknowledged himself deeply indebted for the generous support he bestowed on his work. Mr de Sola, as we have already stated, began, in March 1831, to preach in the Portuguese Synagogue, and his sermons were in all probability the first ever delivered in the English tongue in those precincts. His discourses were received with much approbation, and some of them were published. He translated the whole of the Portuguese Jewish Prayers into English; and he subsequently rendered the same service to the Germans as regards their Festival Prayers. These versions are more lucid and exact than those of David Levi. He began a new edition of the Sacred Scriptures in conjunction with Dr Raphall, with an English translation and critical notes, and he issued the first volume. The work remained incomplete, owing to the removal of Dr Raphall to the pastoral charge of the Birmingham Congregation.

The Rev. D. A. de Sola was an indefatigable worker, and his pen was seldom idle. In 1845 he brought out the "Mishna" in conjunction with Dr Raphall, which comprised some of the treatises of that voluminous work, touching on subjects of daily occurrence. He then produced his well-known "Ancient Melodies of the Liturgy of the Spanish and Portuguese Jews," in conjunction with Emanuel Aguilar. Mr de Sola, in addition to a number of miscellaneous writings and contributions to the Jewish press of England, Holland, and Germany, revised the cheap "Jewish Library," a work issued at the expense of a generous and high-minded lady, Mrs Charlotte Montefiore. This publication, which consisted of stories of Jewish life, was intended for the benefit of the humbler classes, and each tale was retailed separately at a penny. Grace Aguilar, who was a favourite pupil in Hebrew of Mr de Sola, and who was greatly guided by his opinion, wrote one of the tales entitled the "Perez Family." He also was called upon to revise various other works; and he took part in the several movements for rendering known the rich Jewish literature. In 1830 his co-operation was given to the "Society for the Cultivation of the Hebrew Language and Literature," his fellow-labourers in that vast field being Michael Josephs, Joshua Van Oven, Arthur Lumley Davids, Morris Jacob Raphall, and Selig Newman. In 1842 the Rev. D. A. de Sola was instrumental in organising an "Association for the Promotion of Jewish Literature," when he was elected a member of the Provisional Committee with Mr Lindenthal, Dr Benisch, &c. Unfortunately both these societies were short-lived. Mr de Sola left behind him a mass of correspondence of a literary character with most of the highest Jewish scholars of his day, such as Jost, Delitsch, Fürst, Zunz, Rappaport, &c., in Germany; Belinfante, Isaacson, Bassan, &c., in Holland; Carmoly, Cohen, &c., in France; Loëwe, Zedner, Raphall, Dukes, Benisch, &c., in England.

Mr de Sola closed a blameless and busy career on the 29th October 1860 (13th Hesvan 5621), after much suffering. The length of the funeral procession testified to the esteem in which he had been held by his congregation.

No Jewish female author has attained the general and well-deserved popularity achieved by Grace Aguilar. Her numerous literary productions have been read and appreciated in England, America, Germany, and France. Her "Women of Israel" is a work stamped with the most ardent zeal and fervent piety, in every line of which breathe the national sentiment and the true patriotism which are the characteristics of her writings. It is a book teeming with powerful lessons to her own sex, and eloquent exhortations to the opposite sex. She desired to elevate the character of the women of Israel. She has shown that when all the nations of the East degraded females, the Jewish code gave them an equality in civil and religious institutions suitable to women's mind and to their special mission. She has also demonstrated that many women in Israel have been the exponents of the noblest sentiments and the most sublime actions. Her "Spirit of Judaism" and "Jewish Faith" are likewise works of considerable merit, and full of that pious fervour and filial affections which carry the reader along with her, and impress him with profound sympathy for the writer. Her "Jewish Faith" displays signs of no mean acquaintance with Jewish and Christian philosophers and divines, and its logical reasoning is far from betraying the sex of the author. With all her abilities, which were of no ordinary range, she was humble and unassuming, tender and genial to all, and greatly attached to her parents. The ambition of Grace Aguilar was neither for wealth, reputation, nor distinction. The pure consciousness of raising the literary and religious character of the Jewish race, and of her own sex in particular, was at the same time her guiding motive and her reward.

Grace Aguilar was the eldest child and only daughter of Emanuel Aguilar, the descendant of an old Spanish family, and she first saw the light at Hackney, in June 1816. By a not uncommon dispensation of Providence, the strength of her mind was counterbalanced by the weakness of her bodily frame. The shell that confined an over-active intellect was indeed of a frail nature. Grace Aguilar was struggling from childhood upwards through her whole existence with a weak constitution. She was nevertheless very quick of apprehension and learnt easily all she was taught. Her parents seem to have been her principal instructors. In childhood her mother instilled rudimentary knowledge in her bright young mind; and at the age of fourteen her father began a regular course of lessons. The family, owing to Mr Aguilar's health, went to reside in Devonshire: and at Tavistock, amid the beauty of the surrounding scenery, she first gave vent to her thoughts in verse. She was exceedingly fond of music, and became proficient on the piano. From the age of seven she began to keep a journal, and this practice no doubt fostered a spirit of self-communion. She studied the principles of religion, and she carried its precepts in everyday life, relieving sufferings as far as her limited means allowed, and without inquiring into the theological opinions of the afflicted. She herself endured much physical pain; and in 1835 she had an illness which completely prostrated the small stock of strength at her command. In the midst of much mental distress, caused by the sickness and death of her father and by various domestic troubles, Grace Aguilar produced the "Spirit of Judaism" and several other works.

Mr Moses Mocatta, a gentleman who had himself translated from the Hebrew the work entitled "Faith Strengthened," and who was a zealous worker in the cause of Judaism, very liberally came forward, and materially assisted Miss Aguilar in the publication of the "Jewish Faith." She worked hard, and, her health breaking down completely, she was ordered rest and change. In June 1847 she visited Frankfort, where her brother was pursuing his musical studies. At first she appeared to rally, but she became soon again exhausted. She tried the mineral waters of Schwalbach, without success; and, after two months of great suffering, Grace Aguilar passed away in September 1847. Her remains were consigned by the hands of tender friends to that portion of the cemetery of Frankfort which is set apart for Jews. She had loved truly her religion, into the depth of which she entered so fully that her spirit could not rest till she publicly taught it to her sisters and brethren. In addition to her religious works, Grace Aguilar was the successful author of several very pleasing novels which had an extensive circulation, and still maintain their reputation. The principal of these are, "The Days of Bruce," a tale of Scottish history, and some domestic stories, entitled "Home Influence," "The Mother's Recompense," and "Home Scenes and Heart Studies."

Another energetic labourer in the cause of Jewish literature was the late Mr E. H. Lindo. This gentleman, after spending a considerable portion of his existence in commercial pursuits, devoted many years to literary occupations. Mr Lindo, compiled the well-known almanac bearing his name, the usefulness of which is far more extended than would be imagined from the unpretending nature of its title, for it contains a chronological table of the most interesting events in Jewish history. Then in 1842, Mr Lindo published a translation of the "Conciliator" of Menasseh ben Israel, a work which endeavours to harmonise the apparent contradictions in the Bible. The most important production by this gentleman is the "History of the Jews of Spain and Portugal," which was issued from the press in 1848. The author took vast pains to acquire original and authentic information on this interesting subject; he visited the Iberian peninsula, he inspected personally the scenes of the events which he described, and examined many valuable MSS. This work displays much painstaking research and considerable erudition, and was favourably reviewed by the most influential journals of the day. Mr Lindo, in addition, prepared a catalogue of the books contained in the library of the Sephardi Medrash (Religious College), and he completed several translations of Hebrew and Spanish works, in both of which languages he was well versed. Mr Lindo died in 1865, at an advanced age.

Among other deceased Jewish writers who deserve honourable mention, we may name Moses Samuel, of Liverpool, the eminent Hebrew scholar and author of several productions. Moses Samuel was a self-taught man, and he possessed considerable abilities. He was born in London in 1795, and evinced at an early age a singular taste for languages and mathematics. After taking up his residence in Liverpool, he published an address to the missionaries of Great Britain, which was a forcible protest against the attempts of conversion societies to lead the Jews away from their ancient faith. He translated the Book of Jasher, and he brought forth a work on the position of the Jews in Great Britain, while his letters to Lord Brougham and Mr Hume, M.P., were highly commended. He then became one of the joint-editors of a monthly magazine, named "The Cup of Salvation." He was a zealous worker in all that concerned the welfare of his co-religionists, and ever ready to wield his pen, not only on their behalf, but on behalf of the oppressed of all denominations. A rebuke he administered to a member of the bar, and entitled "The Jew and the Barrister," was favourably noticed in several magazines. Moses Samuel, whilst attending a meeting on the emancipation of the Jews, in 1840, was attacked with paralysis, from which he never entirely recovered, but he lived in retirement until 1860. We must also name A. Abrahams, an uncle of Serjeant Simon, M.P., and who translated the "Matinées du Samedi;" and Morris Jacob Raphall, whose versatility, learning, and literary powers were remarkable. We purposely abstain from adverting to the far greater number of literary English Jews and Jewesses who are flourishing at present in our midst; and whom we do not specify by name for reasons that will easily suggest themselves to our readers. Among the Jews of a former generation who distinguished themselves in sciences and in arts, we must give a place to Benjamin Gompertz, the eminent mathematician; Jacob Samuda, the talented engineer, who perished at an early age, the victim of an accident; and Daniel, a miniature painter who in his day achieved a considerable reputation.

No chapter devoted to modern Jewish authors would be complete without including the name, familiar to the Anglo-Jewish community, of the late Michael Henry. The history of Michael Henry offers few stirring events, but it affords an example of philanthropy and self-abnegation such as is seldom witnessed in these days of worldly-mindedness and self-seeking. He was born in Kennington in February 1830, his father being a merchant, and his mother the Miss Emma Lyon of whom we have already spoken in this work. Michael Henry was educated in the City of London School, from which he went to Paris, where he was engaged for a short time in a counting-house. Thence he returned to London, and entered the office of the late James Robertson, patent agent and editor of the *Mechanics' Magazine*. On the death of Mr Robertson, Michael Henry established himself in the same business, which he carried on from 1857 until his death. In course of time he began to assist Dr Benisch in his labours as editor of the *Jewish Chronicle;* and when that journal changed hands in 1868, the editorship, vacated by Dr Benisch, was entrusted to him. Michael Henry was endowed with a strong poetic feeling, which found its vent in fervid verses. At the age of six he composed some lines on a storm; at the age of nine he wrote prayers for his own use; and when he reached thirteeen he produced a short humorous tale. In youth he contributed occasionally to magazines; subsequently he wrote regularly in the *Mining Journal;* and he is best known in connection with the *Jewish Chronicle*. His articles were easy and full of imagination; his style was warm and impassioned, and at times rose to eloquence. His words carried with them conviction, for they were the outpour of an honest, zealous nature, and of one who was an earnest believer in Judaism. In his profession he stood deservedly high for his profound knowledge of Patent Law, and for the perfect conscientiousness with which he carried on his avocations. To his community Michael Henry was a great loss. All the leisure hours left to him by his occupations were employed in advancing the interests of his favourite charitable and educational institutions. Instruction for the young and help for the needy divided his attention, and he was as well known for his love of boys as for his kindness of heart. He was the founder of the General Benevolent Association; the Jewish Stepney Schools owed little less than their existence to his indefatigable labours; and various other Jewish institutions were indebted to him for the support of his forcible pen and eloquent voice. He was modest and unassuming in his deportment; and his geniality and courteousness, added to his other good qualities, won for him a popularity among his race seldom exceeded. When Michael Henry perished in June of the present year, in the plenitude of his mental and physical powers, the victim of a lamentable accident, the respect in which he was held in his community was amply testified, by the presence at the Willesden cemetery of one of the largest assemblages of mourners that for years had followed the remains of a Jew to their last resting-place. As a proof of the esteem and friendship felt for him by his co-religionists, we may mention that they hastened to raise a fund to perpetuate his memory in the manner which would have been most agreeable to his feelings.

CHAPTER L.

THE REFORM MOVEMENT.

Few religious communities have displayed the complete union for which the Jews have been ever remarkable since the days of their last dispersion from Jerusalem. Properly speaking, with the exception of the small number of individuals known as Samaritans and as Karaites, there are no sects in Judaism. The principles of Judaism appear so simple and incontestable, its dogmas so plain and easily understood, that if the Jews numbered a hundred millions, they could never split into a thousand sects like the professors of other creeds. The only differences of opinion existing among Jews are purely confined to matters of practice, and do not affect belief in the simple truths of the Mosaic dispensation. We say it in all respect, there is probably less discrepancy between the Jews forming what are called Orthodox Congregations, and those Jews who are members of the Reformed Congregation of London, than is evident within the bosom of a single denomination of Christians. We venture to assert that a wider and deeper gulf yawns between the Ritualist and the Low Churchman, than separates any two congregations of Jews within the four seas in all that regards essentials. The slight variations in the liturgies of the so-called Portuguese and German Jews, and in the mode of pronunciation of Hebrew, are perhaps inevitable consequences of their residence among different nations, and their adoption of different languages, but in no degree do they constitute a difference in dogma, doctrine, or practice.

The establishment of the West London Congregation of British Jews was doubtless a painful event, which caused much heart-burning at the time of its occurrence, and which is the more to be lamented by Jews, as it might easily have been avoided by the prevalence of wiser and more conciliating counsels, and by a truer perception of the spirit of real religion. It is not within our province to decide on which side to award the greater blame for that which cannot be characterised otherwise than as a secession. We shall treat the question from a purely historical point of view. We shall, in so far as we are able, state the truth, the whole truth, and nothing but the truth. We shall deliver a plain unvarnished tale, adding nought in malice, and extenuating nothing. We shall abstain from offering any comment or remark, even at the risk of rendering our narrative tame and colourless, as we prefer that our readers should form their own conclusions after carefully weighing the facts that we shall bring before their notice.

We have on several occasions adverted to the slovenly and indecorous manner in which Jewish worship was too often celebrated in English Synagogues at a former period. This evil led to serious reflections on the part of those who frequented the Synagogue to commune with their Maker, and not to mumble through, in an indistinct and formal manner, certain prayers which they scarcely understood. All parties indeed desired an improvement in the mode of conducting the services, but all parties did not agree as to what shape the improvement should assume. So far back as the year 5584 (1824), a committee of the vestry of the Great Synagogue, under the presidency of Mr Isaac L. Goldsmid, appointed to propose a plan for the training of some young men for the Jewish ministry, stated in their report that "they are convinced that the small attendance in the Synagogue is, in some measure, to be ascribed to the present mode of reading the service; that it has led, and, if unchanged, will lead, to alterations which they most sincerely deprecate, and which may be fatal to the dearest interests of the Jewish nation." This committee, which consisted of seven gentlemen, all well known in the community for their zeal for and devotion to Judaism, clearly foresaw a rock ahead which they pointed out to the ruling powers of their congregation. The ministers had a happy knack of reading prayers in a mode calculated to disturb and not to arouse devotion. They preferred absurd or exaggerated displays of vocalisation to a solemn rendering of the Jewish ritual. The committee limited themselves, however, according to the restricted nature of their mandate, to recommend the education of some youths for the office of readers, the determination of some fixed and regular mode of reading prayers, and the avoidance of all singing not connected with sacred music. These recommendations were acted upon; but they seemed to have had very little influence on the evils in question.

In the Sephardi Community, the dissatisfaction felt by many members assumed a tangible shape in 1836. On the 4th December of that year, a memorial signed by several Yehidim (members) was laid before the body of elders at one of their meetings. The memorialists stated in that document that they had observed, with regret, the existence of a considerable confusion during a great part of the service; that the irregular singing of the schoolboys and others tended to destroy all harmony, and to impair the solemn effect of the beautiful Jewish hymns; while a constant repetition of some of the prayers seemed to them the cause of a relaxation of the attention and seriousness vitally requisite to the maintenance of a spirit of reverence and fervour. Without presuming to offer any specific plan, the memorialists ventured to make a few suggestions. The singing and recitation of prayers should be confined to the reader, and to a certain number of trained boys; and the introduction of an organ or other instrument, they thought, would insure harmony, order, and solemnity during the whole service. In view of the constant allusions to instrumental music in the psalms, it was not conceived that there could be anything inherent in the Jewish faith to prevent its adoption. They respectfully but earnestly solicited an inquiry to be set on foot. They recommended an omission of the repetition of the *Amidah* and *Musaph*, and especially of *Kadisch* (prayers recited during the service). They entertained an opinion that there was no sanction for the observance of the second days of the Festivals, or of the eighth day of Passover, or of the ninth of Tabernacles. They were convinced that the needless multiplying of holydays was calculated to render the observance of all less strictly attended to; and they ventured to submit the propriety of instituting an inquiry, in order to ascertain whether some steps could not be adopted for limiting the observance of holydays to the days specified in the Perasah (portion of the law) read on these occasions.

This memorial had been signed by members of ancient families, hitherto distinguished for their charity, their liberality, and their profound love and reverence for their faith. On the other hand, at a subsequent meeting of the Elders, held on the 13th December 1836, a counter memorial signed by forty-five *Yehidim* was presented in a sense totally opposed to the former petition. These members expressed an equal desire to see great order, solemnity, and harmony established in the religious services, but conscientiously and firmly differed from the other requisitionists, as to alterations which would set aside or change those observances which for ages have been held sacred, and they firmly believed that if the principle of alteration in Jewish religious institutions was once admitted, it would split the Jewish nation into innumerable sects. This view was supported by a letter to which 109 signatures were appended of persons who said that they were contributing members of the congregation, and of the class depending on their daily labour for the maintenance of themselves and families. They felt at times some hardships and privations from the many observances and ordinances which surrounded them, but which were cheerfully borne; and they declared that, holding in the same veneration as their forefathers the precepts and institutions of their holy faith, they prayed that no measures might be sanctioned or adopted to change them. After much discussion, a resolution, very moderate in tone, was accepted by the Elders, expressing their readiness at all times to receive with attention and to deliberate with calmness on any representations made to them by members of the congregation; that the Elders gave due credit to the first memorialists for purity of intention; that the means of promoting greater harmony and solemnity during prayers, and of infusing more order and decorum in the services, were objects of their best consideration, but that the other suggestions were of a description which they deemed inexpedient to entertain.

It appears evident that the majority of the members of the

Sephardi community were averse to the innovations desired by a portion of the *Yehidim*. Notwithstanding the decision arrived at by the Elders, one of the gentlemen concerned in drawing up the memorial in question circulated a paper, in which he urged the appointment of a committee to ascertain from the ecclesiastical authorities how far those suggestions could be acted upon consistently with the tenets of the Jewish religion. He then used arguments in defence of the proposals for the introduction of instrumental music in Synagogue, and for the limitation of the holydays to the days specified in Scripture. On touching minor points, he mentioned the wish of some members for fixing the beginning of the prayers at a late hour on Sabbaths and festivals, to enable those who dwelt at a distance to attend Synagogue at a proper time. The question was not re-opened by the Elders during that session.

In 1837 attempts were made to introduce greater decorum and order in the Synagogue, and by the assistance of the Rev. I. Almosnino, the senior minister, a choir was instructed. On the 9th December 1837 a joint committee was appointed, together with the Wardens, to extend the measures already taken, and to devise further means of imparting greater order and solemnity to public worship.

Notwithstanding these slight improvements, the existing feelings between the large conservative party and the less numerous party of intending reformers did not assume a friendly appearance. Some members of the conservative party were disposed to grant the concessions sought in the minor points, which probably appeared to them fair and reasonable. But they were afraid that this was but a prelude to further and more sweeping reforms, and they somewhat reluctantly refused to yield an inch for fear that the proverbial ell might be taken. In 1838 stormy discussions took place among the members at their meetings. An unfortunate spirit of contention obtained in the community. A proposal was made in the month of Heshvan in the same year for the appointment of a committee, in which the Readers were to be included, "to inquire into the propriety of altering or curtailing the prayers, and to supply more regular religious instruction." Those who were present on that occasion assure us that the discussion assumed a violent character. Of the formation and subsequent dissolution of the Society of the "Preservers of Sacred Institutions" we have already spoken. Its operations served only to fan the spirit of dissension unhappily reigning in the community. The *odium theologicum* temporarily seized members of the same race, of the same religion, of the same family.

Meanwhile another important grievance was alleged by those gentlemen who were dissatisfied with the existing order of things. The Jews were leaving the districts in which they formerly resided close to their Synagogues, and many of them dwelt in Bloomsbury and other quarters which were then considered fashionable. The German Jews had two or three Synagogues beyond the boundaries of the city. The Portuguese Jews could only pray congregationally within the precincts of their ancient building in Bevis Marks. Some of the more affluent members of the latter community were unable to walk to Bevis Marks, and were equally unwilling to infringe the Sabbath or Festivals by driving to Synagogue. Their desire to possess a House of Worship within a walking distance of their abodes, however reasonable it may appear to us, was considered an unattainable ambition in those days. The Ascama of the Kaal No. 1 (1st Law of the Congregation) forbade, under the severest penalties, the assemblage of ten or more men for the purposes of reciting prayers within a certain radius of the Synagogue. We have seen that this regulation had caused much unpleasantness and ill-feeling on a former occasion, and those who had suffered from its stringency then, were not disposed to treat others with greater leniency than they had themselves experienced.

The difficulty of reaching a Place of Worship, and the regret on reaching it of finding public service conducted in a manner not consonant with their wishes, induced several *Yehidim* to contemplate seriously the practicability of celebrating service in their own neighbourhood, and in their own manner. We have reason to believe that this step was decided upon very reluctantly by those who undertook it, and that they fully expected that it would only be of a purely temporary nature. It must doubtless have been very painful to men who had hitherto strictly followed the precepts of Moses, to disobey the constituted authorities of their Synagogue, many of whom were their personal and attached friends, and still more painful to appear to secede from the traditions of Orthodox Judaism.

On the 15th April 1840, a meeting of twenty-four gentlemen took place, exactly three-fourths of whom were Sephardim and the remainder Ashkenazim, in which the following declaration was signed by the individuals present, who constituted themselves into a separate congregation :

"We, the undersigned, regarding public worship as highly conducive to the interests of religion, consider it a matter of deep regret that it is not more frequently attended by members of our religious persuasion. We are perfectly sure that this circumstance is not owing to any want of general conviction of the fundamental truths of our religion, but we ascribe it to the distance of the existing Synagogues from the place of our residence, to the length and imperfections of the order of service, to the inconvenient hours at which it is appointed, and to the absence of religious instruction in our Synagogue. To these evils we think that a remedy may be applied by the establishment of a Synagogue at the western part of the metropolis, where a revised service may be performed at hours more suited to our habits, and in a manner more calculated to inspire feelings of devotion, where religious instruction may be afforded by competent persons, and where to effect these purposes, Jews generally may form a United Congregation under the denomination of British Jews."

It will be remarked that not a word is here said respecting instrumental music in Synagogues or the abolition of the second days of Festivals ; the two points most objectionable to those who call themselves strict Jews.

Resolutions in conformity with the above declarations were adopted at that meeting, when it was decided that the new Place of Worship should be named the West London Synagogue of British Jews.

CHAPTER LI.

THE WEST LONDON CONGREGATION OF BRITISH JEWS.

THE gentlemen, forming part of the meeting mentioned in our preceding chapter, proceeded to organise themselves as an independent community. They secured the services of an able and eloquent minister in the person of the Rev. D. W. Marks, to whom was entrusted the preparation of a revised book of prayers; and they in due course obtained suitable premises which they converted into a Place of Worship. The conservative members of the oldest congregation in London felt deeply this more than threatened secession; and the Wardens of the Sephardi Synagogue in their address to the Elders, delivered on the 16th of May 1841, thus expressed themselves:—" Several valued and influential members of our congregation have associated themselves with members of other communities in this city, for the purpose of establishing a Synagogue westward. This is already an infraction of the fundamental law of the congregation, which has been our bond of union since our admission into this country, now nearly two centuries since; still it admitted of excuse and palliation in the acknowledged inconvenience experienced by those respected friends and their families from the distance to our Synagogue and the want of accommodation near them. But it is to be apprehended that their contemplated establishment is to be on principles opposed to the received religious institutions and ordinances of our nation, that it is not to be subject to ecclesiastical discipline in religious matters, and that its promoters are engaged in alterations and abridgments of our established ritual to form a new order of prayers and service unsanctioned by any competent or regularly-constituted authority. Then their proceedings thus assume a character of so serious a nature as to call for the united interposition of the Jewish nation." The document closed with the expression of "an anxious and earnest hope" that some course might be devised, in conjunction with the ecclesiastical authorities, likely to conciliate discordant feelings and prevailing opinions, and that "by a temperate and well-digested plan of improvement, and above all, by a cordial and sincere approximation of all parties in so good a cause, the peace and union of the congregation may yet be restored and permanently established." Unhappily these fond hopes were not realised. It rests not with us to apportion the blame nor to decide which side was most in fault. What is obvious is, that whatever opinion may be entertained as to the nature of the demands made by the authors of the movement, some of these demands could scarcely be conceded without proper ecclesiastical sanction.

The following communication was addressed by some members of the Portuguese Congregation to the Elders, under date of 7th Elul 5601—24th August 1841 :—

"GENTLEMEN,—Having so often expressed our sentiments, both to your respected body and to the meetings of the *Yehidim*, on the important subject of the improvements, which in our opinion were so much required in our form of public worship as well as on some other points, and having on so many occasions ascertained your total disinclination to attend to our suggestions, or even to consider our views, we cannot entertain the idea that our present communication will excite any surprise in your minds. In fact, we intimated at the meeting of *Yehidim* in 5599 (1839), on the proposition being made for the abrogation of Law No. 1 of the *Yehidim*, that our object was to establish a new Synagogue on the principles we had so long advocated, and that we adopted this as the best, if not the only, course for satisfying our own conscientious scruples, and for avoiding the repetition of discussions tending to excite and foster ill-feelings. We now proceed before opening the intended Place of Worship to lay a statement of the principles on which it is to be conducted. To secure decorum it is essential that the congregation should assemble before the commencement of prayers and remain until their conclusion. To facilitate this, more convenient hours are appointed for prayers; these being half-past nine in summer and ten in winter. To enable the attention of the public to be concentrated, the service is on no occasion to exceed two hours and a half. It has been found necessary to abridge slightly the prayers; the daily and Sabbath prayers have already been carefully revised, and considerable progress has been made with the festival prayers. To familiarise the rising generation with a knowledge of the great principles of our holy faith, religious discourses in the English language will form part of the morning service on Sabbaths and holydays. That offerings should interfere as little as possible with the devotional character of the place, and that they should not by occasioning interruptions to the reading of the law mar its effects, we have decided to discontinue calling up to the law. On the three great festivals, voluntary offerings will be made on the return of the law to the Ark, to be accompanied by personal compliments and limited to two objects: the relief of the poor and the support of the establishment. It is not intended by this body to recognise as sacred, days which are not ordained as such in Scripture; and consequently the service appointed for Holy Convocations is to be read only on the days thus designated. Gentlemen of other congregations have associated themselves with us, but we have resolved to read Hebrew after the manner of the Portuguese, believing it to be more correct: and to abolish the useless distinction now existing between those termed Portuguese and German Jews, we have given the intended Place of Worship the designation of West London Synagogue of British Jews. These views have been carried into effect not with any desire to separate, and through a sincere conviction that substantial improvements in the public worship are essential to the weal of our sacred religion, and that they will be the means of handing down to our children and to our children's children our holy faith in all its purity and integrity. Indeed, we are firmly convinced that their tendency will be to arrest and prevent secession from Judaism, an overwhelming evil which has at various times so widely spread among many of the most respectable families of our community. Most fervently do we cherish the hope that the effect of these improvements will be to inspire a deeper interest in, and a stronger feeling towards, our holy religion, and that their influence on the minds of the youth of either sex will be calculated to restrain them from traversing in their faith, or contemplating for a moment the fearful step of forsaking their religion, so that henceforth no Israelite born may cease to exclaim: 'Hear, O Israel, the Lord is our God, the Lord is one!' We anticipate encountering considerable difference, and even a strong prejudice against our proceedings, but we venture to hope that on further consideration, our motives and intentions will be duly appreciated, and that those kindly feelings which ought to exist between every community of Jews, will be maintained between the small body, whose views we had endeavoured to explain, and the other congregations. We desire to continue to make through the Elders a contribution towards the relief of the poor, and to devote some of our time and attention to the superintendence of the excellent institutions connected with the parent Synagogue. Influenced as we are by a sense of duty to offer our assistance in these works of charity towards our poorer brethren, we should derive no small gratification, if in thus co-operating with you to satisfy the claims of humanity, we should find that we are thereby establishing a bond and symbol of connection with the old Congregation; and assuring you that its welfare will never be a subject of indifference with us, we shall but express the words which we utter so frequently in our daily orisons: 'May He who maketh peace in His high heavens, in His mercy grant place unto us all, and all Israel.'"

The innovations adverted to in the above document could not receive the assent of the old orthodox community of Bevis Marks, and the friendly and truly Jewish spirit breathing through that letter was not so fully responded to as might have been expected, owing to alarm at some of the unfortunate changes mentioned. It was considered desirable at that meeting of the Elders to express strongly its views on the question; and the following lengthy resolution was adopted. After stating the necessity of making a public avowal of the course it was intended to pursue, the resolution said:—

"This meeting at once declares that in the event of the gentlemen subscribing that letter, or any other member of our congregation combining to erect a Synagogue westward, and to carry into effect therein the principles they advocate in the said letter, either by admitting as their ritual the book of prayers forwarded to this Room (which has already been proscribed by authority) or introducing or allowing the introduction of changes in our established forms, customs, and usages, save and except under ecclesiastical authority, such acts will be considered as a violation of the Askama of Kaal (law of congregation), and render such and every member of our Congregation so acting, virtually excluded from Yahid, and liable to all the penalties of that Askama. Painful indeed will be such proceedings on the part of this Room, for it cannot lose sight of the fact that the members who have addressed them have always been zealous supporters of our ancient congregation and its valued institutions, and that their rank and station in the community entitles them to every consideration; a severance, therefore, from such valued and respected friends, numbering amongst them some who may trace their descent from the original founders of our establishment, must be considered a deep sacrifice of personal feeling to a sense of religious duty. This meeting, therefore, most earnestly exhorts them as brethren, well-intentioned but mistaken in their views, to yield their individual opinions to the united voice of the congregation, to abstain from all objectionable measures, and to recollect that the *Yehidim* of this congregation have given proofs of a desire to grant them their great desideratum—a Synagogue westward—and let them, above all, consulting their own interests and welfare, not lightly discard the protection of their ancient and parent Congregation ; and if they will but seriously reflect on all this, the meeting may yet entertain the hope that the severance so much to be deplored may still be avoided."

Both parties, it thus appeared, professed to be animated by mutual good feeling, which no doubt really existed ; nevertheless the breach between Jew and Jew became wider every day. Nor was the dissatisfaction manifested by Jewish worshippers expressed only by members of the Sephardi Congregation. In April 1842, a meeting of seatholders of several Synagogues was held under the presidency of Mr H. H. Cohen, when a memorial was drawn up to be presented to the respective vestries of the Ashkenazi Congregations. The evils so often mentioned were forcibly pointed out in that document. The then existing system of saying prayers was described as being "as unaccountable as it is unseemly ; as manifestly inconsistent, obviously indecorus, and clearly adverse to that lifting up of the soul in solemn communion with the Creator, which is the effect that prayer is intended to produce." Various suggestions for the amelioration of public worship were made, stress being especially laid on the introduction of pulpit instruction in English. It was not until years afterwards that some of their recommendations were carried out ; and in the meantime several of the memorialists joined the Reform movement.

In April 1841, when the movement had been openly declared, the vestries of the various city Synagogues resolved that no member of any Place of Worship not conforming as heretofore in religious matters, and not recognising the established ecclesiastical authorities, should be eligible to the office of deputy. In September of the same year the Chief Rabbi and the Beth Din of the German Jews and the Beth Din of the Portuguese Jews drew up a declaration against " the forms of prayer used in the West London Synagogue of British Jews, edited by D. W. Marks, printed by J. Wertheimer." This document stated " that the manner and order of the prayers and blessings have been curtailed and altered and otherwise arranged not in accordance with the Oral Law by which we have so long been guided in the performance of the precepts of the Lord ; " and further it was said " We hereby admonish every person professing the faith of Israel, and having the fear of God in his heart, that he do not use or in any matter recognise the said book of prayer, because it is not in accordance with our Holy Law, and whoever will use it for the purpose of prayer will be accounted sinful." This declaration was issued on the 24th October ; prior to its publication on the 9th September 1841, a meeting had been held at the residence of the Rev. Sol Hirschel, attended by the wardens and honorary officers of the several metropolitan Synagogues and by the members of the London Committee of Deputies of British Jews, when the following " Caution " was read and approved, and copies of it were forwarded to the Synagogues :—

" Information having reached me, from which it appears that certain persons calling themselves British Jews, publicly and in their published book of prayers, reject the Oral Law, I deem it my duty to declare, that according to the laws and statutes held sacred by the whole House of Israel, any person or persons declaring that he or they reject and do not believe in the authority of the Oral Law, cannot be permitted to have any communion with us Israelites in any religious rite or sacred act. I therefore earnestly entreat and exhort all God-fearing Jews, especially parents, to caution and instruct all persons belonging to our faith that they be careful to attend to this declaration, and that they be not induced to depart from our Holy Laws.

" S. HIRSCHEL, *Chief Rabbi.*"

The members of the Beth Din of both German and Portuguese Communities countersigned this document.

We are informed by unimpeachable authorities that the Rev. S. Hirschel, as well as the Rev. D. Meldola, senior Dayan of the Portuguese Congregation, signed the above paper with the greatest reluctance, knowing that it would cause much exasperation, that it would sow dissension when peace was sought and desired, and that it would tend to convert a temporary difference into an irreconcilable enmity. But the reverend gentlemen yielded to the powerful influences brought to bear upon them. Even after the Rev. S. Hirschel had been induced to affix his signature to the document, he wished to recall it, and at all events he insisted on its being held back. The "Caution" was not promulgated for some time. On Saturday, the 22d January 1842, it was read publicly in the principal London Synagogues by their respective secretaries, and accompanied by proclamations from the local authorities to the same effect. We may state that the members of the new Congregation deny altogether the impeachment of having renounced the Oral Law. Professor Marks and Mr Elkin, in the earlier days of the Reform, strenuously maintained the general fidelity of their congregation to Jewish tradition.

On the 13th January 1842, the members of the Reform party, before they consecrated their House of Prayer, addressed another communication to the Elders of the Spanish and Portuguese Congregation. In this letter the writers expressed their pain and surprise on perceiving that the conciliatory spirit they had displayed in the former missive had met with so little response; that an Askamah (law), called into existence by other circumstances, should have been resuscitated, and that a determination should have been formed to render them amenable to all the pains and penalties of the law of *Yehidim* No. 1 on their assembling in their new House of Prayer for the performance of divine worship.

The course had been forced upon them of withdrawing at once their names from the list of the *Yehidim* of the congregation. They disclaimed any desire for innovation or schism, and only wished to establish a House of Prayer where they might worship their Creator agreeably to the dictates of their own conscience. They professed an ardent love for the law which they desired to transmit intact to their descendants in perpetuity. They refrained from making the remarks they had intended, relative to the part taken by the Beth Din in the condemnation of their prayer-book, but they avoided doing so, only not to enter into irritating topics. Their communication was thus brought to an end:—

"In conclusion, we earnestly implore Almighty God, who searcheth the inward workings of the heart, to shed His blessing upon every member of the House of Israel, and so to implant His Spirit amongst us, that love, charity, and kindness may ever distinguish the conduct of one Israelite to another. May He cause us ever to bear in mind that we are all sprung from one stock, that we embrace one faith, acknowledge one Law, one God, one Common Parent!

"To all who may doubt the purity of the intentions that have led us to open our Synagogue, we are content to reply in the words of Scripture—'The God of gods, the Eternal, the God of gods, the Eternal, He knoweth and Israel shall know, if in rebellion or if in transgression against the Lord, may we not be saved this day.'"

This touching peroration apparently exercised little influence in the deliberations of the Elders, who in their meeting of the 19th January 1842, in moderate but firm language declared, that the withdrawal from *Yehidim* did not exonerate the parties from the consequences of the infraction of Ascama of Kaal No. 1, which applied to all Jews of the Spanish and Portuguese Communion, whether *Yehidim*, congregants, or even strangers residing in the city.

The more moderate portion of the Sephardi Congregation regarded the penalty of *Herem*—excommunication, or ecclesiastical censure—as opposed to the enlightenment of the age and to the spirit of true religion. Unfortunately less temperate counsels prevailed among the ruling powers. The propriety of abolishing *Herem* altogether was proposed in the assembly of Elders, and lost by a single vote. At meetings held on the 26th February and 4th March, a strong resolution against the retiring members was passed and confirmed.

The offending parties were declared " to have forfeited all claims to the rights and immunities which they enjoyed as members of our community, that the grants made to them of seats in our Synagogue are rescinded and annulled. They are also declared ineligible to act in any religious office or to perform a *Mitzvah* of any kind in the Congregation. Neither shall any gift or offering be accepted from them, or in respect of them, in any way or under any form whatever, during the time they remain in contumacy; they shall not be allowed burial in the *carreira* of our Beth Haim, nor receive any of the religious rites and ceremonies paid to departed members of our communion."

We have stated at the beginning of the preceding chapter that we should offer no opinion and pass no comments on the events which we are relating. We shall therefore refrain from inquiring how far the offence justified the punishment, and whether the authorities of the Orthodox Congregations adopted a just, wise, and conciliatory line of conduct.

On the 27th January 1842, the Reformers consecrated their Place of Worship, formerly a chapel in Burton Street. The Rev. D. W. Marks, now the Rev. Professor Marks, became their spiritual chief. As the members of this community increased in numbers and wealth they removed to a larger building in Margaret Street, and subsequently to their present handsome structure in Berkeley Street. At first the members of this congregation were placed at some inconvenience with reference to their marriages, by the Board of Deputies declining to certify that the Rev. Mr Marks was the secretary of a Synagogue. Young couples desirous of being joined in wedlock were constrained to appear before the registrar, and when that functionary made them one before the law, they went to their Synagogue and passed through the religious ceremony. Eight or ten years afterwards on the passing of an Act of Parliament called the "Dissenters' Chapels Bill," a clause was introduced in the Bill recognising the Reformers' Place of Worship as a "Synagogue," and Rev. Mr Marks as its certified secretary, and empowering the authorities of this Synagogue to certify to the secretaries of other Synagogues which might adopt the same ritual.

The fact that some of their former friends and relatives might be labouring under *Herem*, or religious disabilities was disquieting to the majority of right-thinking members of the Spanish and Portuguese Congregation. Accordingly, on the 14th December 1845, at a meeting of the Elders, it was resolved to ascertain whether the members of that Synagogue who seceded in 1842 were or were not lawfully under *Herem;* and as that body had never sanctioned or desired to sanction the enforcement of that penalty, they appointed a committee to consult with the Ecclesiastical Authorities as to the state of the case. Should it appear that such parties were labouring under excommunication, the Committee were empowered to adopt such measures on behalf of the congregation as might be necessary to absolve them from *Herem*.

The Committee rendered their report on the 19th April 1846. They had consulted the Beth Din, before whom they had laid several documents. It was explained that the *Herem* denounced in the Askama was for the offence of separating from the Congregation, and would have applied equally had the offenders formed another Congregation under the old ritual, or joined any other Congregation already formed. The religious offence of altering the ritual had already been the subject of ecclesiastical censure, with which it was not the purpose of that inquiry to interfere. The answer from the Beth Din stated that the parties in question were labouring under *Herem*, which would remain in force so long as they neglected or refused to abide by the principles of the Jewish religion. So the question remained in abeyance until the beginning of the following year. On the 17th January 1847, at a memorable meeting, the *Yehidim* resolved that the continuance of *Herem* was repugnant to the spirit of modern legislation, and earnestly entreated the Elders to devise some means of effectually relieving the parties implicated from *Herem* and its penalties. At a meeting of the Elders, held on the 28th February 1847, it was determined to comply with the request of the *Yehidim*, by a majority of fifteen votes to three. The parties who were in *Herem* were to be relieved from that penalty, subject to the approbation of the gentlemen of the Beth Din; and a committee was appointed consisting of the Wardens, the Chairman of the Elders, and the Chairman of the *Yehidim*, to confer with the Beth Din, and to carry out in the name and on behalf of the Congregation any religious formality that might be necessary. This resolution, owing to various causes, was delayed in its execution, and *Herem* was not formally repealed until later. Several gentlemen contributed by their exertions to the removal of *Herem*, and among these we may mention Mr H. de Castro and Mr Haim Guedalla. These gentlemen deserve credit for their efforts in this matter. They experienced considerable difficulty in carrying out their pacific intentions, but they eventually succeeded in inducing the seceders, with the exception of two, to sign a request to be relieved from *Herem*. The ecclesiastical authorities performed, on the 9th March 1849, the ceremony requisite to purge the Reformers of *Herem*, in the presence of Mr H. de Castro and Mr H. Guedalla. This act enabled families which had long ceased holding mutual communication, to resume friendly intercourse; and one of the leaders of the Reformers paid at once a visit to one of the chiefs of the Orthodox party, between whom family ties had not prevented the birth of a bitter religious feud.

So ended this the most painful episode in modern Anglo-Jewish history. We in our day can scarcely understand the heart-burnings, the dissensions it caused among a former generation. It is when the difference is small and has arisen between those who were once near and dear to each other, that unhappily the animosity is greatest. Shibboleth does not spare Sibboleth. The Reformers say they would have returned to the ancient Synagogue, even after their own Place of Worship had been opened, if very moderate concessions had been made to them, and if certain acts which they characterised as harsh and unjustifiable had not been perpetrated. The Conservative party aver that those who had left the fold of Israel would never have been satisfied with what religiously could be conceded to them, and that they would have insisted in disregarding traditions held sacred among the Jews, and in adopting practices repugnant to the conscience of the majority of Jews. It is not for us to decide, and the reader doubtless can form his own conclusions without our assistance. What is certain is that most of the reforms asked for by the so-called seceders have been introduced in our days into the Orthodox Congregations. The movement, however, has not greatly spread in this country. A Synagogue was subsequently established on nearly the same principles at Manchester, and in 1874 a small temporary building for a Congregation following a similar ritual was inaugurated in a southern suburb of London.

Time, the great healer of wounds, has meanwhile effected its work. Calm reflection could not fail in the end to remind all parties that discord, with its train of evil consequences, has caused great national disasters, and that Israel, at the present age, needs more than ever union and concord in its onward march towards its glorious future destinies. To forget and forgive is a pre-eminent virtue in the Jewish code of ethics; and we are happy to think that all traces of past animosities are fast disappearing, nay, perhaps, have already disappeared. Wise men have agreed to differ in matters of opinion. Germans, Portuguese, and British Jews meet together to promote the interests of Judaism, of Jewish education, charity, and moral progress. They exchange together social amenities, they assemble at the same social and festive tables, at the same institutional boards; and if they worship in different Synagogues, and with slightly different forms of prayer, yet they pray to the same God!

CHAPTER LII.

THE CIVIL AND POLITICAL RIGHTS OF THE JEWS.

The Jews for many years were subjected to so many disqualifications, that they may be said to have possessed neither civil nor political rights. True, the Jews were not confined in a material Ghetto. But their pursuits were so restricted, the scope of their lives was so cramped, that trading, speculating, huckstering, and bartering, necessarily became the principal occupations of their existence. Not only were they considered unfit to have seats in the national Legislature, but they were thought unworthy of dispensing justice as magistrates, and even of pleading for others in the law courts of the land. As we have seen in a former chapter, to be a Jew was an insuperable bar to a man being permitted to open business premises within the precincts of the City, and even adjuration of the ancient faith did not quite expiate the crime of being born a Jew. Until modern times, the number of Jewish brokers in the City of London was limited to twelve; and we have already stated that the office was purchased, when a vacancy occurred, by a *douceur* to the Lord Mayor, varying from £1000 to £2000, according to the needs or exigencies of that high functionary. The last recorded instance of such a bargain took place in 1826, when Mr J. B. Montefiore bought for 1500 guineas from Sir William Magnay, the then Lord Mayor, the medal which formed the title-deed of the privilege, and which had lapsed by the death of the previous owner. Two years afterwards, this absurd limitation as to number was removed, and Lord Mayors ceased to levy a heavy tax on Jewish brokers. Until the year 1832, a Jew could not be admitted to the freedom of the City of London. Accordingly, he was precluded from opening a retail shop, and was debarred from many other rights and privileges. The removal of these disabilities was owing, to a great extent, to the exertions of Mr Charles Pearson, at that time City solicitor, and of several members of the Common Council. The Court of Aldermen indeed has not always been liberally inclined towards the Jews. We are happy, however, to admit that now, for many years past, the Corporation of the City of London has been justly celebrated for its liberal and enlightened policy, and for its complete freedom from intolerance and prejudice. As evidence of this, we have only to advert to the fact that two Jews have filled the Lord Mayor's chair, and that several have occupied seats in the Courts of Aldermen and of Common Council.

As the Jews during this century progressed in wealth and education, they began to feel their exclusion from civil and political rights, and resolved to struggle manfully to obtain their due. The Board of Deputies, as the representative of Jewish interests, took the matter in hand; and Mr N. M. Rothschild and Mr Isaac Lyon Goldsmid powerfully supported with their great influence the acts of this body. The repeal of the Test and Corporation Act in 1828, previous to which all holders of municipal offices were required to take the Sacrament, aroused the hopes of the Jews. In April 1829, Mr Rothschild informed the Deputies that he had consulted with the Duke of Wellington, the Lord Chancellor, and other influential persons connected with Government, concerning the disabilities under which the Jews laboured, and he recommended that a petition for their removal should be drawn up to be presented as the opportunity occurred.

A deputation waited on Lord Bexley (Right Hon. N. Vansittart) and the Duke of Sussex, and both of them promised to favour the petition. This was prepared by Mr Pearce, the Attorney to the Sephardi Congregation, but the application to the Legislature had to be suspended for that session. Lord Bexley, who was a friend of the Jews, had seen the conqueror of Waterloo, and the result of the interview had been unfavourable. The grounds of objection on the part of the Duke were, that having recently carried so important a measure as the Catholic Relief Bill, which had excited the feelings of all classes of society in the United

Kingdom, he was averse to the creation of renewed hostile feelings against the Government by giving his support to another Bill of the same description during that session. In point of fact, the Catholics, who were strong and numerous, having obtained a rightful recognition, it was not worth while to render justice to the Jews, who were weak and few in numbers. Lord Bexley believed that the Duke of Wellington would certainly vote against the Bill if pressed forward, but that if adjourned to another session the Duke would probably give his countenance to it. So the Bill was withdrawn.

In January 1830, another petition to Parliament was prepared by Messrs Pearce under the direction of Dr Lushington; and it was placed in the vestry rooms of all the Synagogues in London for the signature of British-born Jews. A deputation from the Deputies waited once more upon the Duke of Sussex, who gave the kindest promises of support. The petition was presented in February by Mr Robert Grant, the member for Inverness, in the House of Commons, and by Lord Bexley in the House of Lords. The Jews of Liverpool had signed a similar memorial, and had entrusted it to Mr Huskisson, their representative in Parliament. Moreover, Mr Huskisson presented a petition from 2000 constituents in Liverpool, including several clergymen of the Church of England, every banker and every merchant of importance and influence. Mr Alexander Baring (the late Lord Ashburton) laid before the House a memorial signed by 14,000 bankers, merchants, and traders of the City of London. On the 5th April 1830, Mr Robert Grant moved for leave to bring in a Bill for the Repeal of the Civil Disabilities of the Jews. He stated that the Jews were excluded from practising law and physic, from holding any corporate office, and from being Members of Parliament; and they might be prevented from voting for Members of Parliament if the oaths were tendered to them.

In some large towns, such as Liverpool and Exeter, they were allowed to enjoy civil rights, but in the Metropolis they could not obtain the freedom of any of the companies, nor exercise any retail trade. The motion was carried. The

Board of Deputies bestirred themselves to obtain a successful issue. A number of petitions signed by Christians in different parts of England were collected; and memorials on behalf of the Emancipation of the Jews were found in most of the London and provincial taverns. A committee of the Deputies sat daily between ten and four o'clock, at the King's Head in the Poultry. Nevertheless, on the second reading of the Bill on the 23rd May, it was thrown out by 228 noes against 165 ayes. The expenses incurred were considerable, the solicitor's bill alone amounting to little less than £1000, and the costs were divided *pro-rata* between the various London Synagogues.

The Board of Deputies passed a vote of thanks to Mr R. Grant for his generous efforts in favour of the Bill; but they resolved to take no further steps on the question during that session. Strange to say, that while the Jews of England were making strenuous efforts to obtain their Emancipation, Mr David Henriques sent from New York a communication to the Board of Deputies, in which he furnished a long list of names of Jews holding official appointments in that city. The new country had been readier to render justice to the Jews and to recognise them as citizens than the old country. Some small gain, however, was obtained even in England, for Mr Sugden, afterwards Lord St Leonards, offered to bring in a Bill to enable Israelites to hold land.

In 1833, Mr Grant made another effort in Parliament on behalf of the Jews. On the 17th of April of that year he moved, in a committee of the whole House of Commons: " That it is expedient to remove all civil disabilities affecting His Majesty's subjects of the Jewish religion, with the like exceptions as are provided by the Catholic Emancipation Act of 1829, with reference to Her Majesty's subjects professing the Roman Catholic religion." Sir R. Inglis, a consistent foe to Jewish Emancipation, spoke in opposition to the motion, which was supported by Mr Macaulay, Mr Hume, and Mr O'Connell; and it was agreed to without a division. On the 22nd May Mr Grant moved the second reading of the Bill, which called forth some discussion. Again, honest, narrow-minded Sir Robert Inglis earnestly resisted the Bill, which was as warmly defended by Dr Lushington; and it was passed by a large majority. The Bill was duly read a third time, and it found its way to the House of Lords under the patronage of Lord Bexley. On the 1st August 1833, this liberal-minded nobleman moved the second reading of the Bill before the hereditary legislators of Great Britain. The Archbishop of Dublin, the Bishop of Chichester, the Lord Chancellor, and the Duke of Sussex expressed themselves strongly in favour of the Bill; while His Grace of Canterbury, the Bishop of London, and the Earl of Winchelsea pronounced against it. Dr Whately, the Archbishop of Dublin, made a logical, impartial, and masterly exposition of the case; and the Duke of Sussex brought before the Upper House a petition, signed by 7000 inhabitants of Westminster, who desired the Jews to obtain their rights. The Dukes of Gloucester and Wellington stated that they could not consent that persons who denounced Christianity should be admitted into the Legislature. The noes conquered, and the Bill was thrown out by 104 votes against 54 in the affirmative.

In 1834, another effort was made by the friends of religious tolerance to obtain a recognition for the rights of the Jews. A "Jewish Disabilities Bill" passed through its various stages in the Lower House, and was sent to the Upper House. On the second reading it was supported by Lord Bexley and the Earl of Radnor, and opposed by the Earl of Malmesbury, the Earl of Winchelsea, and the Marquis of Westmeath, who carried the day. The Bill was lost by 130 votes against 38, which were all that the Bill could obtain in that august assembly.

In the Parliamentary Session of 1836, a great number of petitions were presented to the Legislature in favour of removing the Civil Disabilities of the Jews. The latter thought the moment favourable to success, and under the guidance of the Board of Deputies, strenuous endeavours were made to achieve the long-sought-for end. The chairman of that body, Mr Moses, now Sir Moses Montefiore, asked for the co-operation of Mr I. L. Goldsmid and his son, Mr F. H. Goldsmid, who were called in to aid the Board with their counsels and influence. The Board placed themselves in communication with the Right Hon. J. Spring Rice, afterwards Lord Monteagle, who was preparing a Bill for the Relief of Jewish Disabilities; and while thanking him for his kindness, they offered to afford him any information he might require as to the sentiments of the Jews; they being the only authorised body by which the opinions of the Jews could be expressed. A petition was drawn up and entrusted to Dr Whately, the Archbishop of Dublin, who had always manifested a friendly spirit for the Jews, to be presented to the House of Lords. In this document it was urged that those Britons who professed the Jewish religion felt it a great hardship that they should be excluded from stations of trust, by the forms of administering oaths employed on some occasions; and they humbly prayed to be placed in the same condition, as to all rights and franchises, with the other subjects of Her Majesty dissenting from the Established Church. The Bill for the Removal of Jewish Disabilities, which was introduced by the Right Hon. J. Spring Rice, was, as on former occasions, carried through the House of Commons. Mr Alderman Thompson, a high Conservative, presented to the House of Commons a prayer for the removal of Jewish Disabilities, signed by 2000 burgesses and inhabitants of Sunderland. Unfortunately, after the first reading it was abandoned in the House of Peers, partly through the lateness of the season, and partly through the small probability of its meeting with success.

Meanwhile as the struggle for the admission of the Jews into Parliament was proceeding, an important step towards the relief of the Civil Disabilities of the Jews had been gained, by the introduction in 1835 of the Sheriffs' Declaration Bill. The credit of this measure was due to Sir J. Campbell, afterwards Lord Campbell, and then Attorney-General. During that year, for the first time in English history, a Jew, in the person of Mr David Salomons, attained the dignity of Sheriff. That office in London was a double office, consisting of the shrievalty for London, which was a Corporation office, and the shrievalty for Middlesex, which is a Crown office. On the repeal of the Test and Corporation Act in 1828, a declaration was substituted for the Sacrament, which declaration could not be made by Jews, owing to its concluding with the words " On the true faith of a Christian."

This declaration had to be made either before entering upon the office or immediately afterwards; while for Crown offices the declaration was usually made six months or a year after entering the office. The result was, that persons unable to make the declaration were practically excluded from the office of sheriff for the county of Middlesex, an office which in itself did not necessitate the previous taking of the declaration. Sir John Campbell, perceiving the inconsistency of exacting for a non-corporate office a declaration which should have been required only for a corporate office, introduced the Sheriffs' Declaration Bill to set the question at rest. The Jews were not specially named in the Act. Nevertheless it enabled the followers of that faith to enter into the office without violating their scruples of conscience. After Mr D. Salomons, Sir Moses Montefiore in 1837 graced the dignity. Sir Moses was knighted at the same time. In 1841 Queen Victoria conferred upon him, as a mark of royal favour in commemoration of his unceasing exertions on behalf of his injured and persecuted brethren in the East, and the Jewish nation at large, the right to bear supporters to his coat of arms, a privilege usually limited to peers of the realm.

The shrievalty appeared for some time the only office to which a Jew might aspire. In the Parliamentary Session of 1837-8, a Bill was presented to the House of Commons for the purpose of altering the declaration contained in the Act 9 Geo. IV. cap. 17, to be made by persons on their admission to municipal offices. This Bill, however, limited the indulgence to Quakers and Moravians. The Board of Deputies made an effort to obtain an extension of the provisions of the Bill to the Jews. Sir Moses Montefiore placed himself in communication with Lord John Russell, and expressed a hope that the declaration might be so amended as to be rendered available to all classes of Her Majesty's subjects. Lord John Russell, as might have been expected from so consistent a friend to civil and religious freedom, promised his best support to the request of Sir Moses Montefiore. Mr Baines, the originator of the Bill, expressed himself favourable to the claims of the Jews, but he declined to include them in the Bill, for such proceeding would be fatal to its success. He had done so in the Bill proposed in the previous session, and the consequence was, that it was violently opposed and delayed in the House of Commons, and finally thrown out by the Lords. On the 4th December 1837, on the second reading of the Bill, Mr Grote, the historian, and member for the City of London, moved that the benefit of the Bill be extended to all classes of Her Majesty's subjects, and the Jews were especially mentioned by him. Most of the speakers that followed upheld these liberal views. Sir J. Duke, who had been Sheriff for London and Middlesex, passed a high eulogy on his predecessor in the office (Mr D. Salomons) and on his successor (Sir Moses Montefiore), and he bore testimony to the high worth of the Jewish race generally. Mr Pattison, Capt. Pechell, Mr Geo. F. Young, Mr O'Connell, Mr Hume, and Lord John Russell spoke in the same sense. Even Sir R. Inglis, the most uncompromising foe to Jewish Emancipation, expressed his great pleasure in admitting all the high personal qualifications of the two excellent individuals who had been alluded to by gentlemen on the other side. He opposed the proposition, however, on the ground that those who did not believe in a common Christianity should not legislate for it. Mr Baines was not averse to the relief of the Jews, which on the contrary he thought desirable; but on that occasion he did not mean to go further than Quakers and Moravians, though he consented to introduce the term Separatists, thus including another sect of Christians. On a division, Mr Grote's amendment was negatived by 156 ayes against 172 noes. And so the Jews fared no better than before.

CHAPTER LIII.

REMOVAL OF JEWISH DISABILITIES.

Prior to 1841 but little progress had been made towards the abolition of the especial restrictions hemming in the Jews. The only point gained by them was the passing of Sir J. Campbell's Bill in 1835, which enabled David Salomons to serve as Sheriff. The Jews were still excluded from municipal offices and from Parliament. When in 1835 the electors of the Ward of Aldgate chose Mr D. Salomons as their representative at the Court of Aldermen, that body annulled the election; for the first Hebrew Alderman was unable to take the required declaration which was repugnant to his conscience. In 1841, Mr Divett introduced a Bill in the House of Commons "for the relief of persons of the Jewish religion elected to municipal offices," which passed through its various stages in that assembly, but was rejected at the second reading by the higher, if not more enlightened, body forming the second estate of the realm. In 1844, the liverymen of Portsoken honoured Mr D. Salomons by electing him as Alderman for their ward. The election had the same result as before, the Court of Aldermen pronouncing it null and void. However, soon afterwards that Court displayed a more liberal spirit, and made no further objections when Lord Lyndhurst, the Lord Chancellor, introduced in 1845 into the House of Lords a measure relieving the Jews from this disability. This Act, which became law without opposition, substituted a declaration of allegiance for the declaration imposed by the Act 9 George IV. cap. 17. The declaration fixed by the Act of George IV. was itself a substitute for the Sacrament of the Lord's Supper, but could not be taken by a Jew, as it concluded with the words "On the true faith of a Christian."

The benefits conferred by the Act in question were further extended to Jews by the Act of 21 and 22 Vic. cap. 48, in all cases in which Jews were required to make the declaration contained in the Act of Geo. IV. This Act of Victoria substitutes one oath for the oaths of abjuration, allegiance, and supremacy, which were imposed by an Act of 6 Geo. III., and enables Jews to take such oath, omitting the concluding and to them objectionable words. Before the passing of the Act of 1845, the oath and the declarations were both required of all persons holding any office, civil and military, or any place of emolument or trust under the Crown. The oath alone was deemed sufficient for all persons filling offices at either of the Universities of Oxford and Cambridge, and from all foundation scholars and exhibitioners at either of the Universities; while the declaration only was demanded from all persons occupying any office or employed in any corporation.

Mr Phineas Levi, of Devonport, was the first Jew who held municipal office in England; and Mr, now Sir B. S. Phillips, was the first Jewish Common Councilman elected in London. Due credit must be awarded to these gentlemen for their efforts in raising the status of their co-religionists in this country. The attainment of office was not so easy then as it has since become, and to reach even a comparatively humble dignity Mr Levi, and especially Mr Phillips, must have undergone much anxiety and surmounted considerable obstacles. Many Israelites have since achieved civic honours, and have become useful and trusted members of the corporation. They have invariably borne the offices, to which they were appointed by the votes of their Christian fellow-countrymen, with modesty, yet with liberality and dignity. Several Jewish gentlemen, too, received Her Majesty's Commission of the Peace under the Act, and we may name Baron M. de Rothschild, for Bucks; Sir I. L. Goldsmid, Bart., for Middlesex; Sir Moses Montefiore and Sir D. Salomons, for Kent; Sir B. S. Phillips, for several counties; Mr J. M. Montefiore, for Sussex; Mr Benj. Cohen, for Surrey; and Mr Emanuel Lousada, for Devonshire. Some of these gentlemen, however, had already been appointed magistrates before, and they had taken office under the Indemnity Act, which was annually passed, and which afforded exemption in some instances when only an oath was required. Mr D. Salomons in 1845, to commemorate his former election to the office of Sheriff, and as an acknowledgment of the honour conferred upon him, founded a scholarship in the city of London School. Mr Salomons conveyed to the trustees of that institution £1666, 13s. 4d., 3 per cent. consols, to establish an exhibition of £50 per annum, open to members of every religion, towards providing a maintenance of four years at either Oxford, Cambridge, the London University, or King's College, London.

The bar had at this period already admitted Jews to its privileges. The first Jewish barrister was Mr, now Sir F. H. Goldsmid, who was called to the Chancery Bar on 31st January in the year 1833; the second being Mr John Simon, LL.B., of Jamaica, now Mr Serjeant Simon, M.P. for Dewsbury, who was summoned to the Common Law Bar by the Hon. Society of the Middle Temple in November 1842. So many Jews have since that period attained forensic honours in England, that it would be difficult as well as needless to enumerate them here.

In 1846 the "Religious Opinions Relief Bill" became a law of the land. This Act began by repealing the Acts of Elizabeth enforcing attendance at church, all Acts requiring schoolmasters and tutors to obtain a bishop's licence, and the exception against Jews contained in the Naturalisation Act of 23 and 24 Geo. III. The Bill then enacted "that all Her Majesty's subjects professing the Jewish religion, in respect of their schools, places of religious worship, education, and charitable purposes and the property held therewith, should be subject to the same laws as Her Majesty's Protestant subjects dissenting from the Church of England." It also provided "that there should be extended to them (the Jews) the protection of the law against the wilful, malicious, and contemptuous disturbance of religious assemblies and teachers."

A Jew could now become an Alderman, a Sheriff, or a Magistrate. He could administer the laws, but he could not participate in making them. Numerous and prolonged were the efforts necessary to break the last barrier of intolerance.

The first Jew who endeavoured to penetrate into Parliament was Mr D. Salomons, who in 1837 canvassed the constituency of Shoreham. This attempt led to no result. During the general election of 1847, Baron Lionel de Rothschild became a candidate for the City of London. The Liberal party strenuously supported his cause, though it was well known that a Jew could not take his seat in the House of Commons. There were nine candidates on this occasion for the honour of representing the City in the Legislature. The Jews naturally struggled hard to give a good position in the poll to their candidate. A body calling itself the Jewish Association for the Removal of Civil and Religious Disabilities issued an address to the electors and inhabitants of the City couched in eloquent language, and it is certain that the sympathies of friends of religious toleration were enlisted in favour of Baron Rothschild. The Baron was elected after an arduous contest; but he only became a nominal legislator, for he could not vote in consequence of the required oath. There was no direct prohibition to the admission of Jews into Parliament: possibly as some of the opponents to their Emancipation asserted, because it was never dreamt that Jews would claim such a privilege. Only all new members were required to take the oath of allegiance which had been directed against another class of religionists, and which ended in the customary form objectionable to a Jew.

To obviate the difficulty, Lord John Russell, on the 16th December 1847, moved in the House of Commons "That the House resolve itself into a Committee on the Removal of Civil and Religious Disabilities affecting Her Majesty's Jewish subjects." Lord John Russell made an able and exhaustive speech, and the motion was carried by 256 to 186 votes. The Bill brought in, received in the second reading 277 against 204 votes, and at its third reading it was adopted by 234 against 173 votes. Sir Robert Peel, who had at first declared himself against the Bill, finally altered his opinion; and he fully explained to the House the reasons that had induced him to favour the proposition of Lord John Russell, and had placed him in painful collision with many of those friends with whom he had always acted. The House of Lords took a different view from the House of Commons;

and at the second reading the Bill was lost by 163 to 128 votes. Lord Lansdowne had been sponsor to the Bill in the Upper House, and Dr Thirlwall, Bishop of St David's, warmly supported it in a speech remarkable for critical acumen, research, and impartiality. Moreover, Lord Brougham, the advocate of liberty, gave his powerful eloquence to the Jews. On the other side the Archbishop of Canterbury mildly spoke against the Bill, and the Earl of Winchelsea more strenuously opposed it. But the bitterest and most uncompromising foes to the measure were Lord Stanley (late Earl of Derby), the Bishop of Oxford, and the Earl of Ellenborough. In the House of Commons, Sir R. Inglis, Lord Ashley (Lord Shaftesbury), Sir Thomas Acland, Mr Newdegate, Mr Stafford, and Mr Walpole foresaw the direst calamities from the admission of the Jews into Parliament. Mr Gladstone, Mr Disraeli, and Mr W. P. Wood (Lord Hatherley), on the contrary, looked upon the measure as a simple act of right and of justice, only likely to render still more loyal and more attached to the throne, a section of the community already remarkable for its good conduct and patriotism. The arguments on both sides of the question have been urged so many times since that period, and they must be so fresh in the mind of the reader, that it would be tedious and unnecessary to repeat them. Mr Faudel published a masterly reply to the allegations of Sir R. Inglis; and the alleged fear of Judaising the Legislature, by permitting half a dozen Jews to take their seats in an assembly composed of 658 members, disappeared under the weight of well-deserved ridicule. A medal, in commemoration of the services rendered to their cause by Lord John Russell, was struck by some grateful members of the Jewish community.

Mr David Salomons, not deterred by the unsuccessful result of the election of Baron Rothschild, displayed his public spirit by coming forward as candidate for the borough of Greenwich in 1851. Having secured his return to Parliament, Mr Salomons entered the House of Commons, and insisted on taking the oath on the Old Testament, and without the concluding words. He then ventured to take his seat; he spoke and voted upon a division on the very question of his right to remain in the House. Many members and the

Speaker himself loudly denounced his conduct; while a number of other members, among whom were Lord John Russell and Mr Bethell (Lord Westbury), strongly supported him. Mr Salomons was ultimately constrained to withdraw; and an action was brought against him in the Court of Exchequer (Miller *v.* Salomons) for the recovery of a penalty of £500, alleged to have been incurred by him for voting without being duly sworn. After a lengthy argument this action was decided for the plaintiff, when the defendant appealed to the Exchequer Chamber, where the case was reargued and the previous verdict confirmed. The judges present on that occasion were Chief Baron Pollock, Baron Parke, Baron Alderson, and Baron Martin. Mr Baron Martin, it may perhaps be remembered, differed from his brother Barons, and upheld the claim of Mr Salomons.

Several Bills for the repeal of Jewish Disabilities were again brought before Parliament at different periods, but with the same result as in the first attempt in 1847. The House of Commons invariably passed the Bill; while the Upper House, in direct opposition to the will of the people, gave grounds to certain enemies of religious freedom to thank Heaven with the Duke of Wellington that there was still a House of Lords. Finally in 1858 an Act became law (21 and 22 Vic. cap. 49), which empowered the House to modify the oath required of members, by omitting in the case of Jews the concluding words of the oath. Baron Rothschild assumed his seat in Parliament for the first time on the 26th of July 1858. Two years afterwards, by the exertions of the Jewish members, another Act was passed (23 and 24 Vic. cap. 63), dispensing in the case of oaths to be taken by Jews with the words "On the true faith of a Christian," in certain cases not comprised in any of the former Acts. Another Act beneficial to Jews also became law (29 and 30 Vic. cap. 22), abolishing for many offices the declaration required by the Act 8 and 9 Vic. cap. 52, and providing an indemnity for those who had omitted to make such declaration.

Happily in our day a Jew is scarcely subject to any practical disqualifications. Jews have been considered worthy of filling positions of trust. The highest legal offices, with the exception of that which entitles the incumbent to preside over the deliberations of the House of Lords, and to carry the great seal of England, are within the reach of Jews. The Mastership of the Rolls is worthily borne by a Jew, and we shall probably soon see a Jew occupy a seat in the Common Law Bench. Several constituencies have returned Jewish representatives. Social prejudices have disappeared and are disappearing; and the Jew, like the member of any other sect, may fill such place as he wins by his industry and his talents.

The cause of Jewish Emancipation was materially assisted, and a favourable issue was hastened, by the unwearied exertions of some eminent members of the community, who made sacrifices of time and wealth to promote the noble aim they had in view. The great philanthropist, Sir Moses Montefiore, did much to secure to the Jews their civil and political rights, albeit his unceasing efforts were principally devoted to their protection from oppression, to their enjoyment of religious freedom, and to the improvement of their general condition in England and in foreign countries. The services rendered by the Goldsmid family to the removal of Jewish Disabilities are of high importance. Sir I. L. Goldsmid and his son, Mr F. H. Goldsmid, worked strenuously and zealously on behalf of their co-religionists. Sir I. L. Goldsmid, in conjunction with Mr Apsley Pellatt and other members of the Common Council, contributed materially to the admission of Jews to the freedom of the City of London. He zealously urged forward the several Bills brought at different periods before the House of Commons for the relief of Jewish Disabilities, and he spared neither labour nor expense to secure a successful issue. Mr F. H. Goldsmid practically demonstrated that a Jew might be called to the bar : and he wrote several able pamphlets on behalf of Jewish Emancipation. The numerous services rendered by Sir F. H. Goldsmid to the community in latter times are too recent to need recalling to the mind of the reader.

The late Sir David Salomons was the first Jew who obtained the post of Sheriff. He struggled for the civil and political rights of the Jews; he worked hard for the aldermanic gown, and we have already spoken of the great services he rendered to the cause of civil and religious liberty by his election for Greenwich in 1851, and his bold proceedings in the House of Commons. No man deserves more of his brethren than the late Sir D. Salomons, of whom the *Times* said : "At last we have for the first time a Lord Mayor who can speak the Queen's English with propriety." Due credit must also be awarded to Baron L. de Rothschild for his repeated efforts in the same cause, and to Alderman Sir Benjamin Phillips, who has shown to the world that a Jewish Lord Mayor may make an excellent civic magistrate, and may occupy with dignity and becoming modesty the highest office in the wealthiest Corporation in the world. We must not omit to give honourable mention also to Mr Henry Faudel and Dr Barnard Van Oven, who by their energies and talents materially contributed to a successful issue. Some of these able champions of civil and religious freedom are now in a region where all spirits commune alike before their Creator. But those who happily are still amongst their families may look round with pride, and see the position their co-religionists have achieved, as they think of their early struggles for what was deemed by many as almost beyond the reach of probability.

CHAPTER LIV.

THE JEWISH PRESS.

For many years the Jews dwelt in England contented to remain in obscure silence, and without the smallest endeavour to make their voices heard. As this century advanced, and the Jews progressed in numbers, in affluence, and in enlightenment, the want began to be felt of a press which should serve to make known the requirements of the Hebrew community, and should prove a bond of union between its different branches. In 1822, three or four enterprising young men resolved to establish a medium for the circulation of Jewish news, and the first number of the publication was announced for the 1st January 1823. The advent of a newspaper written by Jews for Jews was expected with some curiosity, which was set at rest when the twopenny postman on New Year's Day punctually left the *Hebrew Intelligencer* at the doors of intending subscribers. A copy of this curiosity of literature lies before us at this moment. It bears the same resemblance to the *Jewish Chronicle* of 1874 as the *London Chronicle* of a century ago bears to the *Times* of to-day. The *Hebrew Intelligencer* is a solitary sheet of a small quarto size, and was sold for the sum of sixpence. On the front page of the first number we perceive an Address to the Readers, from which we gather that the journal was to be published monthly. The editors speak of the publication as "a work novel in its nature, and we trust, amusing and useful in its tendency."

The readers are also informed that the writers in the new journal were not moved by a spirit of speculation, for they purposed devoting the gains derivable from the enterprise, after payment of printing and other expenses, to some charitable institution.

This address is followed by an essay very much in the style of Queen Anne's time.

We then come to the news of the day. We learn that the annual dinner of the Society for the distribution of bread, meat, and coals to the Jewish poor during the winter months had been postponed, owing to a number of tickets having been returned by the subscribers. Happily such an untoward occurrence is impossible in our days. Indifference to the calls of charity is one of the things that have been changed since that time. After some editorial comments on this subject, we meet with a short article headed " Proposal of Mr Rothschild to the Committee of the Great Synagogue." We gather from it that Mr Rothschild (of whom we have spoken in a preceding chapter) had suggested to the authorities of the Duke's Place Synagogue the establishment of a fund for advancing to the Jewish industrious poor sums of money to be repaid in small instalments. Mr Rothschild had liberally offered to subscribe £500. We are unable to say whether the fund was actually called into existence, but if so it was certainly not placed on a sound and useful footing. Then under the title of Miscellanies, we have a number of short paragraphs giving scraps of information of a personal nature. The following paragraph we give *in extenso*, as a specimen of the kind of news likely to have been interesting to our grandfathers, or rather to our grandmothers :—

" We are informed that Edward Goldsmid, Esq. of Finsbury Square, is about leaving that neighbourhood for Park Lane, where he has purchased an elegant mansion, which it is supposed with the furniture will cost £10,000."

Finally we have births and deaths. Among the latter we perceive the following :—

" At his house in Finsbury Square, Asher Goldsmid, Esq., aged 70."
" On Thursday, 26th December, Rabbi Luria, aged 76.—(Mr Luria was Senior Dayan in the Sephardi Congregation)."

We cannot tell whether the sanguine expectations of the editors of the *Hebrew Intelligencer* as to the financial success of the venture would have been realised. Their philanthropic designs were certainly frustrated ; a great man in the community considered himself aggrieved by some remarks made concerning him. He exercised some pressure on the printer, J. Wertheimer of Leman Street; and after the issue of three numbers the *Hebrew Intelligencer* came to a sudden and untimely end.

A more serious and important effort to establish a Jewish publication was made in 1835 by the Rev. M. J. Raphall, an accomplished scholar, whose name we have already mentioned. This gentleman, in his *Hebrew Review and Magazine of Rabbinical Literature*, aimed at fostering a love for the higher branches of Jewish literature among his co-religionists. The *Hebrew Review* was a monthly magazine; and taking no cognizance of the small talk of the day, or even of communal events, it devoted its columns to disquisitions on learned Jewish authors of past times; to essays of a philological, exegetical, theological, and literary nature, scarcely likely to be attractive to a circle of promiscuous readers. The *Hebrew Review* was written for the few. It did not seek popularity, and with all its merits it certainly did not achieve it. It continued its career until 1840, when the publication expired for want of support. The magazine was revived in 1859 under the title of the *Hebrew Review and Magazine for Jewish Literature*, but we do not think that much success attended its re-appearance.

The *Voice of Jacob* was the first Anglo-Jewish journal which offered a record of passing events. It was started for the promotion of certain objects, such as the training of a Jewish ministry; the organisation of desultory charities; educational union; the championship and defence of Judaism at home and abroad; the interchange of Jewish opinions with other countries, &c. The founder of the *Voice of Jacob* still survives, and in deference to his known desire, we refer rather to his work than to his individuality. Several accomplished Hebrew gentlemen, all men well known in their community, assembled together at a conference, to meet Mr. J. A. Franklin, who had invited them to attend. They were Mr Sampson Samuel, the Rev. D. de Sola, the Rev. M. J. Raphall, and Dr A. Benisch. Mr Franklin had undertaken to provide funds for the establishment of the journal, which was to be conducted by the

Rev. D. de Sola and the Rev M. J. Raphall. However, these two ministers withdrew immediately from the enterprise, owing to a fear of wounding certain susceptibilities.

The journal made its appearance on the 16th September 1841, and it continued its unbroken course for five eventful years, 5602 to 5606 A.M., inclusive. The first number contained, in addition to the contributions of *Jacob*, its editor and proprietor, some verses by " S. S." (Sampson Samuel), an essay on the vocation of the British Jews by a "Foreigner" (Dr Benisch), and an article proving that Christianity, not Judaism, had first incurred the calumny of using human blood sacrificially, by "T. T." (Professor Theodores). All literary aid was, and continued to be for some time, gratuitous. The undertaking was in no sense a commercial one. Pecuniary losses were foreseen from the beginning, though after a time they were relieved to some extent by a guarantee fund, originated by the late Hananel de Castro. Eventually the journal, except for some of the literary work, became self-supporting. Its founder, after five years of incessant labour, was called upon to proceed to the continent on a filial mission, when he transferred the copyright to Mr H. Guedalla, and Mr Henry Jessel. Dr Benisch was to have conducted the *Voice of Jacob*, but the combination did not work well. After the issue of one or two numbers under the new proprietorship, the *Voice of Jacob* ceased to appear.

The mission of the Jewish Press, always high, had an especially extended scope at that period. Those were stirring times among the Jews. There was a division in the community. Party spirit was rife, and differences of opinion were rendered more irreconcilable by intemperance of language and a spirit of intolerance. There was peace to be restored in Israel, there was goodwill and amity to be preached to all parties, and mutual concessions to be urged. Then the Jewish Press had the opportunity of becoming the medium of communication between Judaism and Christianity, between the descendants of the patriarchs and the outer world. There were civil and political rights to be claimed, and the barriers of disqualification encircling the Jews to be removed.

In most of these directions did the *Voice of Jacob* labour.

That journal was an advocate of authority as based on Jewish tradition, but was far from favouring religious fanaticism. It made known to sincere Christians the religious belief of the Jews; and in a remarkable instance it altered a zeal for conversion to Christianity into a staunch friendship for Israel. It demonstrated the fitness of Jews for civil and religious equality, which was to be considered, not as a boon to an excluded race, but as a gain to the nation at large. The *Voice of Jacob* made for itself some reputation in different quarters of the globe. It was reprinted at Sydney, translated into Judeo-Spanish at Gibraltar, and followed in other parts of the world.

Soon after the establishment of that journal, Dr Ashenheim became one of its contributors, and then its sub-editor. Dr Benisch had not long arrived from Germany then, and he was not familiar with the English tongue; but he quickly acquired a mastery over it, as the readers of that and other journals can testify.

Shortly after the *Voice of Jacob* had spoken, the *Jewish Chronicle* began to note the events of the day. On the 5th of November 1841, one of the Dayanim of the Portuguese Synagogue, the Rev. D. Meldola, a son of the late Haham Meldola, asked permission of his wardens to contribute to a new weekly paper entitled *Sepher Aziccaron*, which was conceded to him. The names of Mr Moses Angel and the Rev. D. Meldola appeared as those of the conductors of this new literary venture, which was not destined to enjoy a prolonged existence. After a few months the Synagogue authorities took umbrage at some remarks made by Mr Meldola, and requested him to discontinue his connection with it, and though Mr Angel was really the editor and principal writer, he did not think himself justified in continuing the periodical.

Mr Angel subsequently joined the *Voice of Jacob*, and undertook the post of its joint-editor with Dr Benisch, under the supervision of Mr Franklin. Mr Angel fulfilled his functions for several years, when he resigned owing to his engagement at the Jews' Free School, the head mastership of which establishment had been for some time under his charge. The contributions of Mr Angel to the Anglo-Jewish

Press, usually signed "A," display great erudition and marked literary powers, and they are most interesting. His "Law of Sinai" which has been reprinted in a separate form, is a valuable addition to Jewish literature.

The *Voice of Jacob* was published fortnightly. Subsequently it was desired to issue a monthly magazine in connection with it, but this part of the programme was not carried out. The journal ranked among its contributors several able scholars and accomplished writers. It has been alleged that the *Voice of Jacob* represented only one section of the community. The problem as to whether one Jewish organ may suffice to reflect the views of all classes of Jews in London has not yet been solved. It is probably impossible to please at the same time Whitechapel, Bayswater, Berkeley Street, and the United Synagogue. At all events, the disappearance of the *Voice of Jacob* left a void in the Jewish world of London. The disinterested efforts of Mr Franklin to maintain an independent and well-conducted Anglo-Jewish Press, have scarcely been sufficiently appreciated.

In 1844 the *Jewish Chronicle* was revived by Mr Mitchell, and started in opposition to the *Voice of Jacob*. At first the new organ sailed under the banners of ultra-orthodoxy, but it gradually adopted more liberal views, until eventually it leant towards Burton Street. The *Jewish Chronicle* at that period was as different from the present *Jewish Chronicle* as the *Mercuries* of old were unlike our *Times* and *Daily News*. Mitchell secured the services of M. A. Bresslau, a ready writer and a man of some attainments. The journal was conducted with ability, but it did not acquire a reputation for independence. Bresslau several times had broken his connection with it, to resume it again at the earliest opportunity. Commercially speaking, the *Chronicle* did not flourish under that proprietorship. On the death of Mitchell, Bresslau proposed to continue the periodical, which happily soon afterwards passed into better and abler hands.

The Anglo-Jewish Press is much beholden to Dr Benisch. No man, next to the founder of the *Voice of Jacob*, has worked so much in its behalf. Dr Benisch, an able scholar and man of letters, perceiving the unpromising condition to which the Anglo-Jewish Press had been reduced after the discontinuance of the *Voice of Jacob*, determined to devote his time and talents to its elevation. We need scarcely advert here to the numerous literary productions of Dr Benisch, which probably are known to our readers, and by them fully appreciated. Dr Benisch established the *Hebrew Observer*, which was subsequently embodied with the third series of the *Jewish Chronicle*. He proposed rendering the new organ honourably self-supporting, and at the same time he did not desire to espouse the opinions of any particular class or section of the community. He advocated a broad Judaism, moderate progress with the age, the spread of education, the study of Hebrew literature, and conciliatory views on religious questions. He aimed at rendering the *Hebrew Observer* the medium for intercommunion between the Jews of the different parts of the British Empire, and, when practicable, the connecting link between them and their continental brethren. The services performed by this gentleman to Jewish journalism in particular, and to the advancement of Jewish interests in general, are too fresh in the minds of his co-religionists to require enumeration here. Resolved to maintain the perfect freedom of his journal, Dr Benisch declined all proffers of assistance, preferring to retain absolute liberty of action. The struggle was doubtless arduous. He purchased the copyright of the *Jewish Chronicle* from the heirs of Mr Mitchell, and he adopted the name as the first title of his journal. With the assistance of his wife, he became his own editor, writer, printer, and publisher. After some years of partial loss, he succeeded in rendering his publication self-supporting; and eventually, assisted as he was by the abolition of duties on paper and advertisements, he placed the *Jewish Chronicle*, for the term *Hebrew Observer* was dropped, on a safe and sound basis. The judgment, moderation, and scholarship displayed by Dr Benisch in the conduct of his journal, have been fully recognised by Jewish and Christian readers.

Another publication devoted to Jewish interests was the *Hebrew National*, started by Mr Filipowski in 1867. It did not, however, enjoy a prolonged existence.

A creditable effort was made in 1868 to establish a Jewish

journal, entitled the *Jewish Record*, intended for family and popular reading, but the venture was not successful, and the periodical did not live long. Since the extinction of the *Record*, another Jewish paper, called the *Jewish World*, has been started. It appears to possess a good circulation, and to be increasing in popularity.

The journal in which these papers were originally published was for some years under the management of an editor to whom the work so admirably performed by Dr Benisch was transferred, and by him as admirably continued. Of the labours of the late Mr Michael Henry in this direction, we have already spoken. He conducted the *Jewish Chronicle* with ability and judgment, until after his death the direction of the periodical reverted to Dr Benisch.

CHAPTER LV.

CONCLUSION.

"Farewell! a word that must be, and hath been,
A sound which makes us linger; yet—farewell."
—*Childe Harold's Pilgrimage.*

ANY act performed avowedly for the last time can scarcely fail to leave behind in the human heart a tinge of sorrow. The prisoner who leaves his gloomy cell, and the emigrant who lands at his destination from an overcrowded and narrow ship, look back wistfully on the stone walls and wooden walls, inside which they suffered many privations, and which they quit for a freer and happier existence without. To look for the last time on any familiar scene or object is painful; and the writer who ends his work which for a considerable period has engaged his attention, and which he has grown to love, feels like a father about to part from his offspring. Even the attentive reader of a book of this nature, however much he may be disappointed at its numerous shortcomings, may possibly feel some slight regret at the conclusion of these chapters, whence at least he has acquired some information he did not possess before, and where he may recognise in earnestness of purpose some atonement for the absence of higher qualities.

Our task is ended. We have endeavoured to follow closely the fortunes of Israel in England. We have seen a handful of Jews immigrate into this country, trembling with misgivings and fears, and we leave them now a peaceful, wealthy, and important community of nearly fifty thousand souls, enjoying the rights and privileges of British-born subjects, and having their full share of public honours and influence. The successors of the few Jews who assembled to pray in

1663 in a room in King Street, find now a dozen Synagogues insufficient. Handsome new structures have of late years been erected in London, and yet the cry is for more extended Synagogue accommodation. We have beheld a Jew debarred from opening a shop in the City of London; and we have witnessed a Jewish Lord Mayor presiding gracefully over the hospitalities of the City of London.

We have caught a glimpse of Menasseh ben Israel eloquently pleading the cause of Israel before the Lord Protector. We have observed the Jews tolerated by Charles II., and favoured by him, possibly aided by the influence of the Queen's Portuguese surgeon, Antonio Mendes. We have found them remaining unmolested under James II., and wisely befriended by William of Orange. Good-tempered Queen Anne, as we know, did not alter their condition, and during the reigns of the Three Georges, we have watched them increasing in numbers and in enlightenment, albeit still excluded from civil and political rights. It was not until the reign of Queen Victoria, as our readers are well aware, that the Jews obtained full justice.

The descendants of the ancient Spanish and Portuguese Jews did not retain their lead in Jewish affairs; and at the end of the eighteenth century they found themselves outstripped in numbers and wealth by the more numerous immigrants from Germany and Poland. With congregations it happens as with families, with cities, and with empires. The glories of Egypt and of Babylon have disappeared. Greece scarcely deserves the name of nation, and Spain has sunk into a seventh-rate power. So the Sephardi Jews, for reasons to which we have adverted on several occasions, no longer occupy the proud position which they once enjoyed, though they are still an important and influential community. Ancient and noble lineage does not necessarily go hand-in-hand with much opulence. The energy, enterprise, and financial genius which, in combination with various other incidental causes, have increased to so great an extent the preponderance of the Ashkenazi Jews, are at least as praiseworthy qualities as Spanish *sangre azul*. The decrees of fate are immutable, and have been recognised as such by all Israelites. Feelings of envy and jealousy have, happily, long ceased to exist among the different sections of the Jewish community in London. The greatest amity and concord prevail now, and we trust the day may come—though it may not be in our time—when the terms Sephardi and Ashkenazi will have disappeared, and when all children of Israel will be known by one name—that of Jew.

We have endeavoured to present to the reader a brief view of the Jews most distinguished for their piety, wealth, high position, or talents, or for the services they have rendered to their co-religionists. The shadows have passed before us of the philosopher, physician, and scholar, Menasseh ben Israel, as he argued on behalf of his brethren before Cromwell, the Privy Council, and the eminent magistrates and learned divines summoned to the presence of the Protector; of Sir Solomon de Medina, the financier, making army contracts with John Churchill, Duke of Marlborough, and paying him a pension of £6000 a year; of Menasseh Lopez, who made a fortune while panic-stricken speculators were rushing to sell stock at Jonathan's under the belief that Queen Anne was dead; of Sampson Gideon, in his threadbare garments, negotiating a loan with Walpole, becoming a millionaire, living like a Christian, and dying like a Jew—a man who wished to be a Christian on earth and a Jew in heaven; of Joseph Salvador, the loan-contractor and patriotic Jew, whose chequered career would serve to adorn a tale; of Abraham Goldsmid entertaining Royalty, and dying rather than the slightest speck should rest on his honour; of Isaac D'Israeli leaving the faith of his fathers on account of a disagreement with the authorities of the Synagogue; of Nathan Meyer Rothschild advancing funds to the principal powers in Europe; of Sir David Salomons firmly maintaining the rights of a Jew to sit in the House of Commons, against the shouts of opposing and intolerant members of the popular assembly.

We have seen a succession of learned men preside over the Spanish and Portuguese Community from the days of Haham Jacob Sasportas to those of Dr Artom; and over the German Community from the time of Uri Phaibul to that of Dr Adler. We have shown the love for his race and faith on the part of Moses Hart, to whose generosity the Great Synagogue owes partly, if not entirely, its existence; and we have not allowed to remain unnoticed the liberality of numerous other members of the same congregation. We have striven to be just and impartial; and even the extravagances of Ephraim Lopes Pereira, Baron D'Aguilar, have been recorded in these columns. Some account has been given of the laws and customs governing the Jews; of their former numerous disqualifications, and of their struggles for the removal of their civil and political Disabilities. A brief history of the original constitution, and of the principal Acts of the Board of Deputies, has been laid before the reader. We have accompanied Sir Moses Montefiore in his glorious mission to the East in 1841, and we have set forth the numerous obstacles he had to contend with, and which were so happily surmounted. We have adverted to the foundation of the principal charitable and educational institutions in the community.

We have devoted several chapters to the development of German Congregations; and if in the earlier part of these articles we have dwelt more fully on the affairs of the Sephardi Congregation, it is, as our readers must recollect, because for a century and a quarter the Sephardi Jews played the principal part in London. It was they who were the wealthiest, most enlightened, and best known. Until the rise of the Goldsmid family, such Jews as were tolerated in high Christian society were, with rare exceptions, members of that Congregation. Necessarily, therefore, the Jews who most deserve a place in the history of those days belonged to the Sephardim.

We have glanced at those Jews who gained a place in literature in England, or who by their writings contributed to the advancement of their co-religionists. We have spoken of the marriage laws that govern the Jews, and of the enactments that refer to them in the statute-book of the country. The Jewish Press has not been forgotten, and a due acknowledgment has been made of the eminent services rendered by Jewish periodical literature to their community. Finally, the division that arose a generation since among the Jews of London, and the separation of a small body into a distinct Congregation, has been narrated as impartially as it may be accomplished by fallible human nature.

CONCLUSION.

We have not continued the history of the Jews until our day, for our task would have entailed upon us discussions and expressions of opinion which we preferred avoiding. Moreover, the present generation of the Jewish community has scarcely witnessed in its midst any stirring events. Indeed, there is little for the Anglo-Jewish historian of the second half of the nineteenth century to chronicle, beyond a steady increase on the part of his co-religionists in numbers, in wealth, in intelligence, in material prosperity, and in moral influence. New Jewish schools have been opened, new Synagogues consecrated, new charities founded, new associations for the advancement of Jewish interests established. Jewish young men have distinguished themselves at college, at the bar, in literature, and in the varied pursuits of modern civilisation. Social prejudices against Israelites are fast vanishing, and the Jews have rendered themselves completely worthy of their improved position, and kept full pace with their Gentile neighbours in the onward march of progress.

LIST OF AUTHORITIES AND SOURCES WHENCE THE FACTS AND INFORMATION CONTAINED IN THIS WORK HAVE BEEN GATHERED.

Annual Biography and Obituary. London, 1817 to end.
Annual Register, from 1758 to end.
Apology for the Naturalisation of the Jews, An. 1753.
Archives of the Congregation of German Jews, Duke's Place, The, from the Middle of the Eighteenth Century.
Archives of the Congregation of the Spanish and Portuguese Jews, The, from the Foundation of their Synagogue, beginning 1662.
Goldsmid, B. of Rochampton, Memoirs of the Life and Commercial Connections of the late. London, 1808.
Biographie Universelle, Ancienne et Moderne. Nouvelle Edition. Mechaud, Paris, 1843.
Blunt, John E., History of the Jews in England. London, 1830.
Burnet, Gilbert, Bishop of Salisbury, History of His Own Time. London, 1766.
Chalmers' Biographical Dictionary. London, 1812.
Collection of the Best Pieces in Prose and in Verse Concerning the Jews, A. London, 1753.
Colquhoun, Patrick, LL.D., A Treatise on the Police of the Metropolis. London, 1797–1800.
Colquhoun, Patrick, LL.D., The State of Indigence, and the Situation of the Casual Poor in the Metropolis Explained. London, 1799.
Confutation of the Reasons for the Naturalisation of the Jews, A. 1753.
De Cheaumont French Ambassador at Constantinople, A New Letter concerning the Jews. London, 1664.
Egan, Charles, The Status of the Jews in England from the Time of the Normans. London, 1848.
European Magazine.

LIST OF AUTHORITIES, ETC.

Evelyn, John, Memoirs comprising his Diaries, &c. London, 1818.
Francis, John, Chronicles and Characters of the Stock Exchange. London, 1855.
Gentleman's Magazine, or Monthly Intelligencer, from 1731.
Hansard's Parliamentary Reports.
Harleyan Miscellany, The.
Historical Treaty concerning Jews and Judaism in England, An. London, 1820.
Hume and Smollett's History of England.
Jewish Chronicle. London, 1841-5.
Jews, A Review of the Proposed Naturalisation of the Jews, being a Dispassionate Inquiry. London, 1753.
Margoliouth, Rev. M., History of the Jews in Great Britain. London, 1851.
Milman's, Dean, History of the Jews from the Earliest Days. 4th Edition. London, 1866.
Nouvelle Biographie Générale. Firmin Didot Frères. Paris, 1855.
Political Mercurius. London, 1655-6.
Records of the London Committee of Deputies of British Jews, The.
Scialitti, R. Moisé, Breve Discurso Politico solve las Espulsiones de los Judios, Letter, &c., 1663, 1675.
Tovey D' Blossiers, Anglia-Judaica. Oxford, 1738.
Universal Museum, and numerous other Periodical Publications of the Eighteenth and Nineteenth Centuries, The.
Voice of Jacob. London, 1841-5.
Wraxall, Sir Nathaniel, Historical Memoirs of His Own Time. London, 1818.

Considerable Information has been obtained from the Inspection of Private Letters and Documents, and from Traditional Family History.

INDEX.

Aben Ezra, 9
Abendana, Jacob and Isaac, 55
Abraham, Eliakim ben, 227
Abudiente, *see* Gideon, Sampson
Adler, Rev. Dr, 291
Act, of 1715, 65; of 1723, 66; of 1740, 67, 87; Naturalisation, 69; Lord Hardwicke's Marriage, 102, 105–112; of 1695, 102; Sir John Barnard's, 219; Prohibiting Marriages of Consanguinity, 128; Marriage and Registration, 112; Test and Corporation, Repeal of, 388, 389; Religious Opinions Belief, 394
Alien Duties, the, 46–51; Aguilar, Baron Ephraim d', 97–99, 110; Grace, 361-364
Almosnino, Hasdai, 193, 271; Solomon, 321
Altona, 319
Amsterdam, Jews of, 25, 31, 35, 43, 45, 53, 58, 145, 169
Andreas, Mrs, 104
Angel, Mr Moses, 404
Anne, Queen, 57, 59
Anti-Gallican Monitor, the, 231
Argus, the, 231
Army, Jews in the, 54, 275
Ascamoth, 38, 40, 191, 296
Ascher, Rev. Simon, 334, 339
Ashenheim, Dr, 404
Ashkenazim, the, 55, 230, 243, 258, 262, 265, 266, 291, 307, 325, 332, 340, 372, 377, 409
Azevedo, Moses Cohen de 192

Baal Shem, the, 245
Banishment of the Jews in 1290, 23
Baring, Sir Thomas, 253; Mr Alexander, 386
Barnard, Sir John, 81
Barrow, Joseph, 273
Basevi, Joshua, 300
Bedford, Jews in, 289
Belisario, Mendes, 107

Benevolence, Jewish, 268, 331, 342
Benisch, Dr. 404
Bensaken, Mr Samuel, 323
Bequests, Jewish, 323
Beracha, 37
Bernal, Jacob Israel, and Isaac, 157
Beth-Din. 107, 111, 170, 208, 214, 294, 322, 377, 382
Betting, 77
208
Bevis Marks, 57, 63, 74, 114, 150, 161, 164, 169, 176, 319
Bexley, Lord, 385
Bible, Hebrew, Text of, 172
Body-snatching. 194
Bonaparte, Napoleon, 69, 273, 275, 281, 234, 319
Braham, John, 231
Bristol, Jews of, 10, 77
Brougham, Lord, 397

Cambridge, Duke of, 267
Campbell, Sir John. 390
Caorsini, the, 15-17, 20
Catherine of Braganza, 44, 103
Cemeteries, Jewish, 226, 235, 320
Charities, Jewish, 75, 76, 136, 176, 245, 260, 273, 323, 332, 401
Charles II., 30, 43, 46
Charlestown, Jews in, 271
Cholera, the, 327, 334
Cohen, Levy Barent, 267; Joseph, 269
Colquhoun, Patrick, 257-260
"Committee of Diligence," 114
Congregation of British Jews.
Conversions, 34, 54, 65, 143, 176, 196, 206, 208, 220, 295, 303 306. 335
Costa, Emanuel Mendes da, 32, 95; Benjamin Mendes da, 89, 95, 155; Moses or Anthony da, 103; Jacob Mendes da, 103
Crimes, Serious, Rare amongst the Jews, 180
Cromwell, Oliver, 25 29

2 D

INDEX.

Cumberland, Richard, 238–240; Duke of, 267
Curry, Elias, 206

Damascus, Jews of, 130, 338, 347–349
Dashwood, Sir James, 87, 88
Davids, Arthur Lumley, 317
Deputies, Board of, Origin, 115, 118; Early Proceedings, 118–121, 385–390; German Jews first admitted, 124
Disabilities, Jewish, 198, 384; Removal of, 392–399; Divorces, 110, 294
D'Israeli, Isaac, 295–301; Right Hon. Benjamin, 300, 396
Dublin, Jews of, 77, 168, 225
Dupass, Mr, 34, 54

Edward I., 20–24, 52
Egmont, Earl of, 88
Elias, D., 333
Elizabeth, Queen, 24
Emigration, Proposed, of Poorer Jews, 153
Ergas, Haham Joseph, 56
Exeter, Jews of, 386

Falk, Rabbi de, 245–248
Foreign Jews, Relief of, 159, 166, 164, 291, 319, 335
France, Laws respecting Jews in, 27, 84, 177
Frey, Rev. C., 342
Funeral Ceremonies, 193, 309
Furtado, Isaac Mendes, 206

Gascoigne, Sir Crisp, 81
George II., 92
George III., 115, 122, 173, 222, 252, 268, 276–278
George IV., 119
Germany, Jewish Immigrants from, 54, 132, 176, 258
Gibraltar, Jewish Immigrants from, 190
Gideon, Sampson, 60–64, 84, 113
Goldney, Edward, 143
Goldsmid, Isaac L., 129–131, 254–256; Aaron, 249, 385, 398; Abraham, 252–254, 259; Benjamin, 249–252; George, 249
Goldsmith, Lewis, 230
Gordon, Lord George, 181–189
Grant, Mr Robert, 386
Grote, Mr George, 391
Guizot, M., 351

Halevy, Yehuda, 56
Hamburg, Jews in, 319
Hardwicke, Lord, 105

Harley, Lord, 88
Hart, Moses, 133
Hartog, Numa, 317
Hebrew, Difference in Pronunciation of, by German and Portuguese Jews, 157, 262, 291, 366; Instruction in, 170, 327, 361; Knowledge of, 279
Helbert, Jacob von, 287
Henry I., 2
Henry II., 4, 8
Henry III., 11–20
Herem, 37, 78, 181, 380–382
Hirschel, Rev. Solomon, 265, 307–310, 350, 378
Hospitals, Jewish, 263
Hunter, Dr

Immigrants, List of the first Jewish, 32
Incledon, Charles, 232
Inglis, Sir Robert, 387
Inter-marriage of German and Portuguese Jews, 157, 265, 325
Interment, Jewish, 216–218, 292
Isaacs, Rev. D. M., 340

Jamaica, Jews in, 53, 120, 353
James II., 46, 47, 67
Jeffreys, Chief Justice, 52
Jewel, Derivation of, 280
John, King, 9–11
José I. of Portugal, 320
Josephs, Michael, 314, 316

Kennicott, Rev. B., 172
King, J., 302

Laguna, Daniel Israel, 56
Langton, Stephen, 12
Languages, the Jews usually possess two, 153, 311, 317, 364, 402, 410
Lara, Mr, 323
Learning, Jewish, 8, 26, 55, 56, 95, 146, 227, 230, 314
Lecture, General, 274
Legacy Fund, the, 267
Leghorn, Jews of, 320
Lemoine, Henry, 229, 278, 280
Levi, David, 228
Levy, Mrs Judith, 96, 147; Mr Phineas, 393
Lincoln, Jews in, 18
Lindo, Miss Esther, 107; Alexander, 273, 328; E. H., 364
Lithuania, Jews from, 54
Literature, the Jews and, 296, 313–318, 359–365
Liverpool, Jews of, 386
London Jews' Society, the, 342
Lopez, Menasseh, 59

INDEX.

Lopez, Rodrigo, 24; Mordecai Rodriguez, 304; Menasseh, 304
Loughborough, Lord Chief Justice 328
Loyalty, Jewish, 67-69, 221, 142, 267, 276
Lushington, Dr, 387
Luzzatto, Philoxene, 317
Lyndhurst, Lord, 392
Lyon, Myer, 147; Solomon, Rev., 285, 314; Miss Emma, 314

Macaulay, Mr, 387
Mahamad, the, 36, 78, 139, 152, 178, 181, 205, 272, 294, 322, 338
Mahmoud II., Sultan, 319
Marks, Rev. D. W., 373
Marlborough, Duke of, 58, 59
Marriage, Three Legal Modes of, 100; Jewish Cases relating to, 106-111; Ceremonies in, 107, 135, 286; Irregular, 107, 293
Matthew Paris, 14, 236
Meat, Measures concerning Butcher's 158, 169, 214-216, 271, 287
Medina, Solomon de, 50
Mehemet Ali, 351, 353-357
Meldola Raphael, 271; Rev. D., 404
Menasseh ben Israel, 25-30
Mendes, Antonio and Andrea, 44, 95; Catherine, 103
Mendoza, Samuel, 212
Menton, Count Ratti, 351
Merchants, Jewish, in London in 1753, List of, 93
Mile End Cemetery, 235
Mocatta, Mr Moses, 326, 363
Mombach, Mr Julius, 340
Montefiore, Sir Moses, 127, 323, 331, 338, 350, 353-358, 388, 390; Abraham, 343
Morocco, Jews in, 173
Myers, Dr Joseph Hart, 222

Naturalization Bill of 1753, the, 80-85; Repealed, 86-91; Squibs on, 90, 91; the Press on, 88; Irish, 114
Navy, Jews in the, 54
Netto, Moses, 151
Newcastle, Duke of, 80, 86
Newdigate, Sir Roger, 87
Nieto, David, 55
Norwich, Jews of, 3, 5, 13, 18

O'Connell, Daniel, 352, 387
Oxford, Jews of, 2, 18, 24

Palmerston, Lord, 351
Parliament, Jews in, 305, 395, 396, 398
Parliamentum Judaicum, 14

Patna, Jews in, 144
Pauperism, Jewish, 152, 257
Paz, Moses de, 179
Pearson, Mr Charles, 385
Peel, Sir Robert, 395
Peerage, Jewish Connections with the, 104, 158, 233
Pelham, Mr, 80, 88
Pepys, Mr, 39
Pereira, Eliau Lopes, 193; Abraham Lopes, 273
Pereire, M. Jacob Rodriguez, 177
Persecutions, Jewish, 3-7, 10, 12-24, 46, 237, 347
Phillips, Sir Benjamin, 399
Pimentel, Jacob Abenatar, 258
Pitt, Mr, 88
Poland, Immigrants from, 258, 267, 341; Jews in, 307
Pombal, Marquis de, 320
Port Mahon, Jews in, 120
Portugal, Jews in, 320
Portuguese Congregation, Foundation of, 36-38; Original Laws of, 40
Press, The, on the Jews, 28, 88, 123, 250, 278, 283, 351, 399
Press, Jewish, 400-407
Pretender, Advance of the Young, 60, 67
Priestley, Dr, 228
Prisoners, Jewish, Exempted from Labour on Sabbaths and Festivals, 243
Prize-fighter, a Jewish, 212
Proselytism, Christian, 143, 203, 241, 283
Provinces, Jews in the, 77
Prynne, 27, 100
Purim Riots, the, 205

Quakers, The, and the Jews, 124

Raphall, Rev. Morris Jacob, 365, 402
Rebello, David Alves, 230
Reform Movement, the, 366-372
Reid, William Hamilton, 280-282
Return of the Jews to England, 25-30
Rhodes, Jews in, 349, 354
Ricardo, Abraham Israel, 220; David, 220
Rice, Rt. Hon. J. Spring, 388
Richard, I., 4
Robins, George, 309
Rochambeau, General, 274
Rome, Jews of, 197
Rothschild, Mr Nathan Meyer, 125, 266, 292, 343 346, 385, 401
Rothschild, Baron Lionel de, 395, 397
Royalty and the Jews, 268, 252
Russell, Lord John, 390, 395, 397

Sabbath, the, 272

Salomons, Sir David, 389, 392, 396
Salvador, Joseph, 162-163
Samuel, Moses, 364
Sarmiento, Jacob de Castro, 56
Saxon Kings, Jews in England under the, 1
Schism, The, in the Portuguese Congregation, 330, 366-383
Schools, Jewish, 41, 154, 170, 201, 261, 270, 321, 332
Scialitti, Moisés, 34
Sedition Bill, 123
Sephardim, the, 31, 258, 262, 266, 272, 320, 322, 325, 338, 368, 372, 409
Sermons, 340
Serra, Isaac Gomes, 342
Services, Jewish Mode of Conducting, 202, 270, 290, 302, 325-327, 367, 381
Shechita, Board of, 271
Sheva, Cumberland's, 238
Shomeré Meshmeret Hakkodesh, the, 329
Shylock, Shakespeare's, 238
Singing, Jewish, 339, 368
Sola, Rev. D. A. de, 327, 359-361 ; Dr Benjamin de, 359
Solomons, E. P. Mr, 217, 220
Solomon, Simon, 341
South Sea Bubble, 60
Starrs, 8
Statutum de Judaismo, 21, 100
Stephen, 3
Stowell, Lord, 107
Surnames, Jewish, 40
Sussex, Duke of, 267, 285, 385-388
Sweden and the Jews, 167
Sweetmeats, Throwing at Marriages, 135
Synagogues in King Street, 30, 33, 39; New, in 1676, 42; in Bevis Marks, 42, 57 ; Number of, in 1804, 266

Talmud, the, 179
Temple, Earl, 86
Terefa, 159, 214, 287
Thiers, M. 357
Thirlwall, Dr, 396
Thomas, Father, 347
Tucker, Rev. Josiah, 90

University College, 255
University, London, 255

Van Oven, Joshua, 259-263, 268, 280, 285, 291
Victoria, Queen, 128, 390
Villareal, Isaac da Costa, 75 ; Mrs Catherine da Costa, 103-104
Volunteers, Jewish, 69, 276

Wales, the Prince of, 277
Walpole, Sir Robert, 60
Way, Louis, 284
Wealth, Jewish, 93, 279
Wellington, Duke of, 385
West London Congregation, the Foundation of the, 372
Whately, Dr, 388
Wilkes, John, 180
William the Conqueror, 2
William Rufus, 2
William III., 48-50, 52, 67, 219
William IV., 328
Witherby, Thomas, 280, 284.
Wordsworth, Rev. Christopher, 284
Wynne, Sir William, 106

Ximenes, Sir Maurice, 303

York, Jews of, 5, 6, 7

www.ingramcontent.com/pod-product-compliance
Lightning Source LLC
Chambersburg PA
CBHW020543300426
44111CB00008B/779